Postconflict Utopias

DISSIDENT FEMINISMS

Elora Halim Chowdhury, Editor

For a list of books in the series, please see our website at www.press.uillinois.edu.

Postconflict Utopias

Everyday Survival in Chocó, Colombia

TANIA LIZARAZO

© 2024 by the Board of Trustees
of the University of Illinois
All rights reserved
1 2 3 4 5 C P 5 4 3 2 1
♾ This book is printed on acid-free paper.

Library of Congress Cataloging-in-Publication Data

Names: Lizarazo, Tania, 1983– author.
Title: Postconflict utopias : everyday survival in Chocó, Colombia
 / Tania Lizarazo.
Description: Urbana : University of Illinois Press, [2024] | Series:
 Dissident feminisms | Includes bibliographical references and
 index. |
Identifiers: LCCN 2024011349 (print) | LCCN 2024011350 (ebook) |
 ISBN 9780252046278 (cloth ; alk. paper) | ISBN 9780252088346
 (paperback ; alk. paper) | ISBN 9780252047633 (ebook)
Subjects: LCSH: Women, Black—Colombia—Chocó—Social
 conditions. | Women, Black—Political activity—Colombia—
 Chocó. | Feminism—Colombia—Chocó.
Classification: LCC HQ1554.C46 L59 2024 (print) | LCC HQ1554.C46
 (ebook) | DDC 305.48/896086151—dc23/eng/20240710
LC record available at https://lccn.loc.gov/2024011349
LC ebook record available at https://lccn.loc.gov/2024011350

Para Justa Germania Mena Córdoba (1960–2013)

Contents

Acknowledgments ix

Introduction Utopias as Why Nots 1

1 Utopian Rehearsals: Ethical Considerations on Moving Beyond Victimhood 26

2 Utopian Stories: Survival Technologies in *Mujeres Pacíficas* 57

3 Utopian Archives: Turning Trauma into Memory 91

4 Utopian Memories: Documenting Collective Territories 125

5 Utopian Networks: Showing Up as a Durational Performance 156

6 Everyday Utopias: Ethics and Care as Peacemaking 184

Conclusion Performing Why Nots 211

Notes 221

Index 245

Acknowledgments

I owe my survival and the materialization of this book to everyone who thought it possible before I did. It certainly would not exist without Justa Germania Mena Córdoba, who believed in me, trusted me, taught me about care and reciprocity, and imagined many audiences for her legacy. I cherish her now ancestral knowledge and her guidance along the way. Todo mi amor y agradecimiento siempre a Banessa Rivas López, Yenny Palacios Romaña, Carmen Aides Navia Mena, Ana Rosa Heredia Cuesta, Luz Adonis Mena Becerra, María del Socorro Mosquera Pérez, Julia Susana Mena Moreno, and Rubiela Cuesta Córdoba, who have been so generous with their time and knowledge to continue this collaboration, and for everything they have taught me about friendship, care, justice, rivers, and life. I am also grateful Rosmira Salas, Miriam Moya Cuesta, and Mariluz (Pancha) Moya joined us in sharing their stories. Thanks to Yessica Monroy, and everyone else in COJUCOMA. Gracias también a Lucely Rivas Espinoza for supporting me and my work in Quibdó and at a distance, inviting me to speak in COCOMACIA Stereo, and trusting me with many projects and events, including Memorias del Río Atrato. ¡Muchísimas gracias a todas!

I went to Quibdó for the first time with Julio César Uribe Hermocillo, and I am so thankful for many trips, beers, and conversations over the years that helped shaped this book. Velia Vidal was incredibly generous with me even before we met, and I am so grateful I got to experience the beauty and community she made possible through Nuestro Motete. Uniclaretiana has supported my work directly and indirectly through their library, events, and invitations to present my work.

I am very grateful to Gonzalo de la Torre, who has been a long supporter of my work and has patiently answered my endless questions for so many years. I am especially thankful I got to meet José Óscar Córdoba Lizcano. It was an honor to present with him in 2021 as part of the event "Comunicación y Cultura, Paz e Identidad." I am thankful for Norma Londoño's (Jamitah) work, and her recommendations of Black women artists, including Hanna Ramírez, whom I also thank for her illustrating the Atrato River, the comisionadas, and the utopian character in this book in ways I was longing for but could not imagine. Many thanks to Justa (Justi) Sánchez and all her students—children and adults—who shared their art with me during my visits to Mama Ú. Sergio Antonio Mosquera Mosquera has taught me a lot through his research, writing, and Muntú Bantú. In Bogotá, I am thankful for Marta Cabrera's mentorship, and her many invitations to present and collaborate at the Universidad Javeriana, my alma mater. Special thanks to my fellow former historians Camila Ashner and Juan Pablo Aranguren, who have invited me to present parts of this book at the Universidad de Los Andes, and to Felipe Arias Escobar, whose public history work keeps teaching me. In Baltimore, I am thankful for Yesenia Mejía-Herrera, Rosalyn Vera, Rocío Herrera, and many others from the Latin American diaspora who have made this place home. Lately, I am particularly grateful for We Keep Us Safe, COVID Safe Maryland, and the Baltimore Student Union for modeling reciprocal care.

This project started as a dissertation at the University of California, Davis. I am thankful for the mentorship and guidance from faculty in Spanish and Portuguese; performance studies; and gender, sexuality, and women's studies. Thanks to Michael Lazzara, Robert Irwin, Lynette Hunter, Luz Mena, Amina Mama, Ana Peluffo, Stefano Varese, and Marta Altisent. My community at UC Davis also shaped me and my scholarship. Gracias a Emily Davidson, Consuelo Cervantes, Tracy Quan, Mayra Sánchez, Diana Pardo Pedraza, David Tenorio, Julia Morales, Magalí Rabasa, Elisa Oceguera, Cinthya Ammerman, Mari Spira, and Carolina Novella. I am particularly grateful to have met Chris Ami, who continues to teach me so much about ethical research and survival.

At the University of Maryland, Baltimore County (UMBC), I am grateful for the support of many colleagues, especially Tamara Bhalla, Bev Bickel, Semhar Yohannes, Rachel Brubaker, Jessica Berman, Courtney Hobson, Carolyn Good, Christine Mallinson, Bill Shewbridge, Omar Ka, Renée Lambert-Brétière, Ana María Schwartz Caballero, Haniyeh Barahouie, Brigid Starkey, Mejdulene Shomali, Milvia Hernández, Fan Yang, John Stolle-McAllister, Catalina Dansberger Duque, Felipe Filomeno, Chris Tong, María Manni, Elisabeth Arévalo-Guerrero, Catalina Shorkey, Bambi Chapin, Kyung-Eun Yoon, and Noor Zehra

Zaidi. I am particularly thankful to the community created by the Faculty Working Group on Latin American Feminisms: Thania Muñoz, María Célleri, Yolanda Valencia, Carla Maenza, Melisa Argañaraz, Julissa Gómez, Viridiana Colosio-Martínez, Andrea Hernández, and Valerie Pasión. I am thankful to all my students at UMBC who have helped me fine-tune some of the ideas I include in this book, especially Charlotte Keniston, Caleb Ruck, Emma Jarvis, Javier de la Morena Corrales, Julissa Gómez, and Viridiana Colosio-Martínez. I am grateful for my research assistants Marcela Hoyos and Liv Smith, who supported this work at different stages and made it so much better. Special thanks to Andrea Hernández, who helped me in many ways during the last weeks of preparing the final manuscript. The research and writing of this book were also supported by UMBC in many other ways, including financial support from the Center for Social Science Scholarship, the Dresher Center for the Humanities, the College of Arts, Humanities and Social Sciences, and the Provost's Office.

This book has benefited from, and been shaped by, many audiences. I am grateful for the feedback received at the Encuentros de Estudios de Memoria. Special thanks to Pilar Calveiro, Ileana Rodríguez, Paola Ovalle, Natalia Escobar, Marta Cabrera, Michael Lazzara, Fernando Blanco, and Ana Cacopardo. I am also grateful for the conversations at the Tepoztlán Institute with Claudia Mosquera, Marisa Belausteguigoitia, Christen Smith, Yoalli Rodríguez, Rosamond S. King, Tito Mitjans Alayón, Nayla Ramalho, Magalí Rabasa, Bárbara Abadía-Rexach, Dina Alves, Alexander Aviña, Yomaira Figueroa, Omaris Zamora, Nzingha Kendall, Matthew Leslie Santana, Itza Varela, Katsi Rodríguez, Natalie Scenters-Zapico, Jorell Meléndez-Badillo, and Nicole Fleetwood. Thanks to Emily Davidson, who invited me to her seminar "The Art of Brevity: Latin American Short Narratives" at Pacific Lutheran University; to Mathilda Shepard, who invited me to present at the "Art and Confrontation in the Americas International Symposium" at the University of Virginia; to Miguel García, who invited me to present at the "Utopian Archives: Turning Trauma into Memory" Mellon Interdisciplinary Seminar at Fordham University; and to all the colleagues who have invited me to classes, panels, and events. I am especially grateful for many conversations with Eduard Arriaga, Félix Burgos, and Camila Daniel.

As a collaborative effort, this book has been shaped by the support of many writing groups and readers at different stages. I would like to especially thank Diana Pardo Pedraza, David Tenorio, Xan Chako, Mike Casiano, cicada inscoe, Yolanda Valencia, María Célleri, Thania Muñoz, Keegan Finberg, Charlotte Keniston, Sarah Fouts, and Nicole King. Thank you to Cathy Hannabach and the team at Ideas on Fire for supporting this book in many stages. Extreme thanks to limón román and Dove ER* who generously shared their accessibility knowledge and time to help me write the ALT text for this book's images.

Many thanks to Elora Chowdhury, Dominique J. Moore, and everyone at UIP who helped materialize this book and to Allison Torres Burtka for her copyediting of the final manuscript. I am particularly thankful for the two anonymous reviewers who helped me restructure and fine-tune some of this book's ideas.

I owe my everyday survival to a growing disability community that started with limón román, whose care and friendship has sustained me. Thanks to Charity Sadé, azucena c., oh, and Semhar, who model the care and solidarity that academia can only imagine.

My extended family has made my existence possible in too many ways to count: ¡Gracias a todxs! Todo mi amor para Tita, mi abuelita Ofe y todas las que han garantizado mi existencia. Nada sería posible sin mi familia nuclear, lxs Lizarazo Morenos, que siguen acompañándome en la distancia y creyendo en mí y en mi trabajo. Gracias infinitas a mi multispecies crip family: David Beard and the past and present bearded lizards Cali, Space, Nova, and Gravity, who give me the safest home nest I need and guarantee my survival every day.

Postconflict Utopias

INTRODUCTION

Utopias as Why Nots

¿Para qué preocuparse? Una sola no puede cambiar el mundo.

Why worry? One cannot change the world by herself.

—Justa Germania Mena Córdoba

Stories are possible because of audiences, present and imagined. I first met María del Socorro Mosquera Pérez in 2008. She was part of a group of nine women: las comisionadas de género [gender commissioners]. Established in 2000, the Comisión de Género has been making women's rights and labor visible as part of COCOMACIA's (Consejo Comunitario Mayor de la Asociación Campesina Integral del Atrato, or the Main Community Council of the Integral Peasant Association of the Atrato River) struggle to defend Black communities and territories alongside the Pacific lowlands' rivers. COCOMACIA is one of the biggest Colombian Black peasant organizations. Over the course of five years, the comisionadas and I shared stories and formed relationships. In 2013, with three additional storytellers, we created audiovisual stories based on their lived experiences. These stories, especially Mosquera Pérez's, inspired the utopian framework of this book.[1] We recorded her story in one of COCOMACIA's offices in downtown Quibdó. Only she and I were present in the room. In her story, Mosquera Pérez addresses women from COCOMACIA, Colombia, and *why not* the world: "Buenas tardes para todas las mujeres del área de influencia de COCOMACIA, y por qué no decir para todas las mujeres de Colombia y del mundo...."[2] [Good afternoon to all the women from COCOMACIA's influence area, and why not say to all the women in Colombia and the world]. This gesture of connectedness exemplifies the relations Mosquera Pérez, las comisionadas, and COCOMACIA build with other spaces, organizations, and people. "Why not" became part of my framework to understand las comisionadas, their stories, and their peace-building work as positioned beyond the city of Quibdó, in Colombia's highly militarized Department of Chocó.

The Comisión de Género is one of eight thematic areas that make up COCOMACIA, "the strongest [B]lack peasant organization in the country."[3] This grassroots organization is widely recognized for its defense of Black communities' territorial rights since its origin. Established as ACIA (Asociación Campesina Integral del Atrato) in 1987, it oversees a portion (695,245 hectares) of the ancestral lands of Black rural communities that were recognized by Transitory Article 55 in Colombia's 1991 Constitution. The collective ownership of this land was legalized in 1993 through Law 70.[4] These territories are governed by 124 community councils, which serve as their highest administrative authority, and are located in eight municipalities (three in Antioquia: Murindó, Vigía del Fuerte y Urrao; and five in Chocó: Atrato, Medio Atrato, Bojayá y Carmen del Darién). It is crucial to note that "'land' is not possessed as property; what is possessed is the long-standing right (*derecho ancestral*) [italics in the original] to the use of various non-contiguous spaces the location of which is determined by the dynamics of the relation between nature and culture."[5] These collective territories are part of Colombia's Pacific lowlands, the biogeographic region also known as Chocó that extends from Ecuador to Panamá. Chocó, known as a biodiversity hotspot, has been the target of numerous extractive industries, ranging from monocultures to industrial gold mining, that have fueled violence against Black communities.

Impossibility defines the boundaries of reality, while ongoing violence restricts what it is possible to imagine. To bet on what is not possible materialized Black communities' collective territories, materialized by imagining what had been thought a legal impossibility: Law 70 of 1993. Everyday utopias reveal that political achievements such as these territories are not static or timeless but demand daily work. Through the Comisión's work, I learned "why not" is a survival strategy and a political commitment to show up and rehearse change. "Why not" is a utopian undertaking in what we long to call postconflict Colombia.

With a Black majority population (85 percent–95 percent, depending on the source), Chocó is often portrayed as a biodiverse or folkloric, or even as an empty region in a country self-defined by mestizaje. Located in the northern Colombian Pacific, Chocó only became a department, one of the country's thirty-two subdivisions, in 1947. Colombia has the largest Spanish-speaking Afrodescendant population in the hemisphere, which explains why "the Colombian Black Pacific was and is one of the main nodes in the racial cartography of the Black Pacific world, offering its own distinct history of [B]lack dispossession and possibility."[6] Chocó is key to comprehending Colombia's Black history and Black people's ongoing struggle beyond national borders. Invoking the world while telling local stories creates a sense of possibility amid historical dispossession.

Before the Comisión's leader Justa Germania Mena Córdoba's death on October 15, 2013, there were nine women working as comisionadas. They all had been campesinas and had faced displacement and violence themselves (some have been forcefully displaced, one of them after a massacre). This Comisión's work has included workshops on women's rights, gender violence, territorial rights, and productive projects in each of the nine geographic areas into which COCOMACIA is divided. Because this Comisión has been funded by international cooperation projects that require applications to access funding, the comisionadas' compensation is intermittent and usually does not sustain their livelihoods. However, the Comisión's office remains open, and comisionadas are constantly on the move. They see each other almost every day, as they meet in their office in Quibdó's downtown, and they regularly travel to rural communities along the Atrato River.

As a country of regions, Colombia has incorporated mestizaje, a blanqueamiento project idealizing race mixture as a conduit to whiteness, into its national narrative of national belonging: "blanqueamiento (whitening), or the racial ideology that embraces mestizaje (ethnoracial mixture), as part of popular and official discourses on Latin American identity provided the population steadily moves toward whiteness over time."[7] Chocó's belonging has been conditional and superficial. Colombia's centers of power are major cities such as Bogotá and Medellín, associated with a homogeneous white and mestizx[8] population that is read and identified as the ideal Colombian citizens. In contrast, Blackness is correlated with the Pacific and Caribbean coasts, disregarding their presence in other regions. Racialized regions are also intertwined with ideas of class, which is embedded with ideas of race: "racialization manifests itself by incorporating socioeconomic differences into a pigmentocratic game . . . classes have (skin) colors, in the sense that, generally speaking, people with greater capital (social, cultural, economic, symbolic, etc.) are 'lighter' in appearance, while those with less capital are 'darker' (which implies that darker mestizos may also be victims of racism)."[9]

The invisible but much-enforced imagined borders within Colombia are particular, not unique. Latin America "developed its own form of eugenics with the concepts of blanqueamiento (whitening) and its correlate mestizaje (racial mixing)."[10] To this day, Latin American national discourses couple mestizaje with multiculturalism, invoking racial mixture as an antidote to racism while erasing ethnic minorities. Colombia's regions are intertwined with preconceptions about national identity's ideal embodiment, reproducing a hierarchy in which able-bodied, light-skinned mestizo men are at the top, presented as the model citizens and leaders. It is common knowledge that power and altitude are intimately connected: "el Centro queda en el centro y además queda en lo alto"[11] [The center is at the center and also at the top]. Chocó and other racialized—particularly coastal—departments are included as repositories of biodiversity or cultural diversity. They are at the margins of Colombia's Andean centermost regions.

Colombia's violence has extended for over six decades, involving legal and illegal armies that expand the political spectrum of left and right. Chocó was not affected by Colombia's civil war between liberals and conservatives, and the presence of guerrillas and paramilitaries was not felt until the mid-1990s. As the only department with coastlines in both the Pacific and Atlantic Oceans, and because of its diversity of fauna and flora as well as gold, silver, and platinum, its natural resources and raw materials did not go unnoticed. After all, corporations benefiting from resource extraction and their relationship with paramilitaries is well known: "Links between paramilitary forces and agribusiness interests have been confirmed by various sources, including the United Nations High Commissioner for Refugees (UNHCR), the Colombian Attorney-General's Office (Procuraduría General de la Nación), the Human Rights Protection Office (Defensoría del Pueblo), Catholic church organizations, journalists and environmental groups."[12] As one of the latest provinces to earn recognition as a department, Chocó has constantly been placed on the margins of the centralist state's gaze. Its inhabitants, mainly Black and Indigenous, along with their cultures, knowledge, and ways of life, have been upturned by extractive practices precipitating their massive displacement from collective territories. To make things worse, when multicultural and multiethnic became official adjectives to describe the nation with the 1991 Colombian Constitution, Black communities officially joined Indigenous communities in the nation's peripheries, making the mestizx as the center even more legible. Not surprisingly, when former president César Gaviria Trujillo (1990–1994) ratified the law that recognized Black communities as an ethnic group in Quibdó in 1993, he stated that "la mayor riqueza que tiene el Chocó son sus gentes y sus bosques"[13] [Chocó's greatest wealth is its people and its forests].

Then again, thinking solely about armed violence ignores the tensions and ruptures of multilayered oppression. Violence is multilayered, victimizing Black and Indigenous women and their communities and territories in particular ways. Plan Colombia (now Peace Colombia), the War on Drugs, and contemporary multinational corporations' interests in the Pacific continue to fuel a conflict that is still active and transcends national borders. The limits between legal and illegal armed groups are entangled with the private and official memories that make national history. In this context, surviving an armed conflict that was not recognized by former right-wing president Álvaro Uribe (2002–2010) sounds like a miracle. Not only does survival seem lucky in the face of omnipresent violence, but also, victims are often revictimized as their testimonies become proof of horror. That most victims live in geographical spaces with no infrastructure associated with progress is read as a justification for violence, making revictimization particularly cruel.

Mosquera Pérez's *por qué no* reorients the center. She imagines an audience for her story that links COCOMACIA's collective territories and the women living there with the women across Colombia (now unmarked from mestizaje as the norm) and even extends her greeting to women worldwide. By centering the Colombian Pacific as the place of enunciation, this book and the stories that made it possible emulate why nots. Each story and node in the networks of knowledge and care that I write about invites the audience to imagine other ways to coexist and collaborate alongside a relentless war. Stories and storytellers are cited and considered knowledge producers in conversation with scholars, especially Latin American feminists, and other sources such as local museums, digital archives, and academic and nonacademic books.

Comisionada de género Luz Adonis Mena Becerra also created a story that urges women to participate in Black political organizing in COCOMACIA. While creating her story, I came to know that she had faced forced displacement and lost all her belongings in a fire many years later. Despite this, she reconstructed her memories for her story through photographs. Mena Becerra's story, like Mosquera Pérez's, is as partial as it is intentional. The willingness to imagine these stories before they had audiences, and despite the absence of personal archives, is utopian. Not because these stories are ideal or unrealistic, but because they rehearse turning what seems inconceivable, a postconflict, into a material reality.

As fragments that do not fully capture the political work of COCOMACIA's Comisión de Género during an ongoing armed conflict, these stories embody Mosquera Pérez's why not to embrace impossibility as challenge, not failure. Comisionadas' stories confirm survival as an everyday commitment. As a collective practice, survival is a promise.[14] And creating possibilities for performing survival opens opportunities for radical imagination in practice to support (and make) each other, in everyday life and in research. The possibilities imagined and enacted in Chocó connect that space of innovation to other spaces and other worlds. These connections are possible because of the narratives we use. In everyday performances of storytelling and survival, solidarity is intentionally imagined. In Chocó, collaboration alongside violence requires an everyday commitment, as the comisionadas will teach us.

Postconflict Utopias as Everyday Knowledge

This book and the digital storytelling archive *Mujeres Pacíficas*—meaning peaceful women and women from the Pacific—developed from a still ongoing collaboration with the comisionadas and other members of COCOMACIA. They document comisionadas' knowledge, who have experienced violence firsthand, and their understanding of their personal journey to becoming activists. For the comisionadas, survival is not accidental but an embodied practice, requiring a daily commitment to existing amid a decades-long (but often denied) war. I use their stories to trace their networks and other spaces that imagine peace in the middle of militarized spaces. As Mosquera Pérez suggests in the introduction to her story, Chocó is linked to Colombia and the world. International humanitarian funding coexists with multinational corporations and local, regional, and transnational feminist organizations. COCOMACIA's Comisión has benefited from alliances with the US Agency for International Development (USAID), the Swedish Fellowship for Reconciliation (SWEFOR), and the global feminist organization Women in Black (WiB), among many others. Peace in this context is not the imposed pacification practices that strive for the absence of disagreement.[15] Rather, peacemaking is the continuous daily willingness of imagining demilitarization while defending life.

Postconflict utopias disrupt the utopia/dystopia and peace/war binaries by exposing the multiplicity of stories, spaces, practices, and performances that exist in between these oppositional pairs. They practice what memory, peace, and justice could look like in a postconflict that has not materialized yet but is rehearsed constantly. Postconflict utopias are reminders that surviving in the Colombian Pacific is intentional but not guaranteed. Postconflict is not a temporal concept to mark the end of war, but a reminder that peace is still pending. I argue that postconflict utopias are strategies that make day-to-day survival and activism possible, despite violence. Postconflict utopias illustrate both impossibility—imagining peace—and the wish for a better world as a motivation for dismantling militarization one day at a time.

I am attracted to the negativity associated with utopia, postconflict, and survival as incomplete concepts. We think of surviving as the opposite of thriving.

Postconflict fabricates an aftermath of violence amid horror. We perceive utopia as naïve and idealistic. In her book *La guerra contra las mujeres*, even Argentinian feminist scholar Rita Segato warns about using the concept of utopia, a Eurocentric authoritarian projection to control the future.[16] But the "no-place" that utopia invokes exceeds an imagined future. Not naiveté, but speculative thinking. I use utopias as a multiple concept that maintains the tension between violence and survival. For me, utopias are gestures beyond the present, motivated by the hope there is a future to imagine after all. As political rehearsals that envision a different world, utopias exceed wishful projections. Utopias are everyday practices of ethics and politics. I start with this contradiction that utopia embodies: to imagine the unimaginable as utopia is creative. Utopia names what does not exist and makes visible the potential of the unknown. Utopias are embodied: they are dreamed and invoked in the repetition of daily actions that make up the collective imagination of a shared future.

I align these utopias more with Aymaran feminist scholar Silvia Rivera Cusicanqui's Pachakuti than with German philosopher Ernst Bloch's utopias. Rivera Cusicanqui defines Pachakuti, an Aymaran concept, as "un momento de inflexión, de cambio, pero que no es una cosa de la noche a la mañana, sino un proceso de acumulación profunda"[17] [a moment of inflection, of change, but not something sudden, but a process of deep accumulation]. Postconflict utopias build on Pachakuti as nonlinear change in time and space that invokes catastrophe and renovation, a slow process that invites change: "*Pachakuti o pacha thijra* [italics in the original] es un vuelco en el tiempo/espacio, el fin de un ciclo y el inicio de otro, cuando un 'mundo al revés' puede volver sobre sus pies"[18] [*Pachakuti* or *pacha thijra* is an overturning of time/space, the end of a cycle and the beginning of another one, when an "upside world" can return to its feet]. I see Pachakuti as an invitation to think beyond the binary, to value academic and nonacademic knowledge to understand the potential of holding multiple truths and temporalities and spatialities at once. As practices in which official narratives of denial and dismissal coexist with their own rupture, postconflict utopias recognize the possibility and difficulty of change as a nonlinear process. As why nots, postconflict utopias describe everyday rehearsals of change as calls to action rooted in processes full of contradictions and potential.

Activism amid militarization is political and risky. It requires planning, alliances, and endless work because of everyday challenges that render it incomplete. Utopia is built in the present and nurtured by individual and collective acts that create a collaborative idea of the world and how to transform it.[19] This world-making and transformative understanding of utopia implies that imagination precedes action.[20] While utopias can be perceived as dreams, their revolutionary potential highlights an unfinished process of doing and being.[21] In larger transnational feminist networks, organizing is a utopian gesture that forms part of their knowledge production. As Mosquera Pérez's why not, postconflict utopias signal what is not yet here. Something to guide desire that does not conceal how difficult it is to materialize it.

As the result of constant performative actions, postconflict utopias are worldmaking strategies for not giving up. Feminist organizing in patriarchal spaces, community caretaking when state infrastructures, such as hospitals and schools, fall short, Afrocentric community museums in the absence of Black national museums, digital archives even when electricity is a luxury. Expanding what we think of as survival and technology opens up possibilities to move from an analysis of technologies of oppression to an approach to agency that considers "survival technology," the practices and knowledge that exceed canonical understanding of knowledge production.[22] Creativity that imagines the survival of people who have everything stacked against their existence is built on Black women's awareness of the threats and opportunities for change despite oppression: "Black women used rhetorical and communicative devices as tools to dismantle oppression, transforming the voice into a technology of survival and resistance."[23] Hacking, remixing, and resisting dominant paradigms and stories are essential to survival in Chocó because they create alternative technologies for survival, a process led by Black women such as COCOMACIA's comisionadas. Postconflict utopias make visible the peace-building potential of activist impulses that sustain life by centering Black women's stories in Chocó, by framing their knowledge as part of "feminismo(s) en-lugar"[24] [feminism(s) in place]— local Black feminist practices and knowledge. Postconflict utopias reveal the contradictions of national narratives beyond Colombia. In essence, Mosquera Pérez's why not is part of larger narratives about collective territories that exceed national discourses. Mosquera Pérez's utopia is to imagine local collaboration and solidarity as part of networks that are not constricted by national borders.

"Es mejor vivir con miedo que dejar de ser por miedo" [It is better to live with fear than to cease to exist because of fear] is often repeated by the comisionadas to explain why they do what they do. Every comisionada has a different iteration of this sentence. At first, the saying seemed powerful, but repetition made it seem a cliché. One day, it clicked for me. Repetition is where the potential for change resides. Fear is present in the everyday when peace is only a promise. Fear is not abstract in Chocó. Every time I have visited the comisionadas in Quibdó, their stories about displacement, assassinations, and new and old armed groups remind me that postconflict and peace are still utopias in Colombia. Hope about what comes next is political when the present reveals the consequences of imagining peace, not as a neoliberal project linked to development but closer to a "paz en pequeña escala" [small-scale peace] and "paz en plural" [plural peace].[25] Or at least as the tension between pacification as a state project and the everyday practice of surviving. As noted, survival requires urgent and nonstop work. Daily rehearsals of peacebuilding work do not guarantee peace, and outcomes are unpredictable. The slow and repetitive drip of everyday persistence accumulates. As an affirmation renewing the importance of the struggle for existing, being is political.

Violence and Survival in Colombia

With the election of right-wing president Iván Duque (2018–2022), the 2016 peace deal with the Revolutionary Armed Forces of Colombia (FARC) continued to be threatened. Acts of repression by the government and other armed actors are still the norm even in pandemic times, where in departments like Chocó, illegal armed groups imposed their own rules on lockdowns. Over 1,100 social leaders have been assassinated since the 2016 peace accords were signed, proving that survival is hard work even in times of cease-fire.[26] As shown by the peace agreement after a popular "no" vote, an historic eight million votes for a leftist presidential candidate on June 17, 2018, and the first Black woman presidential candidate in the 2022 elections, there is space for dreaming of another world. Environmental activist Francia Márquez—who became vice president of Colombia's first leftist government in 2022—embodies the survival technology that materializes what has been historically deemed unimaginable.

Official narratives are not only government-endorsed academic publications, but every attempt to narrate a conflict that is not over yet in a context of denying or confirming the existence of a postconflict. Never-ending political polarization has been renewed for generations, with different actors and escalating techniques to create and narrate violence. In the 1960s, guerrilla groups appeared as a response to social inequality, land appropriation, and state violence. A plan to alternate conservative and liberal presidencies named El frente nacional [The National Front] between 1958 and 1974 was supposed to end political violence, but it only exacerbated corruption and distrust of the government. Confrontations among drug lords, guerrilla groups (the FARC, ELN, and M-19), state-armed groups, and self-defense groups marked Colombians' daily life in the 1980s. Soon after, self-defense groups turned into right-wing paramilitary forces that were legalized during the 1990s and supported by elites and the Army, which has been advised and trained by the United States since the 1960s. Because of these alliances to protect elites' lands, resources, and power, human rights activism and social movements have been historically associated with rural communities and lower classes, or guerrilla members.

Writing about survival in Colombia's unmaterialized postconflict context cannot be separated from the inertia of decades of nationalized horror. These continuities rely on chronologies that are not visible in the everyday and circulate in discourses loosely attached to experience. Violence has been a part of everyday life for so long in Colombia that debates about its historical starting point are still ongoing: 1948, the year in which the infamous historical period, La Violencia, started; 1964, when the best-known guerrilla group, the FARC, was born; and 1985, the year of the Palacio de Justicia holocaust, are well-known dates. And somehow, other important dates for the history of violence in Colombia are not part of every chronology: 1991, when recently amnestied members of the guerrilla group M-19 collaborated in creating a new constitution; and 2000, with the implementation of Plan Colombia, the US military aid aimed to end the "violence." Displacement and horror have marked generations of Colombians, but establishing a background implies selecting some events and discarding others.

The emergence of violentología [the study of violence in Colombia] materialized the ubiquity of violence. The iconic book *La Violencia en Colombia,* published in 1962,[27] included explicit photographs of mutilated bodies as a catalog of technologies of violence: photographs of the cuts inflicted on corpses with their respective names. *La Violencia en Colombia* institutionalized violence as an object and field of study while solidifying La Violencia as a historical period of nationwide conflict between liberals and conservatives following the assassination of the liberal presidential candidate Jorge Eliécer Gaitán. In 1987, the Colombian government created the Comisión de Estudios sobre la Violencia [Commission for the Study of Violence]. Meanwhile, the massacres and techniques of horror worsened with the incursion of drug cartels by the late 1980s and the assassination of three presidential candidates between 1989 and 1990. Academic books have continued to describe and classify violence ad nauseam—at least seven books have been published in English with "Violence in Colombia" in their title. Popular culture includes Colombian telenovelas about drug lords such as *El patrón de mal* and references about "the Colombian necktie" in the US television show *Hannibal*—and in literature, Colombian poet María Mercedes Carranza published *El canto de las moscas* in 1997, in which every poem is named after a town where a massacre took place.

The continuous obsession with violence in practice and writing led to the emergence of a literary genre, inaugurated by Fernando Vallejo's *La Virgen de los Sicarios* (1994). Named sicaresca—by literary critics following Héctor Abad

Faciolince[28]—playing with the word *sicarios* [hitmen] and the genre of the sixteenth-century Spanish novel, picaresca, that traced the adventures of pícaros [rascals]. "The term points to the transformation of a social phenomenon (the *sicariato*) into a cultural one (the *sicaresca* genre), grouping a variety of novels and films about the lives of the young *sicarios*, and in general about the violent and exuberant world of the narcos, that became popular in the late 1980s and are still very well perceived by the public" (emphasis in original).[29] Sicarios becoming mythic creatures, and their adventures worthy of fictional retelling and consumption, reveals the predominance of trauma in cultural representations of Colombia's violence. Thus, representations of Colombian violence are gendered. The commodification of the figure of Pablo Escobar and narcocultura as national symbols[30] and the glorification of masculinist violence in popular music and hypermasculine Colombian performers such as Maluma for global consumption[31] reinforce regional stereotypes as much as gender roles.

Portrayals of activism by Colombian mainstream media as leftist terrorism created a common enemy: guerrillas, strengthening the binary of good (state) vs. bad (anyone against the state). The FARC has been popularized as the public enemy of civilians, making other armed actors less visible to this day. In contrast, according to the Grupo de Memoria Histórica, paramilitaries are responsible for 58.9 percent of the 1,982 massacres documented between 1980 and 2012.[32] Politicians supported the state's paramilitarization, what has been called parapolítica, a process parallel to building an exclusionary state that threatens opposition. Paramilitary groups, in alliance with drug lords and security forces of the state, were responsible for the genocide that killed two presidential candidates for the 1990 presidential elections, and thousands of leftist Unión Patriótica political party's militants (which included former FARC members).[33] The predominance of violence within Colombian society has reinforced ethics and aesthetics that exalt trauma as a symptom of a long process of militarization linking justice and violence. As trauma and its representations have melded and exceed national borders, Colombianist scholar María Elena Cepeda's request is critical: "we must read global Colombianidad through the lenses of racialized regionalism and heteropatriarchy, frameworks that deeply inform the ways in which all Colombians are represented, from both within the community as well as from without."[34]

As Black studies scholar Claudia Mosquera Rosero-Labbé reminds us, the naturalization of state abandonment is explained by an Andean nationalist myth from the nineteenth century that can be challenged by the knowledge of Chocó as the most productive slave-mining region in the eighteenth century.[35] Chocó having the highest rates of illiteracy and poverty in the whole country is by design, which makes ethical production and dissemination of stories and archives alternative to national ones even more necessary. Quibdó, Chocó's capital, and the 100,000 people who live there have been excluded from national narratives through this process of creation as a racialized region.[36] It is no accident that this militarized and isolated region holds the lowest life expectancy and the highest infant mortality rate in Colombia. It comes as no surprise either that in 2022, internal displacement reached its highest point since the 2016 Peace Agreement, and that 62 percent of displaced people are Afro-Colombian.[37] On top of this relentless violence, Afro-Colombian authors have been historically made invisible and undercited in academic publications in the social sciences and humanities.[38]

In Chocó, where Black rural communities' collective land rights have been threatened by both armed actors and multinational corporations, published representations of the area are often written by outsiders and reproduce structures of coloniality. "Si tú las informas y las empoderas, van a ser lideresas" [If you inform women and empower them, they will become leaders], a mestiza nongovernmental organization (NGO) worker told me in 2012 in Bogotá, in reference to collaborating with Chocoan women. She was talking about the positive outcomes of the humanitarian economy fueled by international cooperation funds. Yet, this messianic discourse can be the source of other issues, as it happens alongside a world economy that benefits the Global North at the expense of the Global South; accordingly, the North can help the South and not vice versa. Collaboration, of course, is possible only within an economy of humanitarianism that both motivates and benefits from violence in the first place. Thinking about empowerment as something that can be given strengthens hierarchies and renders the benefits of these claims for funding agencies invisible.

Violence in Colombia has turned into an endless homogenizing abstraction. It does not only name an entire historical period (La Violencia) but conceals different armed groups, and it bleeds into representations of national horror and international interventions. I recognize the historical danger of perpetuating the silence about the continuous trauma of slavery in the multifaceted contemporary Colombian violence, as Claudia Mosquera Rosero-Labbé[39] has warned. This silence exists in the official stories alongside sequelae, which Christen Smith,[40] an expert in anti-Black state violence in the Americas, defines as reverberations of the state necropolitics—using postcolonial philosopher Achille Mbembe's concept to name the state-led distribution of death—against Black women in the Americas. These sequelae are present in the comisionadas' lives and stories, threatened by violent resonance of racial hierarchies that make health care a luxury and mercury from industrial mining a daily encounter in Chocó.

Survival as an intentional practice is not infallible against systematic violence. In redefining survival as a deliberate embodied labor that manifests in multiple everyday actions not always recognized as political, I explore how it can alter entire communities by redefining what it means to live through ongoing multiple instances of violence. I choose survival and not terms like survivance, resistance, or resilience to recognize that survival simultaneously requires intentionality and is only temporary, echoing "La historia de María del Socorro." Mosquera Pérez expresses her commitment to organizing and her community that theorizes survival as an inescapably collaborative project: "Tengo sesenta años cumplidos. A pesar de esa edad que tengo, me siento con ánimo de seguir trabajando, de seguirle aportando a todas y cada una de las compañeras que necesiten mi apoyo.... Porque cada día que uno crece, cada día que uno anda, necesita aún más apoyo de los compañeros y compañeras para poder sobrevivir"[41] [I am sixty years old. Despite my age, I have the strength to keep working, supporting all and every compañera that needs my help.... Because every day one grows, every day one walks, one needs more support from the compañeros and compañeras to be able to survive]. As Mosquera Pérez explains, survival requires collaboration. Survival is a methodical practice, but it is not guaranteed. It requires reciprocity and repetition. Survival is an ongoing outcome of everyday repetitive actions. Survival is both a utopian outcome and rehearsal. Documenting survival is part of valuing the everyday process of resisting and community building.[42] Survival is re-existencia, a collective resistance that does not explicitly oppose power.[43]

As an example of a feminist practice in the making, survival is a political rehearsal based on women's participation. Even if women's actions and stories are still insufficient to materialize peace, they are gestures toward social change. Shared within local, regional, and transnational networks, the vulnerability of women in conflict and postconflict zones does not disappear because of everyday political practices. Daily routines for collective living are a commitment to what is not yet possible, utopian rehearsals for survival in a postconflict where peace is still a wishful projection. As Audre Lorde taught us, survival is not an academic skill but mutual learning to look for worlds where it could be possible to bloom together.[44] Survival values a mode of learning that exists in the everyday and in our bodies. As the comisionadas' embrace of fear reveals, living itself is an embodied choice. A political one.

The Comisión de Género's activism and networks reveal daily survival and ethics as embodied ways of feminist knowing that manifest in the trust of a world that does not exist yet. Their actions and reflections about them echo survival as part of what performance studies scholar Diana Taylor calls "the repertoire," an embodied memory that is ephemeral and requires "being there."[45] As data that cannot be archived, survival is knowledge in practice, a performance. Survival and other postconflict utopias exist only in the doing, a process that might lack precision or planning because of a lack of embodied documentation. Survival as embodied knowledge—the lived experiences of women as survivors and activists—breaks the correlation between womanhood and victimhood in militarized societies. As embodied memory, the accumulation of survival strategies, tools, and knowledge is a collective project, as Mosquera Pérez teaches us.

As embodied knowledge, survival requires showing up, which comisionadas have done for decades, showing up for each other and the communities within COCOMACIA. A durational performance—following endurance art as a glimpse into rituals—survival requires a daily commitment to start over again and to reinvent the strategies and discourses that sustain it. Survival is a practice grounded in the everyday. A daily balance of moving forward and speaking out despite fear that invokes their affirmation: "es mejor vivir con miedo que dejar de ser por miedo," the act of survival is linked to storytelling. As Audre Lorde reminds us at the end of her poem "A Litany for Survival": "when we are silent / we are still afraid / So it is better to speak / remembering / we were never meant to survive."[46] As Lorde does, comisionadas use *we* in their meetings and informal conversations, always representing more than their own experience, and bringing their communities everywhere. Their showing up is rooted in taking up space that historically has been denied to them. Not because of fearlessness. But as a collective promise: a why not.

I understand survival as a feminist issue and a feminist practice. I follow decolonial feminist activist Julieta Paredes's definition of feminism as "teoría de las mujeres"[47] [women's theory] to include women's ways of knowing as feminist theoretical frameworks to understand lived experiences that might not always be framed as feminist. I build on feminist knowledge that calls for a "robust and transformative redefinition of survival,"[48] including the embodied work of the Comisión and its feminist alliances. This understanding is not independent from the conceptualization of the work of survival as a collaborative one, or the recognition of mutual aid (in life and research) as crucial for survival: "We need each other to survive; we need to be part of each other's survival."[49] The work of survival requires transnational frameworks of solidarity practices rooted in a feminist understanding of life, community, and justice.

Survival is utopian when violence is the norm. I approach survival by studying the role of daily performances and alliances, bearing in mind the centrality of ethics in community and research. The research questions that guide my analysis are based on how my ongoing collaboration with COCOMACIA's Comisión de Género has informed my understanding of survival: What does it mean to survive violence in a country in which peace negotiations and "post-conflict" strategies exist alongside still-active war zones? How is knowledge about survival produced and circulated? A transdisciplinary understanding of knowledge as a means for social change informs this book. My work intervenes in the conceptualization of violence in Colombia by continuously exploring who controls its narration and recognizing that narratives are at the intersection of culture and power.

As a transnational and transdisciplinary book, *Postconflict Utopias* takes part in conversations about alternative spaces, stories, memories, and practices that imagine the end of war in Colombia. It also traces embodiment to reveal the networks of solidarity as they create utopias, one of which is the labor of everyday survival, by expanding the practices labeled as activist and feminist. *Postconflict Utopias*' approach to postconflict Colombia as a utopia challenges peace as an ongoing reality after the accords and ongoing talks with the Ejército de Liberación Nacional (ELN) [National Liberation Army]. Peace as a narrative is not only a national one, and it demands our attention to question who benefits from reproducing official narratives that include some ways of knowing by excluding others.

Encouraged by a feminist understanding of knowledge, my research is a product of trust-building and collaboration. In my estimation, a feminist research practice means collaborating with those whose experience I seek to represent. This means recognizing that what I call feminist practices or feminism is community-building for the comisionadas and other collaborators. I also think of research as a performance that requires a daily ethical commitment to avoid reproducing trauma. It is not enough to assume feminism as an everyday commitment if it has not assumed racism as part of its struggle.[50] This book's intersectional feminism[51] requires thinking about ethical practices that are performed every day and interrogate and doubt, instead of assuming a linear morality and ethics. Feminism, then, is not only a theoretical framework but also "a strategy of social mobilization, a practice of solidarity, and a claim for reparative justice"[52] that requires endless rehearsals of insurgent creativity. Whereas decolonial Latin American feminisms have informed my writing and analysis, I do not claim this book to be decolonial or decolonizing. Guided by utopias and why nots, I imagine it to be decolonial-oriented in the spirit of joining those who have imagined other ways to research and exist together outside of the internalized colonial legacies we inhabit.

Utopian Research Methods

In researching and writing this book, I had to negotiate my insider status as Colombian with my outsider status as mestiza. I was born in Bucaramanga, Santander, and named after a guerrilla woman from the Cuban Revolution by leftist parents. Most of my family is from Santander, a department in the East. I grew up in Bogotá, traveling regularly to Bucaramanga and Barranquilla, where my maternal family moved before I was born. As a mestiza, I benefit from the colonial traces of writing-centric research by outsiders about Chocó. I have had access to resources available only in large urban centers where Black and Indigenous people are routinely excluded. I am a Colombian, and I am also privileged by my access to resources in the Global North. As Peter Wade explains, "The repertoire of mestizaje has always been transnational: individuals and institutions continuously make connections with globalizing forms of racism and anti-racism."[53] I negotiated my identity and relationships in different contexts with multiple institutions that have informed my analysis.

Postconflict Utopias is an ethnography of utopian storytelling based on my collaboration with COCOMACIA's Comisión de Género and its networks. This research draws on ethnographic methods that are more networked than multi-sited,[54] as well as a collaborative approach to digital storytelling. I conducted fieldwork in multiple stints since 2008. My trips to Colombia, and particularly Quibdó, have allowed me to take part in COCOMACIA's activities and be in constant communication with the Comisión. I have attended workshops, meetings, and multiple events organized by feminist organizations and local intellectuals and organizers. In multiple conversations with the comisionadas on how they continue working on behalf of their communities, while dealing with the ongoing violent effects and aftereffects of colonialism and capitalism, I have learned the difficult work of surviving. In the process, this research took me beyond the comisionadas' office and even beyond Chocó. Through this ethnographic analysis of the comisionadas' activities and their networks and drawing from different sources, including digital stories, museums, marches, alternative archives, and field notes, I highlight the political significance of local memories, archives, and embodied everyday practices. This allows me to move away from a traumatic narrative that reproduces violence and toward multiple stories beyond victimhood. I focus on how these embodied practices are the means for producing knowledge and imagining a peacetime that includes Black women's lives and territories.

In contrast to voyeuristic narratives of Colombia's armed conflict, *Postconflict Utopias* offers an understanding of peace-building that builds on the everyday.

By valuing creativity, repetition, and improvisation as part of everyday survival, I trace what is imagined, recovered, and dreamed collectively even in situations where trauma has become the norm. My previous research allowed me to think about the disconnection between women's vulnerability in times of war and their strategies for surviving after trauma. Such an approach led me to consider another one: the collaborative creation of survival narratives. Therefore, *Mujeres Pacíficas* was about including Black women's stories in collective memory narratives. Visibility might imply co-optation instead of access to rights or resources.[55] More representations might just mean more representations to confirm already established hierarchies. Representation is not a win in itself if "what replaces invisibility is a kind of regulated, segregated visibility."[56] If segregated visibility is what the regime of visibility leaves for the excluded, then the potential is not staked on visibility itself but on becoming visible. This book recognizes not only knowledge and archives that have small audiences and participate in global conversations about women's and territorial rights but also the importance of Afrocentric stories.

Following three trips of preliminary fieldwork in Chocó and my growing conviction regarding the need to avoid replicating a hierarchical mode of research, the comisionadas and I discussed working together on a project that could benefit both their interests and mine. They suggested working on a documentary together. I suggested a digital storytelling project. We did both. As funding and time were scarce, we had to revise our expectations of the aesthetics and the collaboration. The documentary was a visual strategy to justify the importance of their work in COCOMACIA's General Assembly that would take place in December 2013, while the personal stories were individual attempts to share their life experiences with women from local or global communities. This distinction was also explicit in the process for each product: using a script for the documentary, in contrast to relying on orality and spontaneity in the digital stories. We completed both in August 2013.

My observations are partial and based on observations, conversations, and archives made possible by members of different organizations, mainly from the Colombian Pacific. I avoid "extractive ethnography"—building credibility by using someone else's resources and experiences and giving nothing in return—so I have volunteered and exchanged time, labor, and knowledge with the people I write about. I believe this hands-on collaboration avoids the risk of "top-down" academic knowledge production that situates scholars on risky ethical terrain. It prevents further marginalizing women affected by the conflict from the spheres in which academic and theoretical debates take place, because, through digital stories, they state their case in their own terms. I undertook "collaborative ethnography" as a negotiation process during every step of the research, with my fieldwork and most especially the digital storytelling process making "collaboration... a space for the coproduction of theory."[57] This included recognizing the storytellers' knowledge and valuing their process of organizing and planning their own projects, while emphasizing that documenting their experience can also prove a useful reflexive exercise and tool of advocacy for the Comisión. While *Mujeres Pacíficas*' storytellers are not coauthors of this book, the stories are not only an output of our collaboration but also a structure that nurtured this book's main concepts. Still, comisionadas—portrayed on the book cover—were part of the process of creating the image in collaboration with Afro-Colombian artist Hanna Ramírez.

Ethics informs my recall and writing of words and lives that are not mine. I try to highlight agency, but as the narrator of this narrative, I am the one making the connections between my memory and my readings, and between my perception of the lives I only partially understand and the context that threatens them. In a particular framework of interaction, my body imposes the limits of what I perceive. I am far from unraveling the different strands that have created the Comisión through their constant work. What an everyday understanding of ethics[58] offers my research is the possibility to think about every detour in my collaboration as something that requires my attention, even if it does not seem to be the output I envisioned when I started. At first, I worried about how slowly my collaboration and the different parts of this project were moving. Reading about slow scholarship,[59] critical disability studies, and crip theory, with time, made me realize that because of my and my collaborators' chronic health issues, we had been moving in crip time[60] and rehearsing prioritizing each other. Digital humanist Moya Bailey writes that "the way we treat each other through our work is much more important than the resulting output,"[61] when she discusses the potential of slow Digital Humanities. This slow work is inspired by the comisionadas' work that materializes a crip-of-color critique that centers care in the context of racialized disablement.[62]

Understanding ethics as never finished implies uncertainty. There is hope in uncertainty. Ethics as an everyday repetitive practice calls for a product that includes collaborators as both producers and audience, and not only as primary sources or informants. In essence, this must be a utopian undertaking, because it has the possibility of failure due to the impossibility of empathy and the hierarchy that research presupposes. But instead of embracing failure as unavoidable, we embraced the collaboration as a why not. The utopian potential of collaboration is not possible without the interdependence that Mosquera Pérez conjures. It is uncertain and unstable even if it is positioned toward the future. It imagines the impossible even against the odds, which requires knowledge of the context at hand while hoping for something different.

My methodological approach combines participatory research methods with an analysis of *Mujeres Pacíficas* digital stories, and the process of their production, through the lens of performance. Digital storytelling creates the space for a close reading that values personal, collaboratively created stories. My project brings Afro-Colombian women's stories to the foreground and shows how their knowledge can be deployed as an analytical tool for understanding survival in Colombia as a transnational process. Local networks of care are interwoven with feminist and antimilitaristic feminist movements. And Blackness decenters mestizx identity as national identity by revealing the global links of the Colombian Pacific beyond national borders.

Mujeres Pacíficas, a digital archive created in partnership with comisionadas and COCOMACIA members, documents everyday peace-building efforts of Black women in the Colombian Pacific. This is a utopian endeavor, as "digital preservation requires layers of infrastructure."[63] By embracing digital storytelling's collaborative, non-hierarchical approach, I could imagine into existence some of my own projections about what research could be. As an audiovisual genre, its dissemination could reach different audiences, while its production was aspirationally more democratic. While the digital divide reaffirms the utopia of framing the digital as more accessible, these stories reveal a personal and ethical understanding of survival that is manifested in everyday practices rather than in acts of massive resistance. The everyday becomes a site of political commitment, and the stage to witness the global feminist networks of solidarity imagining peace. These stories perform as alternative knowledge to official history and memory. The website *Mujeres Pacíficas* works to make community-based research on everyday life accessible beyond academia, inspired by the idea of slow archives that "call attention to the multiplicity and plurality of knowledge, storying, placidness, and relational events without reducing practices or systems to binary logics of control or submission, past or present, authority or victim."[64] As an archive of personal stories about what it is like to survive, *Mujeres Pacíficas* documents women's daily survival strategies.

Digital stories materialized this collaboration. The decolonizing potential of audiovisual stories and collaboration is one of the utopias that interest me. Rehearsal and improvisation are integral to a collaborative process. These stories, and the networks they are part of, are glimpses into what we can imagine and dream even in situations where disempowerment seems the norm. Inspired by the emphasis on collaboration and community-building shared by

Mujeres Pacíficas storytellers, I think of collaboration and storytelling as essential for survival and knowledge production. The storytelling process is a source of knowledge beyond forcing questions and assumptions through interviews. It is a rehearsal of everyday ethics, an experiment in imagining otherwise. I value the embodied knowledge of collaboration as utopian to exemplify the optimism and failure of working with others in postconflict contexts. Digital storytelling fit my interest in collaborative research, not only because I had read, reflected, and received training with others in a previous community-based project, *Sexualidades Campesinas*,[65] but because of the possibility for engaging in collaboration within our time and money constraints.

What *Mujeres Pacíficas*' digital stories achieve is a situated knowledge of surviving Colombian violence, a knowledge as trustworthy as it is partial and locatable. The strength of this proposal exists in the worlds of possibility that are imaginable when recognizing the complexity of each woman's experience, and that invokes a theoretical and collaborative utopianism. I use performance studies to discuss the potential and limits of digital storytelling. I start by recognizing performances as ephemeral actions, embodied knowledge that circulates through the repetitive character of lived experience. Using this knowledge, I can see other rehearsals of survival that I group into what I call postconflict utopias.

Digital storytelling is a collaborative method to create stories with multiple origin stories. Digital storytelling is a small-scale genre in terms of its length, technology use, focus on the narrator's personal story, and dissemination. The genre's inherently small scale makes it potentially more democratic than other genres because of the ease of its production and circulation,[66] but this small scale also can be interpreted as an obstacle to its circulation in broad cultural spaces. At its core, digital storytelling is simple: tell a story using images and audio with minimal length. In terms of budget, difficulty, and ease, the digital storytelling method proves convenient. In fact, even its aesthetics show the uneventful character of the everyday that I hope to capture and discuss. These stories result from collaborations done with few resources and little time. They prove the potential of orality for creating new memories. They are about being present, as evidenced by comisionadas rejecting writing a script and reading it. For them, digital storytelling was a spontaneous genre in which their own voices could control the rhythm. Digital storytelling as collaboration-based participatory research allowed us to create narratives that recount women's livelihood and experiences.

In my genealogy of digital storytelling, Joe Lambert, founding director of StoryCenter (formerly the Center for Digital Storytelling), believes that "everyone has many stories to tell."[67] Each of my collaborators had lots of stories, and in the spirit of experimentation with collaboration and openness, we changed digital storytelling. The process used to develop the stories was not the standard digital storytelling process that starts with a storytelling circle and trains storytellers in the technology necessary to assume the role of producers. This workshop-based process lasts one day to one weekend. Participants learn the basics of storytelling and digital tools to make their story an audiovisual product. Although part of the advantage of digital storytelling is its format, the process leads to an outcome that "follows a very Western approach to storylines, which sees the story 'wrap up' neatly within 3–5 minutes."[68] For *Mujeres Pacíficas* we adapted digital storytelling to our collaboration's objectives, and the storytellers' preference of telling stories that can be more associated with "non-Western storytelling forms or traditions, which celebrate stories-in-process and do not require stories to conclude succinctly and fully by the end."[69] This implied flexibility in the process and outcome, which included working one on one to shape and tell the stories. As a bottom-up process, we embraced digital storytelling as a practice where storytellers lead the way, from brainstorming about a story to editing. The process was also adapted around storytellers' preference to tell their stories (instead of writing them). And while they were not particularly interested in the minutiae of hands-on editing, *Mujeres Pacíficas'* storytellers consider the stories to be their own.

The differences among the stories point to the comisionadas' agency in shaping their speech and self-representation for different purposes, using identity as a malleable (and unstable) material. This supports what Geraldine Bloustien and other media scholars have noted: "As part of an overall participatory ethnographic methodology, participatory video can point to the ability to (mis)represent, constitute, negotiate, and play with self-image."[70] In digital storytelling, self-representation is fluid and made up of decisions about what to tell, as much as it is made up of silences and what is left unsaid. Also, it is important to note that genre determines storytelling and how performing personal stories creates different strategies for self-representation.

Sharing, however, differs from public distribution, which might increase storytellers' vulnerability, as they entrusted me with interpreting and disseminating their narratives. Storytellers refused the possibility of anonymity because their commitment to the organization requires the fearlessness of becoming public figures. Their names and pictures are already on social media, books, news, and press releases. Dreaming about using stories as advocacy tools does not cause automatic social change. Stories' distribution and use to motivate civic engagement or policies that benefit Chocoan women can be unrealistic, as media-making is not part of the comisionadas' everyday life. Sharing stories reaffirms the community knowledge behind the practices of keeping going and showing up, usually taken for granted in discussions of organizing.

Even if utopia seems incompatible with digital storytelling, the utopian as "the answer to the universal ideological condition that no alternative is possible, that there is no alternative to the system"[71] is an invitation to picture alternatives. Utopia as simultaneous impossibility and rupture offers an alternative to no opportunities. Creating audiovisual narratives from lived experiences and stories of survival is a utopian endeavor. My utopian methodology documents stories and the embodied knowledge that informs and escapes them. As such, this book engages with storytelling and the coalition work necessary for organizing and surviving as speculative world-making practices. As ways of thinking, everyday storytelling and a collaborative approach to create digital stories are invitations for dialogues and conversations that keep building networks of pushing against what has been presented as the only ways to exist, interact, and do research.

Although I have shared my publications and presentations in Spanish and English about our collaboration with the comisionadas, and they have even attended some virtual events about *Mujeres Pacíficas*, my writing reflects our interactions as much as my own readings, training, and obsessions. My research engages debates within cultural studies, performance studies, and women's studies that challenge writing as the center of knowledge production. Also, the personal stories complicate the supremacy of writing over orality in academic practice, which often marginalizes communities participating in research. I recognize my writing as a rehearsal, an open process of making sense of and producing the stories, places, and networks I explain. Beyond writing-centric knowledge, I hoped the stories could help rethink the limits between academia and community that reinforce languages and narratives that strengthen this binary. I find digital storytelling to be complementary to ethnography. It is a practice that facilitates collaboration. It strengthens my purpose of circulating knowledge beyond writing, even if the ephemerality of everyday practices cannot be completely shown in linear, audiovisual narratives. Instead of assuming or creating narratives about the other's pain, digital stories envision collaboration as the closest we can get to empathic listening, even when the result is distant from achieving a complete grasp. I move beyond "a damage-centered framework," in which "pain and loss are documented to obtain particular political or material gains."[72] Instead, I embrace "desire-based research frameworks" that make "understanding complexity, contradiction, and the self-determination of lived lives"[73] possible.

I keep in mind cultural historian Saidiya Hartman's reminder: utopias are made of disillusionments and failures, as even Thomas More's ideal society was possible only through enslaved labor.[74] While avoiding overgeneralizations of Black women as victims and in centering their stories, this book maintains a tension between denouncing violence and recognizing the daily labor that makes activism (and collaboration) possible. My intervention is centering Black women's experience of navigating militarized spaces by using their own stories to value their lived experience as embodied knowledge of survival. *Postconflict Utopias* expands conversations about the Colombian Pacific in multiple ways. With its focus on digital storytelling, it contributes a methodological approach otherwise rare in this scholarship. Using the stories themselves as part of its theoretical framework makes space for challenging traditional understandings of what counts as knowledge and who counts as a knowledge producer. With the purpose of valuing more than academic and official storytelling, I embrace reflexivity as part of feminist knowledge production, and I value digital storytelling as a tool for feminist collaboration. In the process, I explore how expansive feminist research methods can contribute to academic knowledge production while recognizing that community knowledge transcends academia. I center analog and digital archives as community repositories, finding value in everyday repetitive practices such as showing up as the foundation of social movements. Moreover, this book centers Black women's activism in the Colombian Pacific as part of transnational and global movements that challenge heteropatriarchy and white/mestizx supremacy in Abya Yala and beyond. By exploring how race and region are entangled in Colombia, I also challenge the discourses of difference that reinforce stereotypical ideas about power and nation.

Postconflict Utopias reflects the violence before and after Colombia's peace accords, and the restless work of peace-building. Someone's utopia is surely someone else's dystopia, especially when peace is a wild card. Dystopias make utopias possible, following Rivera Cusicanqui's understanding of the interdependence of colonialism and decolonization.[75] Utopias become blueprints for an imagined peace—not as prescriptive ideals, but as opportunities for community-building and solidarity. *Postconflict Utopias* traces my search for these utopia seekers, and my interest in joining them. More important, as the *Mujeres Pacíficas*' stories, this book is an invitation to engage with the utopias I have collected here, but with a utopian thinking that can add other spaces and stories to the work of imagining together. Furthermore, *Postconflict Utopias* challenges the binary form/content by blurring the limits of writing and books to think about the process of knowledge production within and without these pages.

This book is organized into six chapters. I begin with "Utopian Rehearsals," discussing my first trip to Chocó in 2008 as an opportunity to rehearse writing, research, and storytelling as examples of postconflict utopias. I also rehearse a chronology of violence in Colombia to challenge and move beyond official narratives. As a stage for examining everyday acts as performative (both embodied and creative), this chapter highlights practices of everyday survival. I examine the work of two women's organizations in Chocó: Vamos Mujeres in San Francisco de Ichó and COCOMACIA's Comisión de Género in Quibdó. I argue their activism does not exist in opposition to, but alongside, violence. As I trace my own hesitation throughout, this first chapter underscores the importance and challenges of writing someone else's stories while exploring how untranslatability encourages engaged research.

After rehearsing research and writing to frame las comisionadas' work in chapter 1, I move to tell "Utopian Stories." Taking place mostly in 2013, this chapter is a close reading of *Mujeres Pacíficas'* stories and how the process of collaboration to create them becomes utopian as well. An overview of adapting the digital storytelling process, and stories created in collaboration with women members of COCOMACIA, this chapter traces the discourses of feminism, humanitarianism, and Black organizing that permeate these personal narratives. I also juxtapose narrative elements of mainstream or official narratives with fragments of stories that have not yet been commodified. Such pieces make each story unique and show the storyteller's particular approach to self-representation and community.

Storytelling as the basis of research and *Mujeres Pacíficas* leads me into exploring "Utopian Archives" away from COCOMACIA. In this chapter, I explore additional spaces in Chocó that imagine other ways of knowing and knowledge production. I start with two local public intellectuals, historian Sergio Antonio Mosquera Mosquera and theologian Gonzalo de la Torre Guerrero, and their public archives in Quibdó, who belong to Afrocentric networks of knowledge production alongside violence. As manifestations of utopias, these alternative repositories of memory are spaces of knowledge production and alternative archives of collective memory. This close reading of two independent museums in Quibdó, Muntú Bantú, and a biblical museum, La Muestra Bíblica, exemplifies the continuities between analog and digital memories as much as the vulnerability of these spaces that further contextualize the tension of violence and re-existencia in Quibdó.

In "Utopian Memories," I analyze two digital platforms: the community website Memorias del Río Atrato and the Instagram account Fotógrafas del Pacífico, alongside writer Velia Vidal's cultural project Motete and her epistolary book *Aguas de estuario*. I argue that, while visual memories question the prevalence of writing, their main value lives in creating utopias, as community-based decolonizing projects, alternative archives of memory of Black communities' survival.

These analog and digital archives have the potential to turn embodied knowledge into alternative narratives of memory that center survival and decenter mestizaje.

"Utopian Networks" moves beyond local archives, following the connections among local, regional, and transnational feminist activism. It illuminates everyday strategies of caring for each other by showing up—being there, a requirement for performative practices. I look at three feminist organizations: La Red Departamental de Mujeres Chocoanas, a regional feminist coalition of women's organizations in Chocó; La Ruta Pacífica de las Mujeres, a feminist movement including 300 organizations from eighteen different departments in Colombia; and Women in Black (WiB), an anti-militarist network present in over 150 countries. I imagine showing up as a durational performance that makes transnational solidarity possible as a strategy for peace-building.

"Everyday Utopias" circles back to the Colombian Pacific to frame peace-building and activism as ethical practices rehearsed every day. It argues for an alternative to normative ethics (predetermined based on an abstract morality), using embodied ethics (informed by collaboration and interaction) as a tool to recount the comisionadas' personal lives and advocacy work. As other postconflict utopias examined before, ordinary ethics is an everyday performance that requires constant repetition, rehearsals, and collaboration, and that contains the potential of failure. I also offer insights on the ethical dilemmas and power relations in community-based research as well as the limits of storytelling.

Finally, the conclusion frames utopias as the tension between disappointment and anticipation. The stakes of imagining otherwise in the broader political, cultural, economic, and social landscape of Colombia's violent postconflict imply silences and omissions. By illustrating the limits of both collaborative methodologies and writing to capture embodied knowledge, this final reflection reifies the political potential of everyday utopias, stories, and utopian thinking for collaboration and collective survival.

Postconflict utopias as why nots are transnational gestures that transcend what seems possible and real based on the constraints of the present context. And precisely because they go against what seems rational or logical, a commitment to seeing and enacting them requires ongoing practice. This book rehearses the utopian commitment of narrating and imagining survival alongside violence and dreaming of peace, one day at a time.

CHAPTER 1

Utopian Rehearsals
Ethical Considerations on Moving Beyond Victimhood

> En el 2011 . . . se hizo el encuentro aciático en la comunidad de Tutunendo. . . . Las compañeras por miedo también no hablaron y me dejaron ese tema a mí, del diagnóstico participativo. Yo, sí señor muy animada, y todo, pero cuando yo me paré al frente que yo vi más de 600 personas a mí el cuerpo, a mí me temblaba hasta el cabello . . . me sirvió mucho porque eso le sirve a uno para ir botando el miedo, para ir cogiendo cancha a la hora de pararse ante un público y sí despierta uno, ya para cuando le toque a uno la próxima, ya uno lo hace de forma diferente. Ya sale uno con menos miedo de equivocarse, de hacerlo mal al frente de tanta gente.
>
> In 2011 . . . the COCOMACIA's encuentro was held in the community of Tutunendo. . . . The compañeras also did not speak out of fear and they left that topic to me, the participatory diagnosis. Yes, sir, I was very animated and everything, but when I stood in front of more than 600 people I saw my body, even my hair trembled . . . it helped me a lot because that helps to lose fear, to practice when it comes to standing before an audience and you wake up, by the time you have the next one, you do it differently. One leaves with less fear of being wrong, of doing it wrong in front of so many people.
> —Yenny Palacios Romaña

Fish scales land on the stairs that lead to the Atrato River as women's hands cut rapidly with knives. Boats in all sizes and colors, street peddlers, and people waiting inundate Quibdó's wharf. It is two hours after departure time, but there is no rush. The comisionadas carry heavy sacks of sugar and rice, water bags, boxes of Chilean apples, crackers, candy, and packages of meat and chicken into our weak metal boat, with the help of only one man, the boatman. They do not let me help with the heavy stuff, and when we finally get into the boat, they make sure I am comfortable. We are going to Tanguí for a workshop the Comisión de Género has organized with funding by the UNHCR (United Nations High Commissioner for Refugees). This time, they suggest that I board the UNHCR's boat to avoid burning my light skin. I refuse. I do not know anyone there. We do not talk about not being able to buy food in Tanguí. We do not talk about not following the community's suggestion to feed the workshop participants with what the community produces and prefers to eat: fish, plantains, and local produce. We do not talk about bringing the same crackers and Chilean apples no one likes or about the chicken that went bad last time because of the lack of refrigeration (and electricity) in town. During the last workshop, community members suggested the comisionadas buy chicken, fish, sugar cane, and fruits from Tanguí, but NGOs' funding depends on receipts, license numbers, and authorized signatures that Tanguí lacks. Everyone knows that buying imported goods in Quibdó is not convenient for the community or the comisionadas. But everyone also knows not to fight bureaucracy when money depends on receipts as proof, and food depends on bureaucratically generated money. We stop the boat anyway, next to other boats in the market, to get some green plantains and green bananas to fry later. Bureaucracy might rule, but it does not win every time.

As activists working with displaced rural communities, comisionadas struggle daily with dilemmas and challenges caused by global forces, such as a "humanitarian" economy of "doing good" that reproduces social inequalities and community desires, as financing agents influence what food community members can eat during meetings. This struggle is not unusual. It reveals the spectrum of violence that inhabits daily life in the Colombian Pacific beyond the infamous political violence. New forms of colonialism, embodied by the presence of outsiders like me, strengthen hierarchies of race, class, and gender. Imposing. Suggesting. Helping. Changing the way of doing things. It also reveals that survival is much more than the passive action of existing after trauma. Surviving within a militarized space requires an everyday negotiation of identities that escapes singular explanations. It requires the willfulness to find spaces within structures and systems that impose foreign bureaucracy and food, for healing through known practices, and even local food. Joining forces with institutional and governmental representatives to work with communities is one of many ways in which comisionadas survive and help others survive.

What I see now in the daily practices of COCOMACIA's Comisión is something that I could not grasp in my first trip to Chocó: there is potential in the everyday and the ordinary for revealing characteristics of survival that escape analyses of macrostructures or totalizing theories. By not articulating a forced interconnectedness on experiences that are fluid and changing, we prevent (at least partially) reproducing and imposing models of oppositional politics in which we can read every action as resistance, even if it is not facing hegemonic power. The everyday intertwines oppression and resistance. Their blurry borders require attention to avoid reproducing stereotypical narratives or revictimizing survivors. In between the oppression/resistance binary, survival is a rehearsal of ethics, a committed repetition of practices as creative rituals of imagination.

Before meeting COCOMACIA's comisionadas de género and Asociación Vamos Mujeres' members, I had understood survival as mortality's opposite, with a lingering stickiness of medical prognosis: a random strike of luck for people existing in contexts of violence, not a process that takes daily effort. In Chocó, I have learned that everyday acts reveal more than endurance, the centrality of community, even—or especially—in situations of extreme vulnerability to guarantee survival. Looking closer at where the daily energy is directed uncovers the agency of community members, particularly women, in forging their own paths toward survival in postconflict scenarios, not defined by the absence of violence but through rehearsing strategies of collective survival. Hope is not an abstract concept but a practice of giving through action: workshops and messages about women's rights and territorial rights as much as care and material support for people in moments of hopelessness. "Siempre la COCOMACIA ha estado allí presente"[1] [COCOMACIA has always been present] invokes comisionada Banessa Rivas López in her story noting persistence and presence as essential for community work. Survival is cocreated in this work.

San Francisco de Ichó is one of COCOMACIA's 124 community councils, and my first site of fieldwork. Referred to simply as Ichó, this town is located fifteen miles northeast of Quibdó (the capital of the Chocó department) and is considered part of its municipality. It is a two-hour drive from Quibdó through the road that leads to Medellín or through the Atrato and Neguá Rivers. In 2005, 410 people were estimated to live in Ichó. Two organizations are active in the community: Ichó's local community council and the Asociación Vamos Mujeres [Let's Go Women Association], founded in 1993. As part of COCOMACIA's collective land title, the community is represented by the community council's board. While Ichó's community is majority Black, it coexists with Indigenous and mestizx communities. Two Indigenous reservations coexist with the Ichó community: the resguardo indígena del Alto Río Neguá and the resguardo indígena del Río Ichó. The whole region has been threatened by extractive mining.[2]

During the 1980s, Ichó's agricultural communities embraced the state-promoted project of mining. In 1993, when the mining industry was in crisis and the community's food security and general wellness were in danger, a group of women organized to rediscover traditional agricultural practices. Clashes between Colombia's regular Army, the guerrillas, and the paramilitaries promoted the first families' displacement. By 2000, with the arrival of left-wing armed group Ejército de Liberación Nacional [National Liberation Army] (ELN), only thirty families remained. After this massive displacement, Vamos Mujeres led the community's return and rebuilt the place. Going back meant working in agriculture and mining simultaneously to have food to eat. The activities women led through the organization (working, getting food, and earning money) promoted their partners' greater participation in domestic work.

The activism of Vamos Mujeres and COCOMACIA's Comisión de Género is not best described as oppositional, even though in Colombia, the exclusion of Black communities from political life was a norm until the constitutional reform of 1991 acknowledged them as an ethnic group.[3] The inclusion of Transitory Article 55, requiring legal recognition of the collective property rights of the Pacific coast's rural Black communities, was a product of alliances among Black social movements, academics, and politicians. However, Black communities' displacement from these territories because of confrontations between legal and illegal armed groups reveals the never-ending struggle for inclusion and social justice. The temporary character of alliances, inclusions, and exclusions exposes the need for a new vocabulary to name what escapes the dichotomy of core/periphery and oppression/resistance while valuing the daily contradictions of power, endurance, and identity.

COCOMACIA's members see both the Ichó community's reconstruction and working as comisionadas de género for the organization as collective life projects, and not as struggles against any of the groups involved in the crossfire. Centering their experience places these groups alongside—rather than against—violence. The commitment to carrying on is not positioned toward the state or the armed groups. It is a cocreation that faces the community and its territories as the center. Not the margins. It is a collective effort that requires daily negotiations with insiders and outsiders, as noticed in the comisionadas' reliance on funding for their workshops as well as their refusal to adhere exclusively to the guidelines imposed by that funding. Vamos Mujeres has also secured financial aid and support from NGOs and other institutions, which has helped their commitment to make life livable alongside militarization.

Centering daily rehearsals of survival, I examine everyday acts as performative (as both embodied and creative) practices of survival that exist alongside (not in opposition to) violence. I frame this as a rehearsal of writing about violence in Colombia. First, I locate my writing as part of feminist rehearsals of storytelling. Second, I rehearse scholarly genealogies of Colombian violence to locate my own analysis. Third, I reflect about my failure to grasp the experience of San Francisco de Ichó's community group Vamos Mujeres during my first trip to Chocó and rehearse writing about survival as an ongoing practice to trace the utopias of postconflict contexts. In turn, I embrace the tension between suffering and choosing utopian narratives as a necessary optimism essential for the Comisión's work alongside violence.

Feminist Rehearsals

I am not a survivor of Colombian violence. And yet, somehow, stories of forced displacement, shootings, violent deaths, and insurgency are part of my family history and transgenerational memory. My own positionality gives me the privilege of accessing written narratives and traveling within and outside Colombia to learn about what has been less written or talked about. An outsider in Quibdó, my affiliation to nonprofits and universities has translated into credibility, access, and even safety. As a mestiza who grew up in Bogotá, I also enjoy the privilege of inclusion, of being in the center of national representations. I speak a variety of Spanish that has been historically associated with power and correctness inside and outside Colombia. All these forms of violence contextualize my existence and mobility, establishing a need to rehearse feminist ethics in research, guided by decolonial feminist Ochy Curiel's questions: "What does it mean for white feminists of the Global North to study women of the Global South, or for academic feminists of the South to study the 'other' local women of their own countries? Under what kind of relationships are these investigative exercises done?"[4]

I rehearse feminist frameworks to make violence visible as more than a national history. I move beyond trauma to center less-known stories of survival. This incomplete collage is the framework in which dreaming about peace seems irrational, and there is nothing more rational than the willingness to survive. I see postconflict as not only an unrealized era but also a scenario,[5] a particular way to see what exists and what does not exist yet. Postconflict maintains the tension between trauma and peace. It reinforces national narratives about violence, and it is reproduced by narratives that center the horror.

I locate this rehearsal of finding what escapes the grasp of Colombian violence in a broader context of US hemispheric militarization. Colombia's old war between liberals and conservatives, renewed with the birth of the guerrillas and the formation of paramilitary groups funded by drug lords, has fused with the terrible effects of fumigation and militarism promoted by Plan Colombia since 2000—even though US intervention can be traced to 1903 with the independence of Panamá and the military training provided to Colombians through the School of the Americas (now Western Hemisphere Institute for Security Cooperation). To further complicate matters, three armed actors (guerrilla, military, and paramilitary) have been implicated in the drug trade—which made Colombia's violence famous globally in the 1980s—and the last two have been beneficiaries of US training and aid. Ironically enough, US investment in Colombia has two targets: drug trafficking and insurgency. But this preliminary summary of the conflict already allows us to identify those who ultimately suffer the brunt of the conflict: rural populations, mainly Indigenous and Black communities. It also identifies society's militarization as a constant cause of and response to the conflict, one that further reinforces unequal gender relations. The predominance of armed violence and the impossibility of institutional justice has especially shaped the lived experience of communities excluded from a centralist state that has structured power around urban areas, white/mestizx identity, and the Andean region.

Peace negotiations with the FARC, the oldest and largest guerrilla group, that started in September 2012 have materialized, more than ever, that the so-called postconflict is a continuation of violence as much as an opportunity for imagining peacetime. This process has created a conjuncture for discussing demobilization and creating spaces for debate and discussion about truth and justice in the media, community organizations, and academia. Yet the peace talks were bilateral. They included only the state and the subversive group, excluding other armed actors and civil society. As an incomplete peace process, the FARC's demobilization has prolonged the sense of impunity created by Law 975, known as the "Justice and Peace" law, in place since July 25, 2005, that promoted the demobilization of paramilitary forces, some of which were discovered not to be paramilitaries. Bloque Nutibara's demobilization ceremony, which has been described by former paramilitary "El Alemán" as "a false demobilization with new boots,"[6] is an example. The peace process also invokes the demilitarization of a fake FARC bloc in 2006 staged by then-Peace Commissioner Luis Carlos Restrepo, who fled the country after the attorney general's office issued an arrest warrant for him in 2012. With the relentless targeting and assassination of social leaders and former FARC members since the peace agreement with the FARC was signed, there is nothing more utopian than dreaming of peace.

I argue that both Vamos Mujeres and the Comisión, as part of COCOMACIA, are possible as activist spaces because of embodied practices that are not explicitly oppositional. Despite the impact that the armed conflict can have on the materiality of women's bodies or lives, these groups embody habits and actions to make life livable. Their members' agency creates spaces that do not oppose, or need, the hegemonic understanding of violence as a dualistic process involving (masculinized) perpetrators versus (feminized) victims. I conceptualize this process of empowerment outside of the oppression-resistance logic. Resistance, like survival and the actions of social organizations, should not be reduced to a confrontation or response. It is a concurrent process. Understanding the coexistence of violence and survival allows us to see what exists beside them.[7] As a result, valuing what is alongside or beside (and not in opposition to) hegemonic powers also allows us to embrace embodied knowledge. The knowledge that circulates to make survival possible takes multiple shapes in the everyday practices of care and community building.

When Banessa Rivas López explains her work as a comisionada in her story for *Mujeres Pacíficas*, hope cannot be disassociated from violence. Hope is not an abstract concept. It is willingness to give through action, through solidarity. As a comisionada, advisor for COCOMACIA's youth group Comisión Juvenil de COCOMACIA (COJUCOMA), and later, as a guardiana del Atrato [defender of the Atrato River] and a member of the Foro Interétnico Solidaridad Chocó [Interethnic Solidarity Forum of Chocó] (FISCH), Rivas dreams up a collective future by working with others. She has traveled to every zone of the organization to bring information, supplies, and support. Rivas was born in Isla de los Rojas Negra, Murindó, one of the three (out of eight) municipalities in Antioquia that are part of COCOMACIA. But most of her work has happened in Quibdó, where COCOMACIA's offices are located. Because her family's participation in the organization facilitated her own future work, COCOMACIA is intertwined with her personal life.

In the stage of postconflict, peace becomes a utopian rehearsal. Not performed exclusively by activists, peace is suggested in official narratives, faked by armed actors, weaponized by US intervention, and invoked by chronologies of violence. Rehearsing feminist storytelling sets up the background for imagining genealogies where feminist ethics center survival instead of trauma. Not to deny or suppress the need to grieve or acknowledge the long-standing effects of trauma, but as an alternative to associating racialized communities and regions exclusively with damage and resilience. As hope manifests in the comisionadas' work and their stories, peacebuilding is a process of caretaking rooted in constant presence.

Social movements are will in practice. They can respond to or take part in broader networks, but what assembles them at a micro level is the crossroads of individual motivations in a specific historical and spatial context. Survival is not possible outside of the alliances between daily practices and organized social movements. Workshops led by COCOMACIA's Comisión, for example, mix practices that invoke comisionadas' training by NGOs (games, policy discussions, invited guests), community practices (praying, taking turns cooking, including men and children in meetings, feeding the whole community), COCOMACIA's institutional customs (taking minutes, assigning bureaucratic roles to community members, memorizing information about the organization), and transnational feminist performances (singing an anthem about women's empowerment, stretching, organizing against gender-based violence). Creativity, improvisation, and dialogue inform interactions between the workshop leaders and the communities.

Daily persistence makes possible the continuity of the Comisión and Vamos Mujeres, a process that exemplifies embodied knowledge: an ephemeral, amorphous, and idiosyncratic proficiency in endurance. What seems monotonous in meetings and workshops adds up. Sometimes it is not even the content of these scheduled interactions that makes them valuable. Presence makes some things possible to perceive and transmit only in interaction with others. Being there and showing up are not archivable. They demand intentional repetition. Showing up inspires others to show up, too. Not as an obligation but to be in community, to experience reciprocity. As performative knowledge, survival requires practice and presence. There is no documentation to rely on.

Justa Germania Mena Córdoba attended the workshop in Tanguí in August 2013, despite her pain from metastasized cancer. She died in October of the same year. In her last months, she was at the Comisión's office daily and actively participating in everything she could. Her place was not at home, she reminded everyone, which made me think of Audre Lorde's journals and her writing about cancer and survival: "Survival isn't some theory operating in a vacuum. It's a matter of my everyday living and making decisions."[8] Mena's survival and decision-making are intertwined with her work as part of COCOMACIA and her community. As Lorde taught us: "cancer is political."[9] And as Jina B. Kim writes about Lorde's cancer: "cancer is not an individual property limited to and contained by her body's boundaries, but an extension of the state-sanctioned and extralegal systems that seek to delimit, contain, and exploit [B]lack life."[10] For Mena, showing up was not a denial of her imminent mortality but a choice in how to spend her time and energy in community.

In a video homage comisionadas made to celebrate Mena Córdoba's life, mentions of her showing up, doing the work, and motivating other women to join el proceso (COCOMACIA) reveal the power of presence. "Para Justa" [For Justa] was the title the comisionadas chose. In this video, Yenny Palacios Romaña shared Mena Córdoba's commitment to el proceso as a desire to share a common goal that illuminates and guides bonds of solidarity: "esas ganas de querer que hayan miles de personas que están luchando por un mismo ideal, pero que hay una lucecita adelante que está alumbrando y diciendo es por aquí, por aquí, hagámoslo, mire. Agarremonos de aquí, este es el lazo, esta es la cadena, amarremos lazos. Amarremos, amarremos"[11] [the desire to want thousands of people fighting for the same ideal, but with a light in front of them that is shining and saying it's this way, let's do it, see. Let's grab this. This is the rope, this is the link. Let's bond, let's bond]. Imagining Mena Córdoba as the guide of an endless thread of people who share a common struggle is a visual representation of the process as a collective embodied effort that requires endless repetition. Mena Córdoba's leadership is portrayed as essential, a guiding force, but not only that. Her leadership is part of a collective effort toward a common ideal. This utopian image unravels the collaborative and generational struggle that makes el proceso a community-building practice. An intergenerational bonding practice.

Daily actions disclose tacit knowledge. Comprehensive models that ignore the intricacy of the present cannot rationalize or explain the everyday. Focusing on the structures overlooks the multiplicity and chaos of a present that is not capturable.[12] The singularities of the present can be accessed only when paying attention to how inhabiting the ordinary reveals the value of routine, the transformative potential of daily performances. In a more recent visit to the comisionadas in 2019, when talking about the difficulties of finding funding in a postconflict context, one of the comisionadas mentioned that "el trabajo de la comisión con las comunidades nos mantiene animadas, alimentadas" [the Comisión's work with communities keeps us in good spirits, nourished]. Explaining the work with the communities as motivation for such work makes visible the cyclical experience of performing daily repetitive actions. The "practices of everyday life"[13] are more than the background of politics. The knowledge produced and shared within the organization can be only partially accessed through storytelling and visual commemorations of those who did the work before (Figure 1.1). The everyday is political and demands presence.

Finding well-being in work that does not provide financial security might reinforce ideas about women's labor as free, except, when I asked about plans to receive compensation for their work, another comisionada observed: "pensar en uno, pero también pensar en las mujeres que son las que nos dan la fortaleza" [to think of oneself, but to also think about the women who give us strength]. To keep on going as part of finding strength and comfort in working with others hints at survival as labor even if its output seems counterintuitive. The collaborative work of translating this strength and nourishment into food necessary to survive is left unsaid. Comisionadas take turns cooking and sharing among themselves as part of their everyday routines. They have

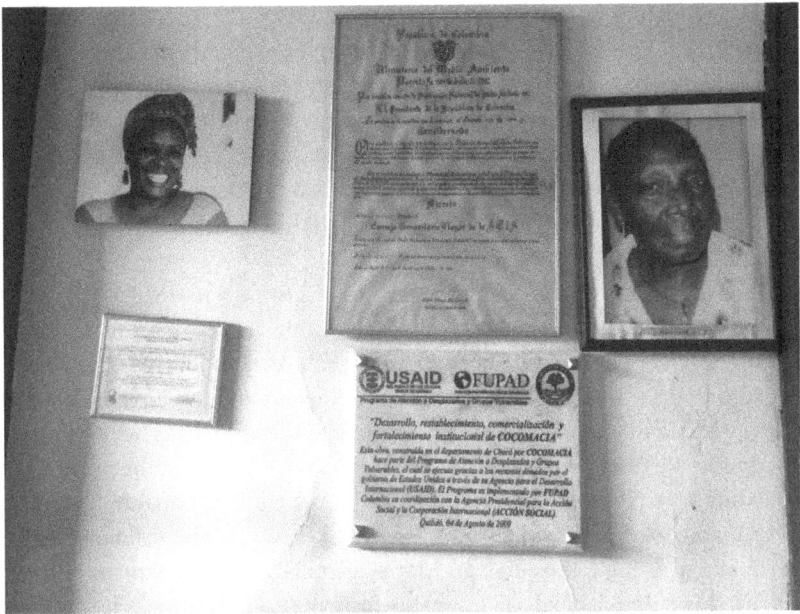

Figure 1.1. Portraits of two leaders: Justa Germania Mena Córdoba (left) and Ana Victoria Torres (right). *COCOMACIA headquarters*, Quibdó, 2016.

included me in these sharing practices when I have been around, making care an anchor for mutual aid.

The ordinary's heterogeneity and multiplicity within war reveals that there is more than victimhood and heroism in women's daily lives. Comisionadas use their energy not to oppose power but to protect their communities, families, and lands. Sociologist Avery Gordon's concept of complex personhood is valuable when thinking about what escapes the label of resistance in their lives: "At the very least, complex personhood is about conferring the respect on others that comes from presuming that life and people's lives are simultaneously straightforward and full of enormously subtle meaning."[14] Comisionadas' lives exceed their work and are as ungraspable as the knowledge that guides their days. By giving value to routine and daily performance, storytelling and ethnography give us fragmented glimpses into the complexity of survival and activism alongside violence.

Rehearsing Genealogies

Myriad research sources exist about the armed conflict in Colombia, a country inextricably linked to violence and with one of the highest numbers of internally displaced people in the world: 4.8 million by the end of 2022, although it had been as high as 6.5 million at the end of 2017.[15] These resources include human rights reports, former FARC hostages' or paramilitary members' memoirs, academic books and articles, chronicles, novels, transitional justice documents, and a seemingly endless list of publications. So what is left to say about violence in Colombia that Colombian humanists and social scientists have not yet said? Why does nothing seem as urgent, but everything written so far seems insufficient? In this section, I rehearse my research genealogies to establish the scenario for moving beyond victimhood.

The will of survival and writing about it in Chocó is a particularly utopian endeavor where race becomes critical. The Colombian Pacific has been central in the study of Black communities in Colombia. After 1998, when the region became a site of military confrontations, fieldwork and research in the area diminished, and research on displacement and urban centers became more common.[16] Researchers continued doing research on the Colombian Pacific, including Mara Viveros Vigoya, Aurora Vergara-Figueroa, Eduardo Restrepo, Peter Wade, Michael Taussig, Kiran Asher, and Ulrich Oslender, following the canonical works of Colombian anthropologists Nina Friedemann and Jaime Arocha. My research builds on my readings of these scholars, and my commitment is inspired by theirs.

More important, my ideas have been shaped by my interaction with Chocoan public intellectuals, such as Velia Vidal, Sergio A. Mosquera, and Gonzalo de la Torre, who research, publish, and live the Colombian Pacific's everydayness, braiding intellectual curiosity with community practice in the intellectual spaces they have crafted. Most of my knowledge about Chocó and survival practices comes from my ongoing conversations with my collaborators, the members of COCOMACIA's Comisión de Género: Justa Germania Mena Córdoba, Rubiela Cuesta Córdoba, Julia Susana Mena Moreno, Banessa Rivas López, Yenny Palacios Romaña, Carmen Aides Navia Mena, María del Socorro Mosquera Pérez, Ana Rosa Heredia Cuesta, and Luz Adonis Mena Becerra, organic intellectuals whose knowledge circulates through their everyday commitment to el proceso. Ordinary spaces in Quibdó become visual memorializations of their work, as has been the case after Mena Córdoba's death. On the second floor of COCOMACIA's headquarters, a picture of Mena Córdoba's I took and printed after her death hangs next to awards and plaques that COCOMACIA has received (see Figure 1.1). On the right, a portrait of the late Ana Victoria Torres has been hanging since 2008, when I first visited this building.[17] These two leaders are considered the founders of the Comisión. On one side of the hallway, visual memories of COCOMACIA's history hang, while the Comisión's office is almost always open on the other side (see Figure 1.2.). From outside,

Figure 1.2. Entrance to the Comisión's office. *Comisión de género de COCOMACIA*, 2019.

the walls unveil pieces of their work and life. Inside, from schedules to pictures of friends and family, including a copy of the same picture of Mena Córdoba visible in the hallway, these pieces become visual collections of their values and commitments. Peace, bodily autonomy, and centering women opens space for what exists alongside violence.

The existence of scholarly work that follows the urgency created by violentólogos [violentologists]—scholars of Colombian violence—and their analysis of the political and social contexts in which violence became part of everyday life in Colombia fuels an ongoing interest in intellectually understanding and denouncing the persistence of bloodshed that has been affecting Colombians' lives for generations. But this concern has also inspired the publication of titles such as *Violentology: A Manual of the Colombian Conflict*,[18] titled to honor violentólogos. A chronological narrative of violence that highlights different historical events and actors, *Violentology* offers an extensive, explicit photographic collection to illustrate the nightmarish details of violence. The beauty of this book—an impressive huge format (11" x 17") sewn by hand, printed on special paper, using a prize-winning press, according to its accompanying website violentology.com—invokes art books made for coffee tables and reveals how violence is made aesthetic.

With a picture of an anonymous corpse taken by an anonymous photographer on its cover—from violentologist Germán Guzmán Campos's explicit photographic collection of atrocities that made *La violencia en Colombia*[19] canonic—I have a difficult time envisioning photographer Stephen Ferry's *Violentology* anywhere close to someone who has experienced violence, even if it aims to "hold the reader's attention through the sense of touch as well as sight."[20] This book embodies the humanitarian rhetoric derived from NGOs such as Human Rights Watch—an explicit inspiration and source for this book—whose function literary critic Elaine Scarry explained so well when she stated that "Amnesty International's ability to bring about the cessation of torture depends centrally on its ability to communicate the reality of physical pain to those who are not themselves in pain."[21] Horror as a tool to stop horror relies on pain's translatability. Empathy relies on translating the pain to those with the power to stop it.

Although I understand the function of these portrayals of trauma, I prefer to rehearse other conversations about violence in which we talk with and not about people we classify as victims, to follow their lead in the stories they want to share. Just as we consider the lack of the state or poverty as causes of violence, a centralist and racist country can normalize violence as an inescapable reality in marginalized spaces by sharing only stories of trauma. Scholarly work on violence can also lead to conversations about violence only as an impartial and distant reality. Ferry's work is useful as a visual linear chronology for advocacy, pedagogy, or humanitarianism, but it circumscribes the conversations of violence within established hierarchies of knowledge in which victims are merely oral sources or photograph subjects/objects.

Research about Colombian violence has reflected critically on the horror that became naturalized as background noise, an accepted part of the soundscape. But studying violence is a difficult task, and, as mass media participates in fetishizing violence, so does research. Scholars in many fields have analyzed violence in Colombia as a cultural problem, a result of a weak state, or as naturalized default reaction to conflict. We have interpretations of violence as a "naturalized" national experience that leads to a "culture of violence" that is not the result of economic factors alone,[22] or violence as a national tradition.[23] This representative line of inquiry builds on the "banality of violence" to describe how violence has been naturalized in Colombia even though a single cause is impossible to pinpoint.[24] In a similar approach, following Italian philosopher Giorgio Agamben's work, others have theorized violence as the result of an extended "state of exception"[25] and as an inescapable part of "being Colombian," even when considering the uneven "geographies of terror" that target spaces like the Colombian Pacific.[26] These approaches to the study of violence in Colombia reveal a deep interest in untangling violence in Colombia to present a logic for its unavoidable presence in the national territory. As much as they have influenced my understanding of Colombian violence, there is still an unanswered question for me: how is the uneventful everyday a scenario of something more than violence, and who are the agents of this struggle against horror through practices that cannot be framed only as oppositional?

My research centers on survival, to avoid magnifying trauma and its effects on daily life. Researching survivors' lives after trauma requires considering its causes, presence, and return while recognizing the challenges of listening and representing the fluidity of daily survival. Black studies scholar Saidiya Hartman might agree that for Blackness, not repeating the trauma might be useful to avoid being complicit in reproducing the ontological association between pain and Blackness.[27] This ethical approach to trauma does not deny the importance of denouncing the violent event, but it is based on the belief that "an ethics of responding to pain involves being open to being affected by that which one cannot know or feel."[28] The vulnerability of not knowing and not feeling what someone else's pain feels like prevents me from appropriating it or internalizing it as my own. Not knowing is the first recognition of an ethical process in which knowing and explaining trauma is not an effortless or guaranteed outcome. Not knowing centers what we see and feel, in the present, beyond trauma and pain.

The genealogies I am interested in center survival as an alternative to reproducing trauma. My work in moving beyond victimhood builds on that of feminist scholars who have centered Black women in their analysis of Colombia's spectrum of violence,[29] and scholars who have explored the everyday life of Colombians in the aftermath of violence using community-engaged methods.[30] I have particularly learned from scholars who have centered the stories and memories of survivors in Chocó,[31] and scholars who center the knowledge of Black Latin American women as contributions to women's movements.[32] These analyses and productions of memory and violence explore the limits and potential of artistic representations of traumatic memories. This scholarship has inspired my storytelling, theoretical, and methodological rehearsals by revealing the instability of narratives of violence and providing new readings and approaches to audiovisual memories. Thinking about cultural productions and their context as embedded in broader spaces of circulation (such as museums, art galleries, and social media) shows that the openness of visual and aural representations that go beyond the wound can provide new spaces of interaction and imagination where we can explore vulnerability and strength.

I summarize the connections among these thinkers from different fields and generations in a broad consensus of the academic production about Blackness in the region: Black communities in the Colombian Pacific have faced multiple threats (economic, violent, and political) and have developed strategies to resist or negotiate with the powers of the state, corporations, or the armed groups. In a conversation focused on the issues of land, race, and social movements, my attention goes to the everyday practices that sustain and inspire life alongside historical oppression. However, awareness of how scholarly representations can reproduce the violence imprinted for generations on Black people reminds us of the ethical responsibilities of research and the need to recognize the social hierarchies from which I benefit as a non-Black researcher in a majority Black department. After my first visit to Chocó, I realized I had joined the privileged Colombians who visit this area for work or research. "Who are you with?" became a routine question, directed at me by other white and mestizx Colombians to find out about institutional affiliation, confirming outsiders as beneficiaries of employment or business in the region.

Moving beyond victimhood, as survival, is not an effortless endeavor. Contemporary violence in Chocó is a continuation of colonialism that constructs histories and realities cemented by intellectual frameworks and concepts.[33] The entanglement of colonialism and academia is one that we need to consciously unlearn through and beyond writing. Chocoan historian Sergio Mosquera Mosquera points out the disembodiment and objectivity associated with modern/European/white/rational/colonial (slaver-capitalist) knowledge.[34] An approach to survival as an object of study maintains the tension between denouncing multiple forms of violence and celebrating the knowledge required to navigate them and imagine their subversion.

Survival is never a complete process or traceable object of study. Survival requires a constant movement in everyday commitment and embodied practices. Instead of searching for objective circumstances to explain violence in Colombia, I center stories and practices that reveal the contradictions of surviving within militarized spaces. People and their actions are not only the mere product of impartial contexts but also the result of agency and a margin of freedom in which we can make decisions, even under oppressive situations. I recognize the process in which decision-making allows a distancing from humanitarian interventions (even in writing), as violence is never abstract. So instead of reproducing the humanitarian impulse, my writing rehearses a space for agency.

Discourses of multiculturalism and integrationism are usually portrayed as ideals of democratic spaces. The historic origins of marginalization of Black communities because of slavery are modernity's inherited and constitutive reality. Therefore, even though the 1991 Colombian constitution recognized Afrodescendants as an ethnic group, this recognition is nothing more than a symptom of the futility of the integrationist discourse for a population that has been historically denied access to humanity. Writing about Black communities requires an understanding of research's complicity in reproducing exclusion or superficial inclusion. This exclusion is not accidental but historical, as Achille Mbembe reminds us: "the slave condition results from a triple loss: loss of a 'home,' loss of rights over his or her body, and loss of political status. This triple loss is identical with absolute domination, natal alienation, and social death (expulsion from humanity altogether)."[35] The mixture between loss and alienation makes slavery the extended state of exception, which allows race to function as a regulator of death's distribution. This exercise of power through dehumanization, within a framework of racial hierarchy, is a useful analytical tool for understanding the politics of distribution of death and the disproportionate suffering in spaces that work as states of exception, like Chocó. But what about surviving against all the odds that necropolitics conceptualizes as the uneven distribution of death? How can we understand will within vulnerability? I look more closely at the specificities of individual and collective processes of survival as a starting point to create more inclusive practices of thinking about Blackness in Colombia.

Rehearsing Failure

This section is a follow-up exercise to my trip in 2008 to San Francisco de Ichó, and my failed attempt to return there to do fieldwork. I was (and still am) concerned with the ethical problems of reproducing power relations through field research: getting information from people who have experienced suffering and translating this experience to academic concepts through theory to make violence intelligible. What did I do to avoid replicating power structures? I wrote about the fear of reproducing power relations. I wrote about me hesitating, about my fear of ethnography. Since then, in my work alongside activist women who have shared truths that take me a while to process, I have been working on methodological strategies (i.e., collaboration) to move beyond the paralyzing fear of "othering," and the need to include ethics as a category of analysis and a research practice. My earlier writing became an account of the difficulties in writing about someone else's experiences with violence. But that writing contained a lot of omissions and silences.

Writing about the problems of writing ended up being a process that did not say much about the women of San Francisco de Ichó. This section embraces doubt and the impossibility of capturing the nuances of everyday survival while welcoming the utopian projections of a better world needed to keep going. Everyday acts ended up being ungraspable, as writing could not track the performative rehearsals of survival. Violence was not all-encompassing anymore.

I went to San Francisco de Ichó in 2008, following one of many workshops with peasants' grassroots organizations in which I took part while working for ECOFONDO, an environmentalist NGO. In meeting Vamos Mujeres members, I encountered survival as an ongoing practice. I learned about the cane sugar transformation center El Porvenir [the Forthcoming] that became a source of food and profit for the community and transformed gender roles when women became providers and prominent members of the community, promoting women's leadership. One image has stayed with me: "no quiero llanto de nadie" [I don't want weeping from anyone] written between cane sugar residue and a big pot containing melao [molasses] (see Figure 1.3). It illustrated the simplicity and complexity of the will to survive: a command phrased as a wish. The reference to tears alongside liquid sweetness exemplified, for me, the coexistence of suffering and strength. This glimpse into the everyday effort of survival challenged my ideas about resistance and victimhood: not crying is possible, but it takes effort.

Later, I found out that the sign was part of a safety campaign to warn Vamos Mujeres' members about work-related injuries at the transformation center.

Figure 1.3. "I don't want weeping from anyone." Transformation center, San Francisco de Ichó, 2008.

Other signs included "cuidado con el de[do]" [be careful with the fing[er]] as a humorous warning to prevent workers from getting injured with the engine used to make harina de popocho (a type of green plantain flour). "No quiero llanto de nadie" was actually a cautionary sign. A reminder that accidents are preventable by following security guidelines. For me, it became a reminder of my endless process of translation and the possibility of misunderstanding. Like Diana Taylor, I embrace untranslatability as a positive reminder of the difficulty of understanding and collaboration: "The problem of untranslatability, as I see it, is actually a positive one, a necessary stumbling block that reminds us that 'we'—whether in our various disciplines, or languages, or geographic locations throughout the Americas—do not simply or unproblematically understand each other."[36]

When I started my preliminary PhD fieldwork in the summer of 2010 as an extension of previous research, I could not stop thinking about the risks of revictimizing my future collaborators. The more I thought about going back to San Francisco de Ichó, the more I worried about my privilege. What privilege? Privilege, I thought, of being the one asking the questions, after thinking and writing a travel grant in the North to research in the South. Even if I am Colombian and I am perceived as being an insider, I carry with me the privilege of growing up in Bogotá, an embodiment of privilege elsewhere in Colombia. During the weeks before my trip, I obsessed about the multiple ways my presence and its accompanying privilege would affect my repeat encounter with the women of San Francisco de Ichó. But when I finally received the news of the death threats some of the Vamos Mujeres members had received and their worries about my visit, it became clear that this research would not happen, and I realized something else.

As my obsessive thinking faded away, the women's refusal to allow my visit due to the threats invoked a utopian understanding. Rather than seeing the inevitable traumatic experiences of women, I was experiencing what to me seemed an example of agency and care politics, as decision-making based on protecting the well-being of the community and its visitors. My privilege, which had been at the center of my worries, blurred when Vamos Mujeres reminded me they had control over their territory. They were protecting the community, and me, even in the worst circumstances, by refusing to host me. I understood that there are other worlds inscribed within what have been called "the margins."

I had received an email from Rosa Rivera, a member of the NGO Vamos Mujer in Medellín (the organization that inspired Ichó's Vamos Mujeres) and occasional member of the community of San Francisco de Ichó, telling me about a list that had been circulating in the town with the names of community members asked to leave. The Diócesis of Quibdó and Red Cross had been in the town to find out more about the threats, but they could not find clear indications of which of the armed groups was responsible for the list. Doubt was the only certainty. Research did not seem that powerful anymore. After being unable to return to Ichó due to death threats that Vamos Mujeres received, I started to work with COCOMACIA's Comisión de género, which claims to have participated in empowering the women of Ichó. As Ichó's community council is part of COCOMACIA, I kept hearing of the community's organizing and well-being without jeopardizing their security. As I rehearse how to capture the everyday survival I have perceived, my researching and writing swing between oppression-resistance frameworks and a relentless intuition that something always escapes it. I choose to be explicit about the preliminary explanations as a further example of an unstranslatability that becomes utopian as I learn to center stories as theories to explain lived experiences.

I could describe the process of organizing and looking for financial aid from within an environmentalist NGO (or international cooperation) as a type of resistance to the cruelty of the capitalist system, embodied by the multinational corporations that used cheap Black labor and then left when there was no more gold. I could describe the effort of communal economic recovery through traditional seeds and organic farms, and the transformation of sugar cane into the sugary liquid melao that the women sell, as evidence of their commitment to anticapitalist and fair-trade practices. But the motivation behind melao production and looking for funding to make it happen is not different from the reason some women and their families still go to the river to make the same repetitive movement with their batea [wooden washing pan] for hours hoping to get a little piece of gold (worth 10,000 pesos, or three dollars). It is about survival. One day at a time.

Classifying daily performances of survival as political resistance would not recognize the strategic use to which the women put the money received from international NGOs, or the hierarchical and bureaucratic practices still in place in the humanitarian economy. Needing receipts for reimbursement might make it more difficult to buy plantains from the river, but it would not stop comisionadas from wanting to feed the communities and themselves what they crave. Even when the melao production or the activism benefits from international funding, this is happening alongside neocolonial practices (such as who is hired to work for NGOs and where industrial mining takes place). In this context of humanitarian exchange, "the West gives to others only insofar as it is forgotten what the West has already taken in its very capacity to give in the first place. . . . So the West takes, then gives and in the moment of giving repeats as well as conceals the taking."³⁷ But, using critiques of capitalism to understand the non-hegemonic community economic practices would frame the process of survival and reconstructing communities within the logic of a greater anticapitalism. Women know of economic inequalities and work constantly for alternatives to what they have experienced (such as dependence on men, territorial conflicts, and forceful displacement). Anticapitalist or environmentalist understandings of inequalities have not inspired the daily effort of Vamos Mujeres' members or the comisionadas. They view humanitarian funding as a necessity to support the political work of empowering more women to be economically independent in a system where money guarantees survival.

I could replicate the interpretation of violence as a traumatic paralysis that marks bodies and immobilizes victims, irrevocably affecting their social bonds and structures. I could describe the 2000 seizure of a nearby town and Vamos Mujeres' actions as a reaction to forced displacement, but this has been done before. In 2005, the Colombian newspaper *El Tiempo* published a chronicle about the group titled "Las 18 mujeres que salvaron a un pueblo de la extinción"³⁸ [The 18 women who saved a town from extinction]. The author described the Vamos Mujeres members as "hembras de piernas fuertes y nalgas empinadas" [females with strong legs and steep buttocks] while also describing their reaction to violence as "[p]ese a la ausencia del Ejército y la Policía, el lugar sigue erguido ante un conflicto que ellas no entienden y al que no han dejado entrar" [despite the absence of the Army and the police, the place remains upright in the face of a conflict that they do not understand and they have not let in].

Benilda Gamboa de Córdoba, leader and legal representative of the Asociación Vamos Mujeres, and Pedro Luis Mosquera Navia, legal representative from the San Francisco de Ichó community council, wrote a letter responding to the chronicle. Challenging the misrepresentation of women, their community, their roles, and their knowledge, they wrote: "Se vive y se entiende el conflicto de diferentes maneras: una cosa es estar en medio del conflicto con los hijos y todas nuestras pertenencias. Otra es verlo en televisión. Existen contextos; por eso no se puede hablar de dejar o no dejar entrar el conflicto. El está adentro"³⁹ [The conflict is lived and understood in different ways: one thing is being in the middle of the conflict with our kinds and all our belonging. Another is watching it on TV. There are contexts; that's why it is not possible to talk about letting the conflict in or not. It is inside]. This letter is more than a counternarrative to the chronicle. It reveals an understanding of a conflict that is ever present and that exceeds its representations.

I could describe the massacre of Bojayá on May 1, 2002, where 119 civilians died in the crossfire between the guerrilla group the FARC and the paramilitary group Autodefensas Unidas de Colombia (AUC) [United Self-Defense Groups of Colombia]. Civilians, the UNHCR, and human rights activists denounced the fear of violence that had threatened the community since April 21, which finally materialized through a transgression of symbols of unity such as religion and the church nine days later, with no state intervention to prevent the massacre. Ironically, people went to the church seeking protection, only to be killed. I could describe the impact of this massacre, and other direct confrontations with the armed groups, that might have influenced some women to organize (one of the comisionadas is a survivor of this massacre).[40]

Choosing displacement can be a practical tool to choose lives over land and leave the town, even if the result is joining the thousands of internally displaced Black people in the cities, also struggling daily with racism and other threats, to survive: "The massive presence of displaced Black people in the capital has brought to light the workings of different forms of racism, as these people were forced into a new inflection of the intersection between Blackness and poverty: being poor, Black, and displaced."[41] As the community response to the 2005 chronicle states regarding the decision to move: "Todos los que pudimos salir, lo hicimos. Aquí nadie juró nada ante el terror"[42] [Everyone who could leave, did. Here, nobody swore anything in the presence of terror], a reminder invoked in conversations with the comisionadas. Displacement takes different shapes (masivo and gota a gota are some of the categories used by the comisionadas), a confirmation that leaving and staying can take the same effort, as staying can also be a temporary state before reuniting with the community. Staying after several waves of displacement can create the same amount of uncertainty. Those who relocate move toward the unknown, possibly motivated by the need to survive before figuring the rest out. Those who stay remain terrorized by the possibility of new violent actions against them or their families, possibly motivated by the hope or nostalgia of a peaceful outcome in the very territory in which they had been investing their energies. Analyzing women's actions as an explicit response to armed violence implies ignoring women's huge motivation to protect themselves, their families, and their territory from future attacks.

Vamos Mujeres' members knew the risks of both leaving and staying, and they chose life for as long as it was possible in their territory. Some stayed; some were displaced and returned right away. It was a political choice, a brave decision. Their motivation was their land, their identity connected to it, and, especially, their hopefulness: hope not like a warm wish but like taking a jump into the unknown. Some comisionadas chose life in displacement but continued to work for their communities.

I could talk about the transformation of gender roles as the cause or motivation for not joining the millions of internally displaced people in Colombia. I could find connections between the feminist NGOs, Vamos Mujeres leaders, and the comisionadas who have constantly survived. I could describe the importance of the transformation center, or the workshops led by women, and the way men supported women's leadership, not without previous conflicts, and started assuming traditional feminine roles: cooking, taking care of children, doing dishes. In my first visit, one story I heard was about the young daughter of one Vamos Mujeres leader, who refused to do the dishes when her mom asked because "that's not a job for women."

But the women of Ichó and the Comisión are not fighting male oppression (at least that is not how they frame their work). Some women have refused to go to the workshops because they don't want to fight with their husbands, and how to avoid problems with the men is still a topic discussed in every workshop led by the Comisión. In the community's response to the chronicle emphasizing the role of women in Ichó, the authors reflect that community solidarity is more important that women's solidarity:

> Sostener que los hombres abandonaron a sus familias, es mentira. Si los poquitos que quedamos, hombres y mujeres, no nos hubiéramos unido no habríamos subsistido. No es sano generar la sensación de mujeres heroínas y de hombres cobardes, con el ánimo de tejer un reportaje amarillista que deja conflictos internos en la comunidad. Cuatro hombres hacen parte formalmente de la organización desde el 2000.[43]

> [To claim that men abandoned their families, is a lie. If the few that remained, men and women, would not have united we would not have survived. It is not healthy to create the sense of hero women and coward men, with the spirit of knitting a sensationalist report that creates internal conflicts in the community. Four men are formally part of the organization since 2000.]

Having men as members of the organization named Vamos Mujeres is a breakthrough in a context in which conversations about gender become critiques of the exclusion of men from workshops organized by the comisionadas: "¿no deberían incluir hombres si género incluye hombres y mujeres" [shouldn't you include men if gender means men and women?] is a common concern voiced by men during workshops. In a workshop the comisionadas led in 2013, one attendee reminded the audience that the aim of learning about gender is "para capacitarse, no para libertinarse o para tomar igual que los hombres" [to train themselves, not for debauchery, or to drink like men do].

Framing these women within a feminist resistance to male oppression denies the complexity of the motivations and multiple experiences within the community. Traditional regional organizations were led by men, and women participated mainly as representatives of their absent husbands. Within Vamos Mujeres, men have taken part as representatives of their wives or sisters. The transformation of traditional patriarchal gender is an important consequence of Vamos Mujeres and the Comisión, but it is not the only motivation for survival and activist work in a militarized space where community might be more important than women's empowerment. Was gender an issue for Vamos Mujeres before or while recovering traditional economic practices after the mining corporations left the community without resources? Was gender equality the motivation for the comisionadas to spend days traveling by the river to get to another community and form networks with other women from COCOMACIA? My rehearsal of incomplete explanations stages the possibility for another narrative that centers the narratives of Vamos Mujeres and the Comisión as the experts in their own work.

Vamos Mujeres has achieved a real transformation of traditional gender roles within Black rural communities. Members did not organize looking for gender equality or to question women's role within the family structure. Gender was not the main issue for the community in this context of economic and social uncertainty. Vamos Mujeres and the Comisión are initiatives that create ways to appropriate and use their territory for the benefit of their families and their community. The groups attempt to use the only assets they have: their land and its resources, and their bodies, their strength, and their volition. And during the time of harsh violence, their confidence in the possibility of using these possessions in their favor, for their survival and the wellness of the community, became their incentive to continue. Single-cause explanations are incomplete, because the closer you get, the more complex people's daily lives get, and the more agency cannot be ignored. What my failure and only nuanced explanations for survival can reveal is how the everyday is the scenario for transformative politics alongside violence.

My conversations with the community leaders and founders of Vamos Mujeres, especially Benilda Gamboa de Córdoba, gave me insight into the complexity of women's lives within militarized contexts. Daily life is not constant grieving or unyielding resistance, but a constant negotiation with partners, armed groups, and local communities. Alongside stories of violence were success narratives of rebuilding the community through hard physical work in the transformation center. Alongside stories of hope were memories of conflicts with men who opposed women's attendance at feminist events in Quibdó or

Medellín. These narratives and the melao sign (Figure 1.3) serve as a reminder that survival is a collective and negotiated daily effort. Embodied in this graffiti-like sign against weeping (a physical symptom of sadness), there is a mnemonic command both acting as a reminder of harm as a constant risk and evading it as a conscious possibility. A survival that is more quotidian and embodied than I thought. A protection from everyday hurt. As a reminder of this never-ending tension, the sign invokes strength by reiterating that bodies' vulnerability exists alongside agency. Agency informs decision-making as a performative action that creates other worlds in which survival is a continuous decision, a daily rehearsal, a never-ending performance.

What my failure to understand and translate the experience of Vamos Mujeres taught me was to look and listen more closely to the contradictions of daily survival practices. Only then was I able to talk with and not about COCOMACIA's comisionadas. And what I learned is that survival is endurance, a cruel daily rehearsal of creating narratives that help communities move forward. I learned that exploring the value that the comisionadas' work incarnates, without forgetting or magnifying the oppression and violence that have marked their existence and their marginalization from democratic spaces, requires constant dialogue and collaboration. Approaching everyday survival as a scenario of utopian potential of the unknown reminds us it is critical to embrace the potential of something we cannot fully imagine. While my rehearsed writing mimics my attempts to look for explanations that could flatten the multiplicity and complexity of the everyday lived experience, Vamos Mujeres and their strategies to survive reveal what everyday peacemaking looks like.

Rehearsing Storytelling

In the Comisión's office, comments about forms of violence that are not related to the armed groups are ever present even if militarization marks the rivers and rhythms of the workshops. During the workshop in Tanguí in 2013, Julia Susana Mena Moreno summarized the debate about sexual violence by saying: "todo el tiempo llevando garrote como si estuviéramos arrendadas en el mundo" [all the time suffering as if we were tenants in the world]. The lack of ownership as a metaphor for suffering reveals both the marginalization and the injustice of Black women's treatment in a world that has not been fully theirs. References to slavery or racism are not uncommon in the workshops that the Comisión organizes about displaced women's rights. But most of their reflections disrupt ideas of survival as a mere consequence of not dying after a traumatic event. The energy derived from the comisionadas' work in rural communities, their pride, and their independence result from their idea to do things right and help others. Moving beyond trauma by highlighting empowerment is the approach of the Comisión's workshops, alongside processes of caretaking and ethical everyday practices.

The comisionadas' daily work includes both denouncements of oppression, like Julia Susana Mena Moreno's, and examples of empowerment through self-representation. Mena Córdoba's intervention of a soccer-themed campaign poster against women's violence saying "La violencia contra las mujeres no va más"[44] [Stop violence against women], with a picture and a personal motto developed in a workshop organized by Carnavalenguas[45] in 2011, blends denouncement and hopefulness. This was one image she used in her personal story for the digital storytelling project *Mujeres Pacíficas*. She titled her story after the slogan: "Mujer que no cumpla su sueño, mujer que no ha nacido" [a woman who does not fulfill her dream has not yet been born], showing the centrality of this image (and optimism) for her self-representation (see Figure 1.4). With a pink wig made of ribbons, Mena's image is an example of the creativity and carnivalesque elements that are part of women's mobilizations against different forms of gendered violence. The immediacy of her performance, as she inserted the poster into the picture and then returned it to the Comisión's office wall,

Figure 1.4. Justa Germania Mena Córdoba's image for her digital story titled "Mujer que no cumpla su sueño, mujer que no ha nacido." *Comisión de Género Office*, Quibdó, 2013.

reveals an interest of preserving an already-public idea and sharing it as part of her legacy.

During one of our meetings before the workshop, Mena Córdoba said resistance is the only way to survive, as slavery and now poverty have threatened Black people's existence. Resistance, she told me, is living without anything but committing to the duty we have as human beings: working with dignity. Of course, I could not help but think about what Marx would say about work as alienation. She went on to explain that the temptation to do "illegal things" arises when there are limited options, but choosing to help others instead is a better alternative. Mena saw the Comisión as an opportunity to not dwell on her health problems (she had been diagnosed with cancer in 2009) as she got to think about others. Collaboration for her was an extension of survival, a community-centered practice. As Audre Lorde writes about her cancer and cancer in her community, and the conscious work of survival, "Our battle is to define survival in ways that are acceptable and nourishing to us, meaning with substance and style."[46] Everyday storytelling about survival was part of the communities of care that the Comisión's office made possible.

From the beginning, Mena Córdoba knew exactly what she wanted to say in her digital story. She wanted to document her life's work to share with her family and community. She knew she was dying, so she was one of those most interested in delegating editing so that she could focus on developing her story. After finishing a first version, she asked to record an introduction in which she would talk about her father and siblings as an example of the patriarchal organization of Chocoan families. She also used her story as a possibility to thank and say goodbye to her family, friends, and community. One of her children and one of her grandchildren could watch her story right after we completed it. Mena's story caused the greatest emotional impact when we screened the stories in Quibdó in 2013, as she thanked comisionadas directly for their help and support during her last years. All the comisionadas cried while listening to her unfinished story at different moments. Listening to Mena Córdoba inspired the comisionadas to organize the video homage, which we planned to screen during a party organized by COCOMACIA in her honor at the end of August 2013. The party was a success, but only Mena Córdoba and the comisionadas could watch the video because of technical problems. She died two months later. Some pictures taken during our project adorned T-shirts and were used during a march and ceremonies realized in her memory.

Mena Córdoba's story, and the comisionadas' celebration of her existence and leadership, center women's experiences without privileging or denying pain. Their refusal to frame empowerment as an undisturbed or linear path deactivates optimist readings of suffering. In a conversation with cultural historian Saidiya Hartman, Frank Wilderson III denounces the questionable optimist tendency in research: "So often in Black scholarship, people consciously or unconsciously peel away from the strength and the terror of their evidence to propose some kind of coherent, hopeful solution to things."[47] In her work, Hartman rejects this optimist appropriation of past violence as a present source of pleasure in relation to multicultural discourses available in integrationist spaces: "That project is something I consider obscene: the attempt to make the narrative of defeat into an opportunity for celebration, the desire to look at the ravages and the brutality of the last few centuries, but to still find a way to feel good about ourselves."[48] As Mena Moreno, Frank Wilderson, and Saidiya Hartman are suspicious of celebrating survival as a happy ending, I have tried to look more closely, zooming into the everyday to avoid obsessing with wounds or supernatural healing.

What I have found is that in the construction of others and ourselves through narratives, we can embrace and reject representations that fit into preconceived worldviews or imagine that we can transform them. Comisionada Rubiela Cuesta Córdoba acknowledged the difficulty of doing the work and not getting paid consistently while validating her commitment to the organization: "Si aquí está mal, en cualquier lugar está mal, pero sin libertad y fuera del proceso" [If it is bad here, it is bad everywhere, but without freedom and outside of the process]. When I asked her about surviving without a constant income, she responded: "Todo el mundo pregunta cómo hacemos. Yo tampoco sé. Lo que sé es que la vida continúa" [Everyone asks how we do it. I don't know either. What I know is that life goes on]. Activists such as Cuesta Córdoba make their agency explicit in choosing where to direct their everyday energy. Instead of centering the contingency of working for el proceso Cuesta Córdoba centers the inevitability of the unknown. Like Cuesta Córdoba, the rest of the comisionadas imagine a change while continuing to use other available narratives and representations to keep envisioning and performing the change they long for.

Daily life is a network of intentionality, negotiation, and chance that transforms daily actions into stories and performances of disidentification, using José Esteban Muñoz's concept. Performing disidentification is a process of using available representations within the dominant ideology as sites of political struggle to make visible non-hegemonic political goals: "Disidentification is a strategy that works on and against dominant ideology."[49] COCOMACIA's comisionadas use available representations (such as victims/vulnerable women) within humanitarian discourse strategically to fund their workshops. Even if it is not a perfect match, because bureaucracy sometimes impedes common-sense decisions, such as buying food from the communities in which workshops take place, as I related earlier, these tactics and negotiations are essential to their work. The tensions between the comisionadas' desires, needs, and strategic alliances inform their daily performances, which is the place where survival resides as a constant process and not only as a result of violence.

Comisionadas' daily life, full of caretaking, learning, and teaching while negotiating their identities and discourses, is ethics in the doing. This ethics aligns with anthropologist of violence Veena Das's ordinary ethics: the "events that shatter ordinary modes of living," in "the small acts that allow life to be knitted together."[50] The interruption of violence can create a glimpse into a different life. Repetition adds up, even if its orientation toward power is not always explicitly combative. In her book *Black and Green: Afro-Colombians, Development, and Nature in the Pacific Lowlands*, Kiran Asher notices that "local strategies of resistance ... are shaped through their active engagement with, not just against, the development and democratic practices of the Colombian state."[51] These local strategies are non-oppositional politics in practice: a strategic movement of words and practices to access spaces and resources that would not be reachable if standing in antagonism. This mode of everyday ethical behavior also resonates with an understanding of ethics where a normative imposition is replaced with a commitment regardless of the outcome, a rehearsal of what life could be. Commitment can be a "survival weapon."[52] And, as one of the comisionadas' friends said in Tanguí: "Todos vamos a morir y no sabemos cómo o cuando, y podemos tomarnos eso a pecho o no" [We are all going to die, and we don't know how or when, and we can take that to heart or not]. In the meantime, we all decide every day how to act to weave our life. Hope is a consequence of showing up, as the comisionadas suggest.

All the workshops organized by the Comisión require external funding. However, the interactions between the comisionadas and the communities extend beyond the topics agreed on with the funding agency. Also, comisionadas' ethical practices include everyday conflict. In 2013, Mena Córdoba reminded the Tanguí community about previous agreements about the workshop and the possibility of negotiation, after some attendees complained about potential resistance from the men in the community: "Porque si esto les va a traer dificultades a ustedes en su familia, en el hogar, hasta aquí llegamos " [Because if this will bring difficulties with your family, at home, we can stop now]. And before the workshop started, she scolded one woman in charge of cooking during the duration of the workshop: "¿Se acuerda que hicimos un acuerdo la vez pasada que usted no iba pa' la cocina? Porque así no la van a certificar, ¿Entonces usted qué aprende allá? Cocinar ya sabe" [Remember we agreed last time that you were not going to the kitchen? Because if you do, you will not get certified. What will you learn there? You already know how to cook]. As an ongoing practice of "being there," activism shapes not only the negotiation of topics and time but also how everyday interactions and decisions are seen as valuable. Gender guides the comisionadas' work, but not at the expense of communities' ties (at least not without the consent of women participants). Cooking makes workshops possible and guarantees feeding not only the attendees but also the whole community. And because comisionadas know the burden of domestic work on women's lives (even their own), they remind women that it should not be their only role.

The determined attitude of the comisionadas' daily work with rural communities shows survival as a daily performance. "Uno no se puede cansar de repetir las cosas" [One cannot get tired of telling things], said Mena Moreno in Tanguí, as a reminder of how crucial it is to continue discussing women's rights and vulnerability in conflict zones, while training community women to do the same. Not because it is easy to change women's situations or even their opinions derived from years of indoctrination and oppression. Doña Juana, one of the most respected women in the community of Tanguí, said during the same workshop: "Los hombres y las mujeres no están en el mismo nivel porque así lo dice la palabra. Pero algunos hombres quieren aplastarnos" [Men and women are not on the same level, according to the scriptures. But some men want to crush us]. But because even Doña Juana expresses this contradiction when thinking about gender inequality, she confirms the importance of the workshops. Mena Moreno's motivational strategy reminds me of Fred Moten's metacritical optimism[53]: we cannot tire of repeating what is wrong as an invocation of what is right, even when the only thing right is not giving up. Repetition is, after all, the essence of the utopia that is survival in Chocó.

Despite facing daily economic and patriarchal oppression, women from Vamos Mujeres and the Comisión practice conscious and unconscious forms of resistance that cannot be explained by structural or general theories of violence and people's response to it. Beyond organized forms of resistance, we find daily survival composed of people's routines, dreams, plans, fears, and even boredom. For the activists of Vamos Mujeres and the Comisión, survival is a process in which living becomes a collective commitment, a resistance that does not mean facing oppression directly or using explicitly political strategies. Resistance, like survival and social organization, should not be equated to a confrontation or reaction that originates social movements, as alliances, networks, and external forces shape them.⁵⁴ Inhabiting a utopian place alongside violence is where the rehearsal of survival centers activists' experience.

The quotidian contradictions of the comisionadas' feminist activism in a militarized space such as Chocó reveal that daily negotiations are necessary to perform survival. Surviving is not a happy accident. Surviving is a constant process that does not hide vulnerability but centers it. It takes agency and will to survive. Surviving does not conceal trauma, and it is not a substitute for it, but it refuses revictimization. It is possible to see the visible and invisible traces of captivity in contemporary Blackness without ignoring the possibility of freedom of agency, as Vamos Mujeres and the Comisión de Género remind us. It is possible to create a space to explore the violent ontology of Black social life without seeing only pathology or vitality. The suggestion that Blackness's existence is indivisible from captivity and the resistance to it is what defines Black studies as a field for Fred Moten, and its object of study: "'Black studies' concern with what it is to own one's dispossession, to mine what is held in having been possessed, makes it possible to embrace the underprivilege of being sentenced to the gift of constant escape."⁵⁵ Moten's critical project values the experience of survival without separating it from the resistance that violence contains in the first place. And, as poet and scholar Alán Peláez López teaches us: "to survive fugitivity is to experiment with the (re)making, (re)shaping, and (re)imagining of our bodies each day."⁵⁶

Postconflict utopias encompass official narratives as much as embodied everyday survival strategies. But writing about everyday survival alongside violence instead of reproducing trauma demands practice. I rehearsed feminist chronologies to create a context that acts as background for stories of survival. I rehearsed genealogies to signal the networks of scholars and texts I think with while writing. I rehearsed failure to signal the limits of the theories and methods when examining what escapes violence. Finally, I rehearsed storytelling to visualize how collaborating to tell stories can rehearse other utopias, including a postconflict. But if survival is a collective endeavor, so is storytelling, as we saw in the multiple stories that coexist in Ichó, Tanguí, and Quibdó. Sharing stories is a rehearsal of collaboration and cocreation, vital tools in the repertoire of postconflict utopias that imagine everyday survival in Chocó.

Chocoans' will to survive is not reflected in the structures of historical oppression that they are forced to navigate. Rehearsing genealogies of knowledge that include stories that grind against colonial ways of knowing exposes the multiple layers of violence in so-called postconflict spaces where international funding and workshops on gender are anchored by receipts and other made-up bureaucracy. Postconflict utopias prioritize intentionality and agency, which are essential for survival and collaboration. This is reflected in the way people make decisions about what to eat or how to show up for each other despite bureaucratic and gendered challenges. We can dream up new worlds and ways to live by telling stories, even if they cannot capture the complexity of surviving every day in militarized spaces like Chocó. Despite the ever-present threat of failure, it is political to imagine together how to show up and attempt to understand each other.

CHAPTER 2

Utopian Stories
Survival Technologies in *Mujeres Pacíficas*

> Descubrir este Pacífico es también ir detrás de múltiples historias, es ir encontrando palabras que me permiten hablar de él, es de cierto modo una lucha por intentar decir lo que parece indecible.
>
> To discover this Pacific is also to follow multiple stories, it is to find words that allow me to talk about it, in a way it is a struggle to say what seems unsayable.
>
> —Velia Vidal Romero

As I walk the streets of Quibdó, the word strikes me. It follows me. Paisa. Paisita. The word used to describe people from Northwest Colombia highlands—usually the departments of Antioquia, Caldas, Risaralda, and Quindío—is used to call me and describe me: paisa. Ironically enough, I am la paisa, apparently an apocope of paisano (countryman), because I am an explicit outsider, a colonizer (even if I am not from Antioquia, the department most closely associated with this identity). Regional identity in Colombia—whether claimed or assigned—is implicitly racialized.[1] Even without the paisa accent, I was grouped into one of the racial categories recognized in Quibdó: Black, Indigenous (pejoratively called cholx), and paisa (mestizx/white). And being part of the racial category of those who tend to be the owners and sellers reminds me of my privilege.

"My appearance confirmed it: I was the proverbial outsider," writes Saidiya Hartman in *Lose Your Mother*.[2] But unlike Hartman, a US citizen in Ghana, I am not a foreigner. And just like Hartman, my position as an outsider is evident even before I open my mouth. Feminist Mara Viveros Vigoya writes about Colombia's regions as spaces for the construction of difference, and mentioning regional cultural differences is a way to discuss race in Colombia.³ My privilege in Quibdó is what makes me an outsider in the United States. The way I look and the way I sound locate me at the crossroads of being a Colombian doing research in her homeland and being an outsider in the space I have built as a home. My double alienness could have worked against me if I had attempted an objective approach, as I would have in my days as a colonial historian. Instead, I embrace my alienness as the only possible site from which to produce knowledge; that is, all knowledge production is mediated by my own embodied, alien experience. My embodiment at first caused mistrust for the comisionadas that took years to dissolve completely. As a student identified with the privileges of Bogotá, access to education and—later—living in the United States, I was read as an outsider, and trusting me could be a threat.⁴

Privilege hides in national narratives that have promoted mestizaje as a proof of a racial democracy. Light-skinned mestizxs have historically embodied the idea of ideal citizens in Latin America, and their racialization has been used as proof of blurred racial borders.⁵ As a mestiza, my simultaneous embodiment of racelessness and racialization associated with Colombia's centers of power marked my presence in the majority Black department of Chocó as a continuation of a historical process of extraction. So even if I call the comisionadas my friends and collaborators now—after more than a decade of ongoing collaboration—research exhaustion informed their first reactions to the calls of another paisa, who might just come to fulfill her own interests. And even if they call me their friend and collaborator now, the question of NGO visitors in COCOMACIA (other paisas or foreigners from the Global North) with whom I come reveals the hierarchy. "¿Con quién vienes?" [Who are you with?] has been a question following me around. At first, I answered with details about who had invited me to the event, meeting, or place. Who do I come with? Later, I realized the question was about institutional affiliation. I understood the different places I have occupied within the local hierarchy. I felt the privilege of being the only one in the office getting paid consistently. My privilege has increased since I went to Quibdó for the first time, as I went from being a master's student in 2008 to an assistant professor in 2015—and as an additional marker of privilege, I got tenure in 2021.

In Chocó, outsiders tend to benefit economically and socially from working with local communities while locals who have been doing community work struggle to find funding. Without the financial support of institutional affiliation to an organization providing funding in exchange for collaboration or information, academic research seemed distant and unhelpful for the comisionadas' causes. Their skepticism was not unfounded, as comisionadas have given testimonials and interviews in the past, and they have been concerned about the lack of control they have over academic narratives about their work. When I first met with them, a sign in the Comisión de Género's office warned: "lo que se habla aquí, se queda aquí" [what is talked about here, stays here]. Long collective silences when I tried to talk about possible collaborative research in 2011 confirmed the skepticism about sharing with outsiders. Building a relationship through reciprocal patience, dialogue, and kindness transformed into collaboration. In every new visit and interaction, we started to find ways to know and trust each other, and eventually to use our knowledge and experiences to learn from each other.

Building trust was a process of years. I shared information about my own life and my intentions to establish collaborative projects beyond my own research. I talked about my dreams of learning from people and not only through books, and my interest in creating and sharing knowledge based on this collective learning. Sharing my own stories allowed me to dispel most of the comisionadas' skepticism about the possibilities of finding commonalities and projects to collaborate on. The first interactions were mainly about getting to know each other and sharing potential stories. After two years of envisioning the possibility of collaborating in developing the digital storytelling project for my research, the comisionadas started to get excited, not only about telling and sharing their stories, but also about the possibilities of working together in other projects, such as a short documentary film about the Comisión's achievements since its creation.

This process of learning to trust and work together led us slowly to explore digital storytelling as a utopian approach to collaborative research. As an audiovisual genre, digital storytelling has been a tool for the comisionadas and other storytellers from COCOMACIA to share their personal stories through the project *Mujeres Pacíficas* (meaning both women from the Pacific and peaceful women) in their own words, document their narratives, and oversee their dissemination to multiple audiences. In this chapter, I explore the process of embracing digital storytelling as an alternative to monopolizing the process of knowledge production with a single story, while being critical of how my own positionality has shaped the process. As a method, digital storytelling offered many exciting possibilities: valuing oral tradition and storytellers' knowledge as much as digitizing pictures and creating audiovisual stories to promote their work, while also embodying the tension between the potential and failure of utopias, some of which I outline here. I start with a close-up of the everyday as the stage for storytelling where the context of Black organizing informs efforts of cocreating Afrocentric narratives. Excerpts from *Mujeres Pacíficas*' stories are the framework to theorize the value of community for survival and storytelling across this chapter. I explore the activism of COCOMACIA members, and in particular the work of comisionadas, as everyday practices of survival and knowledge production, using their stories and words to theorize their political practices. In the process of learning with the storytellers, I use postconflict utopias to connect the life-affirming survival practices alongside violence that connect the political work of COCOMACIA with other people, networks, and spaces imagining peace.

The Politics of Survival Practices and Visibility: Collaborative Storytelling as Willingness

The stories of *Mujeres Pacíficas* are the product of one-on-one collaboration, but they all reflect the centrality of community in the work of COCOMACIA, and even the Comisión de Género.[6] These stories materialize a process of collaboration that precedes my intervention and are not meant to represent the work of COCOMACIA or the Comisión as a whole. But every story invokes COCOMACIA as a referent for personal storytelling. In this section, I explore everyday storytelling and survival as part of collaborative processes that make life possible for Black communities in Chocó and inform both the *Mujeres Pacíficas* stories and the process of cocreating the stories.

The predominance of the written word in knowledge production makes a clear distinction between who historically are the authors of the written record and who are the ones they write about. Writing shapes knowledge and excludes. In Colombia, the naturalization of mestizaje and mestizx identity in the construction of the nation has shaped racial aesthetics in discourses of colombianidad [Colombianness]. National politics has mimicked eugenic understanding of racial superiority sustained by the exclusion of Black communities and the whitening of history.[7] It is not surprising that the effort to research groups traditionally relegated from the writing of history has led to studies of oral tradition.

Orality might be central for Black communities, but representations traditionally highlight "the one who looks and almost never is on the side of the one who is seen."[8] The Comisión keeps an archive of books and pamphlets with the comisionadas' interviews and testimonies. The comisionadas know the importance of using different genres, including writing, to preserve their own stories and experiences. They are creating their own archive and writing themselves into it. María del Socorro Mosquera Pérez, for instance, is a poet and a composer and uses her notebooks to write coplas [rhymes] and poetry that have been compiled and archived in different formats. Since 2019, Palacios Romaña has been working on collecting songs, poems, sayings, and other examples of oral tradition in the Comisión's archive that she wants to publish. As Ulrich Oslender reminds us: "oral tradition functions as a hidden transcript of resistance, which becomes an important political tool when strategically drawn upon in public discourse."[9] The comisionadas know this, and their work takes shape in multiple genres and spaces, with oral culture and Chocó at the center.

In 2013, nine comisionadas that were part of COCOMACIA's Comisión de Género—Yenny Palacios Romaña, Banessa Rivas López, María del Socorro Mosquera Pérez, Ana Rosa Heredia Cuesta, Rubiela Cuesta Córdoba, Luz Adonis Mena Becerra, Justa Germania Mena Córdoba, Julia Susana Mena Moreno, and Carmen Aides Navia Mena—participated in *Mujeres Pacíficas*. The comisionadas also invited COCOMACIA's legal representative Fanny Rosmira Salas Lenis, and two members of COCOMACIA, Mariluz Moya Cuesta, an organizer and Comisión's collaborator, and her sister Miriam Moya Cuesta, who was working at COCOMACIA's restaurant at the time, to participate. After years of discussing the creation of the stories, in 2013 we finally started cocreating them. Alongside this, the comisionadas asked me to support their documentary film about the Comisión. From the beginning, it was clear that each project had a particular audience, format, and goals.

Mujeres Pacíficas documents activism and survival as daily practices, as knowledge that challenges official memory and history about the Colombian Pacific. When storytellers are active decision-makers in the entire process, most stories are narratives of hope instead of trauma. In contrast to voyeuristic narratives about the armed conflict, these stories offer a utopian perspective on the experience of Black Chocoan women as activists, storytellers, and knowledge producers, joining activists and scholars who created and promoted Black studies in Colombia.[10] Through creating and analyzing these stories, storytellers' daily practices and knowledge create unofficial archives of survival. Whereas these stories cannot be understood as empowering by themselves, storytellers understand visibility and public vulnerability as an extension of their work as members of COCOMACIA. The active participation of comisionadas in coproducing these narratives is part of their broad repertoire of practices for communicating, creating, and surviving as part of their community work.

Mujeres Pacíficas is the result of rehearsing a new way of collaborative storytelling. The process was shaped by the connections the storytellers, in particular the comisionadas, were able to establish with the possible use of the stories for their work in COCOMACIA, and our agreement to work on other projects. Every storyteller had a very specific audience in mind, mostly women from the organization, and for the comisionadas, stories became extensions of their community workshops and organizing. The comisionadas welcomed digital storytelling as another way to make visible their work in the organization and beyond. "El proceso," the struggle for territorial rights for Black communities in the Pacific, is a recurring theme in every story. From the very beginning, the comisionadas were excited about the prospect of their stories being shared among many different audiences, including those beyond COCOMACIA's territories, as Mosquera Pérez highlights in her story's introduction.

Mosquera Pérez chose multiplicity in the self-representation she performed for her story:[11] with images of herself and other members of COCOMACIA wearing T-shirts with institutional logos, she shows her role as a comisionada; with an image of her hands crocheting a colorful flower, she shows her work in crafts. Mosquera Pérez also includes a fragment of an alabao [a mourning song][12] she composed and sang about Law 1257, a 2008 law against gender-based violence (during right-wing President Álvaro Uribe's second term) as part of her participation in other feminist spaces beyond the Comisión. The song makes her writing and singing skills visible as she shares the value of her participation in the organization. Her story inspires an understanding of survival as a collective and everyday endeavor. I invite you to watch it before you continue reading. While you listen to Mosquera Pérez's narration, imagine the Colombian Pacific, particularly Chocó, a place where rivers are still the main means of transportation. Imagine a place where camouflage is suspect no matter who wears it, and it coexists with a humanitarian and activist aesthetic where political messages, institutional affiliations, and NGO logos appear in everyday objects, from T-shirts to notebooks. Imagine the cadence of peace-building as a devotion to the intangible. Dream about the performance of survival that I write about.

Some questions recurred during the collaboration: How should we balance storytellers' narratives with the group's broader narrative strategies? How should we understand our interaction as collaborators? How is our collaboration affected by power relations? What would happen after the digital stories were finished? How would we follow up?

Moving forward with our collaboration emphasized the connection between embodiment and knowledge—and what happens when people get together and do something that seems unthinkable. Valuing collaboration is not about the stories as final output, but about the embodied memory that is accessed when thinking about personal experience and is inevitably connected to wishes for social justice or collective activism as "a way to celebrate the individual and the collective, and to lend respect and credence to the lived experiences of individuals through the collective co-creation of individual narratives, and provides participants with the opportunity to work together, tell and share stories, listen to others, and learn."[13] Valuing orality and embodied practices challenges the tyranny of academic writing as the main access to knowledge, and it creates intimacy and a new definition of safety related not to militarization but to care. But something always remains hidden: secrets, silences, refusal, challenges, conflicting stories, and motivations.

"La historia del María del Socorro" is not a story about violence in Colombia. It does not deny or refuse to talk about violence. The story is about life, survival, and community. Mosquera Pérez's narrative is non-oppositional, as it finds value in public policy such as Law 1257, it finds value in the collective struggle, and it centers her activist practice and the practice of her compañeras. It acknowledges women's bodies and territories as platforms of war. This story also reveals the coexistence of our inability to change the world with the need to do it together. Thinking with Mena Córdoba and members of COCOMACIA's Comisión, living, and surviving in Chocó is utopian.

Even though Mosquera Pérez accentuates the importance of community by mentioning the support of both compañeros and compañeras in her life to move forward with her seven children, her story starts by mentioning she is the daughter of a single mother, like herself. So even if, as a narrator, she uses expressions such as "organizing process" and "gender equality" that reveal her experience as a leader and trainer, her narration is anchored in her personal story and her own survival experience. *Mujeres Pacíficas* does not capture the practices that constitute survival—caretaking, chores, forced displacement, choosing life over and over again—but invokes the existence of a knowledge anchored in quotidian practices that can only be reproduced through bodies. Mosquera Pérez highlights the drive needed to work and support others. For her, survival is not independent from her relationships with her compañeras. For her, survival is an everyday rehearsal, and her compañeras are her collaborators in her constant improvisation. Mosquera Pérez's story confirms the importance of "being in everything" that comisionada Cuesta Córdoba articulates (see chapter 5). It invokes the significance of "being there" so emphasized by performance artists and scholars. It is through embodiment that the sacred domain of writing within knowledge production is disrupted. Her idea of survival as collaborative challenges the cathartic powers associated with the testimonial act and genre in the practice of community healing. It exemplifies what feminist scholar Sara Ahmed describes:

The violence that we have to survive is not only gender-based violence, or violence that might take place at home; although it includes these forms of violence. It is the violence of enslavement, of colonization, of empire. It is the requirement to give up kin, culture, memory, language, land. We reclaim willfulness in refusing to give up; and in refusing to forget the severances that have been performed and narrated as the spread of light to the dark corners of earth; to persevere embodies that refusal.[14]

Survival is willfulness. As chosen perseverance, willfulness shapes stories. What any narration includes and excludes is also chosen, and it changes depending on the audience and the story's purpose. The plural in Ahmed's quote is meaningful. Survival, willfulness, and stories involve more than one person. Stories as portrayals of survival and willingness—even if that is not all they do—call for plurality. The comisionadas were aware of the importance of separating personal and public stories and their political uses. Mena Córdoba was constantly reminding the other comisionadas about the format expected for their documentary interventions and the importance of talking about more than COCOMACIA in their personal stories. At the end, the significance of organizing for every comisionada is revealed in how COCOMACIA is the core of most of their personal stories.

Survival performance is world-making. It creates and supports the transformative politics and possibilities that make life possible. Such performance generates worlds of potentiality that change the present and make a future possible. The power of everyday survival rests in storytelling as a process of giving visibility to what disappears as mundane. Making these stories visible has not made the comisionadas' lives easier or their daily efforts more valued outside of their space of action, but it can constitute a bridge to other public or social spaces to continue working toward recognition and understanding of Afro-Colombian women's struggle.

Resistance takes multiple shapes: "Women's acts of resistance, of self-affirmation, as social actors in their different historical and political contexts, are already in themselves subversive to existing power relations; but women have been 'sub-versive' also in another sense: in circumventing, uncoding and denying the various, distinct and multi-layered verses in which their subjugation is inscribed."[15] In this sense, participation and collaboration should be read as achievements in themselves, if only as a way to challenge capitalist ideas related to productivity and results. Storytelling has and creates subversive value, not as oppositional resistance, but as an opening of possibilities for reinforcing the importance of centering Black women's experience. This is the paradox of memory as performance: representation without reproduction because it only exists in the present and becomes something else once it is documented.[16] By challenging the written word as the conventional language of research, thinking about performance is a way to understand an embodied research model that exists only in the doing, in the interaction and collaboration with storytellers. It allows embracing the lack of precision and objectivity, and the role of embodied documentation in the process. More important, it keeps us critical about the dangers of visibility and reproducibility.

Considering visibility is part of this collective exercise of remembrance that subverts the absence of Black women's storytelling in Colombian mainstream narratives even before the digital stories reach the public sphere. Choosing how to narrate lived experiences facilitates conversations about what storytellers care about and their wishes for the future. The images chosen and created for the stories contribute to their utopian character, serving as a political projection of their envisioned worlds. Of course, visual remembrance is not inclusion, as performance studies scholar Peggy Phelan has argued with her critique of the "politics of visibility."[17] Images of underrepresented communities can reproduce the fallacy that representation is power while silence is death, although there can be power in refusal. Hypervisibility can also be obscene, as sociologist Avery Gordon has explained.[18] What these stories achieve is a brief interruption of mestizaje as the center of Colombia's national memory. Even if the supremacy of mestizaje, and its association with neutrality and inclusion, remains intact in national discourses.

Visibility can be used for political purposes only by recognizing its limits and taking advantage of its utopian character, as not all visual representations challenge or are intended to join mainstream narratives. Stories use visual memories to push against what seems impossible; they name what is not yet possible in other representations. Storytelling values a necessary and urgent utopianism that imagines alternative worlds by narrating the past. The political potential of visibility through storytelling is creating space to reimagine the present and the past, which is the essence of activism for social change: "We need to know where we live to imagine living elsewhere. We need to imagine living elsewhere before we can live there."[19] Day-to-day survival, as a practice that exemplifies postconflict utopias, is intertwined with everyday storytelling that can be transformed into digital stories. Sharing stories with others is about making spaces for representations that do not seem possible yet.

Visibility, however, is also limited to storytellers' knowledge and expectations. For instance, Mosquera Pérez's inclusion of her alabao about Law 1257 makes her songwriting and singing part of her story and storytelling. The alabao fragment she included in her story shows the centrality of territories for her and her community: "Ley 1257 es la que ahora nos ampara, de las distintas violencias en contra de las mujeres. Nos sacan del territorio poniéndonos en alto riesgo hasta perder su cultura que es la madre de nosotros" [Law 1257 is the one that protects us from different forms of violence against women. We are pushed out of our territory putting us in high risk until we lose our culture, which is our mother]. She teaches about the law while denouncing the threat of forced displacement. Her personal account of being part of COCOMACIA is both informative and compelling as she shares the particularities of her involvement. Recognizing that survival is a collective effort, she rehearses her role daily. She understands that her individual work is supported by the organization and her fellow comisionadas. Every day is a rehearsal for survival, an opportunity to practice improvisation and collaboration.

Recognizing the challenges of collaboration includes considering collaborators' agency and the possibility of refusal, as research still creates mistrust and exhaustion. Levels of motivation might change according to daily life challenges, or according to storytellers' interest, or lack thereof, in discussing details such as transitions. Collaboration is a daily commitment, subject to change or failure, that is manifested before and beyond digital storytelling. "¿Para qué preocuparse?, una sola no puede cambiar el mundo" [Why worry? One cannot change the world by herself], Mena Córdoba told me in 2012. Her words are a reminder that working together is the essence of any worthwhile transformation, and the starting point to build the world we want to live in. As part of other community-building practices that rehearse what collaboration could look like, the *Mujeres Pacíficas* stories and their process build on the comisionadas' previous knowledge production and dissemination strategies that support their dreamwork.

Collaboration became a process of seeing beyond the stories: the interaction between the stories produced and the spaces in which they were unlikely to circulate, the memories attached to lost or damaged photographs, the secrets and silences that are not perceptible in the stories. Stories became potential tools that the storytellers were interested in for their own advocacy, their own archive, their own family album (in the absence of one), their legacy, or their community. This project followed a similar approach to the one comisionadas use in their own work: embracing life as contingency. Life as change is what allows confronting every day as an opportunity, with the flexibility it takes to produce the change we would like to see around us. But the transformation needs to start with the way interaction within collaboration takes place. Chocó and the

Comisión informed our interaction, as vulnerability was constantly present as background noise and required an active caring for each other. Survival became a practice of ethical paranoia: fearing something could happen but connecting with people and protecting people to care for each other. This collaborative contingency created intimacy and a relationship that extended beyond the planned collaboration. While this seems a new interpretation of survival, it is another manifestation of caretaking that contains the contradiction of ongoing trauma and the willfulness to imagine its end.

Collaboration might seem like the ideal process for any kind of research, but it is necessary to remember that participation is not the automatic result of collaboration, but a never-ending process of being in relationship. The initial skepticism from the comisionadas shows the difficulties of attempting a collaborative methodology. It also serves as a reminder of collaborators' agency and the violence still associated with research that generates mistrust and research exhaustion in underrepresented communities. As a delicate process, collaboration cannot be measured by its output, and the ever-present possibility for failure reinforces its potential as utopian. Participation needs to be understood as a process with value in itself, independent of the outcome. The project's political goal is not to achieve visibility as a means to access power; it is about recognizing that there is power in remaining invisible, in understanding the threats of visibility: surveillance, political fetishization, cooptation, and accepting the dominant ideology in representations.

Digital Storytelling as Utopian Performance

Most of the *Mujeres Pacíficas* storytellers (Figure 2.1) begin their stories by introducing themselves with references to their places of origin, as they do in meetings and events: "Mi nombre es Yenny Palacios Romaña, soy natural del consejo comunitario de Buchadó, municipio de Vigía del Fuerte, zona 7. Mi madre se llama Aurelina Romaña, y mi padre Gabriel Palacios" [My name is Yenny Palacios Romaña, I am from the Community Council of Buchadó, town of Vigía del Fuerte, zone 7. My mother's name is Aurelina Romaña, and my father's Gabriel Palacios]. The zone number refers to the regions COCOMACIA is divided into, and they are routinely part of introductions. The inclusion of parents' names and place of origin locates "La historia de Yenny" as part of a collective history. These introductions acknowledge storytellers' positionality as individuals, part of local communities and the larger organization that is COCOMACIA. They are also examples of everyday storytelling present in community meetings and organizing.[20]

Figure 2.1. *Mujeres Pacíficas'* storytellers: Yenny Palacios Romaña, Banessa Rivas López, María del Socorro Mosquera Pérez, Ana Rosa Heredia Cuesta, Rubiela Cuesta Córdoba, Miriam Moya Cuesta, Luz Adonis Mena Becerra, Justa Germania Mena Córdoba, Mariluz Moya Cuesta, Julia Susana Mena Moreno, Carmen Aides Navia Mena, and Rosmira Salas.

These introductions also reflect storytellers' ongoing commitment to their communities and their local identities' connection with their advocacy, while echoing storytelling patterns within COCOMACIA. At every meeting, attendees share their personal information, including the name of their community and the respective zone. These introductions are common in the organization's internal meetings and in meetings with their networks or collaborators. Storytelling is part of meetings, workshops, and advocacy. It allows connection with others by creating opportunities for solidarity and community-building. Storytelling is, then, an everyday process that has and creates value, and that centers everyday experience. Our collaboration created opportunities to listen to some of these stories. It renewed conversations about what stories to tell, for what purposes, and for what audiences. Instead of assuming that representation (of violence or its victims) was an end in itself, we imagined instead that collaboration could support ongoing work by COCOMACIA and the comisionadas.

The digital storytelling process we used differed from Joe Lambert's StoryCenter.[21] Instead of starting with a story circle and training storytellers to create their own stories independently, we worked one on one.[22] For *Mujeres Pacíficas*, spontaneous storytelling and multiple versions of every story attracted the comisionadas, who embodied rehearsal and improvisation as they do in their everyday practices. In this specific adaptation of digital storytelling, talking and finding the best way to tell and illustrate personal narratives without writing a script or creating a storyboard made space for spontaneous storytelling. Having conversations about each story involved disagreement, negotiation, and collaboration that confirmed the difficulty of dialogue. Continued dialogue was made possible by the power of intentionality and reciprocity.

Digital storytelling practitioner and researcher Son Vivienne defines digital stories as "sites of active social and political negotiation that enact political identity."[23] Interlocking threads of intentions and interactions constitute the crafting of every story, revealing a collective process of collaboration, the construction of selfhood in relation to the Comisión's work. A methodology of vulnerability, in which the range of orality is an acceptable outcome, opens up spaces for threads of incomplete truths, omitting, and interweaving, as sprawling narratives of shared memories and uncertain constructions of the self that are involuntarily connected. The research process and outcome mimic the everyday.

The answer to how to document the everyday for this project's purposes is based on the potentialities of digital storytelling as it "lends itself in philosophy and execution to a participatory research model."[24] Of course, there is a contradiction in thinking that a project based on audiovisual technology is not elitist. "Video itself is not 'innocent.' It, too, is a form of cultural commodity that often stands for a celebration of the self and its powers of invention."[25] The digital storytelling method can be thought of as a compromise to achieve a broader circulation for the stories that include storytellers as producers and audience, while explicitly valuing non-written knowledge.[26] The result is far from perfect, as stories are fixed while their creators continue evolving, and digital stories have a limited audience in comparison to other genres with wider networks of circulation. However, digital stories allow us to explore and imagine spaces where the gap between local knowledge production and academic production can be partially overcome in an instant of mutual collaboration. It might mean little at a macro level, like the everyday practices of the comisionadas, but when you look closer, you can see subtle changes. Tiny traces of collaboration, tiny points of contact might be the utopian instantly needed for motivation to endure, just like the comisionadas' work might generate small but important differences at the micro level.

By showing up every day during every trip, but particularly in the northern hemisphere summer of 2013, I was finally able to start being part of the comisionadas' daily life. I went to the office every day and became an honorary comisionada, helping with homework and reports, and attending meetings and workshops with women and young members of COCOMACIA. We started sharing daily stories, food, and routines, which made me an active participant in the group. My goals for this project started to transform as I realized stories were important but not the priority, when the comisionadas doubted the possibility of continuing to do their job because funding was scarce and organization members were starting to complain about the lack of democratic elections for the positions as comisionadas. Learning about their daily struggles gave context and meaning to their stories, and to their interest in learning and doing things with me that were not related to my research.

In the process, I unlearned a romanticized understanding of digital storytelling and technology in terms of access. When accompanying the comisionadas to lead a workshop in Tanguí, I beelined to an outlet in the community center to charge my camera's battery, as the comisionadas had asked me to document the workshop. Before I plugged in the charger, I remembered—because of everyone's laugh—that there was no electricity during the day. I had been in that community center before and I knew electricity was not reliable everywhere and yet I had internalized that an outlet means electricity. Energy cannot be detached from a racialized organization and distribution of infrastructure and resources worldwide.[27] In the department of Chocó, 83.8 percent of households had access to electricity in 2018.[28] While the percentage is now 86.9 percent, it is still one of the lowest, and it contrasts with the national 96.5 percent.[29] Furthermore, the portion of households with internet access in Chocó was 14.6 percent in 2021. The national total was 60.5 percent.[30] Even though the percentage of people with access to internet from any device in Chocó is higher, this massive digital divide is another example of Colombia's regional hierarchies. That said, lack of access is not destiny. Black and Indigenous communities in Colombia use and demand access through "the articulation of a sophisticated postcolonial subjectivity, negotiating complex and multilayered ways of using space, infrastructure, and technology to achieve political voice."[31]

As the comisionadas were constantly working on designing workshops or writing reports for funding agencies, they expressed an interest in learning about other types of technological tools: word processors to write letters or reports, Excel to make budgets. Rubiela Cuesta Córdoba was also interested in learning how to use a video camera that the Comisión had recently received for a project. She was interested in continuing to document their work through their archive of photographs and documents rather than creating content exclusively for her story. To help comisionadas with their specific technological needs, Doris Moreno—my mother and longtime collaborator of COCOMACIA and its geographic information system (GIS) division—donated two weeks of her time. While I worked with every storyteller, she designed an analog handwritten manual for everyday tasks, and she sat one on one with every comisionada (and even other women from COCOMACIA). Because of different levels of knowledge, short classes ranged from how to turn the computer on to how to make PowerPoint presentations and Excel graphs. After two weeks, this side project became part of our collaboration, and I became in charge of both the digital stories and the technology classes that now included how to set up an email or a Dropbox account. The comisionadas, in turn, felt even more responsible for my safety after my mom left, and they fed me, offered companionship, and took care of me in any way they could in exchange for my labor and my own caretaking of them, which included making food in return, and even giving massages, particularly to Mena Córdoba after long workshops.

Reciprocity is crucial for collaboration. Exchanging time, resources, stories, and personal connections builds an intimacy where affect becomes central in shaping spaces for storytelling and collaboration that exceed any project. Especially during Mena Córdoba's last months of life, crying together as we talked and recorded became a vital part of the process. A collective effort for documenting the Comisión's work and its leader cannot be explained without the process of slowly turning mistrust into affective possibility. As a result, the project not only created an adaptation of digital storytelling (an individual instead of a collective process) but also allowed constant communication about stories and their potential use.

Caring informed the digital storytelling process. After deciding how to co-create the stories, we worked one on one to talk about possible topics for each story to communicate the most relevant experiences for their audience or goal. Initial meetings were followed by questions related to the storytellers' experiences. We developed an oral script and storyboard: each storyteller shared an overview of the story, I took notes, we reviewed the list together, and we started talking about potential images. Within the broader caring collaboration, digital storytelling became emotional labor. During each session, emotions permeated the narration, image selection, and pre/post-session discussions, evoking memories of people, places, and even traumas, shared through painful or nostalgic memories that escaped the final stories.

We recorded the audio after discussing the oral outline of the story. We would stop or repeat as necessary according to each storyteller's needs. Afterward, each storyteller would listen to the audio and decide what to keep, add, or change—at this stage, I took most of the pictures that I have used for a collage of the storytellers (Figure 2.1). After recording the audio, we selected the images in a similarly intentional and collaborative conversation. The storytellers' use of images from their personal archives became an opportunity to preserve and restore family pictures as much as it was an exercise in self-representation. In other cases, the lack of personal archives opened space for creativity where recreating memories visually—when storytellers had lost their visual memories due to displacement or accidents—encouraged collaboration to find or create images. We used a lot of photographs from the Comisión's archive, and the comisionadas negotiated who would get to use some of the group images. Some ended up being included in more than one story. Most of the images used were explicit images, meaning that they mirror what the narrator is saying. For example, images of family became explicit visualization and memorialization strategy for narratives regarding loved ones. Other stories use implicit images as symbolic means to include additional layers of meaning that depart from the narration. Mena Córdoba's adaptation of a poster (discussed in chapter 1) is an example of how creativity can be used to shape photos and video that are already part of personal archives.

Sharing visual memories confirmed that the comisionadas' collective history entails networks of knowledge that constitute a visual archive in itself. Looking at images from the Comisión's and the storytellers' archive turned out to be more of a collective activity than the crafting of each individual story. The daily visitors at the Comisión's office arrived to look at pictures and start conversations. The office also became a headquarters of family photography. The storytellers wanted me to take new individual and group pictures with friends and family members for both their stories and their personal albums. The extensive number of digital photographs we produced and consumed confirmed that photography has transformed "from a rarefied, often elitist pursuit to a mass-popular, fully domesticated and everyday activity."[32] Still, most photographs get lost, through CDs that can't be read anymore, or deleted to make space in phones and computers.

I edited the audio and stories by listening and watching them several times with each storyteller until they were pleased with the content. By telling their stories without interruption, and listening to them before thinking about editing them, storytellers were able to experience the power of "being present" and use their knowledge to share memories they considered important. Even though the editing process was mainly my responsibility, by the time the editing started, they knew exactly what they were telling and how they wanted to tell it. Of course, they were always asking my opinion and agreeing with what I suggested or decided, illuminating my unavoidable mediation. Digital storytelling as a method is not a cure for the reproduction of hierarchies in research, in which the researcher is perceived (or perceives herself) as the source of knowledge. What this kind of collaborative storytelling achieves is the possibility of a constant dialogue about the process and output and a negotiation around the decision-making process.

Editing became a memorialization and preservation project. It included conversations about what each storyteller wanted to see or hear, and how the story's order and structure reflected what they had envisioned. Talking about how images go from one to the next through cutting, fading, and dissolving was not a priority for storytellers. The pacing of the story depended mostly on the rhythm of each individual voice or on the number of images each storyteller wanted to include. Text and soundtrack were not included except for the title of the story, which was almost always "Historia de . . . " and the storyteller's name, except in Mena Córdoba's case, because she had a slogan she wanted to use for her story. Some edits, such as removals of small bits of noise, and additions here or there of snippets of "silence" to fill gaps, affected the stories' flow. Street noise, including construction next door, and even noise from the restaurant, made the quality of the audio a bit distracting. Editing for noise reduction in some cases created a robotic-sounding voice. Nonetheless, edited audio avoided having to rely on a written script. These issues notwithstanding, storytellers seemed pleased with the result, and they enjoyed each other's stories and gave each other feedback at different stages of the process.

Finalized stories were shared with the Comisión and COCOMACIA in a small public screening, where most storytellers were present. The reception was packed with emotional response. Up to this point, the audience for the stories consisted of other women from COCOMACIA and family members. At first, the comisionadas thought the stories would be ideal tools to use as icebreakers when working in the communities, as they usually share their life experiences to promote trust. However, the lack of electricity during the day in most rural communities in the region, and the fact that comisionadas need to share the projector with the whole organization, has made this goal untenable. This same issue kept the comisionadas from using the documentary we collectively produced for COCOMACIA's Gender Assembly in December 2013. To solve this issue, and because the comisionadas are interested in their stories reaching a broader audience, we agreed to publish them online.

Even with the changes to the traditional digital storytelling method that encourages collective storytelling to start the process, and that teaches audio and video editing as part of a short workshop, the aesthetics of digital storytelling remains, with the emotional undertones of a personal voice connecting with universal questions: "These individual stories balance the personal with the universal and the universally accessible, through a combination of familiar tropes and the strong affective resonances created by the warmth and visceral presence of the narrator's voiceover."[33] Each storyteller received a DVD that included her story and most of the stories developed by the other collaborators in *Mujeres Pacíficas*. However, most of them did not have a DVD player at home and were only able to watch the stories at the office. Because the storytellers envisioned sharing the stories with women all around the world, we also decided to create a website in 2015 (mujerespacificas.org), and in 2017 an accompanying Instagram account (@mujerespacificas).

Every finished story is a rehearsal, a glimpse into a temporary moment of storytelling and knowledge production that exceeds the constraints of the genre. And it is also an illustration of existing practices that can be inspiring for other women in the community, and *why not* other women all around the world, as Mosquera Pérez helped us imagine. This wishful thinking about dissemination is the potential of digital media as part of postconflict utopias: sharing as expansive politics, a practice informed by a collective care that is desired beyond the local community. Even after finishing the stories, the process proved neverending as every time we watched the stories, there seemed to be something that could be changed. The utopian character of digital storytelling also manifests in how collaborative storytelling is still insufficient when considering the reparations needed in academia and the Colombian state for slavery—and efforts to make Blackness invisible or reduce it to folklore in its aftermath, which Black women scholars have denounced.[34]

During the process of cocreating the stories and the documentary, the comisionadas decided to organize an event to honor their leader, Mena Córdoba, who had been diagnosed with a terminal cancer two years before. COCOMACIA's department of communications, specifically two men from COCOMACIA estéreo, the institutional radio station, decided to make a video to include messages to Mena Córdoba from each one of the comisionadas. After asking the comisionadas to write two-sentence messages and memorize them, the journalists asked me to record them in the radio station's recording studio, each comisionada reciting their messages standing in front of a huge banner with COCOMACIA's logo. The rest of the comisionadas stood in line waiting their turn, following the men's directions. When we started to record, the men would direct them. They told some to pronounce the final "s" of words properly, and suggested to one to act "natural, like a model." Another one received the suggestion of imagining she was a TV presenter. After leaving the room, we were all frustrated and decided to do our own video, "Para Justa," where comisionadas talked to their friend and leader. No memorization required. Lots of tears, and laughs, and memories. Mena Córdoba died two months later.

Digital stories and video homages are not an antidote to grief either. Yet the collaborative process of honoring created a space to hold our collective grief. "Para Justa" as an audiovisual piece might not be more truthful than the video that COCOMACIA's journalists were envisioning. Our video captured a collective process of expressing gratitude to a leader who was facing death's inevitability: it was emotional and rushed. And the homage video the men imagined was influenced by available media representations that could be read as reflecting ideas about "correct" Spanish and respectable performances of femininity. The constant negotiation and shaping of representation should not be disconnected from the final product. Likewise, the viewers' reactions, based on networks of circulation and consumption, shape meaning.

As an everyday performance, storytelling shapes digital stories. Digital stories are static representations of moving identities and self-representations of survival and activism as embodied knowledge. In fact, even digital storytelling's aesthetics reflect the uneventful character of the everyday. Telling stories with others and sharing them publicly centers oral tradition in the process of memory-making alongside official national narratives. In *Mujeres Pacíficas,* the lack of a written script, and an audio that is not a reading of a script, approximates everyday storytelling. In our collaboration, spontaneous storytelling and multiple versions imitated the rehearsal and improvisation of storytellers' everyday practices.

In times of uncertainty, storytelling is a utopian act that serves as a performance of survival. The stories we tell are important to create new relationships and dreaming alternatives together. While *Mujeres Pacíficas'* stories do not capture the embodiment of storytelling as part of everyday survival, their process created an opportunity for imagining opportunities for existing together and contributing to each other's memories and legacies in less scripted ways.

Collaborative Storytelling and Knowledge Production

Working collaboratively on the production of stories destabilized (briefly) the traditional racial hierarchies that are in place in Chocó. Not as a side effect of digital storytelling but as a result of my presence in community spaces accompanying the comisionadas. In Tanguí, when the comisionadas finished leading the first day of the workshop, one of the participants shared her assumption that I was the facilitator because she had only seen paisas or foreigners leading previous events sponsored by governmental and nongovernmental agencies. She said she felt proud and empowered knowing that Black women with a similar background to hers could have and share so much knowledge. Other women from the community were also surprised that I was acting as audience or helper during the workshop. During my second visit, community members demanded to hear publicly why I was there, even though I had introduced myself and had already stayed and eaten at participants' houses a couple of years before. I introduced myself as a student learning from the Comisión, and their assistant in this workshop as I was documenting it (taking pictures and recording it). The comisionadas confirmed I was assisting them. These interactions were a constant reminder of how knowledge, identity, accountability, and collaboration are constantly performed. The blurry borders between their work and our collaboration's audience in analog and digital spaces since then have solidified our relationship and work together as we continue to explore why nots together.

The Comisión's work already transcends their local networks, as evident in multiple storytellers' references to a global audience, although women who belong to COCOMACIA are still their ideal audience. Some of the stories touched on topics that align with the themes covered in the comisionadas' workshops: family and community, forced displacement, economic inequality, organizing, overcoming obstacles, domestic labor, and the work within the organization. But it is Julia Susana Mena Moreno's words during Tanguí's workshop that express the importance for solidarity that inspire sharing stories: "Da tristeza que mientras sentimos el apoyo y el amor de personas de fuera de la organización, la propia gente de uno no reconoce el trabajo de uno" [It's sad that while we feel the support and love of people who are not part of the organization, one's own people do not recognize one's work]. The need for recognition to counteract criticism reveals once more that community organizing is challenging work, and that solidarity is valued as motivation and gratitude. Working together was an opportunity to appreciate each other's knowledge and share it with others.

In *Mujeres Pacíficas*, multiple stories are woven to create a personal narrative with some points of connection to other stories and what exists beyond them. Each storyteller recounts several topics that she believes are significant to share publicly. Imagining a global audience acknowledges digital storytelling as a performance as well as the performative power of digital storytelling by creating transnational connections—or at least invoking the utopian networks (chapter 3) to which storytellers already belong. What we gain from zooming into el proceso that is captured in the stories is the mundane practices that are needed when knowledge production is a collaborative experience. bell hooks teaches us that "learning and talking together, we break with the notion that our experience of gaining knowledge is private, individualistic, and competitive. By choosing and fostering dialogue, we engage mutually in a learning partnership."[35] This partnership does not fix issues of representation. It creates the possibility to imagine future opportunities to learn and produce knowledge together.

In "La historia de Adonis," you can imagine yourself as the audience Mena Becerra imagined. Imagine being invited to witness the reconstruction of her archive. Imagine being invited to participate: "Mi llamado es para las compañeras mujeres, que cuando nos inviten a las capacitaciones no seamos ajenas a las invitaciones, que nos hagamos presentes porque esas capacitaciones le sirven mucho a uno para su vida personal, para aprender a reclamar sus derechos"[36] [My call is for women compañeras, that when we are invited to workshops we do not ignore the invitations, that we are present because these trainings are useful for our personal life, to learn to demand our rights]. Mena Becerra talks to her COCOMACIA's compañeras directly, especially those she does not know yet. The decision to interpellate women directly is not unique to this story and shows storytelling as an invitation to be in community as much as self-representation.

"La historia de Adonis" shows the comisionadas' conscious ability to shape their speech and self-representation, using identity as a malleable (and not stable) material. In Mena Becerra's decision to recreate her personal archive and interpellate women directly, storytelling can be a process of self-discovery and self-representation. Storytelling as a performative action is part of organizing, and creating memories outside official channels. Comisionadas as storytellers show that they are not just passive recipients but also active creators of knowledge and alternative archives.

But representing activism as legacy is not the only performative action of storytelling and self-representation. Mena Becerra's story is about remnants. Her mom died when she was a baby, and years later, she was forcefully displaced from her community in Munguidó. As is usually the case in the experience of displacement, few objects remained. Some years later, the few objects left, including photo albums and mementos, were lost in a fire in Quibdó. Mena Becerra did not have any photographs to digitize, as most of the storytellers did. The images that illustrate her story are reconstructions of her memories, taken by her direction in a tour of Quibdó she organized so we could visit and capture the spaces she considered central for her personal story. She also used a map she had made during a community cartography training she had received through the Comisión. Her story is not only a call to action but also the materialization of her memories.

If remembering is associated with repositories of memory, how is it possible to remember without a personal archive? Yet the absence of relics does not imply the impossibility of creating, or better, re-creating, personal memories.

A residual memory made of fragments of objects that survived destruction is not an incomplete one. The potential of such a memory is its multidimensionality, the possibility of making connections with other memories. As personal memories, created in the context of the everyday (the Comisión's office with the compañeras de lucha and facilitated by an outsider who is no longer suspect), even reconstructed memories are affective and effective. A patchwork of feelings and snippets of past experiences is stitched together to connect with other women in the struggle. Intentional memories reimagine the past. Not as fate but an opportunity for future change. By using contemporary references and inspiration from other comisionadas' stories, Mena Becerra crafts a utopian reconstruction of her past, an intentional decision-making on memory-making.

In the process of storytelling that "La historia de Adonis" embodies, storytelling is not only about reconstructing memories. Storytelling becomes a tool for organizing. Sharing experiences is a step in the process of inviting other women to join el proceso. Mena Becerra's connection with the audience, engaging with women as her audience and inviting them to participate in workshops and meetings, rehearses communication with a wider audience. Staging memories to illustrate her story is part of identity and self-representation, carefully constructed for community-building. What could be interpreted as the source of distance between the storyteller and her audience is nothing more than awareness about the existence of an audience in the first place. As an exercise in constructing themselves for a very specific "other," an audience that is their own community, storytellers reveal the possibility of imagining their stories visually even if staging is required to make up for the absence of memories and representations.

To tell a story is a strategy for self-representation. To tell a story is performing things that we cannot rationalize. Storytellers reflect on experiences that have taken many years to process, providing only fleeting glimpses of a visceral process of survival that operates privately in the individual and now takes on a decidedly public dimension. Generically freer of ideological structures, performative actions can enhance communication. This project embraced subjectivity to construct and value embodied forms of knowledge. This involved understanding that subjectivity is a product of perception while acknowledging that storytellers hold the power to create gendered relationships. As attentive speakers, storytellers understand that expressing themselves is both a practice of creating an intimate record of their lives and a possibility of interaction with an audience.

Using stories to invite women to el proceso reveals the centrality of COCOMACIA in the storytellers' personal narratives. Rivas López, the youngest of the comisionadas, became part of the Foro Interétnico Solidaridad Chocó (FISCH) in 2014, a coalition space for multiple organizations working on territorial rights. In her story, she mentions that she started attending COCOMACIA's meetings with her mom when she was a child and started formal training in 2004. Even though she has been in the organization longer than other comisionadas, she thought she was inexperienced, and she doubted she had a story worth sharing publicly. After exchanging ideas, she decided to talk about her dreams of going back to school and her son as motivation for her political work. Rivas's story frames her activism as a learning practice, a never-ending commitment to her community. She stresses the importance of knowledge inherited from ancestors and cultural tradition. Even though Rivas had envisioned writing her story before recording it, she ended up improvising it based on an oral script, as the rest of the storytellers did, instead of reading it—as a last-minute decision to represent her life in a more spontaneous way.

In the spirit of Mena Becerra's story, Rivas also included an invitation to join el proceso. This invitation mimics the comisionadas' interaction with local women in workshops. What makes Rivas's invitation different is the explicit references to the different generations that contribute to the process. As Mosquera Pérez and Mena Córdoba explained that survival and social change are collaborative endeavors, Rivas shares the centrality of community for survival and invites young people to participate in defending the collective territories as a common cause that cannot be separated from defending people. More important, she recognizes the knowledge young people have and can share as connected to ancestral knowledge:

> Lo que quiero es pues que día a día las personas nos podamos unir para que podamos contribuir a la misma causa que es . . . la defensa de nuestro territorio, la defensa también de nosotros como personas, que también hacer un llamado que nosotros como jóvenes podamos inculcar a estos procesos, nos metamos al cuento como muchas personas dicen, podamos participar, podamos dar lo que nosotros tenemos y que también nosotros podamos recibir los conocimientos que tienen nuestros ancestros[37]

[What I want is that day to day we can work together to contribute to the same cause, our territory's defense, the defense of people like ourselves. I call on us, young people to contribute to these processes, that we can get involved, participate, and share what we have and that we can also receive the knowledge from our ancestors.]

This invitation for people, particularly young people, to participate in el proceso is part of an effort for generational change that Mena Córdoba initiated and Banessa Rivas López has continued with her role as an advisor for COCOMACIA's youth group COJUCOMA. It also makes the past present by invoking the ancestors as sources of knowledge about the struggle. Making the past present is not only a generational strategy for survival but also a projection of a common cause: the defense of the territory and the defense of life. Choosing a personal narrative that connects the individual struggle with a collective one is part of creating a reality that is interactive as much as it is aspirational.

Thinking about storytelling as ordinary practice implies paying as much attention to the research process as the research outcome, a process in which dialogue sometimes fails even if caring is present and writing is present, even if it is not enforced as the center of knowledge production. By listening during the process, comisionadas and their stories were as important as the dialogue, with all the possible misunderstandings, silences, and indifference. Just showing up and sharing the practice of being there is a political statement about organizing as a priority in the comisionadas' life. And for the storytellers who are not comisionadas, participating is a manifestation of valuing their experiences as part of COCOMACIA's political project. Recognizing embodied practices as knowledge, and interacting with storytellers for extended periods of time, motivates interaction that is itself performance and that occurs before and outside writing.

As a performative and embodied practice, storytelling is an active engagement that creates worlds of possibility. Storytelling is a practice that cannot be reduced to the edited digital stories. Stories surrounded the process—everyday tales about families, communities, partners, needs, fears, and dreams that are absent from the finished stories. Unstructured storytelling was present constantly during the collaboration, but only partially rehearsed and captured. Digital storytelling as a method requires a specific theatrical kind of storytelling that is framed by the genre's limits and the participants' roles. Its practice is embodied through the rehearsal of specific roles (facilitator or storyteller), even though negotiating the specifics of every story with its storyteller requires constant improvisation. Therefore, the decisions made to create each story collaboratively show that identity and self-representation are also daily performances. Every digital story is a shaped representation of images, audio, and events that were carefully crafted by the storyteller, in dialogue with me, to present her life story and identity publicly. In this way, decisions about editing are performative and create the identities and stories themselves.

Storytelling becomes a way to document the cocreation of knowledge. Solidarity and participation are highlighted in the stories as part of long traditions of defending collective territories and, in turn, each other. This collaborative knowledge about el proceso exceeds digital storytelling. Its embodiment is indebted to the ancestors and new generations that are already part of collective survival. Each story offers just a glimpse into interconnected stories and experiences that already circulate in complex networks of knowledge within and beyond COCOMACIA.

Beyond Archives of Trauma: Memorializing Survival

Mujeres Pacíficas stories are narratives of transformation. Avoiding re-traumatization is an ethical practice that explains the absence of stories about pathology: violence as ontology or poverty as destiny. Of course, the danger of optimistic narratives is the potential of reinforcing the idea that intention itself can attract positive outcomes if it is directed properly. Not denying institutional oppression can help avoid individualizing oppression by ignoring external conditions affecting people's lives. The pervasiveness of life-altering events: massacres, displacement, domestic violence, and indiscriminate exploitation of natural resources is not changeable by wishful thinking. Storytellers' stories of overcoming are more complex. Storytellers show that obtaining cultural and social capital does not translate into economic capital. As activists, storytellers reveal that the emotional labor that their everyday struggles require does not always translate into financial stability. Every inconsequential act increases in significance when included in a narrative that revalues it and is susceptible to sharing in a caring context that avoids triggering potentially harmful memories. Each story is different in its multiplicity of topics, but they all include references to the Comisión's work on empowering women. We have seen how some of the storytellers weave personal stories with references to el proceso, blurring the boundaries between individual and collective representation. Mentions of their life before and after COCOMACIA are frequent. Almost every story includes references to what they have received as members of the organization. The collection of issues and the storytellers' ability to connect them with their advocacy practice reveal the political potential of personal narratives to solidify the conviction that another world is possible.

But why is *Mujeres Pacíficas* important if there are so many narratives about violence in Colombia? We have, for example, María Mercedes Carranza's *El canto de las moscas*[38]: twenty-four poems titled after towns in which massacres have been committed. Published in the 1990s, before most massacres on the Colombian Pacific, minimal poetic language about atrocities is a beautiful denunciation consumed by the literate: students, artists, and urban elites. And the Comisión Nacional de Memoria Histórica [Historical Memory National Commission] has dozens of reports based on emblematic cases, collections, and analysis of testimonials as sources for rewriting history and justice. Heredia Cuesta and other survivors of massacres are in contact with the products of research, but there is a disconnect between the writing and her experience. When I asked her about the Memoria Histórica's book about the Bojayá massacre,[39] she got it from the bookcase where all the writing rests at the Comisión's office. She showed it to me, touched it, looked at the pictures of the victims, and closed it again to tell me the story in her own words. She is not the audience or the producer of such narratives. She is more interested in her own story and the stories of the other comisionadas, to which she listened several times before they were finished.

In a national context where archives and narratives do not fully represent Black identities and particularly Afro-Colombian stories, digital storytelling is, in part, an archival project. Reconciling these ideas requires considering what is gained in the process of collaboration, not in the product of this collaboration. Archives and stories require selection, and storytelling as a process is collaborative. Digital storytelling allows us to think about survival in Chocó for its potential and not its efficacy. Survival includes "the vast social worlds and projects that are neither inside nor outside recognition, whose worth and value has neither been nor not been decided, that remain pure potentiality in the actual divisions of the social order, a virtual queue in the seams of late liberalism."[40] In other words, survival is mere potential when value is measured by profit. Politically, potential is relevant only if we start seeing the in-between of survival practices as valuable, regardless of whether they are recognized. What writing and archives exclude might be what is not yet commodified. We can find value in practices that are not profitable, such as the comisionadas' activism and solidarity.

In her story, Heredia Cuesta tells us about her endurance after being forcefully displaced. She included a picture I took of her holding the book about Bojayá as memorialization of the event (Figure 2.2). The massacre served as a backdrop to her transformation into an activist. Loss is part of "La historia de Ana Rosa" of overcoming—but not the center of it. Heredia's self-representation is a performance of independence and endurance that reveals her resolution to create an identity that is not only defined by having survived a massacre. While she references traumatic events she has experienced, her inclusion of a genealogy

Figure 2.2. Ana Rosa Heredia Cuesta reading *Bojayá, la guerra sin límites*.

of her work in the Comisión maintains a tension between suffering and overcoming that is not a success narrative. It reveals how survival is a never-ending rehearsal. A routine exercise of not giving up.

Navia Mena's story also reveals the centrality of COCOMACIA in her identity.[41] The importance of not giving up in a context of displacement and plundering of Black communities' land and resources is centered on her discussion of territory and territorial rights. Especially for Black women, who have suffered the consequences of patriarchal ownership and inheritance of land as much as violence, advocating for land ownership is political awareness and activist practice. By recognizing a history of struggle, Navia Mena shatters ideas about Black communities' dispossession as the result of obliviousness about their rights while using her story as micro-education about political involvement in Chocó. As a rehearsal of imagination, these stories become postconflict utopias in practice, where what is included and excluded creates the possibility of extending their everyday storytelling as part of their work for COCOMACIA.

At first, Navia Mena was unsure about her ability to tell a story. She said she was apprehensive about speaking to an audience, even though she has been leading workshops for years. She constantly asked for my opinion and seemed doubtful about the meaning of her story. Once she started talking, she remembered what was important for her: working for the community as a life commitment inherited from her parents. She decided on her main points: family, organization, and Law 1257, and she committed to tell a personal story of hardship and collective engagement. Recording the audio was challenging. Navia wanted to start over several times and make it perfect. The process revealed the vulnerability involved in storytelling, and the difficulty of tearing apart doubt about the value of practices that are not traditionally considered productive or profitable. However, Navia Mena's hesitation only increased the worth of her story. Her determination to search for strength and to commit to sharing a story mirrors the difficulty of her work with communities. Her courage in moving beyond her own self-doubt comes from a constant reminder about the importance of self-affirmation, not as indulgence but as a political statement. Choosing exposure, even when in doubt, as in Navia Mena's process, is part of what Rivas López and other storytellers do in everyday practice. They perform confidence to report about the Comisión's work in COCOMACIA radio and to lead workshops, even when they sometimes feel they don't have enough training. Improvising in storytelling is an extension of improvising in daily life. Almost every story contains a narrative arc of personal transformation associated with joining el proceso.

Yenny Palacios Romaña talked about overcoming her shyness and graduating from college because of her work in COCOMACIA. Her tale of presenting a report at COCOMACIA's General Assembly, a group of over 2,000 people, reflects the comisionadas' public speaking experience and the effort it requires. Like Navia Mena and Rivas López, Palacios Romaña reveals the pedagogy of social movements and the vulnerability of learning. Also, Palacios shows learning as embodiment and her job for the Comisión as a personal path of empowerment. Her experience as a single mom and her struggles growing up inform who she is, but her construction of identity is based on what she has achieved and what she dreams for herself and her son. Like Rivas López, Palacios Romaña included pictures of her son, reinforcing the importance of motherhood in their motivation for survival.

Palacios Romaña brings up the past as a reference for personal transformation: "Antes era súper tímida, a mí me aterraba hablar en público. Ahorita y gracias a Dios ya soy una mujer que va a los talleres con la Comisión de Género, baja sus temas, mejor dicho, he cambiado para bien. Este es un proceso de aprendizaje de nuevo conocimiento para la vida práctica, para la vida personal, laboral, profesional"[42] [Before, I was super shy. I was afraid of speaking in public. Now and thanks to God I am a woman that goes to the workshops with the Gender Commission, presents her topics. In other words, I have changed for the better. This is a process of learning new knowledge for practical life, for personal, work, and professional life]. Framing personal growth as a consequence of joining el proceso and committing to working for the community exemplifies visibility as part of a political project. Self-representation is intertwined with the process and with COCOMACIA.

During our first meeting, Julia Susana Mena Moreno talked for over an hour about what she wanted to include in her story. Later, we talked about a possible outline to make her story shorter. She highlighted her practice of traditional medicine inherited from her family, her activism in constructing a school for the children in her community, and the vulnerability derived from her activism. Her leadership is manifested in every role but shines in moments like this: "La comunidad colocó su mano de obra. Y yo le hacía seguimiento: desde acá yo bajaba, y miraba la escuela, le tomaba fotografías. 'Está así. Necesitamos que le arregle esto.' yo no soy ingeniera pero sí veo también lo malo" [The community provided their labor. And I would follow up. From here I would go there and would check the school out: 'It is like this. We need you to fix this.' I am not an engineer, but I can also see the bad]. Her humorous takes are intertwined in the three stories in her narrative and the way she chose to present herself publicly. She decided to keep them as one single story even if they exceeded the genre's standard length. Like in "La Historia de Adonis," Mena Moreno included maps of her community made in a recent workshop about community mapping. Several layers of meaning in "La historia de Julia" challenge the need for a narrative arc, but seeing comisionadas' reactions to her story shows that Mena Moreno's storytelling is powerful because she uses her storytelling skills to create affective reactions while discussing difficult issues. "La historia de Julia"'s mini-narratives address multiple topics that recover traditional practices (healing arts, artisanal mining, and fishing), community organizing, and even the history of COCOMACIA connecting her beginning in the organization with Gonzalo de la Torre (see chapter 3).

Mena Moreno revealed ways of knowing beyond writing and used staging to re-create her skills and knowledge. She asked me to go to Quibdó's market to take photographs as she showed me the medicinal plants she mentioned in her story. We also recorded a video of her explaining how gold panning is done, a traditional mining practice she mentions in her story. The visual reconstruction of her past, as with Mena Becerra, not only helps illustrate her story but also creates a visual archive. By staging, they are performing what they like to see, creating what their stories need. In her narration, Mena Moreno even mentions "el secreto," a healing practice that cannot be named or described but invokes the magic of survival, a traditional unknown that can be recalled and shared only partially to ensure that it keeps its power.[43]

Rosmira Salas Lenis shared about her path from literacy education to COCOMACIA's leadership. Like Julia Susana Mena, she established a connection in her story with Gonzalo de la Torre's guidance of missionary work in empowering Black communities. Particularly, she centered on literacy and education as key elements of the political project of COCOMACIA. By including pictures of the literacy booklets used for educating communities about community forests, politics, child mortality, natural resources, media, justice, and other topics, "La historia de Rosmira" values pedagogy as an empowering practice. And in the same way as other storytellers, her children are part of her narrative, revealing the importance of family as an extension of her community.

"La historia de Rosmira" uses sayings that bring her style and daily life storytelling into her story. One expression is particularly memorable: "Ciego no es el que no ve sino el que no quiere saber"[44] [Blind is not the one who doesn't see, but the one who refuses to know]. As Rosmira Salas was COCOMACIA's legal representative at the time of the production, her participation in this project supports the work of the comisionadas, even if in practice her work exceeds the comisionadas' responsibilities. Salas Lenis's support of women's empowerment is not an explicit feminist practice but a support of rural women as part of COCOMACIA's commitment to the autonomy, collective well-being, and territorial protection of Black communities. Her performative language and her narrative reveal the importance of showing up as part of el proceso.

In "La historia de Rosmira," she tells us: "Estamos luchando para que las mujeres se animen a este proceso que necesitamos que haya más mujeres que hombres, porque siempre nosotras las mujeres nos quedamos por ser tímidas, y porque los obedecemos y nos metemos mucho a la ley de los maridos, y no podemos ya estar en esa ley ya de los maridos, si no que tenemos que hacer su vida, como mujer que somos y hacernos valer como mujer" [We are fighting so women join this process because we need more women than men. As women, we stay behind because we are shy, and because we obey men, and we internalize the law of husbands. We can't be in the law of husbands, we need to create our life, as women that we are, and we need to be valued]. Her summary of her work motivating women's participation reveals the tension between women's empowerment and the overarching and internalization of patriarchal rules. Her reference to "la ley de los maridos" echoes women's obstacles in participating in community meetings as much as men's complaints about women's participation. She invites women to participate in el proceso by moving beyond "la ley de los maridos" and finding value in their life, their identity as women, and their agency.

Mariluz (Pancha) Moya Cuesta also uses part of her story as a call to action. Moya Cuesta is not a comisionada, but she is affiliated with COCOMACIA and has contributed to the Comisión as a promotora, an assistant spreading information related to their projects. Her invitation for women to join el proceso matches other stories: "Y les digo a mis compañeras, que se animen al proceso, que no se queden en las casas, que los hombres se sienten orgullosos cuando sus mujeres ya son unas líder[es], que ya no les da temor de hablar en alguna parte, que se capaciten, que por día a día tiene que ir tratando de mejorar, no quedarse hacia atrás, ya eso de uno estar debajo del compañero eso ya pasó"[45] [And I tell my compañeras to get excited about the process, that don't stay in their homes, that men feel proud when their women are leaders and they are not afraid to speak anywhere, to not stay behind, being below their partner is from the past]. While Moya's invitation reaffirms gender roles and heteronormativity, her invitation is a reminder for women about their agency. "La historia de Mariluz" is the only one that explicitly mentions men's perception of women as leaders. Even if men's attention seems to be invoked as a motivation for women to be leaders, Moya reminds her audience that "staying behind" is a thing from the past. "La historia de Mariluz" then echoes the strategic use of digital storytelling for a visibility that is unavoidably collective. Doing the impossible takes multiple shapes. This multiplicity of strategies reaffirms the scope of stories, projections, and representations that are included in the stories.

Mariluz Moya used her story to share her experience in COCOMACIA and in fundraising through her description of a raffle to buy a boat motor for her community. As transportation is an issue for most communities, and rivers are the main routes of transportation, "La historia de Mariluz" is highly local and creates a connection with the everyday challenges of rural communities in the region. Just like other storytellers, Moya uses her personal story of survival to show how family can be a catalyst for dreaming of transformation. Moya's role as volunteer within the organization is analogous to the comisionadas' work as it is motivated by conviction more than it is by individual benefit. She also shares her gratitude for what the organization has given her and her children: "Yo en estos momentos me siento muy agradecida de la organización de COCOMACIA porque he despertado mucho, y le he dado mucho conocimiento a mis hijos también, y viven muy comprometidos con el estudio, porque ellos están en bachiller" [In these moments, I feel very grateful with COCOMACIA because I have awakened a lot, and I have shared the knowledge with my children too, who are committed to studying as they're in high school].

Miriam Moya Cuesta, Mariluz Moya Cuesta's sister, shared her experience about working for her family. Her story expresses vulnerability by explicitly mentioning her housing issues and her lack of resources to solve them. Her story ends by asking for help from her audience, an imagined audience that was very concrete when I was recording the audio: me. Miriam Moya, a former participant in gender workshops in which the comisionadas were trained and working at the COCOMACIA's restaurant in the summer of 2013, tells a story of struggles that are very present. She makes clear that her kids bear much of the injustice brought about by her need to work and her inability to cover her family's expenses. This story shows a different side of survival that reflects the energy consumed in being alive and working for a living without attaining well-being. Story sharing for Miriam Moya is not about educating viewers but about looking for support. Miriam Moya's story might seem the antithesis of the ideal representation of survival, but what it reveals is the complexity and difficulty of existing in a place where the national minimum conditions of life are not met.

The extensive collection of old and recent photographs created a repository of nostalgic remembrances that generated joy, even if briefly. Personal experiences were engaging, and watching the stories became an act of sharing. Each story also reflected embodied skills and knowledge: from making handicrafts to traditional medicine, farming, domestic labor, mining, and organizing. The narratives may not emphasize embodied knowledge, but it forms a crucial aspect of the self-presentation techniques storytellers employed to contextualize their own voices and stories. Choosing to share, in most cases, stories of endurance as advocacy tools shows the comisionadas' efforts in education to make Black communities' survival meaningful. Instead of focusing on reliving trauma, stories provided a supportive environment for sharing fears and hopes, which is accentuated using visual and auditory modes of perception. Moreover, the spirituality and magic woven into the stories reflect community healing practices and embodied solidarity that materialize survival but cannot be contained by written archives.

At the core of every story is an individual struggle and the possibility for transformation. For Rivas López, COCOMACIA works as a support system she is proud to enact. Palacios Romaña traces her personal growth to her professional affiliation with COCOMACIA, and specifically to the Comisión: "Otra cosa que me ha servido mucho para mi crecimiento personal es la llegada a COCOMACIA" [Another thing that has helped me a lot for my personal growth is my arrival to COCOMACIA]. Statements about women's need to challenge traditional gender roles are also common in "La historia de Rosmira," "La historia de Rubiela," and even "La historia de Mariluz." The similarities between the stories could be read as homogeneity or consensus within COCOMACIA, but they can hint at available narratives or the structure imposed by mediation.

Mediated stories are inherently different. There is an audio recorder, a camera, and another person affecting the storytelling process. And there are the implications of self-representation and self-censoring. Self-representation is self-censoring: "What is left out, glossed over or left unsaid is often just as significant as what is included."⁴⁶ Refusing to answer someone's questions in storytelling is one of many possible reactions to mediation. And then, there are secrets that work as a performative refusal that is opposed to silence, as in Rigoberta Menchú's story.⁴⁷ And other secrets work as a performance of religious tradition linked to ritual, as in Julia Susana Mena's story about traditional medicine. Magical secrets perform refusal and survival in Chocó as embodied knowledge that protects from evil and requires protection from co-optation: "Women have their secrets, as men do, but not for gold and not with the devil; secrets to defend yourself, secrets so you can work without getting tired, secrets to cure a snakebite, secrets to staunch the flow of blood, secrets to attract lovers, secrets to climb a chontaduro palm. . . . These secrets are prayers, or what in English we call spells."⁴⁸

The secrets reveal that Black communities were surviving even before the war. The secrets' content is not as important as what they symbolize: survival as improvisation, as refusal. And even if magic has survived the atrocities, it is important to remember that it is not only resistance, or survival, or bravery that informs stories. Every experience and every decision affects the stories and the discourses that inform them. As a common background, the process is a scenario that connects stories and demands silences. As Mena Moreno's secreto, not everything that is important and powerful can be narrated or even explained. Stories are made up of silences as much as they are made of words.

Collaborative creation has limits; in this case, my interest in finishing the stories by my planned departure date restricted the process. My expectations about the stories and conversations about the stories revealed my role as researcher. Internalizing and performing our roles as storytellers and facilitator informed every interaction related to the project with my expectations and the limits of our roles. The collaboration's flexibility was contained by our specific roles and the time constraints. Performances by the comisionadas were naturally informed by their experience as public speakers, as part of their workshops and their weekly radio program. Their stories reflected a close connection with their rehearsed discourses about gender equality and territorial rights, which act as buzzwords for their activism in their personal stories. But spontaneity is also evident when they include laughter, sadness, rage, and emotion within their stories. Palacios Romaña laughs throughout her story, particularly when remembering the first time she had to present information at a large assembly. Mena Becerra starts nostalgic but ends up hopeful. Miriam Moya Cuesta complains about her landlord and her exclusion from the Comisión.

As the stories are told, they are changed by my desires, the storytellers' desires, and the audience's desires. As we invoke ethics and collaboration, we are imagining the ways we hope these stories and practices will circulate. This collaboration has been shaped by ethical practices of care and reciprocity. Such an ethics implies trust in the potential of every individual and their everyday practices. This is a utopian commitment. An attempt to explore worlds of possibility.

Mujeres Pacíficas's focus on storytelling as a performative and intentional practice in daily life offers an alternative to writing. "Being there" and "showing up" are the pillars of the comisionadas' political practice and highlight the importance of valuing daily and repetitive actions as an essential part of the embodied knowledge of activism. Through these stories, we can see just how crucial embodied knowledge is for survival and activism as collective efforts.

The utopian potential of audiovisual methodologies is realized through practices that coexist with hegemonic discourses but are often overlooked or undervalued. Audiovisual stories can suggest what escapes writing and, hence, the archive, by portraying ways of knowing that exist beyond writing. The use of images and digital platforms in depicting survival in Chocó can lead to romanticization, similar to the popularization of stories of Colombia's violence. What floats away and escapes our attempts to make memories (and archives) more accessible and democratic as we have envisioned with *Mujeres Pacíficas* can help us imagine other ways of coexisting. What is left unsaid or forgotten even when we attempt to create collaborative memories. I am trying to be critical of my own collaborative research to push me to think beyond what we have done so far. To me, activism and social change require a constant rehearsal of survival skills and an unwavering determination to not give up. But, as the comisionadas remind us, changing the world is not an individual responsibility.

Of course, *Mujeres Pacíficas* does not hold the nuances of the comisionadas' repetitive tasks that make activism and collaboration in the project possible—showing up to marches and meetings, traveling for days to lead workshops about gender in rural communities, and taking care of each other. *Mujeres Pacíficas'* storytellers embrace the performative and embodied character of storytelling as an unstable process of staging, rehearsal, and repetition where creativity and improvisation are as central as they are in the comisionadas' daily lives. Stories retell the embodiment of survival and agency and, in the process, become an embodied utopia of imagining otherwise. We can imagine other worlds and ways to exist and survive through storytelling, even if it can never capture the complexities of everyday survival. And maybe these worlds we imagine are closer than we think if we look at spaces that are actively working to materialize memorialization beyond trauma.

CHAPTER 3

Utopian Archives
Turning Trauma into Memory

> Yo empecé en el río Buey porque allá llegó el equipo misionero primero. Y yo iba, y yo escuchaba al padre Gonzalo de la Torre. Cuando ya la gente fue a Bebaramá, mi río, que ya existía la organización, ya a mí no me cogía el susto porque ya sabía yo lo que estaban haciendo ... muchas personas le decían a uno "no te vas a meter a eso que esa gente es guerrillera."
>
> I started in the Buey River because that is where the missionary team arrived first. And I would go and I would listen to father Gonzalo de la Torre. When they went to Bebaramá, my river, the organization already existed, and I didn't get scared because I knew what they were doing ... many people would tell me "do not get involved in that because those people are guerrillas."
>
> —Julia Susana Mena Moreno

COCOMACIA's Comisión de Género's office is a repository of images, documents, and keepsakes. Pictures of the comisionadas, their friends, and relatives; posters from campaigns against domestic violence; cards; invitations; letters; awards; and other information hang on the walls and bulletin boards. Depending on the workshops they are attending or organizing, there are maps, calendars with deadlines, forms, posters, or flyers displayed as reminders and souvenirs of their work. The office also has a small library with books. COCOMACIA has produced some of these books in collaboration with NGOs, visible in the logos found on their back cover. Others are gifts from researchers who have interviewed and quoted the comisionadas. The Comisión's institutional archive is made of piles of notebooks, CDs, and paperwork they have kept. After Justa

Figure 3.1. T-shirt with Justa Germania Mena Córdoba's image and part of the Comisión de Género's archive in their office. Quibdó, July 2016.

Germania Mena Córdoba's death, her image became even more present and the office an everyday altar to her memory (Figure 3.1). COCOMACIA's institutional archive is in the room next to the Comisión's office, but other public areas of the building display images of other leaders and collective memories: awards, institutional collaborations, and certificates.

What escapes these rooms is how memories extend beyond the office. Memories of violence, while relatively infrequent in everyday conversations, appear with regularity in everyday spaces and objects. Memory is worn daily. As COCOMACIA's members, some days the comisionadas wear T-shirts with images of leaders who recently died, particularly during the novena—the nine days of prayer that follow someone's death—which in Quibdó includes singing, praying, eating, and drinking together. Other days, they wear institutional symbols (green vests and hats with COCOMACIA in yellow letters) or insignia from the feminist networks they belong to, so they are identifiable as a group. Quibdó's humidity, lack of air conditioning, and constant rain make the Comisión de Género's informal archives vulnerable to disappearing. Analog and digital archives become temporary. Still, efforts to keep memories alive are a daily practice for the comisionadas.

Memory-making in Quibdó might not be institutional, but it is a constant presence and endeavor. Outside COCOMACIA's building, the memories of past political candidates and NGOs' funding materialized in fading images on hats, notebooks, mugs, and wearables that are part of Chocó's landscape and any community meeting. Not only is memory embodied and part of everyday life, but also political and social events are stages for an ephemeral memory that exists in showing up, as I will discuss in chapter 5. Paradoxically, no institution to preserve local, regional, or national memories existed in Quibdó until 2009. In a city that until recently had only one public library and no bookstores, museums, or other official repositories of knowledge, Quibdó's community memory and archives challenge outsider representations of their knowledge and lived experiences.

The absence of official archives and museums is symptomatic of Chocó's association with emptiness, as the concept territorios baldíos [empty territories] has justified colonization and extractive practices. Not only have territories been considered conquerable, but its inhabitants (mainly Black and Indigenous people) also have not been considered deserving of what the region offers. Documentation and conservation happen elsewhere—in large urban centers like Bogotá and Medellín. As a centralist country, Colombia has reproduced the global division of labor: entire regions marginal to the centers of power are still perceived as repositories of raw materials. As one of the most biodiverse regions in the world, the ecoregion of Chocó (which comprises the whole Colombian Pacific from Ecuador to Panamá) is home to fauna and flora that do not exist elsewhere. Extractive capitalism as the norm has promoted the exploitation of the territory and its resources and the assumption that local cultural practices are add-ons to the centralist national identity and serve as evidence for official knowledge production. Information is consistently taken from the region as proof of multiculturalism or humanitarianism, or without efforts to support local knowledge production efforts.

In this chapter, we will see how local initiatives can transform a shared history of Black communities in Colombia into a visual archive in which absence activates connections with transnational representations of Blackness. At the heart of transcending the written through local efforts lies a visual weaving of global ancestors with local social movements in organizations such as Cimarrón Movimiento Nacional por los Derechos Humanos de las Comunidades Negras de Colombia [Maroon National Movement for Black Communities' Rights in Colombia]. As the product of a reading group that discussed Black thinkers such as Martin Luther King Jr. and Malcolm X, Cimarrón embodies the links among transnational and local images, stories, and networks of Black solidarity.[1] Just as is the case with Afrocentric museums, Black organizations create archives that transcend national borders, official narratives, and analog and digital archives: "the ones we create, disavow, critically interpret, reconfigure, leave attended, and pull apart."[2] Their embracing of canonical Black figures troubles the notion of national identity and produces other ways to imagine being Black in Colombia.

The struggle for representation is a political one, and it exceeds the need for inclusion in national memories. Erasure of Blackness is the norm. Colombian national popular culture tends to mimic US popular culture. However, an adaptation of a well-known TV show by African American television producer Shonda Rhimes, *Grey's Anatomy*, cast only white/mestizx actors when it became *A corazón abierto* [Open-hearted], scripted by famous Colombian writer Fernando Gaitán, creator of *Betty la fea* [Ugly Betty]. When Cimarrón found out that the Colombian adaptation's cast did not have any Afro-Colombian actors, in contrast to the racially diverse cast of the original, they published a press release against the owners and producers of RCN (the TV network) that, among other things, invoked Martin Luther King Jr. and Nelson Mandela in their call to boycott the network.[3] This example reveals not only the lack of representation of Black people in Colombian television but also the importance of visual representation for activists. Once again, the construction of Blackness by omission on television motivated a strategic challenge to absence, with activists choosing Blackness over nationality as an organizing principle by finding ancestors in political figures. This connectedness to global representations of Blackness is evident in the adaptation controversy.

From the names of cultural centers and groups (for example, the Frantz Fanon Research Center and Soweto) to stories about members of the Black Panther Party allegedly visiting Colombia in the 1970s, Afro-Colombians have created affinities with Black people in the United States and other parts of the world. Shonda Rhimes, *Grey's Anatomy*, and television became part of this connectedness, symbolically serving as circuits that wired the Afro-Colombian organizations' past to their present and their national politics to their ideological bond with members of the African diaspora. These examples of transnational engagement respond to the marginalization imposed by a white/mestizx national identity. Creating global constructions of Blackness highlighting a shared past and moral leaders is a strategy that does not erase or even question the construction of Colombian identity but offers an alternative to visual representations. Constructing Black history and creating visual representations of Blackness reveals that representations are not neutral and reproduce racial hierarchies and history's silences that keep the social order in place. The political potential of alternative archives and stories lies in their ability to center the experiences of Black communities in Colombia and challenge existing representations of Blackness. Local representations are informed and inspired by the realities of Blackness elsewhere as a response to invisibility. Visibility might not be a magical antidote to oppression and exclusion, but it is central to challenge the violence of intentional invisibility.

In academia, inclusive visual narratives of Colombia's history start with Nina de Friedemann. As one of the founders of the field of Afro-Colombian studies, she is also one of the most important contributors to the field, with an extensive ethnographic work materialized in twenty-seven published books. Her research on Afro-Colombians in Palenque, Providencia, different communities in Chocó, and even in the United States and Africa created an anthropological interest in researching Black communities. Colombian anthropology's focus on the study of Indigenous communities is why, for some scholars, Nina de Friedemann's scholarship was not anthropological enough as it studied Black communities.[4] Still, her influence in the field of Colombian anthropology to date is undeniable. Her use of visual and audiovisual methodologies and outcomes was meant as an antidote to the invisibility of Blackness in Colombia's national narratives. For de Friedemann, invisibility was a control strategy tarnishing science, academia, and politics.[5] Blackness and Indigeneity had been constructed discursively as anchors to the past in the national imagination, obstacles in the mestizo nation's progress toward modernity. De Friedemann's groundbreaking ethnographic research visualized a collaborative and antiracist scholarship to think critically about the silences of official narratives. Anthropological interest in Black communities rapidly infiltrated other fields, creating a significant academic corpus that would culminate in lending the authority to support the demands of Black communities from the Colombian Pacific with Law 70 of 1993 that recognized their collective land rights. De Friedemann can also be considered a pioneer of visual studies. After her death, one of the most important libraries in Colombia, the Biblioteca Luis Ángel Arango, named a visual collection after her that can still be partially consulted online.[6]

Local attempts to create visual archives, such as local museums, provide representations of Afro-Colombians that are alternative to those disseminated in the mainstream media, and they build on narratives imagined beyond academic boundaries. Non-hegemonic reconstructions of memory offer alternatives to the exclusions and oblivion that any memorialization discourse implies. I propose here that local museographic spaces can transform embodied knowledge into narratives of memory that perform and celebrate survival. Alternative rememoration spaces are rooted in everyday practices of commitment to create and celebrate an Afrocentric memory in Quibdó. In the repertoire of postconflict utopias that imagine life in spaces that exist in between violence and peace, I consider local museums utopian rehearsals of archiving knowledge as worldmaking. These utopian rehearsals practice in real time materializing what is not here yet: repositories that turn trauma into collective memories that serve local communities. As utopian archives in a so-called postconflict landscape, they are grouped within the typology of practices that make life bearable, what I have called postconflict utopias.

In this chapter, I briefly discuss the National Museum of Colombia as an example of the silences and omissions of national memory, and its still superficial inclusion of Black communities. Then, I enact a close reading of two museums: Fundación Muntú Bantú, a museographic space founded in 2008 by Chocoan historian Sergio Antonio Mosquera Mosquera, the only national museum dedicated exclusively to commemorate Afro-Colombian history; and La Muestra Bíblica [The Biblical Exhibit] created by Chocoan missionary Gonzalo de la Torre Guerrero, a theological museum grounded in the Chocoan context and Afro spirituality.

Museums and Memory in Colombia

Disembodied artifacts and utensils that once belonged to colonies have plagued museums in former empires. The British Museum online collection database, for example, has 1,745 results for Colombian objects, 365 specifically from Chocó.[7] Needless to say, knowledge production about the past, artifact collection, and cultural spaces are embedded into complex global networks of power hierarchies that define who gets to own artifacts and tell their stories. In Michael Taussig's *My Cocaine Museum*, the gold artifacts at Bogotá's renowned Museo del Oro [Gold Museum] are placeholders of colonization and slavery: "The museum is silent as to the fact that for more than three centuries of Spanish occupation what the colony stood for and depended upon was the labor of slaves from Africa in the gold mines."[8] As the Museo del Oro is a major national symbol and popular tourist site, the silences and omissions of narratives that became national truths are not accidental. The violence of museographic collections is visible not only in the display of artifacts far away from where they belong, but also in the transformation of human remains into artifacts that represent the past even when they belong to communities that already exist, which is the case in the Museo del Oro.

Museums that reify imagined national borders as permanent also reinforce homogeneous racial and cultural identities under the false inclusivity of a national one. What would a memorialization of the centuries-long trauma and survival experienced in Chocó look like? Without official museums in Chocó, and lack of inclusion of Afrodescendants in national museums beyond temporary exhibits, creating and sustaining spaces of Afrocentric memory is utopian. And, even more important, these omissions actively support a centralist narrative portraying entire regions and groups as accessories of a national identity. Until 2020, the Museo Nacional's online request form included eight categories for users to self-identify: afrocolombiano, raizal y palenquero, ciudadano en general, desmovilizado, desplazado, indígena, LGBTI, rom, and víctima de la violencia.[9] "Ciudadano en general" [common citizen] becomes a placeholder for white and mestizx people, and the impossibility of selecting more than one category from the drop-down menu acts as a reminder of narratives that naturalize mestizaje as the center of citizenship. As Peter Wade writes: "elites and middle classes want to re-establish the possibility of making hierarchical distinctions of race (and thus also class and region), distinctions which threaten to vanish if the process of mestizaje were really to reach its ideological goal of homogenisation."[10]

In national narratives and the consumption of culture they require, mestizaje supremacy has crystallized Bogotá and its narratives as the main national dish, while including other regions as garnishes. In her book *Becoming Black Political Subjects*, sociologist Tianna S. Paschel states that Chocó is simultaneously a placeholder for Blackness and not considered part of Colombia. Paschel uses the metaphor of a quilt to visualize how the ideology of mestizaje was about a coexistence of ethnic groups more than an embrace of Blackness as core component of the national identity.[11] The Museo Nacional's drop-down menu represents this quilt while reflecting the inclusion of racial categories (afrocolombiano, raizal y palenquero) alongside categories of ethnic belonging (indígena, rom), categories of sexual and gender identity (LGBTI), and self-identification as a victim or a perpetrator in the armed conflict (desmovilizado, desplazado, víctima). Paschel's quilt is an image of multiculturalism in which identities are add-ons, and intersectionality is impracticable.

The confirmation that rigorous ethnographic work can influence public policy that had historically denied Afro-Colombians access to rights reveals how social movements can strategically use academic research. Jaime Arocha remembers that in the celebration of Law 70 of 1993, social leaders mentioned the importance of de Friedemann's work and how it had encouraged their struggle.[12] The connection between Law 70 and de Friedemann's scholarship reveals the real possibilities of community-engaged scholarship. Instead of reproducing stereotypical representations of entire communities, scholars can choose to support their movements and political goals.

Two decades after the association of de Friedemann's scholarship with Law 70, the Museo Nacional created the temporary exhibit "Velorios y santos vivos. Comunidades negras, afrocolombianas, raizales y palenqueras" [Wakes and Living Saints: Black, Afro-Colombian, Raizal and Palenquero Communities]. Although the exhibit was thoughtfully curated to address the museum's institutional shortcomings, it highlights how the exclusion of Black communities is integral to the dominant narrative of Colombian identity. According to the working group behind this exhibit, its goal was to exalt the aesthetic, symbolic, and spiritual richness of funeral rituals, the relationship with ancestors, and devotion to Catholic saints as renewal of the solidarity of Black communities in Colombia.[13] There are mixed opinions about this and other temporary exhibits as attempts to partially fix the symbolic violence of the Museo Nacional's official narrative. What is clear is that as Arocha Rodríguez states, with this exhibit, the museum filled in the gap about Afrodescendants' contributions for the first time since colonial times.[14]

As an official space, the Museo Nacional has institutionalized mestizaje supremacy by representing the experience of the elite as the referent for national identity. And that the historical—and only temporary—inclusion of Afrodescendants' contributions for the first time was associated with death was a common criticism.[15] Another relevant critique was the decontextualization of sacred spiritualities, altars, and saints that were staged in a museum.[16] What these critiques reveal is the importance of inclusion that is not temporary or superficial. That said, inclusion is utopian: "Presence can be better than absence, but not always. Since present presence leaves much to be desired, its implicit improved futurity is part of its promise."[17]

The utopian archives we will examine temporarily decenter the mestizaje supremacy of national museums and remind us that scholarship is political. Fueling Nina de Friedemann's collaborative visual approach to Black studies in Colombia is a definition of mestizaje as a political ideology used to annihilate diversity and access to rights.[18] This recognition of the ideological power of mestizaje to define who gets to access citizenship rights highlights the importance of methodologies that are not complicit in reproducing this hierarchy. De Friedemann also regards mestizaje as the basis of a caste system built on white supremacy and fueled by an ideology of whitening.[19] De Friedemann's scholarship opposes the ideology of mestizaje as blanqueamiento by tracking African traces in the shape of memories, feelings, scents, images, textures, colors, and melodies.[20] Decentering the museum and the monuments and instead centering sensorial knowledge is utopian.

Cristina Lleras, "the curator of art and history at the museum and part of the curatorial team that produced the exhibition,"[21] confirms in her article about the temporary exhibition that "[Black] communities are not accurately represented in the National Museum's exhibitions or collections."[22] In Colombia, by highlighting racial miscegenation as the standard, Indigenous and Black communities have been othered, and made invisible and hyper visible as fixtures of a centralist nation that has been portrayed as homogeneously mixed. Even Lleras, in her concluding remarks about the importance of including Black communities to the official narrative of the Museo Nacional, reinforces Blackness as otherness: "Many of the staff think it is possible to recognize the other with respect and embrace new practices."[23]

Representation of non-mestizx narratives is not inclusion. Official memory narratives and the institutions founded to uphold them are complicit in defining Blackness as exotic and folkloric, and part of the national patrimony. So even if the temporary exhibit's aim was "to give visibility to qualities that African captives and their descendants have brought to the formation of the nation: spirituality, social organization, aesthetics, and symbolic universes,"[24] its temporary character is a symptom of imperfect structures and institutions that need to be reimagined. Lleras writes that "[i]t was also thought that this inclusion would acknowledge the museum's complicity in making Afro-Colombian communities invisible,"[25] a disembodied gesture in the right direction. We cannot measure the incomplete impact of temporary exhibits in undoing historical damages to communities that, for the most part, cannot physically access the museum.

Mestizaje is an embodied knowledge as much as a national visual narrative. Rehearsals of this racialized narrative are not exclusive to museums. Christen Smith explains how embodied practices create racialized categories as much as discourses: "Body language and implicit visual and corporeal conversations produce racial subjectivities as much as what is spoken."[26] Embodiment is performative. As everyday practices, embodied racial subjectivities require constant performances to become naturalized practices and techniques reproduced through bodies and narratives. As Afro-diaspora studies scholar Yomaira Figueroa reminds us, examining racialization as a process creates space for resistance: "while we understand race as socially and politically constructed, making space to trace how and where racialization occurs, and the impacts of racialization and heteropatriarchy, allows for fuller and more strategic forms of resistance."[27] As this chapter focuses on spaces that resist the silences about race in broad national discourses, it is important to note the role of performance and lived experience in creating meaning within silence: "But what of the meaning that fills the silences of racial discourse? There is a relationship between race, performance and the lived political realities of Blackness in the nation that fills this silence with meaning."[28]

Mestizaje supremacy builds on colonial understandings of racial hierarchies and blanqueamiento as a goal. Mestizaje is linked to whitening as the political ideology of Latin American national projects and cannot be understood independently from the exclusion of entire groups: "Mestizaje and blanqueamiento, common throughout Latin America, were supposed to help neutralize forms of diversity considered subversive, challenges to the official nation."[29] Mestizaje's association with multiculturalism "denies racism yet perpetuates gradual violence towards racialized territories and communities through state policies of dispossession."[30] Official narratives reproducing mestizaje ideology have shaped museums and monuments, which in turn become spaces of hegemonic memory-making. Usually attached to particular understandings of what counts as heritage or what deserves to be preserved, curated collections require the selection and exclusion of groups, stories, and spaces that do not serve the interests of the nation. Non-hegemonic museographic and commemorative spaces exist alongside official narratives and focus on issues and events that are underemphasized or even ignored in mainstream museum exhibitions.

Access to rights through public policies has not disrupted the stereotyped representations of Black people in Colombia. As sociologist Melissa M. Valle notes in her analysis of the use of racialized characters in Colombian Caribbean coast carnivals, "Colombian nationhood is able to assert its whiteness by juxtaposing the contemporary quotidian white exemplars of progress with staged, carnivalesque forms of antiquated Blackness."[31] The omnipresent rehearsal of racialized embodiment in Colombia reiterates and solidifies racial categories as much as racist representations.[32] As a response to the Cátedra de Estudios Afrocolombianos, established by Law 70, research about representations of African descendants in textbooks has shown once again that visibility is not a solution to erasure. In educational contexts, "African descent appears as a marginal, if not exotic, issue."[33]

Official narratives that materialize in museums and memorializations build on narratives with political power. Aymara feminist scholar Silvia Rivera Cusicanqui teaches us that political discourses in Latin America have been characterized by a "not saying" that hides racial hierarchies and separates words from actions. She explains that "[l]as imágenes nos ofrecen interpretaciones y narrativas sociales, que desde siglos precoloniales iluminan este trasfondo social y nos ofrecen perspectivas de comprensión crítica de la realidad"[34] [images offer us interpretations and social narratives that since precolonial centuries illuminate this social background and offer us perspectives for a critical understanding of reality]. What official spaces such as the Museo Nacional de Colombia or the Museo del Oro in Bogotá share is the absence of images that decenter mestizaje. The unsaid is political and aligns with those who have historically held political power in Colombia.

Muntú Bantú: Recovering Black History

The noise of motorcycles sets the rhythm of the everyday in Quibdó. Honking, music from cars and houses, and invitations to get a rapi (mototaxi) or get into a bus make navigating the city an always collaborative experience. A building on the Carrera 18 stands out with a yellow façade and a fence with four horizontal Black bodies on each side. Visitors, and even passersby, cannot ignore this explicit representation of the inside of a slave ship even if the ship is only completely visible from the other side of the street, as it rests on the roof. More than a mile away from the Atrato River, the ship is marked with a sign that reads "Lord Ligonier." The sign below the ship reads "Muntú Bantú. Fundación Social Afrocolombiana." Below a balcony on the second story, there is a fence that represents the inside of the slave ship. A blue horizontal stripe that represents water is painted on a step that holds up the fence. Someone who enters the building through the hallway on the right of the fence is stepping into the water and stepping into the ship (see Figure 3.2).

I went to Muntú Bantú in 2011 for the first time, when its founder, historian Sergio Antonio Mosquera Mosquera, offered a private tour for me and my mom, per her request, as she had seen the museum before on one of her previous trips as technical support for an environmentalist NGO. Now I was in the same role. I would take over her temporary contract for three months, hoping to finish my master's thesis with a less intensive job. I had been working as a secondary school history teacher for five years, teaching over 200 students while taking graduate classes at night. Now I was in Quibdó, learning about a history that was not included in the US textbooks I had been using to teach. Muntú Bantú was a place I had heard about because it fulfills different roles in Quibdó: field trips for schools, a meeting venue, a film club, and a community space.

Muntú Bantú materializes this energy into a past that is made present by a personal commitment to sharing knowledge with the communities most affected by the ripples of this past. Mosquera Mosquera has researched Black communities in Chocó for decades. He explains the origin of his foundation's name as the result of tracing the origin of most Afro-Chocoans to the Bantu

Figure 3.2. Fundación Muntú Bantú. Quibdó, 2013.

region in Central Africa in his research, such as his book *Afrochocoanos y troncos familiares*.[35] Muntú is also part of the Afro-Colombian literary canon as Manuel Zapata Olivella's *Changó, el gran putas* establishes a genealogy of humanity, resistance, spirituality, and kinship embodied in the concept of muntú: "el rostro del muntu refleja el alma de todos los seres humanos, como humanos son todos los que se alimentan de nuestro espíritu"[36] [the people face reflects the souls of every human being, as humans they are all that feed our spirit]. The transformative energy of muntú contains the multitudes of enslavement and liberation.

Mosquera Mosquera describes Muntú Bantú as a center of memory. Unlike museums full of artifacts, this space turns absence into a historical narrative, since there are limited sources and artifacts to reconstruct Afro-Colombian history in a museum setting.[37] The visual representations invoke Black history beyond national borders with colorful murals and quotations that embellish the walls of a house that until 2011 did not look different from others in the Nicolás Medrano neighborhood from the outside. To walk into the museum is to replace Quibdó's motorcycle traffic with the evocation of an ancestral African past in connection with contemporary Chocoan identity, and to imagine a common space to create a shared future. The foundation's structure, changed to resemble the English slave boat *Lord Ligonier*, acts as a reminder of a shared history that cannot be understood with only a national or contemporary approach. As the foundation offers not only a museum, but also a cafe bar and an event room where cultural activities take place, at least two ministers have chosen it as the venue for meetings. The popularity of the aesthetic experience has not prevented this space's marginalization as a viable cultural initiative in which to invest state money. Independent of the lack of funding, Muntú Bantú is a memory initiative that reappropriates history and its representation to offer a space of celebratory monumentalization of Afro-Colombian culture. The building's visibility reframes public space and acts as a countermonument to expose on the outside what museums usually conceal: explicit depictions of slavery.

The museum's historical journey celebrates African heritage and Afrodescendant culture and aesthetics. The first murals celebrate the African continent through images of Africa, African proverbs, and nostalgic sentences: "Todo empezó en África" [Everything started in Africa], a pregnant woman's belly, under which it reads "Quiero volver a nacer en África" [I want to be born again in Africa], and the profile of a woman's face within an African map. A colorful overload of representations of Africa foreground, from the beginning, the particularities of this space of memory. Africans and the African diaspora are no longer an accessory but the history. This visual introduction acts both as a reference framework for the Afrogenetic narrative that centers Africa and as a space for knowledge production. It is an homage, a historical reconstruction, and an interruption of the present to explore survival outside of the everyday urgencies of life in Chocó. As cultural anthropologist and decolonial scholar Hilda Llórens writes, "the reconception and remembering of Africa as motherland has been a steady, if at times muted, feature of Black life."[38]

Memory becomes the foundation of a collective future. "Que no se te olvide de dónde vienes o nunca llegarás a dónde vas" [May you not forget where you come from, or you will never get where you are going] reads another mural close to the entrance. Africa as origin is solidified as a promise. This is a utopian proposal because remembering is used as a political strategy to imagine possible worlds. Utopia here is a hypothetical projection of what could be, as much as a push against impossibility. A rejection of naïveté. And it is only the beginning.

Portraits of Martin Luther King Jr., Abraham Lincoln, Luis Antonio Robles (the first Black congress member in Colombia), Candelario Obeso (nineteenth-century Colombian poet), Diego Luis Córdoba (twentieth-century Chocoan student leader and senator), Toussaint Louverture (and his words), and Bob Marley adorn the walls next to the stairs that go to the first room of the museum. As we go down, we see a framed photo of Malcolm X facing us. Below it is his quote: "Vean por sí mismos, escuchen por sí mismos, piensen por sí mismos" [See for yourself, listen for yourself, and think for yourself]. Nelson Mandela's image is strategically located behind a fence, which can be moved to reveal the whole image, to release him. Below each figure is a brief bio including places and dates of birth and death. Teaching and learning become interactive and collaborative, as Mosquera Mosquera leads us on a guided tour that has the right balance of information and space for observation and conversation. He does this with every group.

By centering Black people, this museum creates a concrete history that goes beyond the soft multiculturalism of Colombia's national narratives as it challenges national boundaries, national identities, and national narratives. Two young Chocoan artists, Fernelis Navia and Leison Rivas, are the creators of most of the murals. Their work is possible through what Mosquera Mosquera calls "un proceso de desentrenamiento de la éstetica occidental para pintar cuerpos negros" [a process of untraining from Western aesthetics to paint Black bodies]. The thought put into the murals' technique and content is evidence of creating images in the reconstruction of a transnational collective memory. Invoking Black identity beyond national borders is not new. When it was founded in 1976, Movimiento Cimarrón was named Soweto, as homage to the struggle against apartheid in South Africa. It is now an antiracist association centering Afro-Colombian knowledge and leadership through programs that include a transnational understanding of Blackness.

At first sight, a collage of transnational celebrities might seem kitsch, but for those who until this moment have not seen a connection among these figures or have never seen so many images of famous Black people in the same place, it differs from the history they know. We witness Black history in the making. Different from traditional representations of Afro-Colombians that fill textbooks and magazines, where they are portrayed fishing, mining, or serving white/mestizx people,[39] this museum's images create utopian visibility. Offering representations beyond iconographic clichés, they encourage visitors to rethink and reimagine Black identity, and they invite a critical approach to Afro-Colombians' representation. This does not mean that pictures of fishermen or miners are more or less real, but that the celebration of Blackness in

Muntú Bantú is a rehearsal of transnational solidarity and visibility. It is not a superficial national initiative but an example of the diversity of Black experience, and an invitation for a critical and autonomous reflection about Afro-Colombianness. Transnational icons do not replace the ordinary but expand the range of representations. This transnational approach also helps imagine Black diasporic connections.

Muntú Bantú addresses some silences around slavery as an institution that scholar Claudia Mosquera Rosero-Labbé[40] highlights: denial of Afrodescendants belonging to the nation, and the deadly abuse of enslaved people as a labor force. As Mosquera Rosero-Labbé states, social inclusion requires not only cultural and symbolic but also antiracist public policies with economic redistribution.[41] As a communitarian space for Black memory, Muntú Bantú recognizes the importance of cultural and symbolic reparations when the state is not committed to real reparations for the atrocities committed against Black people in Colombia. Unlike national memories presented as neutral in institutions such as the Museo Nacional, Muntú Bantú does not reinforce the forgetfulness and silence about slavery that Mosquera Rosero-Labbé denounces. The temporary exhibit "La Esclavitud en Colombia: Yugo y libertad 1553–1859" [Yoke and Slavery in Colombia: Freedom 1553–1859] exemplifies the interest in bringing slavery into the forefront while maintaining the tension between freedom and oppression, even in the present. This exhibit included reproductions of archival documents such as the "Real cédula del año de 1733 sobre la población de los negros en Chocó" [Royal decree of the year of 1733 on the population of Blacks in Chocó] and restaging of atrocities as the embodiment of slavery in the figure of a kneeling mannequin being branded next to a colonial wall. In this same room, a wall on "el barco negrero" [slave ships], with reproductions of *La Providencia* and *Amistad*, stated the dissonance of an education that promoted memorializing slave ship names but has never addressed the consequences and continuities of slavery.

Museographic collections are about exclusion as much as inclusion. The global imaginary of Blackness created in Muntú Bantú that repeals the erasure of Blackness in Colombia and elsewhere can perform its own erasures. Even though the identity emphasis of this museum makes it a pioneer, it is an incomplete space, because just like any museographic exercise, it implies selection, edition, and exclusion according to the curator's interests. Even though the museum includes a controversial figure like Abraham Lincoln, who decreed slavery abolition but is famous for his racist remarks, omitting controversy is likely a conscious choice. While transnational Black men offer a pedagogy of the connections between local and global history, the predominance of men can also signal the inevitable reproduction of a heteropatriarchal canon. Black women become visual representations of Africa as the motherland or unnamed representations alongside famous Black men.

The memory created by Muntú Bantú is a celebration of survival that works as a conscious attempt to reaffirm Afro-Colombian identity even if it continues to reproduce some of the nation's erasures. Memorializing collective survival reinforces a group identity that has historically been erased and distorted, which explains in part why trauma and internal conflicts are not portrayed. In *Decolonizing Methodologies*, Linda Tuhiwai Smith explains: "Events and accounts which focus on the positive are important not just because they speak to our survival, but because they celebrate our resistances at an ordinary human level and they affirm our identities."[42] These representations move beyond iconographic clichés in both remembering survival and resistance and celebrating them as an essential part of a collective identity.

Religious images of Black saints, Black angels, and a Black Jesus reveal an intentional break from the whitening of religious iconography (see Figure 3.3). A whole room for religion and spirituality stages its centrality and the importance of images for worship. The central image is a Black Jesus crowned by sun streams and framed by two Black angels and three human figures. A background of clouds from the floor to the ceiling immerses visitors into the scene. San Antonio de Padua, San Martín de Porres, San Benito, and Santo EcceHomo (see Figure 3.4) are next to images of funerary rites such as alabaos [mourning

Figure 3.3. Black Angel and Black Jesus. Religious mural detail. Fundación Muntú Bantú. Quibdó, 2011.

Figure 3.4. Sergio Antonio Mosquera Mosquera, founder of the Museo de la Afrocolombianidad, in Muntú Bantú's religious room. Quibdó, 2011.

songs] singers. Catholic saints are Afro-Americanized and embraced as mixtures of Yoruba and European religiosities.[43] The research experience of Sergio Mosquera about the African diaspora and spirituality, in particular about slavery and spirituality, is clear in the nuanced and complex representations of religious imagery in this room, inspired by his book *Visiones de la espiritualidad afrocolombiana*, dedicated to Nina de Friedemann.[44] The Afro-American religious tradition is characterized by a belief in secrets and saints, which are imbued with a sense of magic and willingness. These are the secrets invoked by comisionada Julia Susana Mena Moreno in her story, prayers associated with knowledge about plants that blur the boundaries between spiritual and material worlds.

The contrast between religiosity and trauma creates a continuity between life and death present in everyday practices, and it emphasizes a holistic celebration of Afro-Colombian identity by making it simultaneously a recognition of a traumatic past and a celebration of survival. Next to the saints are mutilated corpses inside and next to a church in ruins, as a reminder of the 2002 Bojayá massacre (see Figure 3.5). Standing close to a wooden coffin, alabaoras [alabao singers] invoke funerary rites that blur the boundaries between life and death with music and prayers that accompany the dead and grievers, while guiding the spirit with a collective call-and-response singing as both memorialization and political demand.[45] In a context with the lowest life expectancy in the country, making death a daily occurrence, the visual representation of the life-death spectrum regarding the armed conflict and religious beliefs is not a revelation.

The memory offered by the museum is not only a nostalgic idealization of African roots as a common past, but a reminder of shared pain and survival. Slavery depictions strengthen this link between death and life, and trauma and memory, performing Afro-Colombian identity in a long-term context that complicates historical reconstruction as an approach to cultural roots and, also, to ancestral pain and the mourning process, as visible in the contrast between the massacre's ruins and the alabaoras. It is not about using history as a therapeutic tool, but about acknowledging, rather than minimizing, pain and trauma as part of identity constructions. Portraying trauma as denunciation and not destiny avoids revictimization while educating communities and offering a memorialization and a space for grief that the state does not provide.

In Muntú Bantú, memory exists beyond its contemporary distinctiveness as reconstruction of past national trauma in times of transition, especially in a "postconflict" context where violence changes but does not disappear. History is not a living memory but can be inherited without being distant. Transmission of memories from one generation to the next and their consequent appropriation and internalization as inherited memory is not an automatic process. Knowledge about traumatic memory that escapes collective identity can be a political strategy to understand the causes of Black people's marginalization from hegemonic spaces while fighting the internalization of hierarchies promoted by mainstream narratives. Muntú Bantú creates a space for learning and unlearning with multiple narratives and multiple topics.

Muntú Bantú's visual statement does not simply oppose Colombia's Andean-centric multiculturalism; it decenters it by focusing on local religiosity that is deeply connected to diasporic spirituality. It is not a coincidence that in the religiously oriented room, trauma coexists alongside the syncretism of Chocoan Catholicism, and other spiritual and cultural practices center survival despite the intentional exclusion from national memories. Opening a space for the materiality of religious rituals and images is making space for divinity in the everyday of believers and practitioners. The "Blackening" of religious figures challenges a generalized and naturalized whitening of religious iconography and stresses the significance of Saint Francis of Assisi, who is lovingly known as San Pacho in Chocó.

Muntú Bantú provides glimpses of survival alongside a commitment to freedom by centering Black culture and knowledge production. Looking through a window placed in the middle of the alabaoras and the Bojayá's massacre, visitors can glance into the insides of a slave ship with rows of heads and shoulders

Figure 3.5. Alabao singers and the 2002 Bojayá massacre. Fundación Muntú Bantú. Quibdó, 2011.

followed by rows of feet. Past and present colliding in the tension between slavery and freedom. In *Scenes of Subjection*, Saidiya V. Hartman asks: "How does one survive the common atrocities of slavery yet possess a sensibility, a feeling, an impulse, and an inexplicable, yet irrepressible, confidence in the possibilities of freedom?"[46] Muntú Bantú maintains this tension throughout. To make the past present is a pedagogical strategy to present a nuanced understanding of history, and it aligns with Sergio Mosquera Mosquera's scholarship, which highlights Afro-Colombians as "agentes de su propia libertad"[47] [agents of their own freedom], which is not a euphemism but the actual struggle of enslavement, fugitivity, and its aftermath.

Mourning the unwritten loss of roots and citizenship caused by slavery and mourning the loss of lives because of the armed conflict, these images are subtle representations of trauma that do not fetishize wounds or violence. Even in one of the most violent scenes of the museum, the representation of the Bojayá massacre, the mural highlights the ruins over the blood. The Christ of Bojayá, a mutilated statue preserved after the 2002 massacre (Figure 3.5), is a recognized figure associated with survival, and more recently with forgiveness during the peace process with the FARC.[48] This subtle representation of trauma signals a particular act of mourning that promotes a collective memory beyond the nation's interests. Challenging the silence and invisibility that surrounds Black suffering in Colombia, Muntú Bantú acts as a memorial in which mourning is a celebration of survival as an intentional everyday practice.

Survival as collective memory becomes a reminder of shared pain and potential. The multiplicity of slavery representations challenges easy dichotomies. Afro-Colombian identity becomes a historical process. Muntú Bantú's memory is about pain more than it is about nation-building, or about the pain needed for nation-building that is strategically hidden. Memory in Muntú Bantú is about community-building processes that recognize a common historical pain in the struggle to move forward: "The remembering of a people relates not so much to an idealized remembering of a golden past but more specifically to the remembering of a painful past and, importantly, people's responses to that pain."[49] Shared painful memories make way for collective survival narratives that do not hide or silence pain in the effort to present a homogeneous representation of "the nation." And while the museum centers Colombia as a territory, its narrative transcends borders. A poster from Cincinnati's National Underground Railroad Freedom Center reads "You cannot restrain the human spirit" next to a wall displaying instruments for punishment and torture of enslaved people.

This exhibit's re-creation of images as a form of curation questions the historical narratives that have excluded Afrodescendants from Colombia's national identity until recently. Creating an alternative historical discourse does not translate as justice: "We believe that history is also about justice, that understanding history will enlighten our decisions about the future. Wrong. History is about power. In fact history is mostly about power."[50] And that history is power does not mean that an alternative history has the potential to invert power relations, nor that its existence implies its inclusion within debates or decision-making. Instead, its existence creates situated knowledge relevant to the specific context in which it is located. The incomplete promise of mestizaje becomes a new promise in Muntú Bantú's slogan: "unidad en la diversidad." Diversity is not an overused buzzword in Colombia, unlike multiculturalism. Unity in diversity is a challenge of the hierarchies within the homogeneous national identity. It is an invitation to solidarity across difference that encourages other ways to narrate Colombia's history. For Sergio Mosquera, for example, mestizaje and whitening are processes of "mulataje consciente" with a strategic purpose of speeding the achievement of freedom or class mobility for future generations,[51] an important reminder of the interlocking mechanisms of racialization of class. In contrast, an excerpt from a definition of Ubuntu on one of Muntú Bantú's walls that reads "'Soy porque somos.' Una persona se hace humana a través de las otras personas" [I am because we are. A person becomes human through other people] cannot be read anymore without thinking of Francia Márquez 2022 presidential campaign. Solidarity is not possible without reciprocity. And more important, survival and coexistence are collective commitments that make history possible.

The room "Cine Bantú Conciencia Afro" is a visual homage to Black film and Black authors, a companion to Mosquera Mosquera's publication *Afro Cineastas*.[52] A Nollywood sign is portrayed in the mural on the other side of the wall where films are projected. Black-and-white images of Halle Berry, Danny Glover, and a film strip with faces of Black actors and actresses mostly from the US (including Denzel Washington, Will Smith, Whoopi Goldberg, Beyoncé, Spike Lee, Olivia Spencer, Forest Whitaker, and even Hattie McDaniel, Sidney Poitier, and Dorothy Dandridge) were added in 2014. Mosquera Mosquera has described this room as a space to educate. A contrast with the predominantly white and mestizx representations in Colombian television and films, this room confirms Muntú Bantú as a cultural space and a space of encounter. The film club has not only screened films such as *Eli's Book*, *Panther*, and *Rapsodia negra*, but also consistently organized thematic film festivals. "Mambrú no va a la guerra," a renaming of the children's song "Mambrú se fue a la guerra" [Mambrú went to war] took place in 2014 as an exploration of the effects of militarization. In November 2015, Muntú Bantú organized "No le pegue a la negra" after a verse in Joe Arroyo's famous song "Rebelión," denouncing the violence enslaved women faced. This festival ended on November 25, the International Day for the Elimination of Violence Against Women in solidarity with local feminist groups.

Muntú Bantú's pedagogical—and not prescriptive—potential is an example of the collaboration between academic knowledge and organic knowledge sustained by the organizing experience of Black communities in the Colombian Pacific. It also reveals the importance of looking for dissemination forms that transcend writing. New additions of local political leaders in the entrance murals include prominent Afro-Colombian women, such as Paula Marcela Moreno (former minister of culture) and Piedad Córdoba (former senator) who have filled in some of the gaps of this space (the absence of women). The launch of the book *Afrocolombianas visibles. Un enfoque de género y etnia*, by Zulia Mena García—Quibdó's mayor between 2012 and 2015—and her husband Sergio Mosquera Mosquera[53] on March 8, 2015, also reveals a commitment to a memory that includes Black women. The updates and additions to this site of memory show that memory is contextual and temporary, and that archives and museographic spaces are not static but knowledge in motion.

Most collections are not static, but Muntú Bantú is explicitly a collection in motion, as Mosquera Mosquera constantly adds and rearranges murals, objects, and figures. Walls that he had dedicated to pictures and quotes in the main meeting room, where the space's mission and vision are displayed, have been slowly filled with images and artifacts over the years. A wall of Desmond Tutu. A wall of Malcolm X and Martin Luther King Jr. A wall of Bob Marley. A wall of masks and drums. In 2015, Mosquera Mosquera opened a new room about animals in Chocó, based on his book *Antropofauna afrochocoana: Un estudio cultural sobre la animalidad*, published in 2009.[54] Human-nonhuman relations invoke the ecological politics that we see in the ways the comisionadas talk about their rivers.

Muntú Bantú also challenges the digital/analog dichotomy by using different social media platforms to strategically share content with a broader audience and advertise events and programs. According to a Facebook post from April 2019, Muntú Bantú has a collection of over 800 Afrocentric films. Muntú Bantú's online presence includes a recently redesigned webpage,[55] a Facebook page, a Twitter profile, an Instagram account, a Flickr account, and a YouTube channel, even though some of these platforms are inactive as a symptom of the rapid change in platforms' popularity. As a space of encounter, events with recognized personalities are not only common but also shared on social media. In 2016, US Congressman Hank Johnson attended a meeting with the Consejo Nacional de Paz Afrocolombiana (CONPA), which included an ethnic perspective on the peace talks with the FARC. Richard Moreno, CONPA and FISCH coordinator has also participated in the Comisión de Género's workshops with his legal expertise. These solidarity networks create an exchange of knowledge that makes policy change possible. In February 2019, Afro-Colombian poet Mary Grueso Romero visited Muntú Bantú to read her poetry and lead a workshop on Black dolls for students.[56] In May 2019, Tejiendo esperanzas, the fifteenth encounter of peinadoras (hairdressers) and contest of Afro hairdos, took place in Muntú Bantú. References to augmented reality and artificial intelligence are the most recent additions to the space, which are advertised on its website.

What Muntú Bantú achieves is creating a space to imagine what memory can be outside of institutionalized and official spaces like the Museo Nacional in Bogotá, which is a way to enact postconflict utopias. To materialize an Afrocentric memory into existence has been a slow and steady process, threatened by multiple forces. On January 13, 2023, Muntú Bantú published a communiqué on Twitter, announcing its closure following extortion threats.[57] It made the mainstream national news.[58] Letters of solidarity, including formal statements by the Latin American Studies Association[59] and Scholars at Risk,[60] have circulated since then, condemning the threats and expressing solidarity with Sergio Mosquera and María Fernanda Parra, the museum's director. While its closure confirms the vulnerability of unofficial spaces of memory, Muntú Bantú's position as part of local, regional, and global networks of knowledge production and politics is a reminder of its importance.

Muestra Bíblica: Memorializing Spirituality

I walk from COCOMACIA's headquarters to Uniclaretiana—formerly FUCLA—the university of the Claretian congregation, through the Carrera Primera, taking a long route. I see both the Atrato River and the movement of people and products around the malecón. Walking through the outside of the market, the smells of fresh fruit, herbs, and fish mix with the frying plantains and food scraps outside rotting under the afternoon sun. The sounds of men playing dominoes and competing music from different vendors become the soundtrack for two blocks until Carrera Primera becomes Carrera Tercera. Alongside Carrera Cuarta, chicks and kittens from pet stores are part of a landscape that becomes progressively more residential and less commercial. White railings and a sign with golden letters announce the university's main entrance. Gonzalo de la Torre is waiting for me and my mom, as he has offered a private tour of La Muestra Bíblica. We cross the reception area and an inside patio with birds of paradise and other colorful flowers until we reach the stairs. On the fourth floor, a dark hallway leads us to a brown metal door. The door leads us to a big room full of light artistic reproductions, signs with quotes, and architectural models (Figure 3.6). It reveals the materialization of de la Torre's knowledge about history, theology, and Chocó.

Uniclaretiana was founded by Gonzalo de la Torre and other missionaries in Quibdó, Chocó, in 2006. In the article "En memoria de cien años: Los misioneros claretianos y sus cien años de presencia en el Chocó," de la Torre traces the genealogy of the Claretian presence in Chocó.[61] It traces the Vatican's adjudication of the province as a prefecture in 1909, meaning that this Catholic congregation was directly dependent on Rome. In 1953, Chocó became Apostolic Vicariate and in 1990, Quibdó Diocese. During these years, missionary work included supporting Indigenous and Black organizing, such as the creation of OREWA (an organization of four Indigenous groups: Embera Dóbida, Katío, Chamí, and Tule) in 1979 and COCOMACIA in the 1980s.[62]

Figure 3.6. La Muestra Bíblica's entrance. Quibdó, 2013.

Missionary work as spirituality grounded in cultural contexts and with the purpose of serving local communities informs La Muestra Bíblica, a biblical exhibit with a collection nurtured from de la Torre's studies in Rome and Jerusalem, and his desire to educate by creating a space for spiritual reflection rooted in local contexts. From the beginning of the guided visit, de la Torre warns that this space is not meant as a tourist visit, as he has designed it as a stage for classes, and undergraduate and graduate programs in Bible studies. A complete tour can take as little as six full days to a whole semester. De la Torre invites youth groups, scholars, and other members of the community to get a glimpse into this materialization of what he calls "the content of sacred scripture" in the context of scientific and local knowledge. Silence, questioning, reflection, and debate are welcome in this space, where his role as a Claretian missioner is sharing knowledge that is not meant only for religious people or members of a specific religious community. As the Bible has so many landscapes, characters, and themes, this material summary is structured in twenty themes for the Old Testament and twenty-one themes for the New Testament. I write this reconstruction based on my notes from one single visit in 2013 and, even though numerous conversations with Gonzalo de la Torre have helped capture some of the nuance, the limits of my description might help capture the unrepeatability of the experience of "being there."[63]

La Muestra Bíblica uses methods derived from biblical archeology, social theology, and hermeneutics to interpret the Bible as a historical document, which starts with a visual representation of the universe's origin next to an illustration of human evolution. Surprising anyone who ever thought that creationism is the only biblical interpretation possible, the exhibit starts with visual representations of gods and goddesses from the Neolithic. It includes original and duplicate archeological pieces, and displays and architectural models of palaces, temples, and traditional houses from Egypt, Israel, Assyria, and Rome to visualize the differences between accumulation societies, where the state and the monarch enjoy wealth, and egalitarian societies, where equality and fraternity are promoted. In this way, La Muestra Bíblica is a thought-provoking journey through prehistory and ancient history, besides being a theological space.

Below masks and small sculptures, a statement about the genocide of Afrodescendants emphasizes the church's complicit silence alongside the pride for the ancestors' survival. The selection of images is a reconstruction of a religiosity that does not mimic imposed doctrine but rather is informed by the responsibility of explaining contemporary religious beliefs, including references to historical events that problematize religious institutions, such as enslavement and imposed evangelization. In this museographic space, Catholic dogmas and their colonial imposition coexist with Black communities' resistance and the syncretism that characterize Chocoan Catholicism. The similarity with Muntú Bantú's religious room exposes a continuity of a collective knowledge production based on historical facts, as much the recognition of humanity that has been historically denied to Black people.

Like Muntú Bantú, de la Torre's La Muestra Bíblica establishes a Chocoan history narrative that reconstructs traumatic memories and inverts center-periphery hierarchies to bring into focus local diversity and spirituality. Even though the theological interpretation of the Afro context that this museum presents can be read as an appropriation that reproduces the active role of the church in the oppression of Black communities, the narrative it offers is a critical approach to the historical context of the Bible's mythical language and the social challenges of theology in Chocó. The Claretian theological project that La Muestra Bíblica illustrates can be better understood with the help of de la Torre's words. He defines ethno-education as "el derecho a que la propia historia y la propia cultura de toda etnia sean valoradas como fuentes de conocimiento, como medio de creación de pensamiento y sabiduría y, por lo tanto, como instrumento apto para educar a quienes se identifican con dichos valores u optan por los mismos"[64] [the right that every ethnicity's own history and culture are valued as sources of knowledge, thought creation and wisdom, and, therefore,

Figure 3.7. Gonzalo de la Torre explains some excerpts from "The Song of Songs." Muestra Bíblica. Quibdó, 2013.

as tools to educate those who identify or choose those values]. The right to recognize more than one history and culture as sources of knowledge to educate shows a commitment to challenge traditional models of learning and teaching.

The image selection within the Muestra Bíblica reflects a political commitment that attends not only to aesthetics. The exhibit is more than an archeological study of the Bible or its historical contextualization. It is a construction of a non-imposed religiosity informed by the responsibility of explaining the particularities of Chocoan spirituality: an Afrocentric religiosity informed by the influence of and resistance to colonial oppression. As the result of links between a progressive church and local advocates, La Muestra links spirituality to initiatives of social change. Including images of what de la Torre calls "the resigned Jesus," as the famous Ecce Homo, contextualizes its appropriation as a revolutionary figure. He points at a painting to clarify it is a reproduction whose original can be found in the town Raspadura, where locals report healing properties. In Pogue, a nearby town, Santo Ecce Homo, as this figure is called, has protected its inhabitants from the arrival of paramilitaries, responsible for the forced displacement of communities in Bojayá since 2002. Illuminating resistance within the church's supportive discourse of Black organizing process, suffering, passion, and religiosity are intertwined in the same way as in the everyday.

De la Torre's experience as an active participant in the Black communities' organizing process is explicit in the plural religiosity that the exhibit contains. Thinking that future theologians and missionaries may visit this space as part of their academic training, as the exhibit is directed to theology students, allows us to dream about new utopian collaborations that do not reproduce colonial hierarchies. Imagining connections between the Bible and the Chocoan context is to promote spaces that value the knowledge that flows differently from the centers of power. De la Torre writes about organizing as the contemporary way to evangelize, joining the voice of the people instead of speaking on their behalf: "Organizar es la forma contemporánea de evangelizar: no hay otra forma de que el pueblo reclame sus derechos ni los viva, sino es en una organización que haga sentir su voz. Nosotros los evangelizadores nos preciamos a veces de ser la voz de los sin voz. Sin embargo, tenemos que dejar de ser la voz de los sin voz, para que el pueblo tenga su propia voz. Nuestro papel como Iglesia debe ser más bien sumarnos a la voz del pueblo, sobre todo cuando éste ya está organizado[65] [Organizing is the contemporary way of evangelizing: there is no other way in which the people reclaim or live their rights, but in an organization that makes their voice heard. We, the evangelizers, claim to be the voice of the voiceless. Nonetheless, we need to stop being the voice of the voiceless so the people can have their own voice. Our role as a church instead should be to join the people's voice, especially when they become organized]. This linguistic move away from being "the voice of the voiceless" to "join the people's voice" is materialized in de la Torre's work as much as in La Muestra Bíblica.

Gonzalo de la Torre's biblical exhibit embraces a religion that accompanies the people and not vice versa. That is why the walls are full of paintings by Afro-Colombian artist Freddy Sánchez, and Black representations are everywhere, establishing a connection between biblical topics and local social issues. A painting by Freddy Sánchez portraying a crying woman holding a dead or dying man invokes the religious iconography of Jesus's death; it is a reminder of local massacres. Black women's representations, used to illustrate quotes from the Bible (see Figure 3.7), balance feminine archetypes, such as Jezebel and Rizpah used by the prophets, and become reminders of current prejudices anchored in patriarchal hierarchies reinforcing the prostitute/mother dichotomy. The predominance of women in the biblical exhibit is crucial in the critical consciousness de la Torre hopes to promote with additional context and counternarratives.

By showing misogynist tendencies in religion and the ecclesiastic hierarchy, La Muestra Bíblica shows that not allowing women's official participation does not have a traditional, rational, or religious explanation. In contrast, the exhibit uses a visual and discursive integrationist language. It emphasizes the role of women in primitive churches with reproductions of goddesses and reminders that power and justice are not givens. There is a predominant visual message of inclusion that de la Torre put into words during my visit: "Hoy tenemos que vivir la madurez de las Iglesias primitivas que, por su proximidad a Jesús, fueron evangélicamente libres e inclusivas" [Today, we need to live the maturity of primitive churches that, for their proximity to Jesus, were evangelically free and inclusive]. The celebration of the past is more than a nostalgic description. It is a reference frame for an ethical religious practice that promotes gender equality and inclusion as moral values.

The exhibit practices inclusion and values embodied spirituality by celebrating a rebellious, free, open, and critical woman as the ideal one, reflecting the constant presence of women in the Bible. A sculpture of a Black woman is next to quotes from "The Song of Songs," which celebrates Black women who know how to love (see Figure 3.7). The celebration of women's bodies and sexuality contrasts radically with official contemporary religious discourse and allows an appropriation of a spirituality that is not based on what, for many in Chocó, would seem to be an anachronous body-soul dichotomy. It not only describes a religious practice that resembles the Chocoan context but also can be interpreted as an "ontological restitution" that responds to the exclusion of Black communities from the writing of history and power in Colombia. This restitution seems an ethical exercise of reconstructing a non-hegemonic memory that recognizes the overlapping of embodiment and spiritual practice. Invoking Black women's bodies suggests the agency of women within Chocoan religious practice.

La Muestra presents war and violence and the effects of militarization simultaneously to illustrate massacres by paramilitaries and the effects of leaders' acts on the daily lives of people, with additional paintings and images alongside detailed displays of scripture. Gonzalo de la Torre contextualizes Samuel, Saul, David, and Solomon as warnings about monarchy as an exploitative regime. Being a prophet is then explained by de la Torre, not as seeing the prophet but as being critical and outspoken to denounce leaders' actions. Popular leadership achieves accountability, which is why for de la Torre, real prophets are eliminated.

Theology is plural for de la Torre. Social theology, he says, is not part of the church's official doctrine. And it should not be. Religious practice should always exceed official doctrine, according to de la Torre. La Muestra Bíblica materializes the potential alliance of social theology with the work of grassroots organizations such as COCOMACIA, including defending life, educating its members, incorporating women in its leadership, defending the territory, and understanding faith as a commitment to their community.⁶⁶ In a YouTube video posted on Misioneros Claretianos Colombia Venezuela, published on October 29, 2018, de la Torre mentions his desire to make La Muestra Bíblica accessible virtually.⁶⁷ This wish became a reality as Museo Bíblico Claretiano (MUBÍC),⁶⁸ a recognition of the potential of digital platforms to democratize content. And while there is still a physical collection, it is now located in the Parroquia Claretiana de Jesús Nazareno in Medellín. These new versions of the exhibit have diluted the local connections made possible by de la Torre's vision.

The painting at the end of the exhibit depicts a missionary holding a large cross, piloting a paper boat, alongside a conqueror, devil, policeman, pirate, and bishop, framed by two animal figures reminiscent of those in Picasso's *Guernica* serving as a reminder of the dangers of the church's association with power. Some curatorial texts refer to the violence committed against Black communities, a reminder of de la Torre's conviction of the need for a paradigm shift to center Afro spirituality. For de la Torre, spirituality requires a broader definition: "Se refiere al mundo de las grandes preguntas que el ser humano se plantea frente a su existencia, frente a la construcción de su felicidad . . . con el propósito de humanizarse"⁶⁹ [It refers to the world of the big questions that the human being asks about her own existence, about her happiness . . . with the purpose of humanizing herself]. Spirituality cannot be independent from power relations or history. And because we do not exist in isolation, de la Torre would also agree with bell hooks: "Spirituality and spiritual life give us the strength to love."⁷⁰

The pedagogical narrative and the connections between the biblical themes and the Chocoan context seek not to catechize but to provide a space for connecting spiritual practice to social issues beyond the church's official dogmas. The ultimate aim seems to be to develop a critical consciousness, a spiritual ethical practice that functions in such a way that, as de la Torre puts it, "freedom doesn't become the exploitation of the other." The ethical (but not prescriptive) tone of this exhibit exemplifies the collaboration between missionary initiatives and grassroots activism that achieved territorial rights for Black communities in the early 1990s. For de la Torre, the goal is "to develop a critical consciousness about violence and spirituality to avoid the infantilism of seeing miracles or punishment in everything." The exhibit emphasizes an ethical practice of care, and the quest for justice, not as a unitary and finite concept, but as a product of autonomous decisions and critical thought. Those in power cannot define ethics, Gonzalo de la Torre explains, but people should. Such an ethics implies seeing the potential of every individual in religious practice and exploring worlds of possibility, while remembering the church's participating in and benefitting from colonization. Remembrance and ethical practice are utopian commitments, a daily performative practice of love that fuels Afro spirituality, survival, and activism: "No es la fe lo que salva. Es el amor" [It is not faith that saves. It is love], de la Torre told me.

Turning trauma into memory is not a linear process. La Muestra Bíblica uses spirituality to imagine a pedagogical narrative where writing and images coexist to bring theology to life. Valuing local knowledge and creating space to memorialize the Bible in a local context, this space of memory creates an alongside space to celebrate and critique religion. This utopian space imagines an ethical practice that is not prescriptive. The absences of institutional spaces become opportunities for creating collective memories. These alternative archives and the alternative narratives of memory as postconflict utopias interrupt nationalistic memories with highly local memories.

Absences, Ethics, and Utopias

The museums presented here offer cultural spaces in Chocó created for thinking about Black history. Sergio Mosquera's and Gonzalo de la Torre's museums show a commitment to share their knowledge and interests outside the status of the written text and to take advantage of the predominance of the visual and the oral in Chocó, where the literacy rate is the lowest in Colombia. Their use of visual narratives is informed by local communities, and it decenters the predominance of writing in knowledge production. In Chocó, where there are few cultural institutions, these museographic spaces remember, educate, and celebrate cultural heritages, even the painful ones. Telling the story of Afro-Colombians, which remains uncommon in mainstream Colombian museums, is itself an achievement. Ahmed describes the connection between narratives of injury and entitlement: "Given that subjects have an unequal relation to entitlement, then more privileged subjects will have a greater recourse to narratives of injury. That is, the more access subjects have to public resources, the more access they may have to the capacity to mobilize narratives of injury within the public domain."[71]

But if producing representations or narratives is not an effective means to access power, what is the use of making visible those who have been excluded from normative citizenship? It is probably possible to measure the effects of such visibility only in what is intangible and desired, if we think visibility is a starting point to assert the importance of groups that are affected by the decisions of the powerful or to redraw or subvert power relations within better-known narratives. The existence of these spaces shows the possibility of creating history and promoting remembrance within and despite vulnerability. In consequence, even though local attempts at memorialization receive only modest levels of attention and resources from national and international initiatives that provide temporary relief for vulnerable populations, the possibility of creating and disseminating empowering representations of trauma and memory are not only possible—they exist.

As one chant from the 2013 mining strike summarizes, "Chocó es un departamento empobrecido, no pobre" [Chocó is an impoverished department, not a poor one], and the material conditions that differentiate this region from any other can be traced and narrated historically. Creating a memory that highlights the history of surviving oppressive conditions shows the political potential of remembering. The non-hegemonic exercises of appropriating and creating memory narratives like the Fundación Muntú Bantú and La Muestra Bíblica are revitalizing because they create connections that center the local context as a scenario of solidarity, remembrance, and survival. They materialize postconflict utopias as projections amid violence, as they also emerge as local archives, utopian repositories of narratives that imagine other ways to live and remember.

Emblematic museums of history, such as the British Museum, are powered by the imperialism that secured the artifacts displayed. Even the national museum in Bogotá displays a predominance of usurped pieces and celebration of whiteness/mestizaje that inspired Afro-Colombian artist Nelson Fory Ferreira to create an intervention of white headstones with Afro wigs to commemorate the bicentennial of Colombian independence in 2010.[72] The optimistic reading of minimalist museums such as Muntú Bantú and Muestra Bíblica derives from the fact that their collections are not the result of plundering or colonial appropriation, but they come from the construction of what is not available, by using murals or displays. Their political potential lies in creating memories as an antidote to absence, in listening to what has been silenced, and in promoting an ethics about the other's pain. As collaborative creations of local community members, these museums have a close link with the other's pain. And, as the work of privileged members of the community (Sergio Mosquera and Gonzalo de la Torre are university professors), the museums reflect an explicit practice of a dialogic narrative that is meant to be shared. Pain is not for a pleasurable spectatorship or for the denunciation of violence to promote action. Pain is not for consumption but for remembrance, the starting point of community education that could open spaces for dialogue and creative remembering.

Answering to the impossibility of listening or representing the other's pain with visual creativity requires not imposing a static narrative. As non-hegemonic reconstruction of memories, community museums materialize the constant process of making and unmaking a memory unavoidably incomplete, as it includes diaspora, violence, and a reconstruction of Black history. As a quilt of scenes and fragments of history, the museums display an incomplete memory that requires asking questions and interacting with the curator. Such an interaction between audience and curator happens only through the willingness of Sergio Mosquera and Gonzalo de la Torre to lead tours for high school and college students, and unexpected visitors like me.

Murals of Black personalities and reproductions of historical photographs and artifacts of slavery can be seen in Muntú Bantú, while scale models of historical temples, farmers' houses, and personal items from religious sites in Europe and Chocó are situated next to each other in La Muestra Bíblica. Images of replicas, souvenirs, and original paintings by local artists in both museums serve as performances of absence of original artifacts that were few. The lack of excess is woven into visual memories to remember local traumas and celebrate Black history.

Moving beyond a purely discursive multiculturalism, Muntú Bantú and La Muestra Bíblica perform Black history by centering the representations and experiences of transnational Black communities. Nelson Mandela and Martin Luther King Jr. alongside other local figures are included in the ancestors' political shrines portraying the willingness to continue performing Blackness, or at least to perform it as will, as imagination seeking to create a community that is defined by something other than trauma. These utopian archives create memories that celebrate Afrodescendants' culture and survival in a space of vulnerability.

In a conversation with William Rivas, legal adviser and member of COCOMACIA, I asked him if he knew Muntú Bantú and La Muestra, as I knew that not all the comisionadas had been there, even though they have known Sergio Mosquera and Gonzalo de la Torre for decades. He said that the main absence in both spaces is the memory of the organizing process in the region, which means the absence of activist leaders in the genealogy of liberation. This criticism emerges from a different approach to Black culture in the Colombian Pacific. Instead of framing dances, music, and stilt houses as culture, Rivas, like other Chocoans, believes that the performances and materiality that are classified as culture are, instead, evidence of creativity in interacting with the environment. The absence Rivas criticizes shows that these museums' strategy is to create straightforward narratives that can be embraced by visitors without creating too much controversy about exclusions or alliances with known political figures.

According to William Rivas, every strategy for survival should be evidence of intelligence instead of culture. Following this idea, solidarity can be seen as a survival strategy. In this vein, working without earning money, in exchange for future help, has been a common practice in Chocó. Rooted in collaboration, solidarity has been a response to capitalistic and individualistic practices that have appropriated Chocoan resources for the benefit of foreign processes. Beyond absence, these museums exemplify the creativity and solidarity that Rivas talks about, as they are collaborative constructions of alternative histories and memories. While the comisionadas are familiar with the existence of the two museographic spaces, and have known their founders for decades, most have been there only to attend meetings or events. They have not had a guided tour, as I did. That the comisionadas are not the audience of these spaces makes visible the limits of the spaces' audience and reaffirms their political work as utopian. It also affirms the need for spaces that center Black women's knowledge as part of local movements and networks of knowledge production.

If digital amnesia is the forgetting associated with the internet's overuse, these utopian memories, created to fill in the gaps of a national amnesia that now is predominantly analog, coincide with and intrude into an official memorialization of an ongoing armed conflict. While these countermemories are insufficient as everyday peacemaking strategies, they wish into existence the possibilities of a visibility that centers joy instead of trauma. This visibility, as we have seen, does not guarantee access to power or dismantle violence or the mainstream narratives circulating about it. As utopian gestures, these archives and spaces create stories that support survival by remembering that it has been possible before, that violence does not consume all.

Structural violence is not solid and stable. The two museographic experiences—Muntú Bantú and La Muestra Bíblica—weave trauma-driven narratives together with transformative politics and speculative possibilities for memories and spaces that interrupt partially mainstream national narratives. These exhibits question official national narratives and their silences and concealments. The 1991 Constitution and Law 70 of 1993 reflect years of grassroots organizing by recognizing Black rural communities, both by incorporating ethnic diversity into constructs of nation, and by granting these communities territorial rights. Black communities and their history remain marginalized in mainstream national narratives that are predominantly centralist and "white."

The internal colonialism under which, according to Rivera Cusicanqui, words hide reality is sustained in the association between writing and knowledge.[73] Through concealing racial hierarchies, even public policy promotes the hegemony of mestizaje without explicitly naming race, because it brands everything that has been excluded while obscuring itself under the category of multiculturalism or diversity. The role of Law 70 in recognizing Black communities' collective ownership of territories reflects the centrality of writing in marking difference. That collective territorial rights are thought analogous to Indigenous groups makes clear the outlasting power of racial binaries (neutral/not neutral) in a context that thinks of itself as multicultural. The racialization of those who do not conform to mestizaje is perpetuated through traditional memorialization and museographic spaces. The work of postconflict utopias includes challenging narratives that present mestizaje as neutral or desirable, which requires creating more narratives. But museums and archives need to stay open to narratives that are contextualized in practices of solidarity beyond national discourses and allegiances. Storytelling, as survival, is not possible in isolation. It requires networks of support and care, as much as infrastructure, that make the work possible in the long term.

Stereotypical representations of Blackness are not unavoidable, as the comisionadas and other storytellers have shown. Likewise, scholarship can challenge the naturalization of mestizaje as the center of narratives about memory and history in Colombia. As a utopian undertaking, non-mainstream archives, in their analog and digital forms, are pedagogical opportunities for collaboration and learning together. Museums and memory in Colombia are not limited to what is visible and available in Bogotá or other big cities, but challenging what archives look like could be the first step to create and acknowledge memories that challenge mestizaje. What pedagogical and community spaces of memory in Quibdó offer is the potentiality of Afrocentric perspectives. Afrocentric memories and archives have a political and ethical potential to resignify life amid militarization. By exceeding the compulsory multicultural inclusion, these local initiatives are synchronic negotiations of memory, history, and national identity that decenter mestizaje and mestizxs. That said, the closure and displacement of these museographic spaces to other geographic or digital places reinforce the vulnerability of imagining otherwise amid ongoing violence.

CHAPTER 4

Utopian Memories
Documenting Collective Territories

> He tenido tropezones en mi vida, dificultades, hay momentos que me ha dado ganas de no estar, de irme, que nadie se dé cuenta. Pero yo creo que el mejor legado que uno deja a la familia y a los amigos es la resistencia.
>
> I have had setbacks in my life, difficulties, there are moments that have made me want to not be there, to leave, when no one notices. But I believe that the best legacy that one leaves to family and friends is resistance.
>
> —Rubiela Cuesta Córdoba

In Quibdó, rain is the source of water for showering, doing dishes, and laundry, but flooding can also be an obstacle to going home. Death and solidarity are present everywhere. Even after the rain stops and I try to go back home one day, streets seem like rivers and there are fewer motorcycles, cars, and people. After a long wait, I get on a very crowded minibus and stand next to the door until a woman shouts from the back: "Dele mami, que si en el cementerio cabemos, cabemos aquí" [Come on, dear, if we fit in the cemetery, we fit here]. We laugh, and I sit next to her. Casual references to death are not exclusive to the Chocoan context. But I cannot help but to connect my memory of this gesture of solidarity that reminds of death's inevitability with a wish for postmortem recognition and community. Working on stories about survival forces us to confront the complexity of individual experience and the difficulty of grasping the layers of violence that are part and parcel of the Chocoan context, and that shape collective memories. Everyday relationships are as important as creativity and solidarity to imagine the postconflict.

Surviving in Chocó requires an awareness of its difficulty. Death is not only present in casual conversations but also part of people's everyday experience. In her discussion of the aftermath of the 2002 Bojayá massacre, Aurora Vergara-Figueroa describes how the community prepares for future violence by: "delineating escape routes, protesting, strengthening religious beliefs, struggling to preserve their cultural practices, opening legal procedures against the government, registering as victims of FARC or Paramilitary so they can demand compensation, and giving truthful accounts of what happened."[1] The labor of survival seems knotted with the work of community-building, which in violent contexts includes bureaucratic tasks as much as collective efforts to remember past violence. In a centralist country where narratives rarely center Chocó, memory-making about traumatic events becomes a community exercise in creating alternative narratives to the national ones.

Memories as narratives about shared pasts, where trauma and the longing for collective futures coexist, become utopian in a context where remembering also reproduces exclusion and violence. As anthropologist María Victoria Uribe explains: "Memory is highly contested terrain in Colombia. A battlefield unto itself, it encompasses hegemonic, subordinate, and contradictory memories, as well as the silenced and relegated memories of women, [I]ndigenous peoples, and communities of African descent."[2] As we saw in chapter 3, memory is as multiple as it is political. Remembering becomes part of the postconflict utopias, performative actions—as genuine expressions of what they summon and not insincere engagements—that pave the way for materializing peace, and memorializations that challenge violent exclusions and revictimization.

In a race-denying context in which institutionalized memories such as the ones promoted by the Grupo de Memoria Histórica reinforce national myths, the homogenization of mestizaje is doubly cruel. As members of this group, Pilar Riaño and María Victoria Uribe have noted: "el proceso para documentar la memoria histórica de la guerra [tiende] a homogenizar la noción de víctima, mientras que aún cuesta trabajo darle cabida o comunicar narrativas plurales que reconocen disputas sobre la memoria y voces disidentes"[3] [the process to document war's historical memory tends to homogenize the notion of victim, while it is still difficult to include or communicate plural narratives that recognize disputes about memory and dissident voices]. Although the competition of memories and narratives is still an ongoing process, digital archives disrupt official narratives by preventing the existence of a single historical memory.

The inevitable incompleteness and inadequacy of memories of ongoing processes of dehumanization not only reinforce the impossibility of postconflict utopias but also contextualize the urgency of these grassroots memorialization efforts. Black studies scholar Christina Sharpe poses a necessary question to the efforts to memorialize processes that are not over yet: "if museums and memorials materialize a kind of reparation (repair) and enact their own pedagogies as they position visitors to have a particular experience or set of experiences about an event that is seen to be past, how does one memorialize chattel slavery and its afterlives, which are unfolding still?"[4] Sharpe's question brings to mind the political implications of memorializing ongoing processes. In postconflict contexts, such endeavors can reinforce the use of "postconflict" as a denial of an unending violence that targets Black communities specifically.

The visual construction of Afrocolombianidad cannot be considered independently from the role of Black Colombians as social actors and the struggles for state recognition of their rights. In my search to understand Afrocentric knowledge production about Blackness in Colombia, I identify three methodological approaches to study Blackness: first, the ethnographic paradigm, exemplified in the work of Colombian anthropologist Nina de Friedemann; second, the local paradigm, represented by the museographic experiences analyzed in chapter 3, Muntú Bantú and La Muestra Bíblica in Quibdó, Chocó; and third, the collaborative paradigm, illustrated by the collaborative digital storytelling project *Mujeres Pacíficas* discussed in chapter 2, and other local collaborations with a digital component, including the ones discussed in this chapter. This methodological typography is not chronological nor exhaustive. These projects coexist and are part of networks of knowledge production that transcend academic and disciplinary borders.

Afrocentric memorialization and its political potential are negotiated locally, nationally, and globally. Visual memories and archives of Afrocolombianidad have potential political uses that do not always align. In the same way, the methods used for their creation and the ethical implications of their construction are negotiated by creators and consumers. Nonetheless, Afrocentric memories that fracture the compulsory character of multicultural inclusion work alongside national narratives. Collaborative knowledge production is not only an intellectual typographic exercise, but also a public materialization of the documentation that communities have had to learn as part of their technologies of survival. The documentation of violence has been part of the political potential of the digital for Black communities: "many types of violence suffered by Afrodescendant communities in Colombia because of the armed conflict and the implementation of the peace agreements have been made visible with the aid of digital tools and networks."[5] Memory is not only about the past, and any effort to construct memories encounters the challenge of creating a self-contained narrative.

The homogeneity of national memories relies on representations by omission that feed from invisibility and erasure, excluding what is perceived as a threat to the myth of mestizaje (such as Blackness and Indigeneity). Invisibility becomes a blank canvas on which to project desires beyond inclusion. As a projection, inclusion might never come, but collective memory is more than remembering the past, as it can be the basis for crafting future-oriented narratives that are inevitably linked to a collective past and present: "memory—and the construction of memory from multiple perspectives—becomes central not only as a means of remembering (past) and narrativizing (present) but also as a way to embark on the creation of Black futures."[6] Local narratives of Blackness are about not only rewriting an Afrocentric past but also imagining an Afrocentric future beyond the imposed national boundaries of creativity.

A close reading of the website Memorias del Río Atrato and the Instagram account Fotógrafas del Pacífico, and associated hashtag #fotógrafasdelpacífico, shows that digital tools can both disrupt official national memories and be used to denounce violence against Black communities. Eduard Arriaga and Andrés Villar use "Afro-Latinx digital connections" to name analog and digital networks of knowledge production that make up "spaces of agency and modularity in which Black communities in the Americas innovate, propose alternative models of existence, and share experiences with other communities of the African diaspora."[7] The interconnectedness that digital projects promise is not stable, permanent, or universally accessible, but its potential is not less powerful. As alternative archives, these digital Afrocentric spaces reveal an imagined possibility for a memory that, without explicitly challenging official memories, moves beyond national memories and characterizing Black lives as folklore, in ways similar to the museums explored in chapter 3. Alongside these two collaborative digital memory initiatives, Motete, a cultural center and literacy program in Quibdó that I found first at a distance through its digital presence on Instagram, confirms the creativity of future-oriented survival. I use Motete's founder Velia Vidal Romero's own words from her book *Aguas de Estuario* [Estuary Waters] to connect these digital repositories of local memories with analog efforts of imagining otherwise.

As examples of dissemination that transcend writing, digital archives such as Memorias del Atrato and Fotógrafas del Pacífico are collaborative and create representations that center Black people, and frequently Black women, as knowledge producers, and their collective territories as spaces of Afrocentric knowledge production. While I understand that "[f]or archivists, preservation and description are key ingredients in making a collection of records 'archival,'"[8] a utopian framing of these digital connections as archives recognizes the labor and knowledge of creating them: "the material infrastructure and labor required by digital archives demand resources—natural, human, financial."[9] Motete and *Aguas de estuario* connect these digital spaces with ongoing efforts of reading and writing as exercises of collective memory-making. In the journal article "Luchas del buen vivir por las mujeres negras del Alto Cauca," Charo Mina Rojas, Marilyn Machado Mosquera, Patricia Botero, and Arturo Escobar define teoría socioterritorial en movimiento (TStM) as a non-institutional and transdisciplinary theory. It finds a place of enunciation in the thoughts, narratives, memories, and knowledges of communities in movement, and it interacts with critical tendencies in the intellectual landscape of the continent.[10] Memorias del Río Atrato, Fotógrafas del Pacífico, Motete, and *Aguas de estuario* are theories in movement that contribute to contemporary debates on extraction, humanitarianism, climate change, and peace-building, as part of what Eduard Arriaga calls Afro-Latinx digital connections.

Simultaneously to the creation of analog centers of memory such as the ones I discussed in the last chapter, the use of digital tools and platforms to create projects around memory and identity has been popularized in the Colombian Pacific. As my presence in Chocó since 2008 has been sporadic, I rely on digital platforms to continue communication with my collaborators and keep up to date. That said, while COCOMACIA and the Comisión have online presence through Facebook and an institutional website, they still prioritize in-person engagement—even after 2020, as the digital is not always accessible. Yancy Castillo and Dora Inés Vivanco, members of Conferencia Nacional de Organizaciones Afrocolombianas [National Assembly of Afro-Colombian organizations] (CNOA) address the digital divide affecting Black communities: "Colombia does not have internet coverage in all of the national territory. . . . Also we understand that due to the lack of digital literacy and to economic constraints, among other factors, not all Afrodescendant communities have access to digital tools."[11] With this context in mind, in this chapter, I will analyze two digital projects that exemplify the use of online platforms to create utopian memories: the website Memorias del Río Atrato and the Instagram account Fotógrafas del Pacífico. I discuss them to reflect on what digital memories can look like and do while also challenging the uncontested description of the digital as implicitly accessible or democratic, while also recognizing its potential for imagining otherwise.

I do not position these memories as counter-discourses to official narratives of memory and monumentalization. These memories reveal that spaces are not oppositional or resistant and that rehearsals of utopias contain the energy for social change. These collaborative archives and narratives are ethical, visual, and even written reinterpretations of the embodied and invisible memories of community care that has been historically excluded from the lettered national history. While not absolute answers to counteract official discourses, digital spaces have potential for transnational solidarity: "As a space for intercultural exchange and for the construction of shared artistic and political strategies, cyberspace affords unprecedented opportunities to build shared visions from all over the world."[12] These spaces materialize what it means to imagine another way to remember and learn together.

As utopian archives, the digital memory-making spaces discussed in this chapter serve as repositories of what is worth preserving. In an interview with Eduard Arriaga and Andrés Villar, Afro-Colombian performance artist and member of Cartagena-based Colectivo Contextos Alí Majul talks about the utopian in relation to digital projects as future-oriented: "Utopian is to keep believing that our lives will be better and different."[13] Digital archives that resist humidity, flooding, and the subsequent disintegration become utopian when their failure is baked into the obsolescence of digital platforms and tools that make them possible. "Resources are equitably distributed neither in society as a whole nor, unsurprisingly, in archives."[14] And yet, the fleeting character of the digital is a perfect match for the impossibility of grasping the everyday actions that make memory and survival possible. Reframing reading and writing as spaces of potentiality for community-building and memory-making confirm the importance of imagination in practice.

Memorias del Río Atrato:
The Power and Vulnerability of Digital Memories

Memorias del Río Atrato is an online repository of memories about the armed conflict in the 124 community councils that are part of COCOMACIA as much as a celebration of Black collective territories in the Pacific by centering oral and music traditions as storytelling of Afrocentric memories and traditions. Stories include many of the 124 community councils and Indigenous communities alongside the Atrato River and its tributaries. Owned by COCOMACIA, this website was created in 2013 as a result of the Centro Nacional de Memoria Histórica's "alfabetizaciones digitales" [digital literacies], which was included on the home page as part of Memorias del Río Atrato's story (Figure 4.1). Funded by USAID and the International Organization for Migration (IOM), this three-year program's goal was to promote community journalism and the production of digital media by communities affected by violence directly. As important as

Figure 4.1. Screenshot of Memorias del Río Atrato website, 2016.

this digital repository is, the website was down for a couple of years because the benefactor, a local priest, moved away and could not continue sponsoring the hosting and domain payments, proving that digital platforms are temporary and prone to disappear as they require constant funding and maintenance. Digital humanist Sonya Donaldson's questions are pertinent to think about the ephemerality of the digital: "So, what happens to a digital object disappeared? What might we gain by considering digital materials created by those in the African diaspora as archives of knowledge—and what does it mean that these archival materials are themselves ephemeral, subject to the vagaries of ownership, copyright, access, and resources?"[15]

While the website was still down as of January 2020, fifty-three stories were still available on the Memorias del Río Atrato YouTube channel, which had 102 subscribers at the time. My reliance on YouTube to access some of the Memorias del Río Atrato's website content as I was writing about it also reminded me of another quote from Donaldson: "my misreading of YouTube as a site of permanence and freedom made me susceptible to loss."[16] As I framed YouTube as a backup archive, Donaldson confirmed its instability even before thinking that all digital platforms have expiration dates. But just as abruptly as the website disappeared, it reappeared, confirming the unpredictability of what is conserved.

By the end of 2020, the website was partially reconstructed with the effort and advocacy of Lucely Rivas Espinoza, webmaster and community journalist who has led the initiative and produced most of the content. We worked together to reclaim the domain, and I have been supporting the project since then.

COCOMACIA's ownership of Memorias del Río Atrato is highlighted in the descriptions of the project's participant communities as the organization's 124 community councils—although Rivas's leadership is clear on the website as her email is prominently listed on the right top corner of every page. In the original website, all content was labeled as "escrito por COCOMACIA" [written by COCOMACIA], emphasizing the centrality of Black collective ownership of memories. Still, the mention of Indigenous communities from the Atrato River and its tributaries as participants also highlights this repository as an inclusive space, with this description of the website's imagined audience: "Los contenidos que creamos van dirigidos a toda la población sin discriminación alguna" [The content we create is directed at the entire population with no discrimination]. Imagining everyone as potential audience echoes *Mujeres Pacíficas'* invitations embedded in some of the stories, and particularly María del Socorro Mosquera Pérez's proclamation of "why not all women in the world" as an imagined interlocutor, discussed in the introduction. This utopian gesture in Memorias del Río Atrato to join memorialization narratives is more than a creation of counternarratives, a decentering of centralist memories by creating local and collaborative memories accessible to all.

The collective character of Memorias del Río Atrato is an intentional framework that connects it with other Afrocentric digital projects. According to the website's "Quienes Somos" [Who We Are] section,[17] the site is a response to the mainstream media coverage of the Bojayá massacre and its lack of attention to victims' everyday life. The project is then linked to "la necesidad de visibilizar la realidad de las comunidades, recoger la memoria histórica con las mismas víctimas y documentar el conflicto armado y sus consecuencias" [the need to make visible the reality of the communities, to collect historical memory with victims themselves, and document the armed conflict and its consequences]. The effort to document what mainstream media ignores reaffirms Memorias del Río Atrato's memory-making as more than memorialization of atrocities. This section uses "we" and "our" consistently, as most of the content—"nuestras memorias" [our memories], "nuestros territorios" [our territories], and even the award that Memorias del Río Atrato received in 2015 is collective: "Nos ganamos el premio de comunismo comunitario"[18] [We won the award for community journalism]. The Premio Amparo Díaz Uribe al periodismo comunitario [Amparo Díaz Award for community journalism], a yearly national recognition for regional journalists, accredited the merits of place-based journalism by confirming that Memorias del Río Atrato's memory-making is a community effort.

In an interview, Rivas confirms Memorias del Río Atrato as a memory-making digital space: "I think the website and the content we publish on the Internet make memory. We have made memory with our videos and stories."[19] In an article she wrote for *Semana*, a weekly Colombian news magazine, Rivas explains memory-making further: "en este medio estamos construyendo y re-construyendo nuestra memoria... al recordar un pasado marcado por hechos violentos y un presente de resistencia contra el dominio del poder armado en nuestros territorios"[20] [in this medium we are constructing and reconstructing our memory... by remembering a past marked by violent events and a present of resistance against the armed power in our territories]. Rivas confirms the role of memory in a continuous struggle that is informed by a shared past and oriented toward a collective future that is rooted in COCOMACIA's collective territories.

The acknowledgment of the aftermath of violence as worth documenting reiterates the labor of survival, and the role of memory in the reconstruction of communities. I see this digital archive as an example of what digital feminist Catherine Knight Steele calls, following Rayvon Fouché, "survival technology": Black people's creative uses and knowledge that subvert the oppressive character entrenched in technology's design and practice. For Steele, oral culture, hair care technologies, and the use of digital spaces are examples of Black women's technological agency.[21] As a woman-led website, Memorias del Río Atrato embodies "survival technology" by documenting and using innovative and creative tools and knowledge designed or repurposed for collective survival.

"De mi tierra no me quiero ir" [From my land I do not want to leave], a song detailing forced displacement by Etnia Company, and interpreted a capella by band member Johnier Palacios Paneso, is one of Memorias del Río Atrato's most watched videos. Recorded by Rivas on a boat in the Munguidó River, one of the Atrato River's tributaries, the video documents the song with a close-up of the singer and brief glimpses of the boat, in what seems a routine trip, and its surroundings, the rivers and the tree-lined shore. A still shot of the video where Palacios Paneso is in the middle of singing, with eyes closed and mouth open, is featured in the Museo de Memoria de Colombia's website, a museum of memory whose opening in Bogotá has been announced for years, and now might open in 2025 because of some delays due to inadequate construction process. Titled "Bojayá 12 años—De mi tierra no me quiero ir," the short accompanying narrative describes the song as part of a commemoration of the twelfth anniversary of Bojaya's massacre.[22] This appropriation of local memories as part of a national memory museum reinscribes the contradiction of utopian memories: creations that both are products of survival and contribute to make survival possible, while being fleeting artifacts vulnerable to co-optation as part of mainstream narratives.

Utopian memories also recount the efforts to materialize peace. In 2016, Memorias del Río Atrato published a brief note about "Atratiando por la paz," a journey through the Atrato River in September 2016 in support of the peace treaty between the Colombian government and the FARC. From Quibdó, Chocó, to Murindó, Antioquia, this boat caravan organized by COCOMACIA traversed the river visiting communities from the collective territories it administers. Held from September 25 to September 28, Atratiando was a celebration of the peace negotiations between the government and the FARC that started in 2012 and led to the agreements signed on September 27, and a movement to promote voting yes on the referendum that would ratify these agreements on October 2. Published on the same day as 50.2 percent of Colombians voters chose "no" to answer the question "¿Apoya el acuerdo final para la terminación del conflicto y la construcción de una paz estable y duradera?"[23] [Do you support the final agreement to end the conflict and build a stable and lasting peace?], Memorias del Río Atrato's "Atratiando por la paz, la vida" symbolized the commitment to peace that led to 79.76 percent of Chocoan voters to support the accords, the highest departmental support for the ratification. As Eduard Arriaga and Andrés Villar explain, "Memorias del Río Atrato becomes a way for the people of the region to showcase what they see as a possible future for their own lives in connection with complex identities that are in constant construction through their everyday life experiences."[24] As a reiteration of the stark difference between the country's centers of power—where the no vote won—and its peripheries—where the yes vote won—memories of this event expose the complex identities that Black communities in COCOMACIA's territories, including five municipalities in Chocó and three in Antioquia, negotiate daily.

A majority of no votes for Colombia's referendum by Colombians in the United States connects these negotiations with a global context. With Brexit, the UK's referendum that led to it leaving the European Union, and the 2016 US presidential election's fueling of hate speech, conspiracies about "gender ideology" that had circulated across Europe and Latin America contributed to the triumph of *no* in the Colombian referendum. Led by former president Álvaro Uribe (2002–2010), right-wing groups who opposed peace negotiations, and especially the discussion of gender in the accord, promoted voting *no* as a choice to defend Catholic values and their corresponding incarnation in the nuclear family. These controversies make evident the difficulty of materializing peace. Nonetheless, after the government and representatives of the accord's opponents renegotiated, the new text of the peace agreement was signed on November 24, 2016. As the peace accords that almost were not, the intense labor of peace-building in the Colombian Pacific exemplifies the burden of communities that have been victimized most by war and enthusiastically voted *yes* in continuing rehearsing what does not exist yet.

Thinking about postconflict utopias makes visible the messiness and vulnerability of imagining peace. Memorias del Río Atrato's utopianism is also observed by Arriaga and Villar when describing its outputs as utopias: "Armed with smartphones and trained in multimedia storytelling, the communities started to name and therefore to articulate utopias in the form of videos, songs, and oral stories to define their territories and identities."[25] These utopias are not new and not exclusively digital. Lucely Rivas Espinoza's role in COCOMACIA's communications team started with its radio station COCOMACIA Stereo. With the slogan "la voz de las communidades" [the voice of the communities], the radio station shares with Memorias del Río Atrato a vision of reaching and embodying the multiplicity of the organization's membership. As part of their outreach, the comisionadas had a weekly show in COCOMACIA Stereo.

The heterogeneity of COCOMACIA and its connections with other organizations and territories are also visible in the video "Mujeres de Ríos Tejedoras de Paz" [River Women Weavers of Peace], which was published on Memorias del Río Atrato's YouTube Channel in April 2019, after the Memorias del Río Atrato website disappeared. Black and Indigenous—Embera and Wayuú—women tell their stories about women's traditional gender roles in their communities, and what women can do in, and beyond, their territories when working together. Multiples forms of violence—including the humanitarian economy—are weaved into the stories with strategies for survival and solidarity beyond COCOMACIA, from other organizations: Mesa de Mujeres Indígenas, part of Mesa de Diálogo y Concertación de los Pueblos Indígenas del Chocó, a coalition of different departmental Indigenous organizations created in 2011; Fundación Mujer y Vida, a local feminist organization part of la Ruta Pacífica de las Mujeres, a national feminist coalition; Asociación Dos de Mayo (ADOM), an organization of displaced people from the Bojayá massacre that occurred on May 2, 2002, that is also part of la Ruta. At the end of the video, fourteen women participants are visible,[26] although the collaborators from the UN are only present as names in the video's final rolling credits.

This video makes visible the networks of feminist solidarity present in CO-COMACIA's collective territories that transcend its limits. Three of COCOMA-CIA's comisionadas de género, Luz Adonis Mena Becerra, Julia Susana Mena

Moreno, Rubiela Cuesta Córdoba, and her daughter Yessica Monroy Cuesta, are seen in the video alongside Rivas Espinoza, participating in the documentary's production (from lighting to interviewing and recording). The video includes footage of them behind the camera and asking the interviewees questions, materializing what is described in the credits as "metodología de video participativo y edición participativa" [methodology of participatory video and participatory editing]. The involvement of these leaders from various organizations and initiatives in making this audiovisual piece is not uncommon and emphasizes the overlapping boundaries of different spaces and the networks of support that connect these digital archives, not to mention a testament of the international funding behind the materialization of digital archives and content in Chocó. This video was produced in collaboration with UN Women, as part of a project about participative research on gender in Bangladesh, Colombia, Uganda, and Jordan, also confirming the global arrangement of humanitarian aid. The collaborators' presence is not even part of the B-roll that shows the collaborative production of the documentary.

The act of documenting the present is a vital aspect of honoring and protecting communities and their collective territories. One thing that stood out to me as I watched the video was Julia Susana Mena Moreno's introduction. As we saw in chapter 2, it is very common in COCOMACIA, and the Pacific lowlands, to identify rivers as part of individual introductions in meetings and videos, as was the case in most *Mujeres Pacíficas* stories. In "Mujeres de Ríos Tejedoras de Paz," Mena Moreno states, "Mi río es Berabamá, lo quiero mucho" [My river is Berabamá. I love it so much], right before starting to talk about humanitarian aid. Identifying with a river and loving a river makes clear the centrality of non-human beings when discussing communities and even peace. It might exemplify the community knowledge used in the arguments that made possible the 2016 T-622 sentence that declared the Atrato River as a legal entity with rights in need of protection as part of Black communities' biocultural rights, and created the Guardianes del Atrato as well as the Comisión de Guardianes.[27] Mena Moreno's river, a tributary of the Atrato River north of Quibdó, and her statement are examples of how Memorias del Río Atrato's utopian memories share knowledge that circulates through COCOMACIA's territories, rivers, and beyond.

As embodied strategies for linking past and present in the process of materializing a future for all, these memories are not only symbolically "of the river" but also highlight the centrality of non-human beings in reconstructing local identities. As a repository of local knowledge and cosmologies, Memorias del Río Atrato "explores the links between humans and non-humans—particularly territories—and the way digital tools can reinstate or re-invent the humanity of

Afro-Latinxs."[28] Other videos on their YouTube channel showcase members of COCOMACIA, mostly women such as Rivas Espinoza and comisionadas Julia Susana Mena Moreno and Yenny Palacios Romaña, discussing mining, rivers' pollution, territorial rights as part of conversations about ongoing violence, funerary traditions, and women's rights. By documenting the importance of rivers when discussing extractive industries' impact on territories and communities, Memorias del Río Atrato illustrates the use of digital tools as "survival technology" committed to defending communities with narratives that reimagine who counts when discussing memory in Colombia.

Julia Mena Moreno's intervention in this video is intensely honest as she criticizes humanitarian aid not reaching rural women, who are doubly oppressed, because of the lack of contact between humanitarian workers and the communities they claim to serve:

> No me siento recogida con algunas cosas que se hacen porque en su momento me he sentido utilizada... porque a veces vienen unas cosas muy duras tajantes desde allá sin siquiera mirar la necesidad que tiene la mujer entonces uno que hace un trabajo rural [sabe que] no es lo mismo la mujer urbana que la mujer rural.... La cooperación internacional llega... cuando llegan, porque nomás se queda en lo urbano... se queda en la teoría y la práctica es otra... no se sientan a concertar con la persona que sí sabe. Cogen a un tercero, a uno que tiene la corbata blanca, uno que habla bien bonito, un profesional que no se da cuenta la vida del campo cuál es.

> [I don't feel represented in some things that have been done because at some point I have felt used... because sometimes there are hard and sharp things that come from there without even considering women's needs.... International cooperation arrives... when it does because it usually stays in urban areas... it stays with theory and the praxis is different... they do not negotiate with the people who know. They choose a third party, one with white tie, one that speaks very beautifully, a professional that does not know how rural life is].

Mena Moreno's critique makes visible the contested relations with humanitarian aid by revealing the disconnect between NGOs' goals in Chocó and the choice of hiring outsiders to serve as intermediaries with local organizations. The hard and sharp things from elsewhere reveal the friction of local politics and international politics invested in respectability rather than life in rural spaces of the global South.

Rivas Espinoza concludes this short documentary with a suggestion to humanitarian organizations to guarantee that Black and Indigenous women are considered when writing guidelines for funding, to guarantee that humanitarian aid is transparent and fair. Rivas argues that applications for funding should recognize the knowledge of local leaders over that of professionals: "No necesitan un experto porque a veces los expertos pueden tener un título pero no tienen el conocimiento... que se tenga en cuenta ese conocimiento empírico que tienen las mujeres líderes de acá del territorio... que la parte económica que ese reconociemiento se haga a esas mujeres... a su trabajo... es bueno también que se pueda empoderar a otras mujeres pero que lo hagan ellas mismas... y sigan siendo más fortalecidas hasta poder llegar a asumir una presidencia de la república" [They do not need an expert because sometimes experts can have a title but not the knowledge... the empirical knowledge of women leaders from here, the territory, should be taken into account... it is also good to be able to empower other women but that's done by the leaders themselves... so they can be strengthened so they can achieve the republic's presidency]. Rivas's critique of humanitarian funding processes ends with a wish that might have seemed impossible at the time: a local woman leader becoming president.

With her bid for presidency in the 2022 elections, Francia Márquez made progress toward Rivas's dream with a powerful campaign slogan: "Soy porque Somos" [I Am Because We Are]. While Márquez is from Cauca and not from Chocó, her belonging to the Colombian Pacific's Black communities and her leadership as an environmental activist embodies the empirical knowledge to which Rivas refers. Márquez also has the titles Rivas associates with outsiders in her critique, and nonetheless has faced racist criticisms stating her lack of experience because she had never held political office before becoming vice president. With an outcome that brought Márquez close to Rivas's vision, bringing issues of environmental justice, extractive practices, and gender violence while centering Black and Indigenous women as part of ongoing national debates despite relentless racism is essential. The result of collective struggle against multiple forms of violence, Márquez's presidential candidacy and vice presidency might not surprise Rivas, who has been witnessing and documenting the power of local leadership while renewing her wishes for more.

The collective framework also influences the sharing of knowledge created in collaboration with other projects and organizations, as well as publications highlighting the organization or the region. In the reconstructed site, repostings of others' writing become part of the collective memory. For example, three recent posts are excerpts of a book, *Comisión de Género en la COCOMACIA. Las mujeres en la gestión del territorio en el Medio Atrato*,[29] with individual profiles of five women leaders, including comisionadas Luz Adonis Mena Becerra, Ana Rosa Heredia Cuesta, and Rubiela Cuesta Córdoba, as well as Lucely Rivas Espinoza.

In Memorias del Río Atrato's website, the introduction and the profiles of two comisionadas are reposted alongside a link to access the full document. The collaborative character of memory-making in Memorias del Río Atrato reveals the networks that make memories and survival possible. That said, like Donaldson, Rivas is also aware of the limits of the digital as she discusses these memories' lack of accessibility to their own creators, in her profile in that same book: "Todavía hay mucha gente en comunidades como Bellavista o Vigía del fuerte que no ha podido ni siquiera leer la historia que contó porque no hay internet o acceso a computadores o alguna iniciativa que permita que esta labor sea retribuida en su totalidad a las comunidades del Atrato"[30] [There are still a lot of people in communities such as Bellavista or Vigía del Fuerte that have not been able to read the story they told because there is no internet or access to computers or any initiative that allows this labor to be rewarded in its totality to the Atrato's communities]. Rivas's awareness of the digital divide confirms the utopian character of Memorias del Río Atrato as it is a project that continues to imagine and enact the Afrocentric memories that the Atrato's communities deserve and do not have yet.

Fotógrafas del Pacífico: Social Media as Digital Storytelling

Fotógrafas del Pacífico is a project by graphic designer and photographer Andrés Mauricio Mosquera Mosquera, known as Waosolo. This Instagram account is part of a larger collective and collaborative platform to make the Colombian Pacific visible. With a first post from February 20, 2016, these visual memories offer not only images that challenge stereotypes about Black and Indigenous women and girls, but also daily life scenes that challenge the images that circulate about spaces and inhabitants of the Colombian Pacific in popular media. As of February 2022, Fotógrafas del Pacífico's Instagram account @fotografasdelpacifico had 233 posts and 1,625 followers, which is impressive considering its numbers almost five years before (see Figure 4.2). Enamórate del Chocó is the most recognized piece of Waosolo's platform with the Instagram account @enamoratechoco, which had reached 28,200 followers and 5,440 posts around the same time. Other accounts of Waosolo's initiative include Enamórate del Pacífico (@enamoratedelpacifico) and Enamórate de Buenaventura (@enamoratebuenaventura). I focus on the Fotógrafas del Pacífico profile as it is managed by Afro-Chocoan women and it publishes images of Chocoan women, mostly Black and Indigenous. In Colombia, a whitening aesthetic still disproportionately dominates traditional cultural productions such as television and film. Even the aesthetics celebrating mestizaje

Figure 4.2. Screenshot of Fotógrafas del Pacífico's Instagram account, 2017.

are oriented toward explicit beauty standards closer to whiteness: light skin, straight hair, and light eyes.³¹ The popularity of these accounts shows the need for these digital archives, even if @fotografasdelpacifico has considerably less attention and content than the other accounts. "Being Afrolatin@, whether in the US, the Caribbean, or Latin America, is a state that is 'performed' and, as Peter Wade has argued, 'lived as an everyday experience,'"³² Eduard Arriaga reminds us. This performance marks race as embodiment and reveals the unavoidable interaction with a live audience with internalized ideas about who is racialized and who is not.

Like Memorias del Río Atrato, Fotógrafas del Pacífico is a digital archive that enacts and documents Afrocentric knowledge production while decentering mestizaje. With visual representations that challenge writing as the natural output of memory, Fotógrafas del Pacífico joins Waosolo's goal with his trademark Enamórate del Chocó: "cambiar esa percepción negativa de Colombia, del mundo, y en especial de este territorio"³³ [to change this negative perception of Colombia, the world, and especially this territory]. As collaborative repositories, these online platforms expand what digital storytelling as a genre means. Sharing these archives with a broader audience, memories are not place-bound, and they cease to be national or even regional. These global memories, then, exemplify a utopian time that challenges linearity and practice to share local knowledge online as a project and not only as an extension of a physical space. Territory is still central to these memories as an ancestral presence that keeps making existence imaginable. As Black studies scholar Paul Joseph López Oro writes, "Ancestral memory is multisited as it can manifest in multiple spaces and forms such as dreams, oral traditions, storytelling, visions, spiritual possessions, and reenactments of passed-on generational rituals."[34] While digital memories can only partially grasp the multimodality of ancestral memory, they interrupt hegemonic memories that claim to represent the whole nation.

Fotógrafas del Pacífico documents the everyday. "Mujeres que miran y narran el territorio del Pacífico Colombiano" [Women who see and narrate the territory of the Colombian Pacific] is @fotografasdelpacifico's bio, a succinct rewrite of the bio from 2017 (Figure 4.2) that seems more inclusive of outsiders. The previous bio, "Miradas de mujeres del Pacífico Colombiano, con fotografía exponen el territorio" [Views from the Colombian Pacific women, with photography expose the territory], implies that all the photographers are from the Pacific. While both bios center the territory as the object of the photographs, the updated bio suggests an interest in creating alliances with visitors and outsiders, even though the account has only posted images by local photographers so far. The centrality of the territory makes these memories local, while their imagined audience and their opening to collaborators reminds us of Mosquera Pérez's why not.

The first photograph on the Instagram account Fotógrafas del Pacífico was posted on February 20, 2016, a year before I took the screenshot of the account. This first photograph was a portrait of Quibdó's Cathedral San Francisco de Asís and surroundings. Taken by local photographer Paula Orozco (@pau_orozco8 on Instagram) from the malecón, the image acts as a postcard of the city. The commotion of Carrera Primera's traffic and pedestrians is only suggested with a couple of trucks and a line of rainbow parasols as placeholders for street vendors. The six images visible in the screenshot from 2017 (Figure 4.2) are also by Paula Orozco and serve as a 360-degree view of the malecón, the Atrato River, and the cathedral at different times of the day. As visual records of daily life, these photographs of students going to school, people enjoying the sunset, and the cathedral at night uncover what can be captured in a single spot by looking around patiently. The logo visible at the top left of the image "canoas desde arriba" [canoes from above] was introduced with a post on October 28, 2016. It is an eye made of canoes of different colors. Ripples of water hint at what could be eyelashes. "Miradas de paz" [Gazes of peace] is displayed under the image. The mention of peace after 50.2 percent of Colombian voters rejected the peace accords with the FARC is a utopian nod that reemerges with every post refusing to stop seeing peace in the everyday.

The image used as a profile picture for Fotógrafas del Pacífico until 2020 was an illustration of a Black woman with natural hair. A yellow butterfly (with white and Black markings) resembling a mask was covering her face. The background was pink. No words were part of the logo until recently, when the words that name the account on a white background became the logo and profile picture alongside a new bio: "Narrativas Visuales y Sonoras desde la Mujer del Pacífico Caribe Colombiano" [Visual and Sound Narratives from the women of the Colombian Caribbean Pacific]. While the previous bio suggests that not only people from the Pacific create content for the account, the previous profile picture and the current bio center Blackness. The account's malleability reinforces the shifting spirit of collective memory. Social media platforms are ever changing, loosening any prospect of permanence. Digital archives are fluid and performative. They are unstable, while they enact narratives that might not exist elsewhere. As theories in movement, both Memorias del Río Atrato and Fotógrafas del Pacífico coexist with multiple forms of violence that are also world-making: "Racism is performative; it literally enacts the very conditions it articulates."[35] By centering Blackness while imagining a global audience, Fotógrafas del Pacífico's local memories are also performative: they rehearse the peace they desire.

Recognizing knowledge production from people and contexts that have been traditionally studied, but not centered as knowledge producers, requires expanding how knowledge is defined and what outcomes and audiences define them. In "Afrolatin@ Digital Humanities or Rethinking Inclusion in the Digital Humanities," Eduard Arriaga writes that "[i]f the productive connection between computing and humanities helps us to think 'how we know what we know,' what some Afrolatin@ communities and individuals have been doing is investigating not only how they know what they know but also how others know what they know about them, and the way they have been represented to construct their own representations/counter-representations through digital means."[36] Fotógrafas del Pacífico documents ancestral memory and the everyday while creating knowledge about the Colombian Pacific's territories and communities, which destabilizes preconceived ideas about who produces knowledge and where knowledge is produced. As a collaborative archive, this visual collection also operates collectively, creating solidarity among people committed to changing mainstream narratives and representations about the Colombian Pacific.

Digital platforms such as social media blur the boundaries between consuming and producing cultural products, and they make collaboration possible through the use of hashtags and comments. Real-time production of images on a platform such as Instagram also allows real interaction with a deterritorialized audience. This is ideal to make visible activist motivations and intervene directly in creating visual representations and archives that are multiple and invite spectators to contribute and interact with the content. Captions work to contextualize images and even to link the account with other hashtags such as #fotografasdelatinoamerica. "Hashtagging is a practice that first emerged on Twitter in 2007,"[37] Steele reminds us; and, as Roopika Risam teaches us, hashtags in social media work as archival tools and are part of a "postcolonial digital archival practice."[38] Hashtags make it possible, even for people without administrative access to the accounts, to create collaborative archives. As anthropologists Yarimar Bonilla and Jonathan Rosa write about #Ferguson, "social media participation becomes a key site from which to contest mainstream media silences and the long story of state-sanctioned violence against racialized populations."[39] In the multiple iterations of #fotógrafasdelpacífico—with variations in accent mark placement or lack thereof—there are over 350 posts. Quibdó's cathedral and the Atrato River are summoned and captured alongside sunsets, sunrises, boats, faces, flags, and clouds when clicking on the hashtag. Even the lack of consistency in spelling acts as a reminder of the limits and subjectivity of archiving.

Social media, frequently described as unproductive, can be reframed as political as digital spaces challenge knowledge production hierarchies that reinforce writing and academic publishing as privileged outputs associated with centers of colonial power. Thinking about social media as tools with revolutionary potential to connect spaces and narratives that seemed distant confirms the importance of local stories and narratives. In "Social Stories: Digital Storytelling and Social Media," historian Jessica Marie Johnson invokes digital storytelling as a starting point to think about storytellers and stories in social media: "social media can disrupt and construct inclusive narratives, highlight marginalized histories, and empower users."[40] In #fotógrafasdelpacífico, digital storytelling, defined broadly, takes different shapes and creates visual memories that are circulated and consumed alongside mainstream narratives. The interaction that is made possible through platforms such as Instagram augment the democratic potential of a dissemination that, besides being interactive, allows for potentially instantaneous communication through likes and comments. The blurring between media producers and media consumers is influential in rewriting the narratives about who produces knowledge about/in the Colombian Pacific.

Beyond the tension between omnipresence and deterritorialization that users of digital platforms experience, the asynchronous character of social media, for example, makes interactions flexible. Eduard Arriaga's "temporalidades en red" [network temporalities] help theorize a utopian time where multiple temporalities, particularly of African and Afrodescendant representations, escape colonialism's linearity. Where past and present overlap,[41] their coexistence creates the possibility for imagining a future without forgetting the past, a change in space-time, as Rivera Cusicanqui's Pachakuti. Digital archives' contingency and temporality produce utopian memories that are interactive, deterritorialized, and unstable.

Fotógrafas del Pacífico exemplifies "la temporalidad en red" [networked temporality] as a utopian collage that mixes what the Colombian Pacific is with what it could be. Fotógrafas del Pacífico's posts include portraits, landscapes—the Atrato River is highlighted over other rivers that are included—and the documentation of San Pacho (a yearly festival celebrating St. Francis of Assisi) and other religious festivals.[42] These bits of daily life highlight differences with other regions of Colombia, such as the centrality of rivers and territories in the everyday, and similarities, such as religious images and celebrations. Fruits are also abundant: green and ripe plantains, pineapples, limes, chontaduros, marañones, and mangoes create an abundance that has been denied in dominant representations of Chocó. Although Quibdó is the main scenario, other spaces such as Beté, Carmen de Atrato, and Tumaco y Tutunendo are also part of this photographic collection. Local artists, including photographers Paula Orozco and Luisa Paredes, singer and songwriter Marsh Waris, and actress Mayra Luna, who have their own accounts and followers on Instagram, have created some of the most popular posts.

These forms of knowledge, alternative to official memory and history, do not exist in opposition to mainstream narratives, but they challenge their historical imposition of invisibility and exclusion. As a process of knowledge production, with public output, the agency of contibutors and users is essential. The audience can actively take part in the whole process of creation by using the hashtag or interacting with the content. Unlike constructed narratives from outsiders, these localized memories offer a utopian vision of Afrodescendant existence. The last post on @fotografasdelpacifico is by Buenaventura-based photographer Luisa Paredes, published in January 2021. Social media's immediacy and ephemerality reward constant posting, and somehow this account's following audience has kept increasing. The lack of recent updates only confirms that engagement with platforms and content can take multiple shapes, and that not all engagement might be synchronous.

Centering visual storytellers and stories that have been historically absent from official memories and archives is a political commitment with a network temporality that rescues the past and attaches it to an inclusive vision of the future. But, as we know, technology is not neutral. Even though we associate digital platforms with democratic potential and higher dissemination, what can the digital achieve when technology is not reliable, and the internet access required to use or contribute to digital archives is still a privilege? Digital literacy and internet access could limit who sees these collections, but this lack of access for followers does not mean that archives stop existing locally in smartphones or hard drives, or that previous posts do not continue shaping visual representations of the Colombian Pacific.

Sharing and creating narratives that materialize what communities have imagined despite violence and lack of accessibility is part of the utopian practice of transforming collective memory. Collaborative memories can create a shared accountability for what is yet to come. The future's unpredictability is used to change the unknown into a canvas for projections. What steers these prophecies is not personal gain or lack of knowledge of constant threats to social leaders in the Colombian Pacific, but concern with the generational wellbeing of strangers and future populations. The dream of another world roots the commitment to building and maintaining these utopian archives.

Nuestro Motete: Reclaiming Writing as Peacemaking

I found Nuestro Motete on Instagram, and I started to get to know its founder, Velia Vidal, virtually and by phone before I met her in Quibdó when I visited the cultural center in 2019. We messaged on Facebook as she was helping the comisionadas update and manage their Facebook page for COCOMACIA's Comisión de Género. We talked on the phone once when I asked her if she was interested in writing a text about Nigerian writer Chimamanda Ngozi Adichie's visit to Colombia. I had been asked to write it, but I felt that, as a mestiza, it was not my place to do so, especially because I was not in Colombia and had only experienced the visit on social media. Vidal was not interested because of all her commitments. She encouraged me to write it and told me something that stayed with me: "Si solo la gente negra puede escribir sobre otra gente negra, no tendríamos tiempo o energía de escribir sobre todas las otras cosas que queremos escribir" [If only Black people can write about other Black people, we would not have the time or energy to write about all the other things we want to write about]. Notwithstanding my not writing that text, what she said made me appreciate the value of engaging in conversations with the people I desire to be in a relationship with, and holding myself accountable to them. By the time we met, we knew each other a bit.

As I was revising this chapter, I found out *Aguas de estuario* [Estuary Waters], Velia Vidal's epistolary memoir, was available as an e-book. I started reading it during an insomniac night and soon enough, I was underlining passages that exemplified what I had been hoping to capture about Chocó's postconflict utopias. Vidal's words and work helped me understand the role of Motete in shaping local memories and narratives, as much as her motivations in committing to reading and writing. Before reading her book, I had started to write about Motete's Instagram account @nuestromotete. But in 2021, the account archived all previous images. I thought it was a great example of the digital's vulnerability to disappearance, and the malleability of digital presence to change. Before speculating more, I contacted Vidal, who explained the archiving of previous posts as part of a communication strategy suggested by a public relations firm for Motete's strategic plan in the next years. In turn, I decided to use *Aguas de estuario* as documentation of the theory and praxis behind Vidal's work that I had experienced on Instagram first. Motete and Vidal's writing are part of the networks of postconflict utopias as multimodal memory-making in Chocó. Vidal is an example of what Catherine Steele calls digital Black feminists, who "translate this ability to curate images of the self online to new publishing opportunities apart from Twitter or Instagram, producing steady income and respect as professional writers."[43] Whereas Vidal's career as a journalist precedes social media, she has strategically used her digital self-representation as much as the online visibility of her analog projects to create a career as a professional writer. Since 2021, she has been the principal investigator of *Tributaries*, a project funded by the British Museum's Santo Domingo Centre of Excellence for Latin American Research (SDCELAR).[44] In 2022, she became a columnist for *Cambio*, a Colombian magazine, and was included in the BBC's 100 Women list.[45] In these different roles, she has centered Chocó as a center of knowledge production where she—and others—challenge global and national narratives about Black people in Colombia.

As Vidal writes to her anonymous friend in *Aguas de estuario*, we get glimpses of the process of her moving from Medellín to Quibdó—a reverse migration route, as Medellín is the home of many Chocoans—and leaving her established career as a journalist to create something from scratch. Her words about this move as part of her life project reveal similarities with the comisionadas' narratives: "Necesitaba sentir que mi existencia tenía sentido, que estaba dedicando cada día a algo que valiera la pena para mí y que al final de la vida me hiciera sentir orgullosa"[46] [I needed to feel that my existence had meaning, that I was dedicating every day to something that would be worthy for me and that at the end of my life would make me feel proud]. The simplicity of this commitment makes it incredibly powerful in the context of capitalist exploitation of local resources, and competitiveness in getting ahead.

What she built started with a local everyday object turned into a symbol: motete. Motete, Vidal explains, "es un canasto de los que usan los indígenas para cargar la comida y lo llevan con un bejuco que cuelgan de sus cabezas"[47] [is a basket used by Indigenous people to carry food and it is secured to their heads using a rope]. This common word rooted the project locally and reimagined what a motete could be: "El asunto es que toda la vida los motetes se han usado para cargar comida para el cuerpo: plátano, carne de monte, pescado. Nosotros proponemos llenarlos con comida para el alma: arte, cultura, libros"[48] [The issue is that motetes have always been used to carry food for the body: plantain, bush meat, fish. We propose to fill them with food for the soul: art, culture, books]. And she has materialized this proposal, starting with reading groups for kids, teenagers, and teachers in different Quibdó neighborhoods and schools,[49] and moving to consolidate the Fiesta de la Lectura y la Escritura del Chocó (FLECHO), [Chocó's Reading and Writing Party], a literary festival that had its sixth annual iteration in March 2023.

In her opening speech for the first FLECHO, reproduced in one of the letters of *Aguas de estuario*, Vidal reimagines Chocó into a space for reading and writing: "Los chocoanos tenemos ya una buena parte ganada con nuestra oralidad, y que se completa con esto de escribir para perpetuar. Escribir sin pensar en que se publique, sin soñar con ganar dinero con ello, solo escribir, como resultado casi natural de leer, luego pensar y entonces plasmar lo que nos dicta el deseo" [We Chocoans have accomplished a lot with our orality, and it is completed with writing to perpetuate. Writing without thinking about publication, without dreaming about making money with it. Just writing as an almost natural result of reading, to then think and capture what our desire dictates]. Centering Chocó as a place for knowledge production and consumption creates a powerful narrative about its potentiality and particularities. Writing as an enhancement rather than a replacement of orality. For Vidal, writing cannot be thought of independently from the specificities of the territory and its multiple waters: "Escribir sí con la sospecha tantas veces confirmada de que al hacerlo desde nuestro lugar en el mundo aportamos una mirada especial, que solo es posible en la esquina donde se encuentran el Pacífico y el Caribe, y reciben las aguas de tres grandes ríos que nacen pequeños y se van haciendo grandes al recibir a miles de afluentes que son el amor que los engrandece" [Writing with the suspicion, confirmed so many times, that doing so from our place in the world we provide a special gaze, that is only possible in the corner where the Pacific and the Caribbean find each other, and receive the waters of three big rivers that start small and get bigger by receiving the thousands of tributaries that are the love that enlarges them]. As Julia Susana Mena Moreno does, Vidal highlights the centrality of rivers by invoking love and invoking, as Gonzalo de la Torre did, its power.

Vidal's description of Chocó denaturalizes the borders and othering implicit in Colombia's national and regional discourses: "El Chocó es Caribe, el Chocó es la Colombia indígena y, como bien dicen nuestros hermanos Embera, es al mismo tiempo Eyábida (de la montaña), Dóbida (del río) y Phusábida (del mar). Y con cada partecita de eso que somos se va formando una amalgama donde la cultura ya no tiene límites, siemplemente es" [Chocó is Caribbean, Chocó is Indigenous Colombia, and as our siblings Embera well say, it is at the same time Eyábida (from the mountain), Dóbida (from the river), and Phusábida (from the sea). And with every little piece of all we are an amalgam takes shape, where culture does not have boundaries, it simply is]. The recognition of Chocó as convergence is rooted in local knowledge. Using Embera epistemology and language, Chocó's geography is described as its culture: multiple things at once.

Vidal's exploration of Chocó's diversity exceeds discourses of Colombia's multiculturalism. In her speech she returns to "motete," this time as an example of the multiplicity of Chocó in terms of the coexistence of Black, Indigenous, and mestizx people who share ownership of the word: "Pongo el ejemplo de 'motete,' la palabra que bendice nuestra organización, donde tuvo génesis esta FLECHO. Es tan cierto lo indígena y lo europeo como lo africano de la palabra motete; es una palabra Caribe y Pacífico, tiene equivalente exacto en el embera y es natural para afros y mestizos. ¿A quién podríamos decir que pertenece entonces?" [I use the example "motete," the word that blesses our organization, where this FLECHO has its genesis. It is true its Indigenous and European character as much as how African the word motete is; it is a Caribbean and Pacific word, it has the exact equivalent in Embera, and it is natural for Afros and mestizos. Who could we say it belongs to then?] Reading this made me see Vidal's Motete as belonging to the repertoire of postconflict utopias, the comisionadas' everyday work and networks, and the local archives and memories, that imagine and create more inclusive narratives about Chocó and its people. More important, Vidal is theorizing what scholars such as Peter Wade write about mestizaje: "the structural processes of mixture are multivalent.... In the same network or assemblage, there are diverse social elements (acts, actors, things, ideas) that can be worked by people into different overlapping sets of connections and articulations."[50] Vidal's words center the lived experience of Chocoans by emphasizing cultural sharing instead of racial difference. And she does it without erasing the particularities of ethnic groups but celebrating points of contact and commonality.

Vidal's writing disarms official hierarchies that reinforce purity and separation, ideas that use mestizaje's ambiguity to promote invisibility and marginality of anything and anyone outside its norms, while denying their marginalization. Racial fusion associated with mestizaje has a dual character: its democratizing potential is in tension with its potential to reinforce preestablished racial hierarchies.[51] Vidal's creation of counternarratives to a racially homogenized national history and visual representations of national identity that equate mestizaje with inclusion is an outcome of a historical exclusion. As Arriaga notes: "People who had been left out or neglected from national, regional, or transnational conversations (due to racial issues) resort not only to the power of traditional communication media—books, articles, letters, manifestos, constitutional reforms, etc.—but also to the increasing importance of new digital technologies for questioning existing representations of Blacks and Afro-descendants in the Americas and create new self-representations."[52] Vidal's writing works with her use of social media to create new narratives and representations that emphasize a territory that, like its inhabitants, can be multiple things at once.

The multiplicity of Chocó is similarly performed by Vidal in *Aguas de estuario*'s different personas that exemplify coexistence of various personhoods instead of what we think of as a single personal identity. Vidal's letters are signed in different ways, including Velia, Veliamar, and la seño Velia. Velia suggests familiarity and friendship, although Vidal uses her full name when discussing the role she would like to be known for locally: "Quiero que sea Motete y no Velia Vidal. Yo solo quiero seguir siendo la seño Velia"[53] [I want it to be Motete and not Velia Vidal. I only want to be la seño Velia]. In this distinction, la seño Velia appropriates the apocope of señora [Mrs.] used affectionately and respectfully by Chocoans, especially kids in school settings, to identify with and center public reading for kids in Motete's work: "Seguiré trabajando por ser la seño Velia, la que lee cuentos"[54] [I will continue working on being la seño Velia, the one who reads stories]. Vidal also uses Veliamar to enact the playfulness and symbolism of making sea part of her name: "Yo soy como el mar Pacífico, que presiona con sus mareas al río y lo hace ir contra corriente, que se mete abruptamente a la tierra cada vez que sube y va ganando centímetros a su antojo"[55] [I am like the Pacific Ocean, which presses with its tides the river and makes it go against the current, that gets abruptly into land every time it rises and gains centimeters at will]. This description, inspired by Bahía Solano, her hometown, is also intertwined with other local memories and the reciprocity of writing to her recipient: "Recordé también que a mi vida la llenan de poesía el mar, los atardeceres chocoanos, el agua que cae y que corre, y esta bella costumbre de escribirte y esperar una respuesta" [I also remembered that my life is filled by poetry by the sea, the Chocoan sunsets, the water that falls and runs, and this beautiful routine of writing you and waiting for a response]. The centrality of water in Vidal's description of Chocó, and her own identity, renews the importance of the local, and the different shapes it can take as background and character in the work of willfulness.

Vidal's work—through Motete and her writing—exceeds the recognition and creation of spaces for coexistence. Motete and its reading clubs also enact peace-building, as Vidal writes in another letter: "Insertamos en nuestras sesiones de trabajo en los clubes de lectura los 'Actos pacíficos' y los 'Momentos de juego.' Ha sido muy bello darnos abrazos, decirnos las cosas bellas que tenemos y sacar desde adentro nuestra idea de lo que es la paz"[56] [We inserted in our reading clubs' work sessions the "Pacific acts" and the "Play moments." It has been very beautiful to hug each other, to tell each other the beautiful things we have, and to bring from inside our own idea of what peace is]. Thinking about peace, affect, and beauty as part of reading clubs and everyday exchanges confirms the importance of rehearsing the world we want to create, as part of rehearsing postconflict utopias. In Motete's slogan, Vidal also sees a connection between her project and her life: "El slogan de mi Proyecto es 'contenidos que tejen'; cada día me gusta más. Cada día me doy cuenta de que esos contenidos tejen en mí la realización y la felicidad"[57] [My project's slogan is "contents that weave"; I like it more every day. Every day I realize that these contents weave in me fulfillment and joy]. Weaving reading together with fulfillment and joy in the context of community-building, Vidal joins a commitment for self-determination built on local knowledge and collective work.

If it seems utopian to think about peace during reading groups, Vidal knows so and describes it beautifully: "Lo que yo hago, se trata de leerle a otros en voz alta el cuento que nos alienta cada día, ese que dice que ahí no más, a la vuelta de una decisión o de un poco de esfuerzo, escrito en la página de un libro, en el aroma de unas plantas sembradas o en el sabor de un plato servido está la vida que siempre hemos anhelado"[58] [What I do is about reading to others out loud the story that encourages us every day, that one that says that there, at the other end of a decision or a little bit of effort, written in the page of a book, in the scent of some potted plants or the taste of a served plate is the life that we have always wished for]. For Vidal, explaining what she does every day—reading to others—as part of other mundane and highly sensory experiences—the scent of plants, the taste of food—contains the potential of the life we wish for. Crafting a future life in collaboration with others is part of the utopian energy needed to enact change in Chocó. In the process, embodied memories and archives are created. As Black Dominican studies scholar Omaris Zamora explains, "Bodies and archival memory are linked to form an embodied archive, a place where memories are kept."[59] Acknowledging the sensorial as part of rehearsing life opens space for thinking about embodied memories and archives.

Vidal describes the background where her work and Motete exist: "A veces percibo un afán de las personas del sector social y cultural por sobresalir a costa de lo que sea, observo también la creación de unas élites negras o unas élites quibdoseñas, que me parece que fraccionan más esta ciudad ya bastante fraccionada"[60] [Sometimes I perceive a rush from people in the social and cultural sector to stand out no matter what, I also observe the creation of Black elites or Quibdó elites, that I think fracture more this already-broken city]. Thinking about Quibdó as a fractured city where there is competition and emerging elites that create additional fractures makes it possible to visualize the challenge of imagining otherwise. For Vidal, how she sees herself and her work goes against the available frameworks: "He tenido que irme haciendo un estilo propio de vivir mis relaciones aquí, y del lugar que se va haciendo esta organización. No soporto ser muy visible, no soporto la idea de convertirme en lo que acá llaman 'referentes.' No quiero ser líder de nada"[61] [I have had to make my own style to live my own relationships here, and the place that this organization is making for itself. I cannot stand being too visible, I cannot stand the idea to become what they call here "references." I do not want to be a leader of anything]. Finding alternative ways to exist and work together, Vidal and Motete imagine different relationships and even the potential for a different Quibdó.

It is not surprising that while Vidal was finding herself and Motete's place in Quibdó, she worked with the comisionadas, whom she credits as leaders promoting women's political participation within COCOMACIA: "Después de recorrer este territorio colectivo río a río, vereda a vereda, han logrado que las mujeres tengan puestos en la junta directiva y que sean representantes de varios de los consejos locales"[62] [After traversing this collective territory river to river, village to village, they have achieved that women have positions in the governing board and are representatives of some of the local councils]. While I had known of Vidal's collaboration with the comisionadas and their work, I was surprised to find them in her book. Vidal's description of the comisionadas' work also maintains the tension between the value of their everyday practices and the challenges they face: "Hace dos años que no tienen un proyecto que les permita generar ingresos, y siguen saliendo cada semana a las comunidades, siguen haciendo marchas, plantones, talleres, así vengan desde sus casas a pie, para seguir caminando por la dignidad de las mujeres. Tienen un restaurante y un taller de artesanías, pero los tienen cerrados por falta de capital, de orientación y unas cuantas otras cosas"[63] [It has been two years since they have had a project that allows them to have an income, and they continue visiting communities every week, they continue organizing marches, vigils, workshops, even if that means walking from their houses to continue walking for women's dignity. They have a restaurant and a crafts workshop, but they are closed for lack of capital, orientation, and some other reasons]. The connection between Vidal and the comisionadas reinforces both the difficulty and the importance of activism in Chocó without infrastructure and financial support.

When discussing the 2018 armed strike organized by the ELN in Chocó, Vidal discusses the presence of outsiders in Quibdó as part of humanitarian NGOs, and their conditional presence: "Por motivo del paro armado, las organizaciones que hacen presencia acá decidieron llevarse sus profesionales. 'Sacarlos' es la expresión que usan"[64] [Due to the armed strike, the organizations present here decided to take their professionals away. "Get them out" is the expression they use]. The choice of opting out when things get difficult exposes the limits of humanitarian aid, and the boundaries and hierarchies that separate people when risk increases: "Cuando más duro se pone todo, más solos nos quedamos. Siento que es como si hubiera unas vidas que valen más que otras. Las que valen más merecen ser protegidas, se las llevan a lugares seguros, les impiden venir a donde puedan correr riesgos. Pero nosotros no tenemos a dónde irnos, nos quedamos aquí, a nuestra suerte"[65] [When things get harder, the more alone we are. I feel that there are some lives that are worth more than others. The ones that are worth more deserve to be protected, they are taken to safe places, they are stopped from coming to where there are risks. But we do not have anywhere to go, we stay here to our fate]. The unequal distribution of safety and access to resources and logistics to opt out affirm the hierarchies that humanitarianism underlines. The choice of leaving or receiving support declares whose lives are worth saving.

Vidal takes her reflection on the divide that the humanitarian economy reinforces further with a comparison of how she and Motete had to stop some of the activities during the armed strike, including her reading groups: "Lo que más duele es que eso que siento yo con relación a la gente de los organismos internacionales o las instituciones públicas, en cierta medida lo causamos a los niños" [What hurts the most is that what I feel in relation to international organizations or public institutions is what, to a certain extent, we do it to the children]. This is not the only time she questions her work; she also asks a hard question in the middle of describing a traumatic situation involving one of the kids attending a reading group: "¿De qué sirve leer cuentos en una vida tan dura?"[66] [What good does it do to read stories in such a hard life?] This heartbreaking question underscored the everyday violence that is the backdrop of her work in the Colombian Pacific. That said, Vidal's self-reflective and introspective letters give us, from the beginning of *Aguas de estuario,* access to a vulnerable understanding of the motivation to resist and keep going despite everything: "Me pregunto otra vez sobre lo que me hace resistir cuando decido hacerlo y qué cosas me derrumban todas las resistencias. Al parecer la respuesta sigue siendo la misma: el amor"[67] [I ask myself what makes me resist when I decide to do it and what things crumble all my resistances. It seems the answer remains the same: love]. Vidal's resistencia aligns with re-existencia as everyday insurgencies serve as a means of community survival.[68] The glue that holds a community together is love, and our survival depends on it. We do need each other.

When I visited Quibdó in 2019, Motete as a physical cultural center was preparing to close, confirming Vidal's fear that Quibdó was not ready to support a space centering reading and books. Vidal wrote about the city's preferences as part of her reflections about Motete: "No se van los días en los que no viene nadie, porque la ciudad sigue prefiriendo beber y emborracharse y lucirse en la zona rosa, en los establecimientos lujosos que se han hecho con la plata de orígenes dudosos"[69] [The days where no one comes are not going away because the city still prefers to drink and get drunk and show off in the partying zone, in the luxury establishments that have been built with dubious origins]. Connecting Quibdó's nightlife with local illegal activities, as much as with Motete's lack of consistent support, gives us a glimpse of the utopian thinking needed to create a space for books and cultural activities in Quibdó.

Aguas de estuario not only imagines a Quibdó in which reading and writing are worth it. It also narrates the Colombian Pacific, maintaining the tension between its multiple beauty that has been overlooked and the everyday violence that threatens it. More so, Vidal rehearses a type of personal writing that is rooted in and extends the potential of orality and helps us imagine future written representations of this territory made of water. Oceans, rivers, rain, and humidity set the stage for *Aguas de estuario* as part of materializing a collective identity. First in Quibdó: "Es mucha humedad la que habita ese pueblo. En realidad somos agua" [It is too much humidity that inhabits this town. In reality, we are water]. And later in Bahía Solano, her hometown: "Esto no es pacífico. Pero debo decir . . . que nada me da más paz que estar aquí" [This is not peaceful. But I have to say . . . there is nothing that gives me more peace than being here]. Maintaining the tension between peace and violence, Vidal's commitment is a commitment to showing up and being there in the same way that the comisionadas and her networks continue imagining: "Seguimos adelante, firmes, convencidos de la importancia de estar aquí" [We continue moving forward, firm, convinced of the importance of being here].

Utopian Archives and Memories

Memorias del Río Atrato, Fotógrafas del Pacífico, Motete, and *Aguas de estuario* are examples of "survival technology." As digital and analog archives that intervene in representations of the Colombian Pacific as part of a collective struggle for creating and documenting knowledge that makes survival possible, these projects destabilize the hegemony of mestizaje in national narratives. In the process, they also open space for imagining the potential of local memories in manifesting peace. They reclaim genres, platforms, and technologies that have been used to oppress Black communities in order to resignify and reclaim them to imagine otherwise. What this survival technology achieves is creating interactive engagements with content that represents Chocó and Colombia from a non-centralist perspective. Mestizaje is also challenged as the standard or even desired outcome of multiculturalism. Its oppressive potential is revealed when recognized as a process of whitening that has been naturalized and promoted by national narratives.

Unlike the Museo Nacional that, until recently, had presented a homogenizing history as part of a national identity project, Memorias del Río Atrato, Fotógrafas del Pacífico, and Motete create Afrocentric archives in which memories do not reinforce stereotypical and homogenizing ideas about the African diaspora, and mestizaje is no longer the standard. As Christen Smith reminds us, "The transnational Black condition in the Americas is a political condition defined by the memory of colonialism/slavery and its continued resonance."[70] So even if, as cultural repositories of memories, these spaces share knowledge for local and global audiences, they are competing with other popular analog and digital dehumanizing narratives that have never disappeared. Velia Vidal's recent work on the British museum's Chocó collection further exemplifies the coexistence of conflicting narratives of memory around collections.[71] Speculative thinking and the political potential of what is not yet creates utopias as blueprints where present, past, and future collide. In the worlds created by these narratives of memory, it is possible to imagine new ways to avoid reproducing—while changing the hierarchies that have made us naturalize—mestizaje as a mutation of white supremacy.

In the same way, the cultural objects discussed in this chapter become collaborative archives that offer collective representations of the Colombian Pacific that challenge homogenization and victimization. Social media produces, circulates, and incentivizes the consumption of Afrocentric images and narratives absent in mainstream spaces and discourses. And these projects connect new narratives to existing analog and digital spaces. By looking at and narrating the territory, these cultural productions reveal the potential and limits of digital spaces as memory repositories in a centralist country where most museums and archives are in Bogotá or other major cities, which make them inaccessible to most of the population. And while Muntú Bantú, La Muestra Bíblica, Motete, and other newer cultural spaces confirm that local memory initiatives are possible, they are still located in Chocó's capital, inaccessible to rural populations.

Memorias del Río Atrato, Fotógrafas del Pacífico, Motete, and *Aguas de estuario* act as Afrocentric narratives not bound by physical locations, fundamental to expand representations of Colombianidad. Their content makes clear that the diversity and multiculturalism celebrated in national narratives is incomplete. They help evaluate critically why Afrodescendants are included in national narratives only as an accessory of multiculturalism and not as part of a national history built on the oppression of ethnic minorities and the creation of a mestizaje myth as erasure of racial hierarchies.

An ancestral energy flows through these analog and digital sites of memory in the shape of sounds, smells, tastes, and images that are captured or invoked. Meanwhile, the national and transnational layers of historical oppression that inform these initiatives are more threatening than ever. Industrial mining is threatening artisanal mining as much as the rivers that sustain life in the Colombian Pacific. And capitalism is not only about extracting resources anymore, as material culture is constantly commodified and appropriated by and for outsider consumers. These utopian archives do not exist outside of capital and academic extractive practices, and even attempts of symbolic reparations by institutions such as the Museo Nacional uphold the colonial ontology and ideology that make national identity possible.

The public appropriation of Afrocentric symbolic and cultural narratives, with the purpose of decentering mestizaje from official memories, centers knowledge from Chocoan contexts to complement existing initiatives of struggle and liberation. The audience of this appropriation is first local, as these archives have a pedagogical purpose of unlearning. As non-oppositional narratives, these repositories supplement well-known narratives that reproduce racial, knowledge, and power hierarchies. Self-representation is possible because of autonomous community networks and not because of the digital platforms or the technologies that make them feasible. Despite not having the corporate funding of mainstream media, social media and community networks create small local audiences that connect to larger networks that amplify the utopian potential of creating and imagining new ways to represent and memorialize Chocó and its histories. As collective goods, memories and archives, and their process of construction and reconstruction, require collective and collaborative negotiation. This collaborative production of public knowledge becomes antidote to erasure by imagining new memories, archives, and narratives. And just as rain's malleability is transformative, it is possible to coexist and make space for each other in the elasticity of memories that narrate Chocó from the collective territories.

CHAPTER 5

Utopian Networks
Showing Up as a Durational Performance

> Las mujeres también tejen redes de resistencia. ¡Escuchémoslas!
>
> Women also knit resistance networks. Let's listen to them!
> —Ruta Pacífica banner during Women in Black encounter in Bogotá, 2011

After I could not return to San Francisco de Ichó in 2011, Rosa Rivera from Vamos Mujer, a feminist NGO based in Medellín, invited me to the encuentro of Women in Black, a transnational antimilitaristic feminist organization. The event would take place in Bogotá in August 2011. I contacted the organizers, mainly members of La Ruta Pacífica de las Mujeres. I offered to volunteer while I was in Bogotá, waiting to visit las comisionadas and other potential collaborators in Quibdó. I translated a symbolic script for the event before traveling, and I helped as an interpreter during the event's breakout sessions that would not have simultaneous interpretation.

What I saw in my brief contacts with organizers was the complexity of the logistics and all the moving parts needed to make the event happen, even if at the time I did not see all the connections that make local, regional, and transnational alliances possible. What I learned was that no matter how bad things get, women keep striving to change the world. They show up. The first practice I noticed over and over and wrote regularly in my field notes was showing up: "Why do women show up?" What is behind the logistics and energy that make alliances that transcend linguistic, cultural, and national borders possible? I thought about the commitment that makes showing up possible as a durational performance, a subgenre of performance art that highlights time and requires endurance. As immersive and collaborative, the everyday rituals that make showing up possible are embodied knowledge. At the end of "Mujer que no cumpla su sueño, mujer que no ha nacido," Justa Germania Mena Córdoba shares: "He pasado mucho trabajo. La lucha mía ha sido incansable por salir adelante, por ser alguien, por superarme, por servir a las personas"[1] [I have faced a lot of trouble. My struggle has been tireless to move forward, become someone, get ahead of myself, serve other people]. Her narrative braids her struggle with her personal goals and her desire to serve other people. In Mena's story, her acknowledgment of patriarchal ideologies and structures coexists with her struggle to work in COCOMACIA and her own family to imagine alternative ways to live and love. Showing up is world-making.

Showing up accentuates the potential of the mundane, and it acknowledges what is left of agency, as what escapes violence, when dispossession is the pattern. It also means centering what is often excluded: what is not written or could not be written, or what does get written but flattens the actual embodiment of commitment. The non-written becomes a flow of energy, one that is unfixed, even if repeated. It is always what could have been—but not as nostalgia. Embodied knowledge escapes mainstream knowledge and culture. Mena's commitment to showing up even when she doesn't have to is not fully captured by her story, and even less in writing. Working with terminal cancer seems laughable in the face of violence, but it seems "it is only another battle for self-determination and survival that Black women face."[2] Showing up for Mena Córdoba creates unimaginable possibilities of what being in community can do. Her commitment to COCOMACIA, her family, and her compañeras exceeds the promises of labor within capitalism. What sounds like the cliché of hope is a manifestation of transformative politics: everyday actions that can lead to change as people choose to work together, to survive together. To show up. To care for each other.

This chapter explores the possibilities of embodied performances, through the concepts of care politics and showing up in feminist spaces, as examples of postconflict utopias. Here I refer to the practices of imagining what is not yet possible yet is rehearsed amid violence. In the Colombian Pacific, violence shape-shifts from lack of infrastructure and access to education as inheritances of historical exclusion to land dispossession, extractive practices, and militarization. As abolitionist geographer Ruth Wilson Gilmore teaches us, "Racism, specifically, is the state-sanctioned or extralegal production and exploitation of group-differentiated vulnerability to premature death."[3] Mena Córdoba's story, finished months before her death, confirms that violence is more than what the euphemism "armed conflict" can describe. Survival is much more complex than we think when the threats are relentless: "Racism. Cancer. In both cases, to win the aggressor must conquer, but the resisters need only survive."[4] I use postconflict utopias to name the tension of working toward a future that requires active imagination, and commitment to show up in a context in which anti-Blackness is the weather, and premature death and debility the norm.[5] Building on Diana Taylor's repertoire,[6] I argue that looking at the embodied everyday practices as part of local, regional, and transnational networks gives us glimpses into what happens alongside violence. Both the militarization of daily life and women's survival strategies when their existence and livelihood is threatened reveal the value of everyday solidarity in the face of violence. Performance studies guides us to think beyond written knowledge. Valuing existence and daily routines as attempts to reconstruct communities and lives illuminates embodied knowledge. Thinking about quotidian practices such as organizing meetings and making signs and banners as transformative politics decenters writing. It is not the medium itself but its use that turns it into archive or repertoire. The visible is archivable, as seen in chapter 3, but visibility can be used for other purposes. To show up is embodied visibility that cannot be archived as presence. As a performance, showing up's potential depends on the audience and the engagement.

I include different levels of activist actions as examples of embodied performances that belong to feminist networks of solidarity. While these networks include the local museums that embrace absence and revise history that I explored in chapter 3, this chapter traces the embodied practices of different organizations to which the comisionadas belong. Museums that turn absence into collective memory work similarly to groups of feminist women that cannot communicate in the same language but move as one. The two become spaces that create potential for social change with sustained practice. La Ruta Pacífica de las Mujeres, a feminist regional network, turns mourning into politics, and Women in Black, an international antimilitarist network of women, performs silence to oppose wars all over the world. These networks exemplify the performativity of showing up. The apparent dissonance that results when weaving these experiences together can only be reconciled when thinking about embodiment as a democratic tool linked to existence in spaces of vulnerability.

As strategies of postconflict utopias, showing up and care politics create communities of practice in the absence of the state or other institutions. Showing up, then, is not only about attending events but also about being present for each other. Showing up is possible through care politics, in which caretaking is viewed as a community practice instead of an individual one. In a postconflict context, taking care of each other is not only a daily practice but also one that makes existence possible. Over 1,000 social leaders had been assassinated in

Colombia by 2020,[7] and ongoing human rights violations have been reported since the peace accord with the FARC.[8] Francia Márquez Mina, Afro-Colombian human rights activist, winner of the Goldman Environmental Prize in 2018, and vice president of Colombia, survived an attack in Cauca against her and other leaders. Even in "postconflict" times, peace is a challenging task.

To show up is a commitment in practice that requires embodied presence. To show up is politics in action. It is about challenging the boundaries between public and private spaces. To show up is about building communities and making networks real. It is about protecting each other and building power in numbers, as organizers say. It is about solidarity and visibility. To show up is also a process that requires constancy, and its end is not palpable, as social change seems endless. To show up is embodied theory or "[t]heory in the flesh . . . one where the physical realities of our lives . . . fuse to create a politic born out of necessity."[9] What makes showing up utopian and part of care politics is the material realities of existence (having a body, a family, and a community with ever-changing needs) that make showing up in the first place necessary.

Care politics builds on re-signifying care as feminist ethics in contraposition to care as feminized labor. In her *Mujeres Pacíficas* story, Rubiela Cuesta Córdoba tells us: "Las mujeres siempre planificamos y calculamos bien las cosas, y siempre pensamos en los demás. La mujer siempre piensa: '¿cómo hago para colaborarle al vecino?, ¿cómo hago para colaborarle acá al primo?, ¿cómo le colaboró a la tía?' Las mujeres siempre estamos ahí en ese lugar" [As women, we always plan and calculate things, and we always think of others. A woman always thinks: 'how can I help my neighbor? how can I help my cousin? how can I help my aunt?' As women, we are always in this place]. While the association of women's labor in caretaking is present in her story, she sees care as part of everyday solidarity that materializes in intentional practices of planning and sharing. These practices support communities and make survival and activism possible.

Building on the ambivalence of care—a ubiquitous need marked as feminine and continually undervalued—I define care politics as intentional and ethical collective caretaking that makes life possible, a postconflict utopia. As a feminist project about reciprocity and creativity, care politics is utopian. As Sara Ahmed explains, "[a] feminist project is to find ways in which women can exist in relation to women; how women can be in relation to each other. It is a project because we are not there yet."[10] Caretaking, traditionally associated with the nuclear family and thought of as a feminized activity, is reclaimed as feminist. Care politics reclaims women's labor for their own communities. Quilt-making, chants, T-shirts, body paint, banners, and signs invoking motherhood and womanhood tropes become tactics for materializing a collective of women that can embrace and challenge their inherited domestic roles in public. Through care politics, domesticity and womanhood become compatible with social change. Women's roles expand in spaces where they recognize each other as political subjects. Unlike feminized caretaking, care politics is about reciprocity, intentionality, and community-building.

Care is sustained by networks, or what disability justice writer Leah Lakshmi Piepzna-Samarasinha calls "care webs" in disability communities.[11] Care is performative, as it creates and materializes the support needed to be in relationship long-term for a common cause: "care work . . . is essential to building movements that are accessible and sustainable."[12] Care is political and sustained by—usually women's—labor as valuable and world-making. Feminist theater critic Jill Dolan explains that the "utopian performative" can be found "in feelings of pleasure and hope that often come before the security of articulation, that require a process of arriving in speech, the sense of possibility for something never before seen but only longed for, that glimpse of the no-place we can reach only through feeling, together."[13] Women's organizations, networks, and care webs exemplify Dolan's utopian performative, which, outside theater, takes the shape of showing up. To show up, to be present, requires being able to imagine what can be possible.

The popularity of the term "network" to describe women's movements and organizations that bring together actors with different politics reveals formal and informal connections across national borders. These movements are not defined by a stable membership, but rather by a sense of motivation and duty that's expressed through showing up and performing care work. In her *Mujeres Pacíficas* story, Banessa Rivas López stresses the importance of community involvement in the struggle, recognizing the link between collective territories and ancestral knowledge, as explored in chapter 2.

In this exchange of knowledge that Banessa Rivas López imagines between the youth and the ancestors appears a network of solidarity that makes activism possible in the first place. A conviction that showing up is a long, transgenerational practice of knowledge production and dissemination. Following Rivas and the comisionadas, I explore the embodied practices of feminist solidarity that create memories, imagine truth, and create temporary communities that support transnational women's political engagement. I discuss La Ruta Pacífica de las Mujeres and La Red Departamental de Mujeres Chocoanas as regional and national networks where memories are performed, and truth is imagined as a feminist practice. Part of the comisionadas' local context, networks' practices exceed Chocó through time and space. I move to an analysis of Women in Black and their encuentros in Bogotá and Montevideo to show the potentialities and limits of care politics and showing up.

Regional Alliances as Embodied Memories

San Pacho is what Chocoans call Saint Francis of Assisi. Every year since 1648, from mid-September to the beginning of October, people dance, pray, sing, and celebrate Quibdó's saint in the Festival of Saint Francis, known in Quibdó simply as San Pacho.[14] I have never been in Quibdó during the festival. I have not experienced the chirimías [bands including percussion and wind instruments], rebulú [crowds], biche [homemade sugar cane alcohol], disfraz [floats representing social or political issues], caché [outfits incorporated into the parades in the last decades], or even the accompanying violence hyperrepresented in national news about this religious festival. But I have seen the pictures that the comisionadas took and decided to include in their stories and sampled the biche that is part of most celebrations I have attended. Every year since I met them in 2008, I have heard about La Red Departamental de Mujeres Chocoanas' meetings where local women talk about the year's theme, colors, fabrics, and messages of the outfits they will wear. Not only women who are part of La Red wear the outfits. Men and women, members of COCOMACIA and La Red, join the group wearing messages of social justice to dance for hours in a parade.

Since 2012, San Pacho has been included in UNESCO's Representative List of the Intangible Cultural Heritage of Humanity. Scholars and locals have already written about the festival: a community practice for musicians to rehearse, learn, and even construct their masculinity,[15] and as a collaborative celebration that brings the church, corporations, government, and neighborhoods together every year to keep traditions alive.[16] Building on the idea of San Pacho as a shared space with possibilities for rehearsing and creating, the festival materializes connections to Chocoan women's organizations through dancing while wearing messages defending women's rights. Messages have included "por una vida sin discriminación y sin violencias contra las mujeres" [for a life without discrimination and forms of violence against women] in 2009 and "la mujer campesina hace grande al territorio y fomenta el desarrollo del Chocó" [the peasant woman gives value to our territory and promotes Chocó's development] in 2012. As an example of how activist networks work together and organize around ideas of transformative politics, San Pacho exemplifies the connections and solidarity among women's organizations and networks in Chocó. Organizing a parade requires collaboration and energy, and the emphasis of sharing information about laws that protect women on T-shirts and banners signals the vulnerability to violence that affects Chocoan women even during celebrations.

Participating actively in the festival has not stopped members of COCOMACIA's Comisión de Género and La Red Departamental de Mujeres

Chocoanas from denouncing violence against women even during the festival. Teresa Quejada Palacios, a leader from COCOMACIA's zone 4, was killed by her husband on September 19, 2009, in Bocas de Amé, a small community in the Medio Atrato. In a press statement, comisionadas condemned the death of yet another woman in her own home. Other signatory organizations included ADOM (May 2 Association, displaced people from the Bojayá massacre), La Red Departamental de Mujeres Chocoanas, Fundación Mujer y Vida, La Ruta Pacífica de las Mujeres, ADACHO (Victims' Association of Chocó), and Asociación Mujeres por una Vida Digna y Solidaria. As supporters of Law 1257 of 2008, against gendered violence, and Auto 092 of 2008, protecting the rights of internally displaced women because of the armed conflict, these organizations use strategies to call attention to the violence Chocoan women experience daily (see Figure 5.1).

The construction of a regional community of women is the basis for resignifying San Pacho as a space for living together. Participation embraces cultural traditions. And questioning tradition to imagine ways of political participation in celebration to denounce violence against women blurs the public/private binary that has restricted women's politics. As Taylor explains, "By emphasizing the public, rather than private, repercussions of traumatic violence and loss, social actors turn personal pain into the engine for cultural change."[17] Press statements, workshops, conferences, and written documents are not enough to

Figure 5.1. Banner of Law 1257 at the Comisión de Género's office (including photographs of members of women's organizations in Chocó). Quibdó, 2013.

denounce the naturalization of violence against women that makes femicides, sexual violence, and displacement constant threats. Performative actions such as parades put traumatic memories in movement. They turn trauma into warnings and reminders of the importance of working together and protecting each other. A recognition of the inevitable daily tension between violence and peace. Showing up is political community care.

In 2012, I volunteered in the after-school activities organized for children of the neighborhood led by Justa Sánchez—lovingly known as Justi—a Claretian missionary and director of Mama Ú,[18] the cultural center of Uniclaretiana, the university of the Claretian congregation. Young kids would paint glass bottles or write rhymes. Teenagers were working on painting local plants and animals on fabric for the tenth Feria Alternativa Justa y Solidaria, an annual fair that is part of the Semana por la Paz, a yearly celebration in Colombia since 1987. After working with the kids, I used to visit with Claretian missionary Gonzalo de la Torre. One day, he introduced me to Teresa Ochoa Palacios, one of the leaders from La Red Departamental de Mujeres Chocoanas.[19] La Red, a network that includes fifty-two organizations from twenty municipalities in Chocó, had been part of the fair since 1994. COCOMACIA's comisionadas de género had also been part of the planning and organizing committee led by María del Socorro Mosquera Pérez, who crochets mochilas and headbands nonstop for months every year. Members of La Ruta Pacífica have participated through Mama Ú and Justa Sánchez.[20] Even Gloria Uribe, who always allows me to stay at her place in Quibdó since I visited with her brother in 2008, has participated in the fair. The spheres of where I did research and where I socialized, which I had considered independent from each other, had more connections and ramifications than I had thought and envisioned.

In discussing women's place-based politics, Wendy Harcourt and Arturo Escobar use the concept of "meshworks" to describe networks that are "non-hierarchical and self-organizing" and "created out of the interlocking of heterogeneous and diverse elements brought together because of complementary or common experiences."[21] While Chocoan women's networks that make possible planning and participation in marches and events share some of the heterogeneity and non-hierarchical interweaving of meshworks, they are not oppositional to dominant networks, as meshworks tend to be. That said, meshworks that oppose oppressive development discourses are also part of the weaving that make these women's networks glimpses into alternative economic and transformative practices.

The fair's aim is to promote a solidarity economy allowing women's and youth groups, some of them part of the displaced population in Chocó, to showcase art, handicrafts, and even food. With the support of Mama Ú, FUCLA, and

NGOs, groups offer handmade crafts made from local materials and artistic products such as clothing painted with images of heliconias, orchids, drums, and birds; baskets, bags, and accessories of multiple materials and colors circulate through local networks before, during, and after la Feria. Handmade products require an embodied knowledge that is transformative, creating spaces within capitalism to value women's labor that is traditionally exploited and undervalued. The fair and other projects by La Red, such as community banks and funds to support women's small businesses, exist alongside extractive industries such as mining and agribusiness that the national government has promoted in the region as the "locomotive" of the economy. The cost of development has been the exploitation of resources after the convenient forceful displacement of thousands.[22] Spaces in which solidarity is valued, instead of solely profit, requires a consistent effort through daily practices that imagine other ways to live to sustain them. Bureaucracy, politics, and violence exist concurrently with these transformative spaces, illustrating how alternative processes imagine other ways of coexisting. La Red, in its interactions with local organizations, is a solidarity network highlighting traditional practices.

Teresa Ochoa Palacios told me she started working with literacy programs in rural areas. She developed pedagogical materials for adult learning. This is a similar story to one Julio César Uribe, who introduced me to San Francisco de Ichó's Vamos Mujeres, told me. Rosmira Salas, the legal representative of COCOMACIA between 2013 and 2016, also highlighted literacy programs as part of her organizing beginnings. Teaching and learning are political, and they create networks where knowledge is created and shared. Literacy teaching is one of many political strategies, such as community training, that promote knowledge as the basis for organizing. It is linked to the workshops about legislation that protects women's rights and territorial rights, and about productive activities that have promoted transformative politics in the region. The overlapping efforts of local activists reveal a network of community efforts and organizations that work to make information and knowledge available in rural communities. These regional feminist networks create spaces, such as la Feria, or make use of institutionalized celebrations, such as San Pacho, to highlight traditional feminized activities as knowledge.

Solidarity networks that make feminist events possible challenge models of power such as core/periphery.[23] Boundaries that reinforce these power distinctions require that the observer's position remains static and remains in the center, something that is impossible when considering collective practices and changing identities. But margins are not static. They are changing and regularly contested. Conceptualizing space by locating people or spaces at the margins will reinstate the center as unchangeable reality. But there are always multiple centers and multiple peripheries. And sometimes, there are also webs, nodes, gaps, and cracks. A further challenge is that collaborating across marked places, according to arbitrary hierarchies, implies a constant placing and displacing. Within collaboration, power relations remain, but there is not a static center; locations are constantly negotiated.[24] When made visible, such locations are not markers of identity. Their recognition in the process of collaboration is only a confirmation of distance. How to explain, for example, the power of attending an event in the Global South with Global North funding while attempting not to reproduce essentialized identity hierarchies?

Trust cements the public presence of groups of women refusing to stay silent and refusing to stay home. A constant creation of gastronomic, traumatic, performative, and carnivalesque memories is both the output and the starting point of trust building. However, that women have become participants in public events, discussions, and political spaces, and not only inhabitants of private spaces, does not mean that women's vulnerability has diminished. Violence is still a daily occurrence. Showing up does not protect women. Showing up might even make them more visible and vulnerable. Individual decisions to participate require support by networks of care and solidarity that make showing up possible. Communities of care become nodes of action that work as assemblages and express the potential and source of activism in local spaces alongside survival technology: "places and embodiment have by no means ceased to be important—and one must not forget that there are many embodied aspects to activism; activism is not only about sharing information or technology—one needs to think anew about the productive capacity of places and bodies for difference, that is, how difference is mobilized politically."[25]

Regional alliances in Quibdó become visible in the everyday. For San Pacho, and other community events like la Feria, women's organizations work together to support each other. While every group has specific goals and alliances, working as part of regional and national women's organizations strengthens practices of feminist solidarity that transcend local contexts. Showing up requires a sum of collective efforts in the everyday and a commitment to community care that takes different shapes. Care becomes political when it is shared collectively by working toward imagining other ways of living together.

La verdad de las mujeres: Performing Utopian Truth

Local networks are nodes in larger feminist webs. COCOMACIA's comisionadas and members of La Red are part of La Ruta Pacífica. La Ruta won the Premio Nacional de Paz [National Peace Prize] in 2014. This recognition gave visibility to eighteen years of work for a negotiated resolution to Colombia's armed conflict. Awarded during unprecedented peace negotiations in Havana, this prize recognized women's activism and leadership in contemporary politics. Awarded one year after La Ruta's Truth and Memory Commission released its report, this prize has been interpreted as a tribute to victims and survivors who shared their testimonies. Women's vulnerability and their role in rebuilding their lives and communities after trauma are evident when the collective body that is La Ruta insists: "¡Ni guerra que nos mate ni paz que nos oprima!" [Neither war that kills us nor peace that oppresses us!] Decolonial feminist Ochy Curiel has described La Ruta as women who make memory alive and struggle for the demilitarization of their lives and territories: "Las mujeres irrumpen desde el más recóndito rincón para mantener viva la memoria, el olvido nunca le llega a sus vidas y luchan por la desmilitarización de sus territorios y la vida civil porque entienden que NO HAY GUERRA QUE LAS DESTRUYA NI PAZ QUE LES OPRIMA"[26] [women appear from the farthest corner to keep memory alive, forgetfulness never arrives to their lives and they struggle for the demilitarization of their territories and civilian lives because they understand that THERE IS NO WAR THAT KILLS THEM NOR PEACE THAT OPPRESSES THEM].

La Ruta's goal is to demilitarize not only the country but also peace. La Ruta's Truth and Memory Commission's report, based on the testimonials and group work with over 1,000 women, values subjectivity by collecting both the factual and the experiential truths embedded in women's narratives of violence. The commission's documentation is an alternative to the symbolic violence of official narratives; the commission stresses reparations based on giving value to victims' testimonies to reconstruct communities' memories.[27] It materializes the work of local organizations and networks of women struggling for peace, truth, and justice. Not as abstract concepts or institutionalized and legal processes, but as lived realities.

La Ruta's Truth and Memory Commission is an example of postconflict utopias. As a rehearsal of a peace that is not possible yet, the process and outcomes of this commission reveal peace-building as an everyday embodied practice. The process is the product of a collaboration that takes many shapes even if women's class privilege is implicit in the different roles. Without the women who fight daily for the lives and territories threatened by a violence that is not only political, truth telling and peace-building are not possible. Hierarchies are not completely abolished, as the roles of researchers and reports invite conversations different from the public demonstrations. They have different audiences and goals.

Memory for Life maps the research process that started in 2010 from the perspective of the women who participated in the research project in different roles—from interviewing to coding. The narrative starts with questions that exemplify the complexity of this work amid an ongoing armed conflict: "What does a Truth Commission mean for women? Would it not be better to talk of women's Memory in the conflict since a truth commission should be something official, to be carried out later as part of the process of social reconstruction after the end of the armed conflict?"[28] These questions frame the legal and temporal limits of both the officiality of La Ruta's Truth and Memory Commission and the challenge of memorialization within war. The utopian undertaking of an unofficial truth commission is only possible because of the networks of women's organizations that belong to and trust La Ruta. In the epilogue, a quote from one of the research team's coordinators is used as an epigraph: "Violence kills desires. It kills life. A person who does not have wishes does not live."[29] If wishing is living, wishing is political. Collecting women's testimonies while imagining a collective truth illuminates the cracks in the violence.

What does peace without women look like? As the late inclusion of gender and women in the process of negotiation and materialization of the peace accords with the FARC reveals, even peace is patriarchal. In 2018, I found an image from Colombia's High Commissioner for Peace's website explaining that the accords represent Colombia's multiculturalism as a collection of identities represented where people can be only one thing at a time. With the title "¿Quiénes han participado?" [Who has participated?], nine cartoonish figures summarized the participants of the process. Víctimas [victims] were represented by a feminine figure with a side braid, earrings, and distressed clothes. Empresarios [businessmen] were literally masculine, as the gendered word in Spanish, with a figure of a light-skinned bald man with a suit and tie. Indígenas [Indigenous people] were portrayed with a long-haired figure with darker skin than empresarios in what looks like traditional regalia from the Kogui community. Afros, not Afrodescendants or Black communities, were embodied by a figure with short curly hair, dark skin, and a crossbody bag. Mujeres [women] were depicted with white skin and long hair. LGBTI appeared as a long-haired figure with bangs, and a black-and-white pride flag in the background. Académicos [academics] were gendered by the word and a bearded man with glasses and darker skin than the empresario. Campesinos [farmers] were also gendered and represented by a light-skinned man with a mustache, a hat, and what seems to be a ruana [a poncho associated with rural Andean communities] carrying something on his back. The last category was expertos internacionales [international experts], with the figure of a dark-skinned, balding man with glasses wearing a collared shirt and tie and some kind of identification. This visual representation of the national peace process demonstrates the importance of acknowledging women as integral parts of each group, rather than only as victims or women. As anthropologist Kimberly Theidon writes: "Women belong at the peace table because they have a stake in the conflict and thus a stake in its resolution."[30] Showing up is about challenging invisibility with presence, political mobilization, and truths alternative to the official ones that limit identity, participation, and representation.

According to documents available on La Ruta's website,[31] the Women's Truth and Memory Commission reflected a commitment to justice as a goal that started with the design and a process that included women at every step and used feminist approaches to achieve truth and justice. Participatory action research, a community-engaged approach to data collection and analysis that emphasizes collaborative action, informed the process that took place in nine regions and was led by nine different groups. In each team, there was a regional coordinator, two interviewers, and one encoder. The result was the collection and coding of 932 testimonies from women between the ages of seventeen and eighty-three. Forty-seven percent of the participants identified as mestizas, 26 percent as Black, 6 percent as Indigenous, and 21 percent as other. The creation and training included workshops to streamline the process and the data collection through interviews. Some of the questions were: What happened? Who was the victim? What was her story? Who was responsible? What impact did that have on your life? What happened next? What did you do to face the facts? Why do you think it happened? What were the responses of the state? What to do to avoid the repetition of the facts?[32] As a result, the report includes nine collective cases to summarize the testimonies, presenting facts, impacts, coping and resistance strategies, causality, state response, prevention, and reparations.

Feminist objectivity was the goal of La Ruta's commission. Testimonies' collection reconstructed facts by considering women reliable narrators. A script was used to ease the interaction between interviewers and interviewees, but even if testimonies are coded after being collected, the process values women's knowledge and memories as sources of information and brainstorming about prevention and reparation of violence. Beyond the traumatic event, telling a truth that includes discussion of coping mechanisms highlights the responsibility of the perpetrators and the state, and it reports on the impacts of trauma. This truth exemplifies what believing women and including them in conversations about peace can look like. Commitment to truth telling as nuanced and complex collective storytelling results in three written documents in Spanish and one in English.

In La Ruta's Truth and Memory Commission report *La verdad de las mujeres* [Women's Truth], peace and justice appear utopian, as road maps for the end of violence. Truth telling centers women's narratives. The participants are all women, and more than a third belong to women's organizations[33] manifesting the importance of solidarity and organizing. Feminist truth telling is both an alternative to patriarchal narratives and a pacifist tactic to disrupt the peace/war dichotomy. It not only reveals violence as a continuum but also imagines peace as an outcome. Truth telling is also transnational, as it uses models from other conflicts and imagines a global audience for the reports. Truth is humanitarian and exceeds humanitarianism with a commitment to outcomes that redistribute resources through reparations. Narratives that center women's experience enact different kinds of justice. The report might never materialize the reparations it supports, but it dismantles a patriarchal justice system that is punitive and reproduces violence.

So why is justice utopian? The impossibility of guaranteeing an outcome that benefits victims makes the tension between the creation of the Truth and Memory Commission and its outcomes merely symbolic. In a context where social leaders are still being threatened and assassinated, truth is complicated, dangerous, and incomplete. As a durational performance, peace demands extended collective rehearsals, endurance, and repetition, but its vulnerability to failure remains. Justice is materialized in the process and dissemination. The testimonies collected do not reveal a truth that cannot be accessed through other genres, but they are glimpses of the embodied and affective character of memory. In *La verdad de las mujeres*, references to coping take the shape of dance, and affect beyond individual feelings, crying, and weeping when collecting testimonies abounds. Truth and justice are incomplete. Guilt, silences, and ideas for what they could look like include reparations as part of multivocal self-reflective reports.

La verdad de las mujeres as a concept, a process, and a report is a fragmented embodied process, a postconflict utopia. It strengthens solidarity among women and solidifies the networks that La Ruta makes possible through marches and other events. It is not a conclusion, and it does not prevent repetition of what it denounces. What makes the initiative meaningful is a commitment to truth. La verdad de las mujeres acts as if truth telling were possible. As if women's voices and knowledge were enough to denounce violence. An additional step makes information from the reports available for a wider audience. Dissemination takes different shapes, including 1000 Voces, a website and a collection of thirty-four audio clips that were shared between September 2017 and April 2018 as "un ejercicio de memoria y reparación"[34] [an exercise of memory and reparation]. The clips are excerpts from the testimonies collected, and they create the possibilities of reaching a wider audience, and while they are still available, the project's website is no longer active—which, once more, confirms digital collections' vulnerability to disappearance when there is not a plan or infrastructure for preservation.

As the pressure of women's organizations helped create a gender commission in the negotiations taking place in Havana, La Ruta's commission enacted a symbolic pressure that imagined the materialization of an official truth and reconciliation centering women and including multiple agents of violence even before peace negotiations with the FARC started. From the beginning, this process denounced the lack of women's inclusion in official peace-building efforts, while creating an alternative feminist peace-building. Dreaming about peace is a durational performance as much as activism. As a process that takes place over an extended period, peace-building relies on a community (or many communities) and requires improvisation, repetition, and endurance, as failure is an endless threat. Peace is not guaranteed or likely. For those who strive for it daily, peace embodies im/possibility: it is both achievable and elusive. As an idea that has yet to be realized, it requires both a belief in its ultimate possibility and an acceptance of its current nonexistence.

Transnational Alliances: Women in Black

Over 300 women from Belgium, Bosnia-Herzegovina, the Democratic Republic of Congo, Ecuador, Spain, the United States, the United Kingdom, Honduras, India, Israel, Italy, Mexico, Palestine, Perú, Serbia, Tunisia, Uruguay, and Colombia met August 15–20, 2011, in Bogotá, Colombia. I found out about the event two weeks beforehand when I started to volunteer as translator. I wanted to learn more about the women's movement in Colombia and its connections to global networks. While talking to the comisionadas in Quibdó, I found out that Ana Rosa Heredia Cuesta and a group of Chocoan women associated with La Ruta and La Red were attending the event. With the slogan "No a la guerra y a las violencias contra las mujeres" [No to war and violence against women], the XV Encuentro Internacional de Mujeres de Negro [fifteenth Encounter of the International Network of Women in Black] took place in downtown Bogotá. The first day of the event in Bogotá, held at the Centro Cultural Gabriel García Márquez in the historical center, I saw that most of the women had traveled for hours by bus to attend. Only a minority of Colombian women were from Bogotá.

In translating documents for the international women before the event, I learned about the chronology of Women in Black and its connection to La Ruta. Women in Black International Network was founded as a group of antimilitarist feminist women in 1994. In Jerusalem, Palestinian and Israeli women wearing black carried signs against the occupation since 1998, creating two of the main elements associated with the movement: silence and wearing black. In 1992, the first encounter of Women in Black was organized. In 2000 and within the context of the alliance between La Ruta Pacífica and the Organización Femenina Popular de Barrancabermeja [Barrancabermeja's Popular Feminine Organization], Women in Black in Colombia and the National Movement of Women from Colombia against War were born.

I learned of the expectations for participation and, especially, about the event's logistics by translating the guión simbólico [symbolic script]. The objects selected and described in the script were carefully displayed as planned in the Centro Cultural Gabriel García Márquez's auditorium: a fishnet decorated with colored origami butterflies surrounded by candles, flowers, banners with slogans of Women in Black (WiB), La Ruta, and the Encounter, and handmade dolls and necklaces. Although the candles, which were to create a fire to surround the fishnet, were lit only briefly because of the venue's fire code, most of the national and international women (following the categories created for the event) brought dolls, seeds, and even soil to contribute to the symbolic staging. The organizers (mainly women from La Ruta based in Bogotá) chose colors to represent important concepts for the movement: black (for WiB network), white (for justice), yellow (for truth), blue (for reparation), orange (for peaceful resistance), green (for hope), and purple (for feminism). Other symbols had a double purpose: as decoration for the venue and the collective mobilization with mothers of the so-called false positives (a euphemism to refer to state killings of young men falsely identified as guerrilla members), victims, and members of WiB on the last day (see Figures 5.2 and 5.3). The briefly lit candles represented the number of delegations with the colors associated with each continent. They were placed on paper plates with water surrounding the fishnet where pinwheels were placed. Women from different places in the world and Colombia brought handfuls of soil that were also placed around the fishnet, representing their territories. The four elements represented the movement as coalition across difference.

Four fairies performed as mimes during the encounter. They were completely silent during the duration of the event, referencing the silence of the traditional WiB's weekly vigils. Each fairy represented one of the four continents present in the encuentro: Africa (wearing orange), Asia (yellow), America (green)—thought of hemispherically as is common in Latin America—and Europe (blue). Although the initial script was stereotypically specific about the race of every woman representing a continent, to highlight the attendees' ethnic diversity, all but one of the fairies were young Colombian white/mestizas. Most participants from every country wore black. Some dressed in official black T-shirts with the slogan "Cuerpos y territorios sin guerras ni violencias" [Bodies and territories without wars or violence]. Others wore insignia from their own organizations and networks. It was suggested that every woman wear a bandanna or a flag of the same color worn by her continent's fairy. Many, especially those from the international delegations, ended up wearing hand-painted clothing and local artisanal jewelry. Colombian women sold these crafts outside the auditorium and during the breaks to fund their present or future trips. These transactions were reminders of economic hierarchies and the layers of participants' experiences and resources to fund and participate in the encuentro. We all show up, but we show up in different ways.

To promote collaboration, La Ruta encouraged attendees to write and draw on the huge butterfly wings that one of its members would wear during the last day's demonstration (Figure 5.2). Members of the Colombian delegation wrote most of the messages on the wings, revealing the spectrum of motivations, demands, and reasons to show up. "No al secuestro" [no to kidnapping], "no al feminicidio" [no to femicides], "participación = autonomía" [participation = autonomy], "equidad" [equity], "justicia" [justice], and "Saquen mi cuerpo de la guerra," [take my body out of war]. Images of women and family members who have been assassinated were next to anonymous messages with no identifying information about where events took place. A hand-stitched message read "mataron a mi hijo y a mi sobrino y nos desplazaron" [they killed my son and my nephew and displaced us]. Millions of Colombian women could have written it. Another read: "Todo lo tenía. Una casa, un río, comida y vivía tranquila. Hoy me siento triste. Me duele el alma" [I had everything. A home, a river, food, and I lived calmly. Today I feel sad. My soul hurts]. The bottom of the wings read "Ruta Bogotá," grounding these traumatic memories in the place of encuentro. As an embodied archive of mourning, these wings were worn by many during the march, and they appear in almost all the pictures I took that day.

In addition to the orange dolls made with pins and strips of wool to represent women's bodies, described as muñecas de resistencia pacífica [peaceful resistance dolls], Colombia's delegations also created purple necklaces with bags made of veil to hold local seeds representing women's territories. In the opening ceremony, women from Colombia's regional delegations gave one of the resistance dolls to every participant as an amulet of protection. "Para que me la cuide" [so it takes care of you], a woman told me while putting one around my neck. Every participant also received another necklace with seeds. The same woman that put the necklace on me asked me to plant them as soon as I went home. I never did. While I failed in materializing the request of planting the seeds, what seemed arbitrary requests from the organizers for every delegation took shape and helped build a community for the five days of the event. The care politics surfaced as a practice of solidarity and reciprocity. Care for each other

Figure 5.2. On the last day of the encuentro, one of the members of La Ruta Bogotá/WiB Colombia wears body paint and butterfly wings with signs against violence and militarization. Bogotá, 2011.

enabled the potentiality of finding common ground to keep everyone working together. Caretaking became a political strategy to promote endurance and a connection that fed belonging.

Each international delegation, by country, brought banners, videos, songs, and presentations with testimonies of women on the effects of militarization on their lives, territories, and bodies. Chocoan women, for example, sang alabaos [mourning songs] to remember the victims of massacres, deceased family members, and ancestors. Every national and regional delegation also brought letters to share their personal stories with other women who have been struggling against war and militarization. They also brought pictures and videos to share their battles and actions as WiB in their specific countries. Anti-war signs and banners with anti-militarization were present, with messages such as "¡No a la guerra, a los guerreros, a la militarización y a las armas!" [No to war, warriors, militarization and weapons!]. A myriad of colorful peace symbols and anti-weapons symbols from Red de Mujeres de Negro in Colombia (including La Ruta Pacífica) were visible in the auditorium, and especially during the last day's mobilization (Figure 5.3). Four hundred women participated in the event, according to La Ruta. Cameras from national and international TV news and networks (RCN, CM&, Telesur, and Cablenoticias) and political leaders such as former senator Piedad Córdoba (which explained the media coverage in the first place) completed the staging of the event. Denunciations of women's rights violations and memorialization of victims and disappeared tested the borders of the private-public divide constantly.

When I was translating the instructions for international delegations, I imagined every symbol, object, and request as an extra hassle for stressed women dealing with domestic logistics while packing to attend. But by the first day of the encounter, in a packed auditorium, I realized every little detail contributed to the creation of a sacred space filled with rituals that made communication possible, even without the help of simultaneous interpreters. Prayers, songs, and storytelling invoked hugs and shared tears that created a temporary community, reminding everyone why they do what they do. Even this description of the universality of the community created is inspired by the energy surrounding women's participation. Every intervention, particularly those of countries' delegations, proved to be a puzzle whose completion illustrated the extent of the solidarity and community the WiB network created. WiB London, for instance, created a video not only presenting their group's vigils and projects, but also explaining that the reason why only two delegates were present in Bogotá was because other members decided to donate their money to fund the participation of some of La Ruta's members.

Figure 5.3. Quilts with memories, slogans, and images from delegations from different provinces (Cauca and Nariño) were carried by demonstrators on the encuentro's last day. Bogotá, 2011.

Academic talks were not as well attended as workshops. Breakout sessions had the additional obstacle of not having simultaneous interpretation. But in every session in which personal stories of violence were told, even when the translation came through the whispers of a volunteer like me, hugs and body language became the way to communicate sympathy and solidarity. Translation created places of contact with malleable boundaries, where listening does not guarantee understanding. The eagerness to communicate made the transfer of knowledge possible: from misconstrued fragments to embodied bonding. My role as translator/interpreter was a reminder that writing is also translation and repertoire and that navigating different frames of reference will always alter what we are trying to explain.

"You are not alone," "we are not alone" became mantras of survival. The last day of mobilization included marching, singing, hair braiding, face painting, drumming, hand-holding, and chanting. Physical contact and the vulnerability of marching and protesting in Bogotá's historical downtown strengthened relationships as the practice of care was actualized. The five-day encuentro was a durational performance, an experiment in community-building, a rehearsal of survival. Everyday activities work as place of encounters, and spaces for community-building. Becoming Women in Black was possible through the collective relationships among members and their audience during their vigils.[35]

The last day, during the march, interaction with passersby included indifference, curious staring, and short conversations reflecting a mix of solidarity, mostly coming from young people; and prejudice, voiced specifically by older men who suggested that women should look to their families if they wanted to feel safer. This experience mimics what Tova Benski[36] found in her participant observation of the Haifa vigil of WiB Israel, where, weekly, rage was directed at the women participating in the silent vigil. What stood out, after hours of standing and walking together, as a group of over 100 protesters, was the weaving of memories invoked and atrocities denounced from all over the world. Global networks were visible, and solidarity seemed more than an abstract ideal. Yet, as is the case with the quilts from different organizations that are displayed and carried around during marches, networks are an uneven mixture of individual fragments that are only integrated by intentional design to reach a common goal.[37]

The encounter differed from the silent vigils associated with the movement's original gathering of women protesting the Israeli occupation of Palestine. As every delegation has adapted the objectives and symbols of WiB's peaceful resistance to war to the specificities of the violence at hand, their performances differed. European groups, such as WiB Belgrade, founded in 1991, seemed to have repeated the self-imposed silence and minimalism for which the movement has been famous, while groups in Latin America have created more public theatrical performances informed by Latin American social protest and exemplified by La Ruta's symbolic feminism. Experiences, routines, and actions developed in different spaces became usual narratives during the encuentro, showing that there is no constant communication among delegations. Every group develops different strategies, projects, alliances, and causes derived from the specific contexts they inhabit. The encuentro seemed to spark interest and collaboration in a collective process of teaching and learning. Staging and performance of different groups also revealed different ways in which the anti-militarization activism of WiB public constructs feminism.

The encounter's embodied character can be seen in the messages that were worn and carried by the participants. Some T-shirts read: "mi cuerpo primer territorio de paz" [my body, first territory of peace], which was also a multicolored quilt with a piece of fabric per letter. "¡Qué vergüenza la guerra!" [War, what a shame!] read another. As in Quibdó, women participating in the event used their bodies to bring their messages wherever they went. Signs, part of the vigil, scaled up the impact of the messages in downtown Bogotá. A sign held by one of the mimes read: "oposición a la militarización de la seguridad nacional e internacional" [against the militarization of national and international security]. Another read: "Parar la guerra es un asunto / tuyo, mío, / nuestro. / ¡Negociación ya!" [Stopping war is my, your, our business. Negotiation now!] These embodied archives are temporary. While women wore these messages constantly during the encounter, they relied on the power of presence to be communicated. In the march, multilingual banners became alive with chanting (see Figure 5.4). Showing up is essential to fully experience the messages.

During the last day in Bogotá, delegations offered to organize the sixteenth encuentro. India and Uruguay were the strongest contenders. After public deliberations, Uruguay became the host for encuentro 2013, as distance was one determining factor for attendees. Colombian women promised to attend. Delegations from the Global North mentioned the option of donating what one delegate would spend to fly from their countries to fund the trip for multiple women from Colombia, as WiB London's delegates had done this time. Women from rural areas in Colombia started talking about renting buses to go to Montevideo two years later. The role of promise was not as utilitarian as it tends to be in traditional political campaigns: promising to do something in exchange for votes or power. Here, instead, women exchanged promises to imagine seeing each other again. For some attendees of Bogotá's encuentro, intention materialized two years later. But the Colombian delegation in Montevideo consisted

Figure 5.4. Banners from the international delegations. Bogotá, 2011.

of only three women; the absences intertwined with memories of hundreds of Indigenous and Black women who wanted to attend the encuentro but did not have the resources to do so. This act of promising embodies postconflict utopias as an act of survival. It is an optimistic act that suggests a hopeful future where everyone can see each other again, even though the reality was that many were not able to go.

Economic privilege and institutional support were evident determinants of participation, as only Marina Gallego, the director of La Ruta; Roseli Fiscue Chavaco, Indigenous leader from Mujeres Indígenas del CRIC, Consejo Regional Indígena del Cauca [Indigenous Women from the Regional Indigenous Council of Cauca]; and Teresita Gómez Murillo, leader from La Red Antioquia, were able to attend the sixteenth encuentro in Montevideo. By the end of the first day, I was also considered part of the Colombian delegation. That I was able to travel to Montevideo to attend the encuentro, while thousands of women who are active members of La Red and La Ruta, including COCOMACIA's comisionadas, could not, made visible our placements in global hierarchies. As a graduate student in the Global North with a yearly stipend of less than $20,000 in exchange for my labor—which was not a lot in California—I was more financially stable than any of my collaborators in Chocó, and most members of La Ruta and La Red. Who has access (or not) to these encuentros exemplifies Chicana studies scholar Maylei Blackwell's claim: "The political project of feminism in Latin America and the Caribbean has long grappled with the challenge of 'inclusion' and, conversely, its practices of exclusion based on class, sexuality, and race."[38]

Non-Spanish-speaking participants quickly adopted me as their personal interpreter when simultaneous interpretation was not available, as had been the case in Bogotá. My knowledge of English as a second language, which marked me in the United States as a first-generation immigrant, here was a mark of privilege among other Latin American women. Not only did women benefit from my being there, but everyone made sure to make me feel included and part of the WiB sisterhood. Delegates from WiB Baltimore gave me clothes and shoes, as my suitcase had been lost. Delegates from Palestine and Israel walked me to the hotel one night, as I was not staying with the rest of the delegations. I benefited from the networks of solidarity and care. And through this exchange of an endless chain of favors, I became part of a global feminist network of reciprocity in which showing up is not guaranteed.

In Montevideo, feminism took a different shape. Staša Zajović from WiB Belgrade refused to speak next to a Serbian flag in the opening ceremony of the encounter, held in Montevideo's City Hall. Zajović's rejection of national symbols as representation for Serbian women invokes the power of disobedience and anarchy to counteract sexism, patriarchy, and militarism. For her, the antidote for war is a constant radical autonomy from the state, the church, and the government. "Cuando los nuestros llegan al poder, no son nuestros" [When our people achieve power, they are not ours anymore], said Zajović, rejecting the usefulness of traditional institutions for advancing the networks' beliefs or representing women's interests. "Los únicos héroes son los desertores de guerra" [The only heroes are war deserters], she continued, exemplifying an explicit rejection of war and her participation in the Network of Conscientious Objectors and Anti-militarism in Serbia. Staša Zajović's intervention does not exclusively represent the WiB movement. Her antiwar and antinationalist views intersect with other delegations' approaches to feminism and exemplify WiB's alliances and commonalities with other causes and organizations as much as the heterogeneity of these networks' ideologies. Most important, Zajović's words reflect the transnational alliances that make it possible to reject national and ethnic identities that support political polarization and military confrontations. In turn, what Zajović and others propose as WiB members suggests an ethics of care as a political option that creates solidarity with and among victims of violence as a resistance to national discourses.

The antinationalist and antifascist feminism of WiB Serbia[39] echoes in other delegations that use the shared identity of womanhood to make visible the disproportionate violence against women. While the encuentros create opportunities for dialogue and community-building, WiB's network structure makes the multiplicity of discourses possible, while uncertainty about membership is the norm: "It's impossible to make an accurate census of 'membership' because groups come and go, not all of them record their existence on the website, and we do not know how many women are involved in each."[40] The impossibility and the not knowing associated with WiB make showing up more uncertain—and more powerful.

"There is a war against women, even when there is no war" was the message different delegations repeated, denouncing different types of violence haunting women globally, along with femicides and sexual violence in war zones. Violence takes the form of poverty, illiteracy, lack of agency, and an economic crisis that is nothing more than a social war against women. WiB Uruguay's focus on domestic violence reminded us that peace is nothing more than a permanent state of pre-war in which women experience the violence of patriarchy that limits their access to education and employment. Delegations dealing with the militarization of women's daily lives, such as that of Colombia, emphasized how military structures are accomplices in keeping women down by bolstering traditional gender roles and justifying the use of violence. Some delegations and participants thought domestic violence or political violence was the most urgent issue, depending on their personal and collective experiences.

Networks of affect and tenderness were created in Bogotá that were reactivated in Montevideo. As a product of a learning experience from women from the Balkans, Palestine, Colombia, and Italy, the reencounter in Montevideo reinforced the importance of talking, looking, listening, and touching as part of an embodied practice of resistance. The encuentro's conversations challenged the mainstream approach to gender-based violence as a domestic or private affair, paying attention to the internalization of military ideas and the militarization of women's lives and consciousness. Stories of survival and resistance, such as that of Nora Cortiñas, one of the Madres de la Plaza de Mayo, exemplified the blurriness between the personal and the political. Performative visual acts, such as a flash mob organized by the youngest members of WiB and Chile's delegation call center to get information about autonomous abortion after it was made illegal, as part of "Lesbianas y feministas por el derecho a la información" [Lesbians and feminists for the right to information], highlighted the importance of direct action. The worlds of possibility the WiB network created during the encounter challenged the grammar of the core-periphery by showing that nodes of action burst and crumble organically all the time. The exchange of stories and experiences of distant actions reanimates the networks, contacts, and energy, sustaining the global network.

The minimalistic and silent character of WiB in Montevideo was in stark contrast to the theatricality of the Bogotá encuentro. This highlighted the fleeting and unrepeatable nature of activism as performance. Although the local and regional groups may share some beliefs with global networks, each gathering, protest, and encuentro is uniquely crafted through action. In the present, by showing up. The heterogeneity of this global movement expresses how every event is situated. Local groups use and develop their own activist tools to resist militarization in response to their unique circumstances. The practice of getting together and telling personal stories makes survival possible when others have survived, and we might, too.

And yet disenchantment, dispossession, and displacement haunt every conversation. Stories about activist actions against war meant retelling traumatic experiences that are not interchangeable and can be only partially compared or understood, as time and interest dwindle. Difference and misunderstanding taint everyday interactions as panels and breaks fragment discussions about personal lives and national contexts. Confusion can be at the core of understanding, taking care, and living with each other, especially in a multilingual community where not everyone is bilingual. But misconceptions, partial truths, and misidentifications exist beside learning, compassion, and solidarity that women create when naming violence and finding ways to interpellate each other. Affinity, rather than identity, is what creates a safe space in which alienation becomes belonging, even when discussing trauma, militarization, and alternatives to the artificial discourse of reconciliation. Testimonies and quotes from official reports are part of the program, but most of the panels include personal narratives about struggling and overcoming violence. The impossibility of peace felt during the encuentros coexists with the urgency of stopping war. Postconflict utopias become global when mapping the transnational links of militarization and antimilitarist efforts such as WiB.

When WiB members are together, difference does not disappear, and it might even be accentuated in what seems a large, mismatched intercultural and intergenerational group of women from different races—even though Black and Indigenous women were underrepresented—sexualities, and political ideologies. Identity categories are displaced, interrupted, and reinvented by a more prominent category: feminist women, even if feminism is something different for every woman. A community of women around issues of violence requires constant effort. The archive of suffering blends with archives and repertoires of creativity as political practice. The archive of atrocities includes official narratives where reparations and justice can only be dreamed about. In contrast, alternative archives—worn and chanted—communicate wishful thinking by demanding rights and justice. Imagination is at the core of WiB's community, as the movement's existence depends on envisioning spaces of connection that are created in the doing. As postconflict utopias, these feminist networks imagine peace one day at a time.

By weaving together the subjective and the objective, pain, politics, and poetry can dialogue with deeper layers of knowledge about military budgets, humanitarian aid, and postconflict peace-building. Corinne Kumar, from WiB India and the World Court of Women Against War and For Peace, stated that imagination is the only way to create new universalism and new ethics as the basis for creating other concepts of justice, summarizing some of what WiB does. For Kumar, it is fundamental that the movement create notions that challenge traditional understandings of justice that are not associated with punishment and violence. The political is reinvented by infusing it with engaged ethics, counteracting contemporary politics where women are collateral damage. Inspired by social movements of the Global South, WiB has embraced the power of the powerless and collaborative practices challenging official and national discourses to stand with women in contexts of war and victimization. For Corinne Kumar, the scientific way is one way to know, but not the only one. Asking how we know what we know, WiB values women's intuition, voices, and practices as useful knowledge to create new definitions of justice. All this is possible when women decide to care for themselves and for each other in the absence of guarantees for their survival. With the conviction that dreaming is a step in peace-building, they rehearse care politics. Together. One day at a time.

Compassion and reason exist side by side in WiB, by supporting a rebellion of subjugated forms of knowledge that denounce militarization and promote women's empowerment. An ethical understanding of care is part of this formula for creating informed collectives of women challenging dominant knowledge and wisdom that support military interventions in the name of security. Extravagant actions that interrupt the military routines that are part of daily life create spaces for a new political imagination. This is not exclusive to WiB—not only because there is an overlap of membership of different local, regional, and global networks, but also because, for a lot of people, surviving is not possible without networks of support and caretaking that fill in the gaps of lacking public resources.

Showing Up as a Transnational Feminist Practice

WiB creates new cultural narratives and a new radical imaginary that return the ethical to the political by questioning ideas about security and the militarization of feminism. This creates distrust about the unanimous approval of the United Nations Security Council Resolution 1325 in 2000 on women, peace, and security. While feminist groups use official documents like this to educate the public about the impact of armed conflict in women's lives, this resolution's material effects are unknown. Another postconflict utopia. In contrast, horizontality is seen as a strategy to change the world when military spending increases supported by politics do not represent women's interests. Utopia, as a projection of what security could be, is part of WiB. By recognizing unknowability and vulnerability as things we all share, WiB creates empowering strategies based on women's ability to revolt and to create forms of kinship that are not explicitly related to blood, class, or race. How is it possible to get there? What resources and creativity make WiB's kinship possible? WiB is a rehearsal of a community created by women's desire to defend their own communities.

With signing delegations from Argentina, Belgium, Chile, Colombia, Congo, Spain, the United States, Guatemala, India, Israel, Italy, Palestine, Serbia, the United Kingdom, and Uruguay, WiB circulated a resolution in September 2013, following the sixteenth encuentro in Montevideo. By reaffirming WiB's existence as an international movement of feminists against different forms of women's oppression, WiB rejected armed conflicts and preemptive and humanitarian wars. The resolution called for, among other things, the abolition of United Nations peacekeepers' immunity because of their involvement in violence against civilians in Congo, Bosnia, and Haiti; the approval of Boycott, Divestment and Sanctions (BDS) against Israel; and support for Colombia's peace negotiations in Havana. This resolution also included requests about justice in militarized and postconflict contexts, revealing the scope of WiB's dreaming as political practice. The symbolic power of a collectively written document is to strengthen the feminist networks that are visible only as groups sharing a name (Women in Black/Mujeres de negro) until they convene in an encuentro.

Showing up takes different shapes. I saw two simultaneous discourses identifiable in women's participation in activist organizations and networks against war. One is a strategic approach that is not threatening to the established order and that benefits from collaborations in which representations of motherhood and femininity, including women as caretakers, are possible. We see this in the Madres de Plaza de Mayo. I also saw a combative feminist discourse that understands that women's marginalization from political and economic positions is not an accident and needs to be remedied with education and social mobilization. Many other ways to show up exist that do not even require identification as a feminist.

As part of the WiB network, local and regional feminist networks challenge traditional ways of seeing and treating others, particularly women as contributors to politics, peace-building, and reconciliation. This utopian political practice of dreaming of a new order fuels WiB members' activism. Dreams become political, as do questions of affect, friendship, and solidarity. WiB, like other women's networks, creates the conditions of possibility for listening and telling stories as a political practice that transforms vulnerability into activism. The spaces of interaction created by showing up to meetings, marches, or encuentros perform safety outside of militarization and value a feminist knowledge production that rests on collaboration and trust. These networks of solidarity might not be visible after public actions, but documentation makes it possible to build on previous participants' knowledge. Shared accountability through symbols and memories has created movements that mobilize women and highlight their political participation. The vulnerability of women denouncing violence in public reveals the limits of these actions, while providing support for women's narratives and experiences.

Different languages, levels of education, countries, ideologies, challenges, sexualities, and ethnicities stand out in the interactions of La Ruta, La Red, and WiB. What stays with me is the solidarity and the willingness to create a shared history and a shared project, a performance of belonging and inclusion as a response to a militarized world that excludes women. Even if this community is temporary, what remains is the dream of women as a collectivity that embodies the change we would like our political reality to reflect. In the WiB encounters—and the logistics and organizing that precede and materialize them—showing up makes transnational alliances possible, a "space for action and imagination."[41]

Different layers of activism and personhood are present during WiB encounters. Resilience, disagreements, conflicts, exhaustion, excitement, rage, pessimism, hope, and even boredom weigh on activists during and after events, which is a reminder of the limits of bodies and the contingency of activism that make every gathering unpredictable. Access to spaces and networks is not a given, not only because of the resources and energy needed to make everything happen, but because of the difficulties of staying in touch over long distance. WiB embodies the contradictions of collective imagination against war. As a movement, WiB is contingent on showing up. And, as we have explored before, transnational feminist movements are possible only because of the everyday labor of local organizations committed to political goals, ranging from survival to peacemaking. Whereas self-identifying as a feminist is not a requirement for participation in any organization or network discussed in this chapter, showing up exemplifies the process of imagining what feminism and solidarity look like. Not as ideologies, but as everyday practices.

CHAPTER 6

Everyday Utopias

Ethics and Care as Peacemaking

> Es muy grato poder estar acá, poder uno desplazarse a las comunidades, llevarles alguna capacitación, llevarles algún mensaje ... le lleva uno como un voto de esperanza a las personas cuando están por ejemplo en un momento de decepción, o desesperanza o angustia. Siempre la COCOMACIA ha estado allí presente.
>
> It is wonderful to be able to visit communities, to bring a workshop, a message. . . It brings a sign of hope when people are facing a moment of disappointment, hopelessness or anguish. COCOMACIA has always been present.
> —Banessa Rivas López

On our way back from Tanguí in our crowded boat, where boxes and bags of food were replaced by people wanting to return to Quibdó, two men in a speedboat instructed us to stop. I did not see them at first, as the boat they were on was on the opposite bank of the Atrato River. When I finally did, I could not help but notice the weapons and camouflage blurring any possibility of even attempting to identify them. The boatman slowed down, and as we approached the armed men, he revealed that he did not have the documents to drive. The comisionadas knew that one passenger worked as a boatman. They asked him if he had his license and instructed him to fake a headache to explain why he was not the one driving. He did not hesitate. When we stopped, the armed men identified themselves as being from the Navy and asked about the documents. The licensed boatman volunteered his documents. While one man wrote down the information, the other asked us some questions and gave us a stack of flyers, in case we knew anyone who might be interested in the information they contained, he said. I took one. It read: "Guerrilleros y guerrilleras de las FARC: Colombia está lista para recibirlos" [FARC guerrilla members: Colombia is ready to welcome you]. Directed at guerrilla members to promote their demobilization, this encounter was a confirmation that it is unnecessary to take sides to be perceived as a threat. As a group, we were suspect.

Unlike me, what the comisionadas noticed first was the picture on the back of the flyer: men working, surrounded by plants. "Estos no son plátanos" [These are not plantains], Rubiela Cuesta Córdoba said. "Éstas son las palmas de Uribe" [These are Uribe's palm trees], she said more loudly. "Did you know that these palm trees are responsible for the displacement of thousands?" she asked the men. The men looked very young, but they had rifles. They said nothing and seemed puzzled by this woman who dared question them with their very visible weapons. Cuesta Córdoba mentioned just minutes before that people get killed for anything here. Now she was the one asking the questions and directing her complaints at the men in camouflage. The rest of the comisionadas also looked at the picture and made comments about massacres and about the paramilitaries' alliances with the military. The men ignored the comments and questions, returned the driver's documents, asked some questions about the trip, and let us go. I could not say anything until we were far from their boat. I was terrified, even though encounters with the military are common in Colombia. When the comisionadas asked me what I thought, I just said I wondered if we looked like guerrilla fighters or their friends. Rubiela Cuesta Córdoba took all the flyers, except mine, and threw them in the river.

I wish it were possible to classify this kind of encounter with armed men as an "event." But in a militarized country, these random encounters are part of everyday life. So is Rubiela Cuesta Córdoba's determination, a trait that is not only hers. She tells us that her approach to life is that it is better to die fighting than to live on your knees. The other comisionadas have said similar things reflecting on their own daily commitment to speak their mind about war, even in the presence of armed actors, and about gender, even in the presence of misogynist men. It is not only courage. It is knowledge. And, just in case, they wear green vests and hats with COCOMACIA's logos and slogans. "Opción por la vida" [Choice for life] read the comisionadas' vests (Figure 6.1). After the experience traveling back from Tanguí, thinking about life as a choice seems more difficult and meaningful than before.

Life is not compatible with extractive capitalism and its pollution. Violence can take the shape of palms: "Though its expressions are subtle and often taken-for-granted, violence constantly marks women's material, symbolic and affective relationship with oil palm."[1] Knowledge about the multiple forms of

Figure 6.1 Ana Rosa Heredia Cuesta (right) wearing a vest from COCOMACIA. Tanguí, 2013.

violence threatening life every day is the impulse behind Cuesta Córdoba's reaction to the encounter and the flyers' use of oil palms as an incentive to guerrilla demobilization. Although the cultivation of oil palm preceded Álvaro Uribe's administration (2002–2010), Cuesta Córdoba's association of oil palm and Uribe's violence is not random, as oil palm monocultures were presented as a "counterterrorism measure."[2] Monocultures threaten everything COCOMACIA, the comisionadas, and Black communities in the Colombian Pacific fight for: "Law 70 of 1993 called for the protection of biodiversity and Afro-Colombian culture and communities in this region. The establishment of monocultures of any type is a clear violation of this legislation."[3] Everyday encounters are entangled with the day-to-day ethical negotiations needed for survival, as well as with the social movements that guide the collective principles that make life a possibility.

This chapter is a glimpse into the everyday. Not only into the everyday as a concept, but into the Comisión's daily activities—the everyday with all its tensions and power dynamics and day-to-day survival practices. I am interested in the mix of hope and despair that seems to invade daily existence and somehow translates into the commitments that sometimes spark social movements and social change. This chapter revolves around the apparently trivial details of everyday life that get lost when thinking only about historical events that cause large-scale transformations. I center and value the daily energy released in spaces otherwise deemed marginal or peripheral. It is an experiment in paying attention and looking more closely to find value in the banal and ordinary. Building on the concept of showing up, everyday practices are a fragment of the spectrum of postconflict utopias, rehearsals of peace amid violence.

I argue that looking more closely at everyday practices unveils the value of embodied knowledge and daily rehearsals of what a postconflict could be. To do so, I will start with a section that explores the everyday as a scenario of actions that might seem mundane but reveal the political and performative potential of everyday politics. The second section reveals the ethics and affect of the comisionadas' politics of living. Their everyday practices reflect daily engagement, proving that survival is a constant process, a performative one. Finally, the third section addresses survival and failure by exploring the tensions between moving on and giving up that the comisionadas face daily in a context of multiple forms of violence.

The everyday has a life of its own, even if it seems not to be of specific interest for any disciplinary field. There is always something happening in the everyday, so even if it seems the opposite of history, "a historicity that is embodied, shared and ever-changing (repetition does not have to be stale)"[4] shapes every day. Even if the everyday gets obscured in the description of historical events, paying attention to the political potential of the everyday allows us to see what history does not. Feminists have noticed the potentiality of the everyday as a stage for political intervention.[5] Even the repetition associated with the routine of the domestic everyday does not guarantee the duplication of an outcome. The everyday might reveal the constant release of energy that creates commitment to social change. As María Lugones and Rita Segato remind us, change is unavoidable: "With Segato I think that people's customs 'are transformed constantly since a people's permanence depends neither on the repetition of their practices nor on the immobility of their ideas.'"[6] The everyday is change, and in the motion of daily life rests the potential for a new world.

Leaving aside large-scale concepts and issues such as social movements, resistance, and human rights, especially when studying postconflict contexts, creates a promise of togetherness and collective transformation that does not rely on anything other than agency and commitment to being with others in the present. As anthropologist Clara Han notes in her book about everyday violence and care in Chile:

> When we move from the transcendent values of reconciliation, to the everyday, the nature of acknowledgement changes: from forgiveness for a past act, such as the accounting of a moral debt, to arriving at another's present. This arriving

at another's present can be understood as an awakening to oneself and others, in which times for mourning are created and attempts are made to live together again: through absorbing death for a life together, and in acknowledging another's desire, even if doing so means a bitter compromise with oneself. With such labors of self-revelation come fragile promises for an eventual everyday.[7]

What is often most compelling about the everyday are the tensions within it, the coexistence within it of resilience, resistance, and commitment that dissipates the need for a singular explanation or a single outcome. It also renders the everyday more challenging to relay. The everyday is unstoppable and ungraspable because it resists boundaries and works against the solemn linear chronology of history, which makes thinking about the threat of failure and daily life a process, a necessity. Therefore, choosing what seems an optimistic frame for this analysis is not to impose a false happiness or sense of closure on the comisionadas' experience. Analyzing the everyday should not be complicit in oppressive ideas that impose untenable promises of what is only available in, or only benefits, privileged spaces. Instead, I accent the everyday to emphasize the value of nonoppositional practices.

In 2012, when discussing his role as Claretian missioner and pioneer of social organizing through the comunidades eclesiales de base [grassroots ecclesiastic communities], Gonzalo de la Torre emphazised that women have been the original leaders and organizers of Black communities. A couple of weeks later, during a conversation with Jesús Albeiro Parra Solís, former director of Pastoral Social [Social Care Ministry] and later missioner of Pastoral Indígena [Indigenous Ministry], he also mentioned women's leadership. He told me that even though most Chocoan women suffer a triple oppression (for being poor, women, and Black or Indigenous), they have been at the forefront of activism for territorial rights. Organizing and achieving collective land titles for Black communities is fueled by women's everyday activities, their social reproductive labor. As anthropologist of violence Veena Das asks, "So how should we think of habits and customs that form the texture of everyday life?"[8]

In the context of Chocó's patriarchal society, it is remarkable that in the election for the Main Council that took place in the Community Council of Buchadó between July 25 and 29, 2012, six women were elected (ten spots were available in the junta directiva). Fanny Rosmira Salas Lenis won the position of legal representation, the highest one. In the context of this election, COCOMACIA's economic problems were part of many conversations. For some (inside and outside the organization), they were caused by so-called bad management decisions in the past and might have influenced the decision to include women as actual leaders. Others thought that women in decision-making positions were not necessarily an outcome from the Comisión's work to empower women. The elected women—like many other leaders in the organization—had been working for decades as organizers, educators, and advocates of their own communities. Without the same opportunities as men to be in positions of power, their election was possible because of the women's experience and the Comisión's advocacy for women's representation. But, until the organization provided opportunities for individual recognition—which within the organization has been associated with access to resources as much as power—through leadership roles, women were predominantly occupying supporting roles. Ironically, with women in leadership positions, COCOMACIA has been able to pay off previous debt and even secure its headquarters as cultural patrimony so it cannot be taken away.

The Comisión de Género does not claim direct responsibility for the women's official presence in COCOMACIA's leadership positions. Yet it is not possible to ignore the powerful transformation that derives from the Comisión's daily work. It is important to remember that most of these leaders—like the comisionadas—have experienced violence themselves, and their ethical everyday practices are informed by an accountability to the communities they come from as much to el proceso. Like the comisionadas, women in leadership positions rehearse ordinary ethics in their everyday, even if outcomes do not align with everyone's interests—especially when they're in positions of power. That said, women's participation in the organization at all levels is a bet on the future, even if there is no guarantee of anything beyond the present. The tension between Chocoan women's oppression and their world-making practices is better summarized by Betty Ruth Lozano Lerma: "Afro-Colombian women who are subjected to multiple oppressions, resist them nonetheless, persist, and imagine insurgent processes in order to create and recreate their worlds."[9] Persistent world-making is not an easy path. It requires daily energy and effort to move forward.

The value of *alongside*[10] or *beside*[11] as alternatives to the dualistic center-periphery model that reproduces exclusion is a good framework to hold the contradictions of the everyday. Performance studies scholar Lynette Hunter's conceptualization of alongside was useful for me when trying to move beyond the binary violence/peace to name survival as an intentional performance in militarized Chocó.[12] Thus far, I've tried to suggest that recognizing the limits of writing to capture and describe embodied knowledge invites us to see other cathartic practices (rituals, dance, touch, silence, songs, affect, and unspectacular spaces such as the everyday) that do not require writing. Now I want to build on that by exploring how postconflict utopias are ordinary practices and what alternatives to speaking on behalf of someone we have to study the everyday.

Performing Everyday Survival

Hours finding receipts, preparing a menu, buying food, planning activities, making copies, traveling by the river, meeting new babies, and having conversations about women's issues in different communities exemplify the embodiment of everyday survival. "Aportamos con sus manos, no con plata" [We help with our hands, not with money], said one workshop attendee when saying goodbye to the comisionadas and planning a future event. A last-minute reflection on the importance of collaborative work on community-building that had materialized in all the logistics of housing, feeding, and entertaining everyone who came from out of town. Our panga [boat] with capacity for eight people stretched to fit ten people and a gas cylinder, putting into practice what Comisión leader Justa Germania Mena Córdoba said to the UNHCR representative when we were leaving Tanguí: "No se preocupe por eso que la comida nunca alcanza" [Don't worry about it that there's never enough food]. She was referring to the food that went bad and the concern about not feeding everyone as much as possible, as it is custom. And, more important, she was talking about the commitment to make space and share as an everyday practice.

That women are the ones receiving funding is related to what international funding organizations define as a priority in countries that have overcome the humanitarian crisis, even if this is just a product of government lobbying. For the comisionadas, funding is an important part of their work, even if those funds never reach them directly. And the support of UNHCR and other NGOs (SWEFOR, Diakonia, HECKS, and Mercy Corps) they work with translates not only into economic benefits, but also into the safety and legitimacy of international actors' presence and witnessing in communities where armed actors are still explicitly present or have paid informants. These alliances with the humanitarian economy might seem counterintuitive but are part of the strategic use of identities in the quest for survival. That the Comisión has benefited from such funding does not guarantee its continuity, as there are expenses such as food and transportation that cannot be covered otherwise but require compromises and documentation, and that are not always the priority of funding agencies. The extra labor of bureaucracy does not guarantee reimbursement or continuous support for projects that cannot self-sustain with only community support. Humanitarian funds have also decreased because of the perception of Colombia as a postconflict nation, because of the supposed demobilization of paramilitaries, and the peace treaty with the FARC.

COCOMACIA's Comisión received funds from the UNHCR to create a gender commission in Tanguí. This required planning and leading workshops for women only, even if the Comisión's approach usually includes men, too. The comisionadas could not do the workshops without these international funds, as the only way of getting to Tanguí is the river. They needed gas for the speedboat, and prices change constantly based on supply and demand. It takes nine bombas of gas to get to Tanguí, that is, fifty-four gallons. Food is also needed for the participants. The Comisión, therefore, must use all available funds strategically to continue its work without a guarantee of future support. Every workshop remains vital in the process of a collective wish for something to linger even if funding disappears or reappears for some other issue that someone far away considers more important than empowering women.

As in every workshop, women volunteered their labor, and somehow there was food for everyone regardless of attendance. The labor involved in making a workshop happen extends beyond bureaucratic logistics, budgets, and transportation. And, as the opening vignette for this chapter proves, obstacles do not end when the workshop does. Survival is a full-time, non-remunerated job. At the end of the workshop, multiple people were taking pictures of the attendees, most of them holding their notebooks and folders with their notes and materials, outside of the community center rebuilt with funding from UNHCR in 2011. The signs about sexual violence and prohibiting weapons in this humanitarian space were reminders of the recent forced displacement and the constant threat of a new one. Yet the mood was festive, and hope for what was to come was contagious.

Thinking about performing the everyday is an alternative to concentrating on trauma and reinforcing identity categories associated with traumatic events. Performing the everyday is using vital energy in filling the day, sometimes with repetitive chores, sometimes making up space in the day for things that are meaningful. Following this logic, repeating things would be more valuable than isolated events that are performed just once. Not because there is value in repetition by itself, but because there is a conscious decision to direct the energy in the acts that are performed more than once. The comisionadas' daily performances might be repetitive, but the energy needed to perform is not infinite, and it is not a given. Doing community work that requires traveling through rivers for days or weeks shows how valuable a repetitive performance can be. Unlike trauma, conscious daily performances are decisions that direct agency and intention to materialize change. One day at a time.

Showing up every day at the office or the malecón [waterfront] means something different when the reasons to show up do not respond to the simple capitalist transaction of money for labor. Yet, showing up might not be anticapitalist. The reasons to show up entangle with the lack of possibilities for other kinds of employment, and with beliefs in working for the greater good (women, the organization, the process, the territory, the rivers, peace). It is difficult to measure the impact of showing up, or to calculate the sum of other everyday actions that seem to be unremarkable: being available to say hi or taking care of someone else's children, sharing lunch with someone who cannot afford it, checking on colleagues who are attending an event in Bogotá, or getting medical attention in Medellín. And to this day communicating with me and other collaborators through Facebook and WhatsApp. Could it be that there is value in routine? What counts as a potentially valuable political performance? What is the value in "what we do when we do nothing, what we hear when we hear nothing, what happens when nothing happens?"[13]

Showing up at the office everyday seems like a given; paying 1,000 or 2,000 pesos (less than one dollar) for a rapi (a motorbike taxi) adds up. But once we know the economic implications of showing up, we wonder why the comisionadas even bother or how they do it. When I ask Yenny Palacios Romaña, she simply says: "Ni siquiera sabemos cómo" [We don't even know how]. Spending money to go to work when pay is not forthcoming seems counterintuitive; however, "Lo hacemos porque nos gusta" [We do it because we like it], says comisionada Luz Adonis Mena Becerra. What we gain when approaching the everyday is a shift from grandiose metanarratives to the nuances and contradictions of daily existence. This might mean acknowledging the contextual challenges of the comisionadas' daily existence.

Until I stayed at one of the comisionadas' homes for two weeks, I did not fully understand the endless daily challenges that she and others must face before they even "show up." Rats, mice, and lack of potable water are common in Reposo, a neighborhood of forcibly displaced people, where many survivors from the Bojayá massacre live. But instead of highlighting marginality, the additional challenges of showering and doing dishes on an unroofed patio, or collecting and carrying rainwater to flush the toilet, stress the invisible labor of showing up. The extra energy spent doing these things is a reminder of the privilege of saving time and energy in not having to do them. That the comisionadas go above and beyond what they must already do because of structural inequalities might confirm the need to pay attention to the details of their daily life as political. The encounter on the river as described earlier was exceptional for me, even though I grew up in Bogotá, a militarized city that has normalized daily encounters with armed men. The uncertainty of the encounter was a reminder of my privilege. Showing up for me is optional.

Looking closer at survival means paying attention to embodied practices, the same ones that were not supposed to survive: embodied labor commodified that has never completely enjoyed citizenship. In Chocó, a patriarchal society strengthened by militarization has supported the commodification of Black women's labor. Looking closer allows us to see beyond their exclusion and to value the knowledge and energy that come from them daily. Looking closer reveals that it is possible to center the comisionadas' embodied knowledge instead of discarding it or marking it as marginalized. Thinking about embodied knowledge is a strategy to look closer while questioning the connection between writing and knowledge that has strengthened power and class hierarchies. Stepping away from written knowledge is a tool to explore why every morning the comisionadas channel their energy toward unpaid work.

Daily performances coexist with explicit discourses that center policy. In Tanguí, the comisionadas share information and resources for women who have been displaced or have experienced different kinds of violence. What is unsaid is that while they might identify as victims sometimes, they carry with them all their identities and the ways they have used their vital energy before: Rubiela Cuesta Córdoba used to sell fruits in Nariño after she was displaced, Julia Susana Mena Moreno has been a traditional medicine practitioner for years, and all of them are part of rural communities where physical labor is survival. Why would they use their energy now in planning workshops, attending meetings, writing reports, and talking to collaborators? "Aquí es donde queremos estar" [This is where we want to be], they say. They enjoy working for their communities, and they benefit from NGO resources, even if only sporadically, and sometimes when it is only a payment in kind. The comisionadas invoke el proceso when referring to their work in COCOMACIA to describe being part of a bigger movement, the Black communities' social movement. And "the process" only exists in the doing, like any performative knowledge.

The doing that makes workshops possible starts with showing up even before arriving at the malecón, as we saw in chapter 1. For the comisionadas, showing up is not simple, as it requires securing funding, buying and transporting food, and getting receipts and loans. The comisionadas have used loans to leave food at home while traveling to lead workshops, and even to pay for the food for the communities (even without knowing whether they will be reimbursed). They also have a policy of sharing all income even if the funding received pays only two salaries, and they consider personal circumstances (such as not owning a house and additional caretaking responsibilities or health issues) to divide what they have. Loans become essential for work relying on NGO funding and bureaucracy. The priority is to go to the communities and complete the workshop about land rights and new masculinities. The bureaucratic mess is resolved later.

Workshops usually take place in community spaces, like a community house or auditorium, both considered safe spaces and marked with signs that forbid weapons. To the untrained eye, that would be enough to assume safety. But in a town like Tanguí, where the population was displaced after guerrillas assassinated community leaders, there is no guarantee of safety. The conflict is always present. In some communities, informants of paramilitary or guerrilla groups attend their workshops; in others, husbands complain about their wives' participation because of the new demands the Comisión places on them. The comisionadas know that the topics they talk about—sexual violence, displacement, gender roles, and territorial rights, among others—are controversial and challenge men's leadership in families and communities. But they do not stop talking and sharing their own experiences as displaced women, as campesinas who learned to do something else, while continuing to fight for what they care about: Black rural communities' rights and land. Listening to fellow women in the community speak about this "irrational" commitment makes other women light up and share their stories of discrimination, suffering, and displacement, only to confirm that returning to their town and learning about their rights is a worthwhile endeavor.

For the community members in Tanguí, showing up is also a daily performance that requires negotiating gender roles in domestic responsibilities to materialize an almost all-women space. Singing, praying, taking notes, and creating a space where babies can sleep and nurse and kids can play is survival in action, rooted in care politics that values women's time and different competing roles. This political work is invisible to outsiders but essential for reconstructing a community like Tanguí after forced displacement, and to support it as part of COCOMACIA. More important, the everyday is more than an abstract concept. The everyday is grounded in the geographical context of daily actions, which for Black communities cannot be removed from a relationship with the land.

The comisionadas' struggle is not independent from the Black communities' struggle in the Colombian Pacific in defense of their territories. Black feminism in Colombia is not separate from Black organizing: "Para las mujeresnegras, afrocolombianas, palenqueras y raizales la construcción de un feminismo decolonial está ligado de forma indisociable a la defensa del territorio y los derechos colectivos como pueblo negro. Se trata de feminismo(s) en-lugar"[14] [For Blackwomen, Afro-Colombian, palenqueras and raizales the contruction of a decolonial feminism is inherently linked to the defense of our territories and collective rights as Black people. It is about feminism(s) in-place]. Lozano's use of mujeresnegras [blackwomen as a single word] makes the impossibility of compartmentalizing the identity of Black women who have been skeptical of identifying as feminists because feminism has never centered them. The intersectionality invoked by Lozano is a reminder that the comisionadas' work exceeds a traditional understanding of feminism. By showing up, their performances reflect their commitment to a struggle that is collective and understands the rights of Black communities as inseparable from their territories. Lozano's feminism(s) in-place describes more than geographical context: grounded willingness to be there.

"Being there" is the only way to be part of el proceso Being present is experiencing the singularity of each action as unrepeatable. It is the political power of participating in knowledge production. Being present means working for the community as a commitment to survival for themselves, their communities, and their territories. Life depends on the small actions adding up. But even participation in community building is gendered. For women, being present in el proceso has meant overseeing gendered work such as cooking and cleaning. However, since the creation of COCOMACIA's Comisión de Género, the questioning of traditional roles within the organization has led to sporadic changes and, at least, to debates about equity and the need to promote women's participation in "espacios donde se toman las decisions" [spaces where decisions are made], as the comisionadas describe them. Traditional roles are still well preserved (and defended) in most communities, and sometimes the comisionadas even assume the role of serving men. We can read these contradictory practices of assuming roles as survival strategies that gain them respect in communities where men are resistant to dialogues about gender violence and gender equity. Performing as leaders who also can perform women's traditional roles in domestic spaces reinforces their message about helping to strengthen families, not tear them apart (even if most of them are single or separated, an irony the comisionadas discuss often). Being present means being on the defensive and the offensive; it means adapting to the community's needs without sacrificing the essence of their work. It means sharing their stories and information with women who are working every day for their communities' survival amid multiple violences. Being present means creating alliances and identities that are malleable and make life livable. One day at a time.

Presence is not guaranteed, and it relies on constant negotiation and alliances with different networks, people, institutions, and funding agencies. Temporary alliances work as disidentificatory performances[15] that have world-making power. Disidentifications allow underrepresented communities to reformulate and transform their identities to match (or not match) available representations as a survival strategy. Performing domesticity can be more than an alliance with patriarchy. In this sense, performativity (as the creation of survival by performing it) is a political force that works in terms of offering recognized models (such as mourning mothers and women as caregivers in feminist movements) that use an identification that mimics traditional gender roles, for example, to identify, misidentify, and counteridentify. As disidentificatory performances create new spaces through the collaboration between performer(s) and audience, they are utopian. Muñoz argues that:

> Disidentification is not always an adequate strategy of resistance or survival for all minority subjects. At times, resistance needs to be pronounced and direct; on other occasions, queers of color and other minority subjects need to follow a conformist path if they hope to survive a hostile public sphere. But for some, misidentification is a survival strategy that works within and outside the dominant public sphere simultaneously.[16]

Under forced displacement, migrating and refusing to migrate are direct actions that comisionadas have used as alternative strategies for survival that have allowed them to be leaders. Being displaced means becoming internal refugees and adapting to new identities, leaving behind their communities and territories. But thinking about daily disidentificatory performances brings to light what could be ignored for not being explicitly opposed to power: feminist activism. As gender has been institutionalized as part of state and NGO-led campaigns, the work of comisionadas and their networks aligns with mainstream narratives. In *Disidentifications*, Muñoz specifically addresses performances by queer artists, and he constantly refers to other minorities located outside spaces of power that use similar survival strategies and long for similar outcomes.[17]

While queerness might not be part of the comisionadas' explicit struggle, and openly discussing sexual orientation in Chocó was not common in the spaces I visited, the comisionadas work daily to challenge gender roles and stereotypes. In explicit conversations about sexual diversity, concerns about LGBTQIA being a set of imported identities is manifested alongside a sincere recognition that everyone should choose how to identify, which reminded me of similar conversations I had with sexually diverse Latinx farmworkers in California.[18] Comisión de Género's alliances with humanitarian NGOs reflect the strategic use of funds available for the work in which they are interested: working with Black women in rural communities. I read this as disidentification. Disidentification for the comisionadas might mean navigating their contradictory identities as Afro-Colombians, refugees, victims, and community leaders, while collaborating with outsiders who have different discourses about these identities. In private, they're skeptical of these categories. In public, preexisting labels save time and energy needed for everyday improvisations, with their communities' future in mind. Comisionadas' discussion of identity as malleable informs both their public and private practices of identification, and even more so the endless tensions between these co-existing identities. As Muñoz explains: "Disidentification's use-value is only accessible through the transformative politics that it enables subjects and groups to imagine. . . . Disidentifications are strategies that are called on by minoritarian subjects throughout their everyday life."[19]

This disidentification process is a daily and embodied one. It might help us understand the comisionadas' activism as a discipline in motion that is constantly influenced by internal and external factors: "'afrocolombianas' subjectivities and organizations are shaped by the language and practices of development institutions and their gender politics, and by broader Black cultural and political movements."[20] And because of the multiplicity of influences that inform the comisionadas' activities, focusing on the daily practices of the group of women that work as COCOMACIA's Comisión de Género might reveal more about the complexity of their survival strategies.

There is something about looking more closely that enables seeing more details, even if that means ignoring the bigger picture sometimes, or perhaps moving intermittently between the details and the whole, the micro and the macro, just to appreciate even more the endless potential of daily life to explain bigger issues. Daily performances' potentiality might not be as visible and explicit as the discourses the Comisión de Género highlights through their work with communities and funding agencies. The potential of what is not said is a political commitment that does not rely on traditional structures or affiliations. It is an everyday utopia that makes living political. An everyday rehearsal.

Politics of Living and Ethical Rehearsals

What I name everyday survival is nurtured by Julieta Paredes's feminist "vivir bien"[21] [to live well] and the Proceso de Comunidades Negras (PCN)'s "buen vivir"[22] [good living], practical concepts that are not aligned with capitalist or patriarchal narratives and do not explicitly oppose them. In my collaboration with the comisionadas, I see what guides their daily life as a practice of solidarity, reciprocity, care, negotiations, and responsibilities. To think about survival as the complex product of fluid beliefs and practices that escape the binary and go beyond the logic of surviving as passive or accidental means recognizing comisionadas as creators. Survival, then, as other daily decisions, is an ethical practice of endurance. Power and knowledge production are also part of the everyday, collective processes that exceed the edges of what we think of as personal life.

Rubiela Cuesta Córdoba has been part of COCOMACIA for over three decades. She shows the consistency that survival requires in the story she shared as part of *Mujeres Pacíficas*: "el motivo de continuar en esta lucha es porque para las comunidades negras, y por qué no decir para el mundo entero [a] la mujer no nos miraban como una persona útil en la sociedad"[23] [the motivation to continue the struggle is because for Black communities, and why not, for the entire world, women were not seen as useful people in society]. The struggle starts with the dehumanization of Black women but creates the possibility of transnational solidarity with other women. Such an old and deep wound requires alliances with institutionalized spaces as much as it needs to construct everyday ethical spaces where Black women's knowledge and existence are valued. Like María del Socorro Mosquera Pérez's why not, Cuesta Córdoba urges a global understanding of Black women's struggle. Collective survival is a political struggle anchored in multiple spheres of women's lives that can't be separated: "women's place-based politics refers to the various political activities carried out by women around the body, the environment, the community and the public arena where women's groups are redefining political action."[24] Politics for Cuesta Córdoba reflect this multilayered understanding that Black women's work intersects with and exceeds racial justice and feminist movements in Colombia.

Cuesta Córdoba's recognition of the global and historic dehumanization of women and the reference to Black communities before clarifying the transnational character or patriarchy locates the Comisión's work in the influence area of COCOMACIA. In her story, the perception of women as a collective phenomenon that precedes their existence shows that her struggle is not an individual one. Mentioning the motivation of her struggle as part of a collective struggle invokes Julieta Paredes's "feminismo communitario" [community feminism] as more than women's rights, and "vivir bien" as a commitment to living and fighting despite fear. Rooting her story in place reveals the solidarity as much as the friction within romanticized understandings of transnational activism.[25]

Cuesta Córdoba recognizes the persistence of patriarchy, but what her story highlights are the changes generated by training women to question the internalization of traditional gender roles. Her long-term commitment to challenge stereotypical understanding of women's roles embodies the Comisión's rehearsal of alternative paths for women within the organization, despite entrenched ideologies. Recognizing her own experience as a leader and trainer as part of a longer antipatriarchal history and struggle confirms the communitarian character of the Comisión's project. "La historia de Rubiela" is the practical side of narratives that invite women to value their own voices, experiences, and decisions:

> Hoy en día que habemos tantas mujeres líderes . . . es una lucha, un trabajo que se ha venido haciendo hace mucho tiempo porque el machismo y el patriarcado que nos han enseñado que la mujer es para la casa y el hombre para la calle, que

la mujer es para tener los hijos y criarlos. No nos daban la oportunidad que estuviéramos en los espacios donde se dan las tomas de decisión. Siempre la mujer callaba, siempre la mujer obedecía, siempre la mujer escuchaba, pero nunca opinaba ni tampoco decidía y hoy en día por medio de todos estos procesos, de estas capacitaciones dentro de su organización, en sus comunidades, ya tenemos esa autonomía y ese derecho de opinar, decidir y que se escuche lo que decimos y que se tenga en cuenta la opinión de las mujeres[26]

[Nowadays that we are so many women leaders . . . it is a struggle, a work that has been done for a long time because of machismo and patriarchy that have taught us that women are for the home and men for the streets, that women are for having children and raising them. We were not given the opportunity to be in spaces where decision-making happens. Women always remained silent, women always obeyed, women always listened, but never gave their opinion or made decisions. And today through all of these processes and trainings in the organization, in the communities, we already have that autonomy and that right to give an opinion, decide, and have what we say heard, and that women's opinion be taken into account].

Transforming women's roles is the constant drive for the Comisión. To commit to women's liberation and the COCOMACIA's vision as much as to the communities that belong to it. What could be seen as a contradiction is narrated in "La historia de Rubiela" as multiplicity and coexistence of struggles. Cuesta Córdoba confirms Black feminist scholar and activist Betty Ruth Lozano Lerma's description of Afro-Colombian Black feminism as the recognition by Black women that inside their communities and organizations, power relations between men and women have been constructed and need to be challenged.[27] In the previous fragment of Cuesta Córdoba's story, it is possible to see what cofounder of the Process of Black Communities and intellectual activist Libia Grueso[28] calls resistencia/re-existencia as part of the defense of the territory where women are protagonists, not only by resisting but also by guaranteeing the re-existence of their communities. Feminism in this context can be associated with the Afrodiasporic feminism as complex, contradictory understandings and uses of theory and praxis led by Afrodescendant women in different times and spaces.[29]

These negotiations of gender roles added to resistance/re-existence aligns with what Veena Das calls ordinary ethics as a survival practice through day-to-day actions. Unlike normative ethics, ordinary ethics is the quotidian manifestation of moral behavior that does not respond to transcendent values (see chapter 1).[30] What I like most about ordinary ethics is that it highlights women's ethical behavior, since women have traditionally cared for others. By focusing on women, ordinary ethics translates morality into everyday use and breaks the monopoly of ethics by humanitarian or religious institutions to value the uneventful.

After achieving territorial rights, survival did not stop. It just adapted to the specific challenges the communities have faced. Women's survival strategies have benefited from broad discourses promoted by the state, NGOs, feminist movements, and Black social movements: "In the post-Law 70 period, Afro-Colombian women's strategies were shaped through their active engagement with and against the development practices of the Colombian state and Black ethnic movements."[31] What this means is that even when looking closer, context plays an important role in defining how stories, discourses, and movements are constructed. In *Sentipensar con la tierra*, Arturo Escobar uses utopia to respond to critics of Law 70 who consider it an obstacle for development, as it keeps Black communities in the past. For Escobar, the ethno-territorial understanding of autonomy and cultural difference in Law 70 and other manifestations of Afro-Colombian social movements is based on "un sentido de *utopía realista en relación con la gran multiplicidad de entramados humano-naturales* [italics in original] que tendremos que seguir cultivando los humanos desde lugares específicos del planeta para promover las transiciones a 'un mundo donde quepan muchos mundos'"[32] [a sense of *realist utopia in relation to the great multiplicity of human-natural networks* that as humans we will need to cultivate to promote the transitions to "a world where many worlds fit"]. I see ethical rehearsals in the everyday as postconflict utopias that dream up what seems unimaginable but is essential for the survival of Black communities and their territories.

The Comisión de Género's ordinary ethics is present in the comisionadas' lives and work. Ordinary ethics allows them to treat every woman in their workshops as a colleague and a future comisionada. They make sure everyone eats, but they also make sure everyone understands and agrees with the process, and they always remind women that the comisionadas were once sitting on the other side, learning. Undoubtedly, conflict and disagreement are part of the process, as lack of resources and lack of participation threatens the workshops' continuity. In addition, misunderstandings of the discussions of gender equality that make women dream about the social and sexual freedom that some men enjoy in the communities, and make men fear the challenging of the traditional patriarchal order, have disturbed the meetings with complaints about fights within families and communities. In her story for *Mujeres Pacíficas,* Ana Rosa Heredia Cuesta shared that women were not attending the events because they did not have anyone to take care of their kids or permission from their husbands: "En las comunidades empezamos a hacer fortalecimiento a las mujeres, porque decíamos

¿por qué las mujeres no vienen a los eventos?, y ellas nos decían porque ellas no tenían con quien dejar a sus hijos, porque los maridos no las dejaban"[33] [In the communities we started empowering women because we asked ourselves, why don't women attend events? And they told us because they didn't have anyone to take care of their kids, because their husbands didn't let them].

Ordinary ethics as a performative practice of survival used to rebuild communities through everyday acts is, therefore, also central to developing personal narratives about survival. Ordinary ethics keeps the comisionadas from giving up, and that inspires them to help other people, even when they themselves have problems covering their personal expenses. When the Comisión de Género was planning a trip to Tagachí, Mena Moreno had to borrow money from her neighbor, who could offer it only if all her chontaduros [fruits of the chonta palm] were sold. While waiting for the money, she had no other option than leaving rice and plantains at home for her children and grandchildren to eat. But she did not hesitate to attend the workshop; her presence would make less of a difference in Quibdó than it would in Tagachí. And, just maybe, she would be able to take something home from the community. Ordinary ethics means fulfilling a commitment, spending energy on things within one's control, and participating in multiple webs of care.

Ordinary ethics also manifest in the comisionadas' critical approach to what they do. They criticize each other and give feedback, noticing that members of their organization are not always completely convinced of their course of action. They fight and remind each other of the importance of working with women and facilitating their education, while behind the scenes they are always trying to respond to critiques about why they are the ones receiving funding and not COCOMACIA. Accountability is part of their practices of reciprocity, and they report to each other and their communities as much as they do to their organization after every grant and event.

In Tanguí, women complained that their husbands thought their participation in the Comisión would generate antagonism. The comisionadas explained that they were not trying to create conflict in the community and that they could stop going to town and doing workshops if the women did not feel comfortable. They explained that the workshops' goal is to empower women and make them feel comfortable, not diminish their opportunities to collaborate with their communities. Later, when the women in Tanguí were asked whether they would continue with the process and whether they thought it was valuable to them, there was a long debate. Some women said the problem was miscommunication about what was discussed in the workshops. Some said only the most radical men felt threatened, while more open-minded men could see the advantages of having a wife who knew about her rights and took part in protests. In the final assessment, the women attending the workshops in Tanguí agreed that those not interested could stop attending, while those who were enjoying the workshops could continue; they did not want the workshops to end before Tanguí created a gender commission.

If el proceso is an everyday utopia, its materialization depends on the intentionality and collaboration of showing up. The negotiation needed to encourage women to take part in the events organized by the Comisión is part of a willingness to imagine women's empowerment. Cuesta Córdoba describes the multiple roles she and other women do as "estar en todo" [to be in everything]. Her leadership despite the trauma she narrates in "La historia de Rubiela" (the assassination of her husband, being a single mom, her forced displacement, and conflicts with members of her networks because of her activist involvement) exemplifies the vulnerability of being in everything. In another fragment of her story, she explains her motivations for "estar en todo," a defense of learning and activism as legacy and collective practices:

> El mejor legado que uno deja a la familia y a los amigos es la resistencia, el querer. Esa espontaneidad, esa dedicación, esa honestidad de hacer las cosas sin que la gente mire en uno esa suspicacia, esa agalla de querer estar ahí porque me quedo con esto o me lo llevo. Todo ese bagaje, esa huella de camino de aprendizaje, de experiencia, de conocimiento, que uno le deja a los hijos, a las amigas, eso va acumulando, se va enriqueciendo uno . . . y entonces uno dice "no perdí el tiempo, valió la pena estar en todo.[34]

> [The best legacy one leaves their family and friends is resistance, desire. That spontaneity, dedication, and honesty of doing things without people misreading the bravery of being there because I want to keep something, or take something. All that baggage, the traces of a path of learning, experience, and knowledge that one leaves their kids, friends, accumulates, it enriches one . . . and then one says "I didn't waste my time, it was worth it to be in everything"].

Cuesta Córdoba's reflection about resistance as desire, being there, or showing up as part of her legacy shows her work as an everyday practice anchored in presence and intentionality. Her daily effort is an embodied experience rooted in a repetitive action: being in everything. And estar en todo is only possible as part of the learning and care networks that transform the world and build peace in real time. Projecting estar en todo as a legacy for the next generation and friends imagines a kinship beyond the nuclear family. It also highlights the quotidian as a stage for enacting the world that is desired, a space where ethics is practiced every day as a rehearsal of what could be. Estar en todo aligns with Lozano's concept of insurgencias cotidianas, overlooked practices with political potential.[35] These quotidian insurgencies add up, and they can make possible what Maylei Blackwell calls "scales of resistance" through interweaving and connecting knowledge and spaces by Indigenous women's organizing moving between scales.[36] Building on Silvia Rivera Cusicanqui's idea of women's identity as a fabric where territories and citizenship are made through women's practice, Blackwell's scales of resistance can illustrate the multiplicity that Cuesta Córdoba is theorizing with the idea of being in everything.

Being in everything is an example of ethics as an everyday performance, as embodied knowledge that requires intention. Simultaneously volatile, temporary, and intentional, being in everything maintains the tension between state violence and organizing. Moving beyond horror and the categories that define people based on traumatic events does not mean ignoring the multiple forms of violence that the concept of postconflict hides. It means giving value to practices that are considered trivial, following the tendency of *Mujeres Pacíficas* stories to prioritize process over outcome, and emphasizing that the struggle is ongoing and every woman in COCOMACIA's territories and—as Mosquera Pérez says—why not beyond is welcome to join el proceso.

Negotiating bureaucracy, local politics, and caretaking responsibilities also raises questions about economies of care and the hierarchy of needs. As examples of ethical behavior in the everyday, the collective practices of showing up and reciprocity might reveal a selfless understanding of what is important and what merits the consumption of these comisionadas' energy. And it might confirm an understanding of the common good in everyday life that shapes surviving as a collective and collaborative endeavor. Working for empowerment and sharing hope and motivation to continue living and demanding rights exemplify what the comisionadas say: "Es mejor vivir con miedo que dejar de ser por miedo" [It is better to live in fear than to cease to exist because of fear]. A recognition that the endless pull between the struggle for freedom and living exceeds what we understand as postconflict. This durational performance, one that values the embodied forms of knowledge that circulate as routine, is a good alternative to reproducing the power of writing as the only valuable knowledge, derived from its colonial imposition. Rubiela Cuesta Córdoba reminds us that giving and receiving support is the "everything" that makes imagining survival possible.

Echoes of solidarity as the pillars of a feminism embodied in daily community practice are also present in a text of *Mujeres creando,* a Bolivian feminist collective, which captures what comisionadas say about their work: "Compartimos lo poco que tenemos y eso es una cosa que hemos aprendido siendo un movimiento"[37] [We share the little we have and that is one thing we have learned by being a movement]. This solidarity belongs to a collaborative practice that challenges colonialized versions of ethics and feminism. The struggle for women's liberation is intertwined with the liberation of Black people and their territories. As Lozano reminds us, for mujeresnegras, the construction of a decolonial feminism is essential to defending Black people's territory and collective rights.[38] The comisionadas might choose el proceso and not feminism as a framework, and yet centering women in their work is essential to defending Black communities' rights and territories.

Women, men, children, and babies attended the events in Tanguí in 2013 (four workshops during four months). At every session there were fewer people. Some women were working in the trapiche [sugar mill], some had been forbidden by their husbands to attend the workshop, and some were not interested anymore. The comisionadas did not seem to care much about the number of attendees. They did not care that most of the town's inhabitants enjoyed the food for the workshop. Some women leaders in the community, who could be attending the workshop, cooked. And, when it was time to eat, everyone in the community wanted to partake, bringing even small pots to share with their families. Facilitators and attendees of the workshop did not mind as long as everyone getting food would sign the attendance sheet the Comisión needed to return to the UNHCR. Feeding everyone was considered an ideal side effect of the comisionadas' presence. Even important topics such as women's rights seemed secondary to being able to contribute to the community's well-being, at least for the day. Building trust and mutual aid is part of the care that makes space for conversations about gender. The comisionadas know that imposing attendance would not yield better results than truly welcoming people to come of their own volition.

Not promoting massive participation in the workshops can also be read as part of comisionadas' ethics as they recognize multiple reasons why people cannot show up consistently. In the difficult tension between imposing their presence and helping interested women, the comisionadas knew they needed to be firm about the content of their workshops, while respecting the community's wishes. This is how they have been able to earn other communities' trust. This is one reason they have been effective at denouncing the effects of mining and the armed conflict on women's bodies. And consequently, they have the support of some men, even when those men do not completely grasp why talking about gender is useful. So they continue organizing community-based workshops, even if that means repeating the same themes and trying not to tire of doing so, as Julia Susana Mena Moreno says. They continue to work for free; their only reward is the freedom to speak their truth and help others.

The work of the comisionadas de género is based on a situated context, and it is not oppositional. By being present, comisionadas work for causes they believe in, even when they do not seem to receive anything in return for their work. Like Mosquera Pérez's why nots imagine a global audience for her story (chapter 1), Cuesta Córdoba's reflection about the importance of "being there" highlights presence as part of her activism. Her daily effort is the embodied commitment to showing up for her communities. Being there is embodied knowledge. Looking more closely at the practices that sustain communities challenges the relation between writing and knowledge that strengthens hierarchies (which are racialized, even if in Latin America the utopia of mestizaje is still very much alive). Valuing presence and consistency as part of the rehearsals necessary for peace-building, and imagining an alternative to violence for their communities requires trust in the reciprocity and power of community work as the seeds for change.

In the foreword to *Jazz*, Toni Morrison describes the "unreasonable optimism" of jazz and explains that "[t]he music insisted that the past might haunt us, but it would not entrap us. It demanded a future."[39] This "unreasonable optimism" of survival and the demand for a future is evident in the stories of *Mujeres Pacíficas*. This unreasonable optimism also motivates comisionadas' daily performances. They hope for a future that may never arrive. Daily life is activism. It is action. It shows where motivation is directed, and which projects matter to people. It is subversive because it is radical to talk about gender equality, and to show up, to be present, to continue to do things even if they do not seem useful, and especially if they have no obvious exchange value in the context of late-stage capitalism.

Surviving Failure: The Limits of Storytelling

"Entonces yo le pregunto: ¿en qué me puede usted ayudar ... pa' ver si yo salgo adelante, pa' ver si Dios me ayuda cómo hacer el rancho?" [So I ask you: how can you help me ... to see if I can move forward, to see if God can help me to build my house?] I stopped recording after the question Miriam Moya Cuesta asked. The question was not rhetorical, and she was looking at me and waiting for a reply. We had followed the same process I had designed with the comisionadas who made up most of the storytellers for *Mujeres Pacíficas*. Only this time, we were inside the restaurant and not in one of the offices in COCOMACIA we had used previously, the construction noises replaced by the clanging of pans and plates. I asked whether she preferred to write a script or tell me the outline of what she wanted to include in her story before recording. I wrote a short list on a post-it and we discussed it briefly before she agreed to record. The main topic of her story was her lack of a home despite her commitment to work for the organization. The question was a natural end for "La historia de Miriam" after having discussed her struggles as a single mom, survivor of domestic violence, and employee living in Dos de mayo, a neighborhood of displaced people in Quibdó named in commemoration of Bojayá's massacre, with less than minimum wage.

Miriam Moya Cuesta was one worker at COCOMACIA's restaurant in 2013, a meeting point where members of the organization and outsiders alike would eat, drink coffee, or come by to say hello. She had been working for the organization in different roles and had even received the same training that the now comisionadas de género did years ago. There was some untold tension between her and the comisionadas as she had attended preliminary workshops about gender led by a feminist NGO and was not chosen to be part of the Comisión. Some comisionadas had previously worked in the restaurant, but even now some of the Comisión's gender workshops emphasized the need for women to question traditional roles as caretakers and domestic workers to embrace leadership roles. It did not help that the Comisión had been seen within and outside COCOMACIA as a successfully funded group and the comisionadas often were perceived as privileged.

Miriam Moya Cuesta participated in *Mujeres Pacíficas* after her sister, Mariluz Moya Cuesta, created her story. "La historia de Miriam" brings to light how tangible the everyday obstacles of survival are: the reality of having to provide for six kids and having to work for 400,000 pesos a month (even though the legal minimum wage was set for 589,500, around US$300 at the time). Other stories, including her sister's, do not explicitly mention wages or a particular problem in need of concrete help. By providing specific details that build the background for her unambiguous request, "La historia de Miriam" reveals the limits, gaps, and silences of storytelling. The process of creating this story challenged my framing of digital storytelling as an alternative to reproducing hierarchies. I could do nothing practical to help her achieve her goal of building a house. My privilege and her oppression were intact even after we brainstormed about ways I could help.

This story made me face failure as part of collaboration and interaction with others. Unlike most narratives from *Mujeres Pacíficas,* "La historia de Miriam" proves storytelling cannot always achieve something tangible. Her interpellation is about what I can do for her in exchange for what she is doing for me. With the Comisión, we had established specific tasks and projects I could do to help their mission beyond my research. This was not the case with Miriam Moya Cuesta. The final question reveals the limits of collaborative research and reciprocity. Violence, poverty, and survival as endless everyday experiences reflect other topics that are not explicitly part of other stories but are fundamental to understand postconflict in a militarized space like Chocó: economic insecurity, colonial practices, racial hierarchies, and precarity within the context of the humanitarian economy.

Visibility as a political goal is insufficient when basic needs are not met. While *Mujeres Pacíficas'* narratives weave discourses of feminism, humanitarianism, and activism with lived experiences of poverty and oppression, the gaps and nuances that "La historia de Miriam" invokes illuminate the pieces in everyday survival that have not yet been commodified and cannot be captured by storytelling: the storytellers' everyday world-making strategies, and even silence and omissions, that have made their survival possible alongside ongoing unmet needs.

Everyday practices escape stories. Their performance contains the political and ethical potential of transformation through survival as re-existence, as an invisible collective commitment. Trauma and memory inform these commitments and remain untranslatable. Untranslatability highlights the limits of language to capture what has been embodied. What it means to survive and live with trauma exceeds storytelling. The difficulty in expressing, explaining, and representing trauma deactivates, or at least neutralizes, the power given to testimonies as ideal genres for catharsis, healing, and denunciation. There is no simple formula for empathy or understanding someone else's pain, and words are insufficient. Failure looms even if we understand difference as the basis for, and not an obstacle to, understanding.

After many years of finishing the stories, their incompleteness is more evident, despite the constant rehearsal of ethics in our ongoing collaboration. The endless threat of failure in understanding each other infuses storytelling, giving us glimpses of survival in every story as examples of enduring performances. There is not a predetermined process or outcome when thinking about ethics as a performative practice. As "La historia de Miriam" taught me, we are responsible for the interactions we start, and assuming responsibility for this process does not guarantee an ethical outcome.

"La historia de Miriam" is not a hopeful story, and it materializes the additional challenges of working outside of the Comisión. The end challenges the script and centers failure as a possibility of collaboration and interaction with others. Unlike the optimistic character of the other stories, "La historia de Miriam" ends with an interpellation that shows the limits of collaboration. The final question reveals violence and survival as never-ending everyday experiences that bring into light other issues that were silenced or forgotten in

Mujeres Pacíficas. I argue the silences and omissions that "La historia de Miriam" underlines are fundamental to understand that postconflict scenarios are not peaceful and to question the usefulness of research and digital platforms to work through everyday violence.

One issue that "La historia de Miriam" points out is economic insecurity as part of the everyday that I have described as the scenario of survival. The comisionadas' labor might be constant, but remuneration is not. As "La historia de Miriam" exemplifies, minimum wage is not guaranteed in Chocó. Colonial practices are still alive, as it is common for mestizxs to be business owners and Black people to be used as labor: "The Pacific region is a laboratory where the global coloniality of power expresses itself."[40] This is true for NGOs that reproduce colonial hierarchies by hiring almost only outsiders to advance their humanitarian agendas. Chocó receives more money from international cooperation than any other department, a republic of NGOs where logos and slogans of nonprofits became part of the landscape. Still, most people working in humanitarianism are outsiders. Lack of accountability and funding of projects that are not self-sustainable create a cycle of dependency that mimics the government's "assistance-based approach."[41]

For the Comisión, sometimes funding for a project does not have a specific budget for the comisionadas' wages. Their criteria of needs (who is sick, has more dependents, or needs help) helps them divide the little they get. This is not explicitly discussed in any of the stories from *Mujeres Pacíficas*. And even if prioritizing activism over remuneration can be read as an example of everyday ethics, the ethical sharing that informs the comisionadas' priorities is an additional emotional labor. Also, it hides the precarity imposed by state marginalization and patriarchal organizations where some women are still responsible for fulfilling gender roles or assume a workload that includes caretaking responsibilities. Survival is never individual, but that does not mean that everyone will survive.

Daily survival works on several different levels for Heredia Cuesta and the rest of the comisionadas. It is present in dealing with persecusión mental, as one of Heredia Cuesta's neighbors describes the trauma of forced displacement after surviving a massacre. It is embodied in the lack of control of mental and physical symptoms that the comisionadas have catalogued in their research of industrial mining: skin rashes, respiratory issues, sexual dysfunction, and infertility. Daily survival manifests itself in the efforts made every day to stay strong and take care of others, even at the expense of being healthy. It is grounded in women's independence and self-reliance, which hides the gendered labor of surviving and caretaking. Understanding the everyday as an archive of survival compels us to think about memories, moving on, affectivity, and not giving up. I see mental persecution as a placeholder for the unspeakable and invisible mental effort of surviving. Trauma challenges the artificial boundaries that distinguish present and past as much as the difference between safety and threat. In turn, survival requires anchors that exist outside of individual minds to repair the ruptures of ongoing violence and the haunting of traumatic memories.

"Yo no lloro muertos no. Los muertos lloran. Yo les pido fuerza para empezar el día" [I do not cry for the dead. The dead cry. I ask them for strength to start the day], Ana Rosa Heredia Cuesta told me the day we recorded her story. Death is an everyday and unavoidable presence. Persecución mental might be as much about the inner noise we associate with paranoia as it is about the rituals created and reproduced to make life bearable when it is destabilized every day. Everyday utopias exist at the intersection of historical trauma and communities' commitment to generational survival. Invoking ancestors for strength at the beginning of the day is one of many examples of enacting survival.

Everyday paranoia is another issue absent from *Mujeres Pacíficas*, even though it exemplifies the reproduction of traditional ideas about femininity. Mental persecution exists outside the digital stories while haunting everyday storytelling about individual and collective traumas. The presence of illegal armed groups made up of demobilized paramilitaries, now named BACRIM (bandas criminales/criminal gangs), creates and renews care practices as a strategy to navigate spaces. The comisionadas do everything possible to leave the office before sunset. They walk together and call or text to check on each other. And when I visit, I am included in these logistics of care and survival. Even if this illustrates the care politics that survival requires, the mental and physical exhaustion of experiencing violence takes a toll on the well-being of Afro-Colombian women that is not quantifiable. These behaviors of care reinforce the role of women as caretakers, which can be naturalized as effortless or mundane actions. And these practices are rarely visible or valued, even by other members of the organization who have different embodied experiences of navigating the city at night.

Internal tensions within COCOMACIA are not discussed in *Mujeres Pacíficas*, partially because comisionadas' ethical behavior manifests in everyday ethics and care politics. But another reason is that storytelling is a conscious staging that recognizes the existence of an audience, which most storytellers in this project have considered mainly women of the organization. To make things worse, not everyone sees the Comisión as a valuable space promoting equality. Men feel excluded, and the Comisión receives less support from the organization than other commissions. A lot of energy from comisionadas within the organization goes to working to show support for COCOMACIA, besides working with the Comisión. Some of this extra work also reinforces gender roles and affects women particularly.

The strategic use of official and humanitarian language to receive funding and as a strategy to survive is an instrumental tactic. Comisionadas align themselves with available discourses. Using available identity categories in official discourses of humanitarianism and official memory might reinforce hierarchies of class, race, and gender. Disagreements and conflicts weigh on the comisionadas when making these decisions, which illuminates the limits of bodies and the unpredictability of everyday life. And, at the same time, outside support is essential for livelihood, motivation, and even credibility. As described in chapter 3, being part of local, regional, national, and transnational feminist networks is essential for the work of the comisionadas and storytellers as part of COCOMACIA.

The performance of silence and forgetfulness in storytelling mirrors the tension of survival and disidentification. Silvia Rivera Cusicanqui reminds us that oral history is not a neutral or passive practice even if it is portrayed as such.[42] *Mujeres Pacíficas* does not reproduce a lament discourse that Rivera Cusicanqui associates with NGOs' practices of oral history and that characterizes other representations of victims, but orality is shaped in the editing and writing process. "La historia de Miriam" reminds us that storytelling has limits, and hierarchies are created and re-created in the everyday. And writing about storytelling also has limits. Storytellers' daily practices of survival in Chocó exceed stories and writing. Ignited by those who did the work before and are no longer here, like Mena Córdoba, the everyday is the stage for political imagination, for a peacebuilding that is accountable only to others who commit to a survival that can only be collective. But as everyday practices cannot guarantee the same output even through constant repetition, storytelling is a rehearsal without a guaranteed outcome. Story work is another why not. Postconflict utopias are the everyday rituals of imagining the impossible while working toward it. Failure is inevitable in the enduring performance of survival, where only showing up and being in everything can guarantee change. One day at a time.

CONCLUSION

Performing Why Nots

> En las comunidades empezamos a hacer fortalecimiento a las mujeres porque decíamos: "¿por qué las mujeres no vienen a los eventos?" y ellas nos decían porque ellas no tenían con quién dejar a sus hijos, porque los maridos no las dejaban. Y ya empezamos en la lucha, y empezamos la lucha.
>
> In the communities we started to do strengthening of women because we would ask: "why are women not attending the events?" and they would say that they did not have anyone to take care of their kids, because their husbands would not let them. So we started the struggle, and we started the struggle.
>
> —Ana Rosa Heredia Cuesta

In 2014, on one of my follow-up visits to the comisionadas after Justa Germania Mena Córdoba died, a rumor began that comisionada de género Ana Rosa Heredia Cuesta had a chola [a derogatory term for an Indigenous woman] living with her. When Miriam Moya Cuesta, one of the *Mujeres Pacíficas* storytellers, saw me walking later that day, she realized I was "la india de Ana Rosa" [Ana Rosa's Indigenous woman]. We laughed at the gossip and the assumptions about Heredia's income that this had caused. It made me consider how spaces influence how we are perceived. I had been a paisa [a term to describe mestizxs and people from Antioquia] in Quibdó for years, on the street, in the minibus, at the market, or at the office. But the only paisas living in this neighborhood were the owners of the store. Other paisas would come only occasionally with Red Cross T-shirts and cars. Why would anyone with the option of being somewhere else decide to be here? I wrote in my notebook: "There's silence, and the thought of never leaving this place. But I will." I was thinking about choice as much as how self-representation is constructed by performing our identity and creating our own stories. Location and performance inform storytelling. I could be a chola or a paisa depending on who was telling the story.

Due to the association of Colombian identity with mestizaje, people like me who are perceived as neutral enjoy an embodied privilege, which becomes even more visible in Quibdó. As a mestiza and outsider, I acknowledge the process of researching and writing about Chocó as one of untranslatability—even more so as I have written most of the versions of this book in the United States, and in English. This book is not the only piece of the puzzle. *Mujeres Pacíficas* and other collaborative audiovisual pieces, as well as the spaces, books, practices, and networks I write about, exist independently from my writing. Narratives are always incomplete. Many details of the lived experience in "postwar" Colombia escape this book. Many silences and secrets, too.

Books are never the entire story. For the comisionadas, books, letters, and pamphlets are part of a collection to be consulted or shown. They are a constant presence in the Comisión's office. The books produced by or about COCOMACIA or the Comisión do not even capture the daily storytelling that makes the Comisión's office a space of encounter. Books were not an aesthetic background, as a library might be in a scholar's headshot. Instead, the Comisión's library came across as a collection of the comisionadas' contributions to someone else's project or research. This book will be there, too, despite its collaborative approach and its emphasis on embodied knowledge. Unlike other everyday actions, the act of writing and reading in the Comisión's office has been linked with the compulsory imposition of bureaucratic practices that come with funding. Until 2013, Yenny Palacios Romaña was the only comisionada to receive a stable salary, having been hired as a secretary to perform tasks such as typing reports, taking notes, and managing correspondence. Comisionadas' notes from meetings, conferences, drafts, and budgets feed the project reports and grant applications. Writing involves collaborating, projecting the document on a wall, taking turns reading, suggesting ideas, rewriting, and keeping each other accountable. Personal stories are present, interrupt bureaucratic writing, and have almost nothing in common with the official stories written in the records that adorn the office.

Along with written documents such as pamphlets and memos in the Comisión's office are photographs of leaders, family members, and friends, and posters received from local and national feminist organizations, NGOs, or other funding partners. The mandatory inclusion of Afrodescendants in the curriculum by the Cátedra de Estudios Afrocolombianos [Afro-Colombian Studies Curriculum] established through Law 70 of 1993 paradoxically reproduces their exclusion as knowledge producers.[1] Obviously, this law that recognized the territorial rights of rural Black communities has not impeded the stereotyped reproduction of Afrodescendants' images.[2] Visual counternarratives to the whitening of Colombian history and identity have always been present in Quibdó. African origins are embraced; orishas' [deities in African diasporic spirituality] imagery and invoking Changó and Elegguá become part of the conversation alongside Catholic saints, destabilizing the historical blanqueamiento of education and visual representation of colombianidad.[3] There are multiple ways of being visible, which do not guarantee inclusion or change in the structures that guarantee exclusion.

Why is visibility useful if it does not grant access to power? We cannot measure visibility as a tool for empowering or resisting marginalization. But visibility is attached to intangible wishes about personal and political goals. Visibility can serve as a catalyst for individuals and communities to position themselves outside or beside the imposed boundaries of representation. It could blur the margins or the power relations present in the centers of power where mainstream narratives originate. My optimistic reading of what postconflict utopias can do, such as reconstructing non-hegemonic memories and archives, and creating spaces for dialogue and learning, weaves stories into the always-incomplete memory of survival. Postconflict utopias remind us that what exists now was only imagined at some point, so we can constantly reimagine and change it. What we do with and for others in the everyday are the seeds of survival.

Even if it is possible to narrate the glimpses of peace contained within Colombia's violent "postconflict," it may still result in omissions and silences. The purpose of this book is not creating grand narratives or models for peacebuilding in postconflict Colombia. This is a study of practices, ways of knowing, and alliances that enable survival, but are not recognized as knowledge production due to their inability to ensure lasting peace or political significance. By centering them, we open ourselves up to seeing beyond just resistance and resilience as political options and to acknowledging the structural exclusions that perpetuate violence.

My interactions with storytellers in the process of cocreating *Mujeres Pacíficas* unfolded in a context of uncertainty due to a civil mobilization against state regulation of mining in August 2013, with protests that even closed off Quibdó's airport.[4] The Comisión promotes the equal division of domestic work between women and men to avoid reproducing traditional gender roles that keep men in positions of power. However, when the miners arrived at Quibdó for the strike, comisionadas Luz Adonis Mena Becerra and Banessa Rivas López, along with other women from COCOMACIA, volunteered to help cook and organize the coliseum, where the miners were staying. The Comisión was still critical of the involvement of the Marcha Patriótica—a leftist social movement that had been wrongly linked to the FARC and threatened by right-wing paramilitaries—in the strike, and the connection between mining and prostitution in the collective territories along the rivers. Comisionadas' willingness to support the protesters is part of their commitment to show up for each other and their communities.

Uncertainty informed our collaboration, as the contingency of violence is part of daily life in Chocó, and the urgency fueled by vulnerability motivates the comisionadas' daily activities. I did not go to the coliseum, but I learned about the details of the strike through storytelling. During a meeting, Rubiela Cuesta Córdoba stated that mining corporations were responsible for prostitution businesses opening in communities, adding to women's victimization. This added additional details to other side effects of mining, including health issues such as skin rashes, vaginal infections, and respiratory issues, but also food insecurity and human trafficking.[5] Multiple additional stories circulated, giving additional details of the unforeseen effects of militarization and extractive capitalism while recognizing artisanal mining as a livelihood.

The comisionadas arrange workshops, attend conferences, partake in the San Pacho celebrations adorned in clothing with social justice messages, collaborate with and are constituents of other women's associations (including the transnational and antimilitaristic Women in Black), and have made a commitment to train the children of leaders (who are now young adults) who express a desire in serving COCOMACIA. The multiple activities that the Comisión organizes and supports make it difficult to capitalize on their work, even when they have tried to be in charge of the organization's restaurant, or sell crafts, as the comisionadas are constantly on the move. Not having consistent funding is also a consequence of the disappearance of humanitarian aid from a country that is not considered high priority anymore. Their daily energy is usually directed toward organizing and attending marches and protests to defend women's rights in Quibdó and traveling to the communities for events planned by the organization or the Comisión. Collective survival is made possible by the intricate choreography of care, ethics, and imagination that underpins collective work. Postconflict utopias are embodied practices of imagination and life. As such, they are performances, in Christen Smith's definition, as the site of both Black oppression and liberation.[6] Here, everyday survival means fulfilling a commitment. It is a bet on what is to come, even though we cannot grasp anything beyond the current moment.

The act of persisting through willfulness enables the conceptualization of survival as knowledge that is embodied. Willfulness's utopian character manifests in the collective and intergenerational struggle for survival. Comprehending the experience of existing within the tumultuous aftermath of peace negotiations, in the space of liminality, depends on recognizing the centrality of the tension between unpredictability and failure, as most definitions of utopia have acknowledged. *Mujeres Pacíficas*' stories deliberately maintain distance from revictimization. The message about legacy found in Mena Córdoba's intervention on a campaign poster against women's violence in her story, "Mujer que no cumpla su sueño, mujer que no ha nacido" in chapter 1, mirrors Cuesta Córdoba's motivation as an organizer, which she refers to as estar en todo in chapter 5.

Storytelling and listening are not healing practices by themselves. As a crucial part of the enduring performance of survival, they serve as invitations to acknowledge and honor the networks of care that enable our existence. Despite changes in immigration status and the ongoing pandemic that have prevented me from traveling, I have remained connected with the storytellers of *Mujeres Pacíficas*. While the stories may be distant memories for most, my interactions with COCOMACIA continue to reinforce the significance of storytelling for sustaining daily life. The willingness to collaborate stems from presence and strengthens community bonds. Stories have the potential to enhance the solidarity that has been fostered through continuous presence at the Comisión. These stories do not possess a greater or lesser degree of authenticity than other depictions of identity. Their value is not reparative. As practices that are fundamentally subjective, storytelling and listening function as extensions of survival. They already play an integral role in the everyday practices that uphold communities.

Stories are a vital component of the comisionadas' funding strategy, and the bedrock for regulations like ruling T-622, which granted the Atrato River the status of "an entity subject to rights of protection, conservation, maintenance and restoration"[7] in 2016. Former comisionada and storyteller Rivas López is one of the fourteen guardians who make up the Guardian Commission established by this ruling. As a guardiana del Atrato, she is responsible for protecting the river and its rights. Shortly before that, the comisionadas had been engaged in the "Atratiando por la paz" campaign, touring through the Atrato River to encourage people to vote in favor of the peace deal referendum. Defending the river entails recognizing the violent effects of legal and illegal mining, which are entrenched in the systems of colonialism and capitalism perpetrated by war.

Other comisionadas are engaged in larger-scale community organizing efforts within the city, aimed at creating and preserving public spaces. They have also assumed various leadership positions within COCOMACIA, as Cuesta Córdoba, for example, was elected as the board's vice president. For those who remain in the Comisión, their daily routine involves seeking funding for the various projects that have been unfunded in the last two years.

As embodied knowledge, survival demands "showing up," which can be understood as "feminismo(s) en-lugar,"[8] as Colombian Black feminists frame organizing rooted in Black territories. It means being there for each other and COCOMACIA's communities. A durational performance requires repetition and presence. Survival requires a daily commitment to start anew, imagining alternative possibilities while using available resources to sustain this commitment. Despite vulnerability, the everyday practice of ethics and survival reveals the potential to create and innovate. Postconflict utopias entail navigating the tension between recognizing the persistence of violence, even within the structure of humanitarian aid, and carrying out tasks beyond established parameters. Comisionadas operate within a context where they must choose between identifying as a victim or activist or becoming an advocate or guardian of rivers. This tireless work does not guarantee their survival or the survival of their communities. And survival is contingent on showing up for this never-ending work.

Survivors rebuild their lives through everyday acts. As a concept, survival conveys an undertone of insufficiency and the potential for empowerment to maintain an essential tension in the need to imagine otherwise and condemn human rights violations in spaces scarred by war. For Brazilian councilwoman and human rights activist Marielle Franco, survival meant more than just the bare minimum of sustaining life.[9] Her assassination by the Brazilian state on March 14, 2018, serves as further proof of the constant risk faced by those who are vocal in the struggle for Black liberation worldwide. Despite the risk, the stories, archives, and marches in this book exhibit calls to action and reframe survival as a political commitment in daily life, beyond individual effort.

The appointment of Francia Márquez Mina, an Afro-Caucan activist, as vice president of Colombia since 2022 underscores the ongoing tension between desire and change in postconflict utopias. Critiques of the vice president's performance, appearance, and politics have put a spotlight on the racism and classism prevalent in Colombia despite the country's self-proclaimed status as a multicultural nation. There is still much work to be done. Those who work toward change understand that progress can take generations to manifest. Despite everything, the message is clear: our actions in our daily lives have the power to either perpetuate or subvert the current state of affairs, and ethical actions matter, even if we do not see their impact immediately. Every day is an opportunity to rehearse our own survival again.

By constructing a chronology of violence in Colombia using utopian rehearsals, I emphasized the importance of performing everyday survival. My first encounter with Vamos Mujeres in San Francisco de Ichó and COCOMACIA's Comisión in Quibdó was a rehearsal of conceptualizing survival as more than just an unexpected consequence of war. I came to understand that these groups' activism exists alongside violence, not in opposition to it. I shared how my collaboration with COCOMACIA's Comisión is a nonlinear process shaped by multiple projects and agendas, as well as untranslatability. I learned that what escapes violence has as much impact as explicit resistance, and sometimes rehearsing collaborations creates opportunities to imagine the impossible together.

Digital stories have value not just as tales about the storytellers' experiences but also in the improvisational aspect of embracing vulnerability during the transformative process of sharing. Unpolished stories, group images, interweaving storylines, shared stories, and all the emotions derived from the digital storytelling process create alternative memories and archives of everyday survival. Storytellers are producers of knowledge about themselves and their communities. As organic intellectuals, they participate in networks of memorialization and affect. They remember together. Solidarity and community are woven into their personal stories. Moreover, many stories are left unrecorded, yet they continue to circulate powerfully in the collective dream world.

Stories helped me find and learn from other ways of knowing that challenged my knowledge of Colombia's history. Through local archives and narratives, I understood how mestizaje and nationalism dominate official narratives, and who benefits from it. The cumulative daily routines for survival, coupled with the influence of transnational networks of solidarity, unveiled to me the local archives in Quibdó as embodiments of postconflict utopias. As comisionada Julia Susana Mena Moreno shares in her story for *Mujeres Pacíficas,* her personal narrative is intertwined with the work of missionary Gonzalo de la Torre, and others who have imagined peace in Chocó. Digital and analog alternative narratives created new avenues for alternative memories and allowed for multiplicity in knowledge production. Muntú Bantú and the Muestra Bíblica challenge official narratives with Afrocentric narratives of collective memory. Despite the lack of infrastructure and funding, and recent threats, these utopian archives still exist, even if mostly in their digital forms.

As digital collaborative archives, Memorias del Río Atrato and Fotógrafas del Pacífico craft connections to utopian memories and local initiatives of memorialization that center Chocó as a space of survival and creativity. Writer Velia Vidal's epistolary book *Aguas de estuario* and Nuestro Motete project offer additional alternative narratives to the discourse of mestizaje as the norm in Colombia. These memories embody the sensory experience of Chocó and Blackness, and in doing so, they reclaim the technologies and genres that have been used as tools of oppression. These analog and digital memories can transform embodied knowledge into performative narratives that focus on survival and self-determination, rather than trauma, through collective and collaborative celebrations of survival.

Local, regional, and transnational feminist activism in the Colombian Pacific taught me the importance of everyday practices such as caring for each other and showing up—over and over again. La Red Departamental de Mujeres Chocoanas, La Ruta Pacífica de las Mujeres, and Women in Black become temporary communities that uncover the support needed for political mobilization. As an enduring performance, showing up is the basis of transnational solidarity and peace-building. Temporary communities emerge and vanish as nodes revitalizing or deactivating transnational networks that depend on local activism to protect women's lives. These utopian networks underscore care as a political practice, one that prioritizes reciprocity and interdependence as seeds for community-building.

Everyday utopias showed us that comisionadas' lived experiences are integral to their activism and storytelling, and that these embodied alternatives can offer new perspectives on normative ethics. Ethics became a daily performance that required constant repetition, rehearsals, and collaboration, and that carried the potential for failure. In the same way community-based collaborative research necessitated constant negotiation, everyday ethics represented incomplete endeavors toward mutual understanding and aid. Collective transformation is achievable only through ordinary actions that require being present with others and making ongoing commitments to each other's survival.

Utopias reveal the tension between disappointment and anticipation. Imagining otherwise is necessary for the postconflict utopias analyzed in this book to exist. Although the ways of thinking that I classify as utopian, as represented in stories, spaces, and daily practices, are incredibly powerful, their lack of a concrete connection to power renders them unachievable in a postconflict context. This final reflection highlights the limits of collaboration and writing to capture embodied knowledge, reminding us that the political potential of postconflict utopias cannot guarantee a specific outcome. The labor of imagining peace is central to utopian visions, which offer a critique of the established structures and narratives that revictimize entire populations in Colombia.

I envision contributing to future storytelling (academic or otherwise) that acknowledges the transnational networks sustained by Black women, and their theoretical contributions to research about their activism. In "La historia de María del Socorro," why nots appear for the first time to imagine women of the world as its audience. In "La historia de Rubiela," why nots reappear to denounce the dehumanization of Black women as a global issue. This book's utopias reveal peacemaking as an everyday labor that takes different shapes. Why nots are not only the driving force behind COCOMACIA's Comisión's work in the Colombian Pacific, but they also connect with Afrocentric archives like Muntú Bantú and La Muestra Bíblica and feminist networks such as La Ruta Pacífica de las Mujeres and Women in Black. Why nots describe the motivation for feminist solidarity in local and global contexts. When no other alternatives appear viable, creativity and imagination become part of everyday political practices to summon change. Why nots are inspirational and anticipative as much as they are defiant. They offer a utopian vision promising what still seems impossible.

Digital or not, storytelling emphasizes the value of ethical practices in envisioning the future. Through their stories and actions, the comisionadas embody a shared feeling: we do things with the support of each other, and we do things every day because we imagine other possibilities for each other. Mosquera Pérez reminds us of the role of support for survival. Cuesta Córdoba explains that community work is an embodied practice where spontaneity and constant work create a legacy transmissible only by being present. Mena Becerra and Rivas López address women directly to invite them to become active participants in the organization's activities as part of the community work that makes collective survival possible.

Postconflict utopias emphasize what war cannot destroy and what the aftermath can bring. Silvia Rivera Cusicanqui reminds us that "nada sería posible si la gente no deseara lo imposible"[10] [nothing would be possible if people did not wish the impossible]. The comisionadas' practices exhibit a commitment to fostering innovative opportunities for collective action and existence, in Chocó and beyond. The political work in Chocó shows how global networks of activism, storytelling, and knowledge production can foster transnational solidarity. Even if solidarity appears to be only symbolic while marching and chanting, a sign from the students' march in Bogotá in December 2018 reminds us that "lo imposible cuesta un poco más" [the impossible takes a little bit longer]. Survival and peace are long-term performances.

My collaboration with the comisionadas preceded the peace agreements with the FARC, as peace was surely a dream in 2013 when we recorded all the stories for *Mujeres Pacíficas*. In 2020, why nots became urgent amid a pandemic that has disproportionately affected Black communities worldwide, and in Chocó where there were no ICU units or ventilators until June. In 2024, the unequal distribution of grief, disability, and death still hangs heavy in the air, a stark reminder of the challenges we must overcome for our collective survival. The stories, spaces, practices, and networks that I highlight are world-making, but I call them utopian to signal their inevitable incompleteness. In a way, my hope with this book and the storytellers and visionaries who shared their time and knowledge with me is to unlock new possibilities for imagining future utopias, and future collaborations to wish what is not yet here into existence. This is an invitation to dream the impossible together.

Notes

Introduction. Utopias as Why Nots

1. I choose to use storytellers' last names when referring to their stories and experiences to recognize them as interlocutors and knowledge producers about the topics I write, in the same way I use last names for scholars.
2. María del Socorro Mosquera Pérez, "La historia de María del Socorro," *Mujeres Pacíficas*, 2013, http://www.mujerespacificas.org/madelsocorromosquera.
3. Ulrich Oslender, *The Geographies of Social Movements: Afro-Colombian Mobilization and the Aquatic Space*, 2016, 2, https://doi.org/10.1215/9780822374404.
4. Law 70 of 1993, also known as "La Ley de Comunidades Negras," is considered an impressive legal achievement for the recognition of Black Colombians' rights. Law 70 has been the legal framework for historical and ongoing social movements working toward materializing these rights. It not only recognizes Black communities' rights to collective property in the Colombian Pacific. It also recognizes socioeconomic rights to land use and natural resources, and it delineates the importance of curricular changes to guarantee rights to an ethnically relevant education. For more on Law 70, see Kiran Asher, "A Retrospective Look at the Winding Paths to Legalizing Afro-Colombian Rights in Law 70 of 1993," *Revista de Estudios Colombianos* 47 (January 1, 2016), https://scholarworks.umass.edu/wost_faculty_pubs/7.
5. Libia Grueso and Leyla Andrea Arroyo, "Women and the Defence of Place in Colombian Black Movement Struggles," *Development* 45, no. 1 (March 2002): 60, https://doi.org/10.1057/palgrave.development.1110319.
6. Yesenia Barragan, *Freedom's Captives: Slavery and Gradual Emancipation on the Colombian Black Pacific* (New York: Cambridge University Press, 2021), 7.

7. María Elena Cepeda, "Putting a 'Good Face on the Nation': Beauty, Memes, and the Gendered Rebranding of Global *Colombianidad*," *WSQ: Women's Studies Quarterly* 46, no. 1 (April 25, 2018): 125, https://doi.org/10.1353/wsq.2018.0005.

8. I use the "x" following the use of gender-inclusive language in Latin American Spanish that precedes and informs the controversy around the word "Latinx" in the United States. The use of "x" is part of a decision to think beyond the gender binary in *Tejiendo de otro modo: Feminismo, epistemología y apuestas descoloniales en Abya Yala*, edited by Yuderkys Espinosa Miñoso, Diana Gómez Correal, and Karina Ochoa Muñoz, and published in Colombia by Editorial Universidad del Cauca in 2014. Another example: Bolivian theorist Silvia Rivera Cusicanqui's 1988 book *Los artesanos libertarios y la ética del trabajo*, using masculine grammatical gender, was republished by Argentinian press Tinta Limón in 2013 as *Lxs artesanxs libertarixs y la ética del trabajo*, clearly using inclusive language to denaturalize masculine grammatical gender as universal.

9. Fernando García et al., "The Formation of Mestizo Nations," in *Against Racism: Organizing for Social Change in Latin America*, ed. Mónica Moreno Figueroa and Peter Wade (Pittsburgh: University of Pittsburgh Press, 2022), 42.

10. Tanya Katerí Hernández, *Racial Subordination in Latin America: The Role of the State, Customary Law, and the New Civil Rights Response* (New York: Cambridge University Press, 2013), 20.

11. "Darío Henao Restrepo Interviews Delfín Ignacio Grueso Vanegas. En Colombia, el centro queda en el centro y además queda en lo alto: Colombia es lo que se ve desde Monserrate," *El Guarengue* (blog), May 23, 2022, https://miguarengue.blogspot.com.

12. Kiran Asher, *Black and Green: Afro-Colombians, Development, and Nature in the Pacific Lowlands* (Durham, NC: Duke University Press, 2009), 167.

13. Julio César Uribe Hermocillo, "Ley 70 de 1993: 28 Años de Vana Letra," *El Guarengue* (blog), August 30, 2021, https://miguarengue.blogspot.com/2021/08/ley-70-de1993-28-anos-de-vana-letra.html.

14. "I love the word survival. It sounds to me like a promise" is a quote by Audre Lorde used as an epigraph in Alexis Pauline Gumbs, "Foreword," in *Beyond Survival: Strategies and Stories from the Transformative Justice Movement*, ed. Leah Lakshmi Piepzna-Samarasinha and Ejeris Dixon (Edinburgh: AK Press, 2020).

15. Diana Pardo Pedraza, "Ethical Disconcertment and the Politics of Troublemaking," *American Ethnologist*, July 6, 2023, https://doi.org/10.1111/amet.13198.

16. Rita Laura Segato, *La guerra contra las mujeres* (Madrid: Traficantes de Sueños, 2016), 26.

17. Ana Cacopardo, "'Nada sería posible si la gente no deseara lo imposible.' Entrevista a Silvia Rivera Cusicanqui," *Andamios* 15, no. 37 (August 2018): 180, http://dx.doi.org/10.29092/uacm.v15i37.635.

18. Silvia Rivera Cusicanqui, *Un mundo ch'ixi es posible: Ensayos desde un presente en crisis* (Buenos Aires: Tinta Limón, 2018), 85.

19. Feministas Autónomas, "Una declaración feminista autónoma, el desafío de hacer comunidad en la casa de las diferencias," in *Tejiendo de otro modo: Feminismo,*

epistemología y apuestas descoloniales en Abya Yala, ed. Yuderkys Espinosa Miñoso, Diana Marcela Gómez Correal, and Karina Ochoa Muñoz (Popayán, Colombia: Editorial Universidad del Cauca, 2014).

20. Gloria Anzaldúa, *Borderlands/La Frontera: The New Mestiza* (San Francisco: Aunt Lute Books, 1999).

21. José Esteban Muñoz, *Cruising Utopia: The Then and There of Queer Futurity* (New York: New York University Press, 2009).

22. Catherine Knight Steele, *Digital Black Feminism* (New York University Press, 2021), 32.

23. Steele, 32.

24. Betty Ruth Lozano, "Feminismo Negro-Afrocolombiano: Ancestral, insurgente y cimarrón. Un feminismo en-lugar," *Intervenciones Latinoamericanas* 5, no. 9 (2016): 45.

25. Alejandro Castillejo-Cuéllar, "La paz en pequeña escala: Fracturas de la vida cotidiana y las políticas de la transición en Colombia," *Revista de Estudios Colombianos* no. 53 (2019): 5.

26. Gimena Sánchez-Garzoli, "Ongoing Protests and Abuses in Colombia," Washington Office on Latin America, August 9, 2021, https://www.wola.org/2021/08/ongoing-protests-and-abuses-in-colombia/.

27. Germán Guzmán Campos, Orlando Fals-Borda, and Eduardo Umaña Luna, *La Violencia en Colombia* (Bogotá: Taurus, 2005).

28. Héctor Abad Faciolince, "Estética y Narcotráfico," *Revista de Estudios Hispánicos (St. Louis, MO)* 42, no. 3 (October 2018): 513–18.

29. Juliana Martínez, *Haunting Without Ghosts: Spectral Realism in Colombian Literature, Film, and Art* (Austin: University of Texas Press, 2020), 12.

30. Aldona Bialowas Pobutsky, *Pablo Escobar and Colombian Narcoculture* (Gainesville: University of Florida Press, 2020).

31. María Elena Cepeda, "'A Cartel Built for Love': 'Medellín, Pablo Escobar, and the Scripts of Global Colombianidad,'" in *Critical Dialogues in Latinx Studies: A Reader*, ed. Ana Y. Ramos-Zayas and Mérida M. Rúa (New York: New York University Press, 2021), 39–50.

32. Grupo de Memoria Histórica, *¡Basta ya! Colombia: Memorias de guerra y dignidad* (Bogotá: Imprenta Nacional, 2013), 36, https://centrodememoriahistorica.gov.co/basta-ya-memorias-de-guerra-y-dignidad/.

33. Grupo de Memoria Histórica, 142.

34. Cepeda, "'A Cartel Built for Love,'" 39–40.

35. Claudia Mosquera Rosero-Labbé, "Reparaciones para negros, afrocolombianos y raizales como rescatados de la trata negrera trasatlántica y desterrados de la guerra en Colombia," in *Afro-Reparaciones: Memorias de la esclavitud y Justicia Reparativa para negros, afrocolombianos y raizales*, ed. Claudia Mosquera Rosero-Labbé and Luiz Claudio Barcelos, Estudios Afrocolombianos (Bogotá: Universidad Nacional de Colombia, 2007), 236.

36. Tianna S. Paschel, *Becoming Black Political Subjects: Movements and Ethno-Racial Rights in Colombia and Brazil* (Princeton, NJ: Princeton University Press, 2018), 43.

37. UNHCR "Colombia: Large-Group Internal Displacement," Global Focus: UNHCR Operations Worldwide, December 2022, https://reporting.unhcr.org/colombia-large-group-internal-displacement.

38. Aurora Vergara-Figueroa et al., *Descolonizando mundos: Aportes de intelectuales negras y negros al pensamiento social colombiano* (Buenos Aires: Consejo Latinoamericano de Ciencias Sociales, 2017), 11, https://doi.org/10.2307/j.ctv253f4t7.

39. Mosquera Rosero-Labbé, "Reparaciones."

40. Christen A. Smith, "Facing the Dragon: Black Mothering, Sequelae, and Gendered Necropolitics in the Americas," *Transforming Anthropology* 24, no. 1 (2016): 31–48, https://doi.org/10.1111/traa.12055.

41. María del Socorro Mosquera Pérez, "La historia de María del Socorro."

42. Linda Tuhiwai Smith, *Decolonizing Methodologies: Research and Indigenous Peoples* (London: Zed Books, 1999).

43. The concept is attributed to Colombian artist Adolfo Albán, though my use follows Black Colombian feminists Betty Ruth Lozano Lerma and Libia Grueso. For more on re-existencia, see: Betty Ruth Lozano Lerma, "Pedagogías para la vida, la alegría y la re-existencia: pedagogías de mujeres negras que curan y vinculan," *[Con]textos* 5, no. 19 (September 26, 2016): 11–19; Libia Grueso, "Escenarios de colonialismo y (de)colonialidad en la construcción del Ser Negro. Apuntes sobre las relaciones de género en comunidades negras del Pacífico Colombiano," *Comentario Internacional: Revista del Centro Andino de Estudios Internacionales* 7 (2006–2007): 145–56.

44. Audre Lorde, "The Master's Tools Will Never Dismantle the Master's House," in *Sister Outsider: Essays and Speeches* (Berkeley, CA: Ten Speed Press, 2007), 110–14.

45. Diana Taylor, *The Archive and the Repertoire: Performing Cultural Memory in the Americas* (Durham, NC: Duke University Press, 2003).

46. Audre Lorde, "A Litany for Survival," in *The Collected Poems of Audre Lorde* (New York: W. W. Norton, 2000).

47. Julieta Paredes, "Hilando fino desde el feminismo indígena comunitario," in *Aproximaciones críticas a las prácticas teórico-políticas del feminismo latinoamericano*, ed. Yuderkys Espinosa Miñoso and Lucía de Leone (Coloquio Latinoamericano Pensamiento y Práxis Feminista, Buenos Aires: En la Frontera, 2010).

48. Alexis Pauline Gumbs, cited in Sara Ahmed, *Living a Feminist Life* (Durham, NC: Duke University Press, 2017), 235.

49. Ahmed, 235.

50. Betty Ruth Lozano and Bibiana Peñaranda, "Memoria y reparación ¿y de ser mujeres negras qué?," in *Memorias de la esclavitud y Justicia Reparativa para negros, afrocolombianos y raizales*, ed. Claudia Mosquera Rosero-Labbé and Luiz Claudio Barcelos (Bogotá: Universidad Nacional de Colombia, 2007), 715–24.

51. Kimberlé Crenshaw, "Demarginalizing the Intersection of Race and Sex: A Black Feminist Critique of Antidiscrimination Doctrine, Feminist Theory and Antiracist Politics," *University of Chicago Legal Forum*, no. 1 (1989), https://chicagounbound.uchicago.edu/uclf/vol1989/iss1/8.

52. Aurora Vergara Figueroa, *Afrodescendant Resistance to Deracination in Colombia: Massacre at Bellavista-Bojayá-Chocó* (Cham, Switzerland: Palgrave Macmillan, 2018), 83.

53. Peter Wade, "Anti-Racism in Mestizo Societies," in *Against Racism: Organizing for Social Change in Latin America*, ed. Mónica Moreno Figueroa and Peter Wade (Pittsburgh: University of Pittsburgh Press, 2022), 169.

54. Jeffrey S. Juris and Alex Khasnabish, "Introduction: Ethnography and Activism within Networked Spaces of Transnational Encounter," in *Insurgent Encounters: Transnational Activism, Ethnography, and the Political* (Durham, NC: Duke University Press, 2013), https://doi.org/10.1215/9780822395867-001.

55. Peggy Phelan, *Unmarked: The Politics of Performance* (London: Routledge, 1993).

56. Stuart Hall, "What Is This 'Black' in Black Popular Culture?" *Social Justice* 20, no. 1/2 (51–52) (1993): 104–14, 107.

57. Joanne Rappaport, *Intercultural Utopias: Public Intellectuals, Cultural Experimentation, and Ethnic Pluralism in Colombia* (Durham, NC: Duke University Press, 2005), 2.

58. Veena Das and Didier Fassin, "Ordinary Ethics," in *A Companion to Moral Anthropology* (Oxford: Wiley Blackwell, 2012), 133–49, https://doi.org/10.1002/9781118290620.ch8.

59. Alison Mountz et al., "For Slow Scholarship: A Feminist Politics of Resistance through Collective Action in the Neoliberal University," *ACME: An International Journal for Critical Geographies* 14, no. 4 (August 18, 2015): 1235–59; Maggie Berg and Barbara Seeber, *Slow Professor: Challenging the Culture of Speed in the Academy* (Toronto: University of Toronto Press, 2016).

60. "We can . . . understand the flexibility of crip time as being not only an accommodation to those who 'need' more time but also, and perhaps especially, a challenge to normative and normalizing expectations of pace and scheduling." Alison Kafer, *Feminist, Queer, Crip* (Bloomington: Indiana University Press, 2013), 27.

61. Moya Bailey, "The Ethics of Pace," *South Atlantic Quarterly* 120, no. 2 (April 1, 2021): 288, https://doi.org/10.1215/00382876-8916032.

62. Jina B. Kim and Sami Schalk, "Reclaiming the Radical Politics of Self-Care: A Crip-of-Color Critique," *South Atlantic Quarterly* 120, no. 2 (April 1, 2021): 325–42, https://doi.org/10.1215/00382876-8916074.

63. Itza A. Carbajal and Michelle Caswell, "Critical Digital Archives: A Review from Archival Studies," *American Historical Review* 126, no. 3 (September 2021): 1105, https://doi.org/10.1093/ahr/rhab359.

64. Kimberly Christen and Jane Anderson, "Toward Slow Archives," *Archival Science* 19, no. 2 (June 1, 2019): 99, https://doi.org/10.1007/s10502-019-09307-x.

65. For more information on this project and this process, see: Tania Lizarazo et al., "Ethics, Collaboration, and Knowledge Production: Digital Storytelling with Sexually Diverse Farmworkers in California," *Lateral*, no. 6.1 (2017), https://doi.org/10.25158/L6.1.5.

66. Nick Couldry, "Digital Storytelling, Media Research and Democracy: Conceptual Choices and Alternative Futures," in *Digital Storytelling, Mediatized Stories: Self-*

Representations in New Media, ed. Knut Lundby (New York: Peter Lang Publishing, 2008), 41–60.

67. Joe Lambert, "Full Circle," StoryCenter, accessed February 25, 2020, https://www.storycenter.org/storycenter-blog/blog/2013/2/26/full-circle.html.

68. Ashlee Cunsolo Willox, Sherilee L. Harper, and Victoria L. Edge, "Storytelling in a Digital Age: Digital Storytelling as an Emerging Narrative Method for Preserving and Promoting Indigenous Oral Wisdom," *Qualitative Research* 13, no. 2 (April 1, 2013): 141, https://doi.org/10.1177/1468794112446105.

69. Cunsolo Willox, Harper, and Edge, 141.

70. Geraldine Bloustien, "Play, Affect, and Participatory Video as a Reflexive Research Strategy," in *Handbook of Participatory Video*, ed. E.-J. Milne, Claudia Mitchell, and Naydene De Lange (Lanham, MD: AltaMira Press, 2012), 115–30.

71. Fredric Jameson, *Archaeologies of the Future: The Desire Called Utopia and Other Science Fictions* (London: Verso, 2005), 74.

72. Eve Tuck, "Suspending Damage: A Letter to Communities," *Harvard Educational Review* 79, no. 3 (September 1, 2009): 413, https://doi.org/10.17763/haer.79.3.n0016675661t3n15.

73. Tuck, 416.

74. Saidiya Hartman, *Lose Your Mother: A Journey along the Atlantic Slave Route* (New York: Farrar, Straus and Giroux, 2008).

75. Silvia Rivera Cusicanqui, *Ch'ixinakax Utxiwa: Una reflexión sobre prácticas y discursos descolonizadores* (Buenos Aires: Tinta Limón Ediciones, 2010).

Chapter 1. Utopian Rehearsals

A previous version of this chapter was published as "Alongside Violence: Everyday Survival in Chocó, Colombia," *Journal of Latin American Cultural Studies* 27, no. 2 (April 3, 2018): 175–96, https://doi.org/10.1080/13569325.2018.1447447.

1. Banessa Rivas López, "La historia de Banessa," *Mujeres Pacíficas*, 2013, http://www.mujerespacificas.org/stories#/banessarivas.

2. Consejo de Autoridades Indígenas Asociación OREWA, "El Territorio Indígena del Resguardo Alto Río Neguá, afectado por la explotación Minera," Comisión interétnica de la Verdad de la Región Pacífico (CIVP), December 4, 2011, https://verdadpacifico.org/el-territorio-indgena-del-resguardo-alto-ro-negu-afectado-por-la-explotacin-minera/.

3. Oslender, *The Geographies of Social Movements*, 1.

4. Ochy Curiel, "Constructing Feminist Methodologies from the Perspective of Decolonial Feminism," in *Decolonial Feminism in Abya Yala: Caribbean, Meso, and South American Contributions and Challenges*, ed. Yuderkys Espinosa Miñoso, María Lugones, and Nelson Maldonado-Torres (Lanham, MD: Rowman and Littlefield, 2021), 54.

5. In *The Archive and the Repertoire*, Taylor theorizes scenario as a framework that defines a perspective, foregrounding some things while hiding others.

6. Stephen Ferry, *Violentology: A Manual of the Colombian Conflict* (New York: Umbrage, 2012), 104.

7. Eve Kosofsky Sedgwick and Adam Frank, *Touching Feeling: Affect, Pedagogy, Performativity* (Durham, NC: Duke University Press, 2003).

8. Audre Lorde, "A Burst of Light: Living with Cancer," in *The Selected Works of Audre Lorde*, first edition (New York: W. W. Norton, 2020), 92.

9. Lorde, 131.

10. Jina B. Kim, "Toward a Crip-of-Color Critique: Thinking with Minich's 'Enabling Whom?'" *Lateral* 6, no. 1 (2017), https://doi.org/10.25158/L6.1.14.

11. Comisión de Génerode COCOMACIA, "Para Justa," *Mujeres Pacíficas*, 2013, http://www.mujerespacificas.org/stories#/justamena.

12. Kathleen Stewart, *Ordinary Affects* (Durham, NC: Duke University Press, 2007).

13. Michel de Certeau, *The Practice of Everyday Life* (Berkeley: University of California Press, 2011).

14. Avery Gordon, *Ghostly Matters: Haunting and the Sociological Imagination* (Minneapolis: University of Minnesota Press, 1997).

15. Internal Displacement Monitoring Centre (IDMC), accessed February 25, 2023, https://www.internal-displacement.org/countries/colombia.

16. Eduardo Restrepo and Áxel Rojas, *Afrodescendientes en Colombia: Compilación bibliográfica* (Bogotá: Universidad Javeriana, 2008).

17. In her chapter about gender, ethnicity, and development, Kiran Asher retells a conversation with Victoria Torres about women's organizing within COCOMACIA with the creation of a women's section, the origin of the Comisión de Género: "Torres told me that the Women's Section did not split formally from ACIA because it is committed to the [B]lack movement's ethno-political project and to implementing Law 70)." *Black and Green*, 138.

18. Ferry, *Violentology*.

19. Campos, Fals-Borda, and Luna, *La violencia en Colombia*.

20. Ferry, *Violentology*, 12.

21. Elaine Scarry, *The Body in Pain: The Making and Unmaking of the World* (New York: Oxford University Press, 1987), 9.

22. Peter Waldmann, "Is There a Culture of Violence in Colombia?" *Terrorism and Political Violence* 19, no. 4 (Winter 2007): 593–609.

23. Gerard Martin, "The 'Tradition of Violence' in Colombia: Material and Symbolic Aspects," in *Meaning of Violence: A Cross-Cultural Perspective*, ed. Göran Aijmer and Jon Abbink (New York: Berg, 2000), 161–91.

24. Daniel Pécaut, *Orden y violencia: Evolución socio-política de Colombia entre 1930 y 1953* (Bogotá: Editorial Norma, 2001).

25. Ulrich Oslender, "Spaces of Terror and Fear on Colombia's Pacific Coast," in *Violent Geographies: Fear, Terror, and Political Violence*, ed. Derek Gregory and Allan Pred (New York: Routledge, 2013), https://doi.org/10.4324/9780203944585-7.

26. Ulrich Oslender, "Another History of Violence: The Production of 'Geographies of Terror' in Colombia's Pacific Coast Region," *Latin American Perspectives* 35, no. 5 (September 1, 2008): 77–102, https://doi.org/10.1177/0094582X08321961.

27. Saidiya V. Hartman, *Scenes of Subjection: Terror, Slavery, and Self-Making in Nineteenth-Century America* (New York: Oxford University Press, 1997).

28. Sara Ahmed, *The Cultural Politics of Emotion* (New York: Routledge, 2012), 30.

29. Aurora Vergara Figueroa and Katherine Arboleda Hurtado, "Feminismo Afrodiaspórico. Una Agenda Amergente Del Feminismo Negro En Colombia," *Universitas Humanística*, no. 78 (December 2014): 109–34; Lozano and Peñaranda, "Memoria y reparación ¿y de ser mujeres negras qué?"; Betty Ruth Lozano Lerma, "The Killing of Women and Global Accumulation: The Case of Bello Puerto Del Mar Mi Buenaventura," in *Decolonial Feminism in Abya Yala: Caribbean, Meso, and South American Contributions and Challenges*, ed. Yuderkys Espinosa Miñoso, María Lugones, and Nelson Maldonado-Torres (Lanham, MD: Rowman and Littlefield, 2021), 155–72.

30. María Eugenia Velásquez Prestán, Natalia Escobar García, and Aurora Vergara Figueroa, "Etnografía Comprometida en Contextos de Conflicto Armado: Lecciones de Bellavista-Bojayá-Chocó y Bahía Málaga-Valle Del Cauca-Colombia," *Anthropologica* 36, no. 41 (2018): 59–92, https://doi.org/10.18800/anthropologica.201802.003; Juan Orrantia, "Momentos de Silencio, Serie 1–8," *Antípoda: Revista de Antropologia y Arqueologia* 9 (July 1, 2009): 217–30, https://doi.org/10.7440/antipoda9.2009.08.

31. Vergara-Figueroa, *Afrodescendant Resistance to Deracination in Colombia*; Oslender, *The Geographies of Social Movements*.

32. Ochy Curiel, "Rethinking Radical Anti-Racist Feminist Politics in a Global Neoliberal Context," trans. Manuela Borzone and Alexander Ponomareff, *Meridians* 14, no. 2 (2016): 46–55, https://doi.org/10.2979/meridians.14.2.04; Grueso and Arroyo, "Women and the Defence of Place in Colombian Black Movement Struggles."

33. Vergara-Figueroa, *Afrodescendant Resistance to Deracination in Colombia*.

34. Sergio A. Mosquera, *La trata negrera y la esclavización: Una perspectiva histórico-psicológica*, vol. 19, Ma'Mawu (Bogotá: Apidama Ediciones, 2017), 24.

35. Achille Mbembé, "Necropolitics," trans. Libby Meintjes, *Public Culture* 15, no. 1 (March 25, 2003): 21.

36. Taylor, *The Archive and the Repertoire*, 15.

37. Ahmed, *The Cultural Politics of Emotion*, 22.

38. Andrés L. Rosales García, "Las 18 Mujeres Que Salvaron a un Pueblo de La Extinción," *El Tiempo*, February 1, 2005, https://www.eltiempo.com/archivo/documento/MAM-1684173.

39. Benilda Gamboa de Córdoba and Luis Mosquera Navia, "Protesta Chocoana," *El Tiempo*, February 28, 2005, https://www.eltiempo.com/archivo/documento/MAM-1677881.

40. For more on the Bojayá massacre, see Aurora Vergara-Figueroa's extended case-based study *Afrodescendant Resistance to Deracination in Colombia*.

41. García et al., "The Formation of Mestizo Nations," 44.

42. Gamboa de Córdoba and Mosquera Navia, "Protesta Chocoana."

43. Gamboa de Córdoba and Mosquera Navia, "Protesta Chocoana."

44. This poster is part of the campaign "La violencia contra las mujeres no te hace campeón" [Violence against women does not make you a champion].

45. Carnavalenguas (Carnaval Nacional de Lenguas, Voces y Letras de Mujeres— National Carnival of Women's Languages, Voices and Letters) Alianza Nacional de Mujeres Libres de Violencia (Alliance of Women Free of Violence) is both an artistic/literary contest and a social movement against gendered violence. As part of *La Ruta Pacífica de las Mujeres*, it reclaims cultural practices (popular music, art, theater, dance, poetry, etc.) to create carnival-like marches and workshops in which women use wigs, masks, body paint, dancing, and singing as strategies for solidarity and memory.

46. Lorde, "A Burst of Light: Living with Cancer," 131.

47. Saidiya V. Hartman and Frank B. Wilderson, "The Position of the Unthought," *Qui Parle* 13, no. 2 (2003): 183.

48. Hartman and Wilderson, 185.

49. José Esteban Muñoz, *Disidentifications: Queers of Color and the Performance of Politics* (Minneapolis: University of Minnesota Press, 1999), 11.

50. Das and Fassin, "Ordinary Ethics," 139.

51. Asher, *Black and Green*, 26.

52. Lorde, "A Burst of Light: Living with Cancer," 92.

53. Fred Moten, "Black Op," *PMLA* 123, no. 5 (October 2008): 1743–47.

54. Arturo Escobar, *Territories of Difference: Place, Movements, Life, Redes* (Durham, NC: Duke University Press, 2008).

55. Moten, "Black Op," 1745.

56. Alán Peláez López, *Intergalactic Travels: Poems from a Fugitive Alien* (The Operating System, 2020), 94, https://www.theoperatingsystem.org/wp-content/uploads/2020/03/Intergalactic-Travels_Alan-Pelaez-Lopez.pdf.

Chapter 2. Utopian Stories

1. Peter Wade, "Territory and Anti-Racism," in *Against Racism: Organizing for Social Change in Latin America*, ed. Mónica Moreno Figueroa and Peter Wade (Pittsburgh: University of Pittsburgh Press, 2022), 102.

2. Hartman, *Lose Your Mother*.

3. Mara Viveros Vigoya, "La interseccionalidad: Una aproximación situada a la dominación," *Debate Feminista* 52 (October 1, 2016): 1–17, https://doi.org/10.1016/j.df.2016.09.005.

4. For more of the hemispheric construction of Latinidad, see Petra R. Rivera-Rideau, Jennifer A. Jones, and Tianna S. Paschel, "Introduction: Theorizing Afro-Latinidades," in *Afro-Latin@s in Movement: Critical Approaches to Blackness and Transnationalism in the Americas* (New York: Palgrave Macmillan, 2016).

5. Peter Wade et al., "Nation and the Absent Presence of Race in Latin American Genomics," *Current Anthropology* 55, no. 5 (October 1, 2014): 503, https://doi.org/10.1086/677945.

6. Stories, previews, and other resources from *Mujeres Pacíficas* are available here: http://www.mujerespacificas.org/.

7. Jaime Arocha, "Ley 70 de 1993: Utopía Para Afrodescendientes Excluidos," in *Utopía para los excluidos: El multiculturalismo en África y América Latina*, ed. Jaime Arocha, Centro de Estudios Sociales (Bogotá: Universidad Nacional de Colombia, 2004), 164–65.

8. Peggy Phelan, *Unmarked: The Politics of Performance* (London: Routledge, 1993), 26.

9. Oslender, *The Geographies of Social Movements*, 47.

10. Teodora Hurtado Saa et al., "Los estudios contemporáneos sobre población Afrocolombiana y el dilema de la producción del conocimiento 'Propio,'" in *Descolonizando mundos: Aportes de intelectuales negras y negros al pensamiento social colombiano*, ed. Aurora Vergara-Figueroa et al. (Buenos Aires: Consejo Latinoamericano de Ciencias Sociales, 2017), 335–60, https://doi.org/10.2307/j.ctv253f4t7.13.

11. Mosquera Pérez, "La historia de María del Socorro."

12. Alabaos are part of the Colombian Pacific's death rituals and are associated with oral tradition, but they have been used as part of collective political action, especially after the Bojayá massacre in 2002. See María Paola Herrera Valencia et al., "El objeto-relato como dispositivo de memoria: El caso del Grupo de Alabao de Pogue, Bojayá, Chocó," in *Lugares, recorridos y sentidos de la memoria histórica: Acercamientos metodológicos*, ed. Laura Fonseca Durán et al. (Bogotá: Universidad de la Sabana, 2019).

13. Cunsolo Willox, Harper, and Edge, "Storytelling in a Digital Age," 132.

14. Sara Ahmed, *Living a Feminist Life* (Durham, NC: Duke University Press, 2016), 80.

15. Saskia Wieringa, *Subversive Women: Historical Experiences of Gender and Resistance* (London: Zed Books, 1995), 1.

16. Phelan, *Unmarked*.

17. Phelan, *Unmarked*.

18. Gordon, *Ghostly Matters*.

19. Gordon, 5.

20. Other examples of introductions include: "Mi nombre es Luz Adonis Mena Becerra. Vengo del río Munguidó, una comunidad que se llama Alta Gracia" [My name is Luz Adonis Mena Becerra. I come from Munguidó River, a community called Alta Gracia], which highlights the importance of rivers in the Colombian Pacific, part of genealogies of belonging to communities and territories. "Mi nombre es Ana Rosa Heredia Cuesta y vengo de una comunidad muy humilde. Yo pertenezco al municipio de Bojayá" [My name is Ana Rosa Heredia Cuesta and I come from a very humble community. I belong to the municipality of Bojayá] is another one where the place of origin is also associated with belonging and class. "Hola todas y todos. Mi nombre es Banessa. Soy de una comunidad llamada Isla de los Rojas, municipio de Murindó, Antioquia, zona 9 área influencia de la COCOMACIA" [Hi everyone. My name is Banessa. I am from a community called Isla de los Rojas, municipality of Murindó, Antioquia, COCOMACIA's area of influence zone 9] is another introduction that reveals a generational difference: using gender-inclusive language (todas y todos) and

not including her two last names, but also using COCOMACIA's zones as a reference, and a reminder that there are Black collective territories in Antioquia (even if, as a region, it is associated with whiteness).

21. For more on StoryCenter's method, including the seven steps of digital storytelling and the three-day workshop timeline, see Joe Lambert and Brooke Hessler, *Digital Storytelling: Capturing Lives, Creating Community* (New York: Routledge, 2018).

22. This adaptation was inspired by my participation in the digital storytelling project *Sexualidades Campesinas*. For more details on the process, see Lizarazo et al., "Ethics, Collaboration, and Knowledge Production."

23. Son Vivienne, *Digital Identity and Everyday Activism: Sharing Private Stories with Networked Publics* (Basingstoke, UK: Palgrave Macmillan, 2016), 44.

24. Adele De Jager et al., "Digital Storytelling in Research: A Systematic Review," *The Qualitative Report*, October 2, 2017, 2551, https://doi.org/10.46743/2160-3715/2017.2970.

25. Martha Rosler, "To Argue for a Video of Representation. To Argue for a Video Against the Mythology of Everyday Life," in *The Everyday*, ed. Stephen Johnstone (London: Whitechapel Gallery, 2008), 53.

26. Cunsolo Willox, Harper, and Edge, "Storytelling in a Digital Age."

27. Ankit Kumar, "Energy Geographies in/of the Anthropocene: Where Now?" *Geography Compass* 16, no. 10 (2022): e12659, https://doi.org/10.1111/gec3.12659.

28. "Indice de Cobertura Energía Electrica—ICEE," Datos Abiertos Colombia, accessed July 13, 2023, https://www.datos.gov.co/Minas-y-Energ-a/Indice-de-cobertura-energ-a-electrica-ICEE/uu67-ffu5.

29. Ministerio de Minas y Energía, "Cobertura de Energia Eléctrica—ICEE Actual," Intégrame, accessed July 13, 2023, https://www.integrame.gov.co/tablero/cobertura-de-energia-electrica-icee-actual/.

30. DANE, "Encuesta de tecnologías de la información y las comunicaciones en hogares (ENTIC Hogares)," Departamento Administrativo Nacional de Estadística, accessed July 13, 2023, https://www.dane.gov.co/index.php/estadisticas-por-tema.

31. Nicolás Acosta García and Katharine N Farrell, "Crafting Electricity through Social Protest: Afro-Descendant and Indigenous Embera Communities Protesting for Hydroelectric Infrastructure in Utría National Park, Colombia," *Environment and Planning D: Society and Space* 37, no. 2 (April 2019): 249, https://doi.org/10.1177/0263775818810230.

32. Son Vivienne and Jean Burgess, "The Remediation of the Personal Photograph and the Politics of Self-Representation in Digital Storytelling," *Journal of Material Culture* 18, no. 3 (September 2013): 280, https://doi.org/10.1177/1359183513492080.

33. Jean Burgess, "Hearing Ordinary Voices: Cultural Studies, Vernacular Creativity and Digital Storytelling," *Continuum* 20, no. 2 (June 1, 2006): 210, https://doi.org/10.1080/10304310600641737.

34. See Claudia Mosquera Rosero-Labbé, "Reparaciones para negros, afrocolombianos y raizales como rescatados de la Trata Negrera Trasatlántica y desterrados de la guerra en Colombia," in *Afro-Reparaciones: Memorias de la esclavitud y Justicia Reparativa para negros, afrocolombianos y raizales*, ed. Claudia Mosquera Rosero-Labbé and Luiz

Claudio Barcelos, Estudios Afrocolombianos (Bogotá: Universidad Nacional de Colombia, 2007), 213–78. Betty Ruth Lozano, "Feminismo Negro—Afrocolombiano: ancestral, insurgente y cimarrón. Un feminismo en-lugar | Intersticios de la política y la cultura. Intervenciones latinoamericanas," *Intervenciones Latinoamericanas* 5, no. 9 (2016): 23–48, https://revistas.unc.edu.ar/index.php/intersticios/article/view/14612.

35. bell hooks, *Teaching Critical Thinking: Practical Wisdom* (New York: Routledge, 2013), 43.

36. Luz Adonis Mena Becerra, "La historia de Adonis," *Mujeres Pacíficas*, 2013, http://www.mujerespacificas.org/stories#/adonismena.

37. Rivas López, "La historia de Banessa," *Mujeres Pacíficas*, 2013, http://www.mujerespacificas.org/stories#/banessarivas.

38. María Mercedes Carranza, *El canto de las moscas: Versión de los acontecimientos* (Bogotá: Arango Editores, 1998), http://babel.banrepcultural.org/cdm/ref/collection/p17054coll10/id/2830.

39. Grupo de Memoria Histórica, *Bojayá. La Guerra sin límites* (Bogotá: Aguilar, 2010), http://centrodememoriahistorica.gov.co/bojaya-la-guerra-sin-limites/.

40. Elizabeth A. Povinelli, *Economies of Abandonment: Social Belonging and Endurance in Late Liberalism* (Durham, NC: Duke University Press, 2011), 77.

41. Carmen Navia Mena, "La historia de Carmen," *Mujeres Pacíficas*, 2013, http://www.mujerespacificas.org/stories#/carmennavia.

42. Yenny Palacios Romaña, "La historia de Yenny," *Mujeres Pacíficas*, 2013, http://www.mujerespacificas.org/stories#/yennypalacios.

43. In 1977, the Spanish philologist Germán de Granda referred to secrets as "formulas orales" included in the "categoría de las *contras* o conjuros de protección contra diferentes males" in his text "Fórmulas mágicas de conjuro en el departamento del Chocó (Colombia)," *Thesaurus* XXXII, no. 1 (1977): 168.

44. Mena Becerra, "La historia de Adonis."

45. Mariluz Moya Cuesta, "La historia de Mariluz," *Mujeres Pacíficas*, 2013, http://www.mujerespacificas.org/stories#/mariluzmoya.

46. Vivienne and Burgess, "The Remediation of the Personal Photograph and the Politics of Self-Representation in Digital Storytelling," 286.

47. Doris Sommer, *Foundational Fictions: The National Romances of Latin America* (Berkeley: University of California Press, 1991).

48. Michael Taussig, *My Cocaine Museum* (Chicago: University of Chicago Press, 2009), 9.

Chapter 3. Utopian Archives

1. For more information on Movimiento Cimarrón, see its website at http://movimientocimarron.org/.

2. Nancy Raquel Mirabal, "Rethinking the Archive," in *Afro-Latin@s in Movement: Critical Approaches to Blackness and Transnationalism in the Americas*, ed. Petra R. Rivera-Rideau, Jennifer A. Jones, and Tianna S. Paschel (New York: Palgrave Macmillan, 2016), 135.

3. Yeidy M. Rivero, "Anatomy of a Protest: Grey's Anatomy, Colombia's A Corazón Abierto and the Politicization of a Format," in *Contemporary Latina/o Media: Production, Circulation, Politics*, ed. Arlene M. Dávila and Yeidy M. Rivero (New York: New York University Press, 2014), 149–66.

4. Inge Helena Valencia Peña and Laura Silva Chica, "Nina S. de Friedemann: Imágenes de la existencia negra en Colombia," *Revista Chilena de Antropología Visual* no. 23 (June 2014): 29.

5. Valencia Peña and Silva Chica, 29.

6. Biblioteca Luis Ángel Arango, "Nina S. de Friedemann-Archivo," Banrepcultural: Red Cultural del Banco de la República en Colombia, accessed February 28, 2020, https://www.banrepcultural.org/coleccion-bibliografica/especiales/nina-s-de-friedemann.

7. "Collection Search: Chocó," British Museum, accessed February 28, 2020, https://www.britishmuseum.org/collection/search?keyword=chocó.

8. Taussig, *My Cocaine Museum*, x.

9. "Módulo de Atención al Ciudadano," Museo Nacional de Colombia, accessed February 28, 2020, http://www.museonacional.gov.co/atencion-al-ciudadano/Paginas/default.aspx.

10. Peter Wade, "Rethinking 'Mestizaje': Ideology and Lived Experience," *Journal of Latin American Studies* 37, no. 2 (2005): 245.

11. Paschel, *Becoming Black Political Subjects*, 46.

12. Jaime Arocha Rodríguez, "Nina S. de Friedemann (1930–1998): La etnógrafa de africanías y cimarronismos," *Revista de Estudios Colombianos*, no. 47 (2016): 140.

13. Juliana Botero Mejía and Sofía Natalia González Ayala, "Velorios, santos y marimbas en el museo Nacional de Colombia: ¿de quién es el patrimonio de la Nación?," *Universitas Humanística*, no. 77 (January 2014): 289, https://doi.org/10.11144/Javeriana.UH77.vsym.

14. Arocha Rodríguez, "Nina S. de Friedemann (1930–1998)," 146.

15. Botero Mejía and González Ayala, "Velorios, santos y marimbas en el Museo Nacional de Colombia," 289.

16. Botero Mejía and González Ayala, 289.

17. Angharad N. Valdivia, *The Gender of Latinidad: Uses and Abuses of Hybridity* (Hoboken, NJ: Wiley Blackwell, 2020), 118.

18. Nina S. de Friedemann, *La saga del negro: Presencia africana en Colombia* (Bogotá: Instituto de Genética Humana, Facultad de Medicina, Pontificia Universidad Javeriana, 1993), 10.

19. Friedemann, 41.

20. Friedemann, 57.

21. Cristina Lleras, "Doors Being Open: Rights of Afro-Descendents in the National Museum of Colombia," *Curator: The Museum Journal* 55, no. 3 (2012): 332, https://doi.org/10.1111/j.2151-6952.2012.00157.x.

22. Lleras, 331.

23. Lleras, 336.

24. Lleras, 330.
25. Lleras, 330.
26. Christen A. Smith, *Afro-Paradise: Blackness, Violence, and Performance in Brazil* (Urbana: University of Illinois Press, 2016), 99.
27. Yomaira C. Figueroa-Vásquez, *Decolonizing Diasporas: Radical Mappings of Afro-Atlantic Literature* (Evanston, IL: Northwestern University Press, 2020), 1.
28. Smith, *Afro-Paradise*, 99–100.
29. Asher, *Black and Green*, 33.
30. Meztli Yoalli Rodríguez Aguilera, "Grieving Geographies, Mourning Waters: Life, Death, and Environmental Gendered Racialized Struggles in Mexico," *Feminist Anthropology* 3, no. 1 (2022): 32, https://doi.org/10.1002/fea2.12060.
31. Melissa M. Valle, "Burlesquing Blackness: Racial Significations in Carnivals and the Carnivalesque on Colombia's Caribbean Coast," *Public Culture* 31, no. 1 (January 1, 2019): 18, https://doi.org/10.1215/08992363-7181814.
32. Nayibe Katherine Arboleda Hurtado and Yolima Perea Perea, eds., *La cátedra de estudios Afrocolombianos: Una apuesta jurídica de justicia étnico-racial en la escuela* (Cali: Universidad ICESI, 2020), https://filcali.com/wp-content/uploads/2020/10/La-Ca%CC%81tedra-de-Estudios-Afrocolombianos-ICESI-Y-EMAVI-Oct.22.pdf.
33. Elizabeth Castillo Guzmán and José Antonio Caicedo Ortiz, "Niñez y racismo en Colombia. Representaciones de la afrocolombianidad en los textos de la educación inicial/Childhood and Racism in Colombia: Representations of Afro-Colombian Identity in Early Childhood Education," *Diálogos sobre educación* 7, no. 13 (July 2016): 9, http://dialogossobreeducacion.cucsh.udg.mx/index.php/DSE/article/view/229.
34. Rivera Cusicanqui, *Ch'ixinakax Utxiwa*, 20.
35. Sergio Antonio Mosquera Mosquera, *Afrochocoanos: Orígenes y troncos familiares* (Quibdó, Colombia: Muntú Bantú, 2014), https://isbn.cloud/9789584651105/afrochocoanos-origenes-y-troncos-familiares/.
36. Manuel Zapata Olivella, *Changó, El Gran Putas*, Biblioteca de Literatura Afrocolombiana (Bogotá: Ministerio de Cultura, 2010), 584, http://babel.banrepcultural.org/cdm/ref/collection/p17054coll7/id/2.
37. Most of the information available about Afro-Colombians during slavery and its aftermath comes from official archives. For a methodological discussion of the use of written documents to study enslaved populations in Colombia, see Rafael Antonio Díaz Díaz, "Esclavos, amos y escribanos. Perspectivas metodológicas y de investigación para el estudio de la población esclava en la Sección Notarías del Archivo General de la Nación de Colombia," *Memoria Colombia*, no. 2 (1997): 82–103. For the most canonical works on Afro-Colombian history, see Nina S. de Friedemann and Jaime Arocha, *De sol a sol: Génesis, transformación y presencia de los negros en Colombia* (Bogotá: Planeta, 1986).
38. Hilda Lloréns, *Making Livable Worlds: Afro-Puerto Rican Women Building Environmental Justice* (Seattle: University of Washington Press, 2021), 76.
39. For an analysis of a well-known photograph that circulated in *Hola* magazine in 2011, see Eduard Arriaga Arango, "Racismo y discurso en la era digital: el caso de la

revista Hola y los discursos en las redes sociales," *Discurso & Sociedad*, no. 4 (December 31, 2013): 617–42.

40. Mosquera Rosero-Labbé, "Reparaciones."

41. Mosquera Rosero-Labbé.

42. Smith, *Decolonizing Methodologies*, 45.

43. Sergio Antonio Mosquera Mosquera, *Visiones de la espiritualidad afrocolombiana*, vol. 5, Ma'Mawu (Quibdó: Apidama Ediciones, 2000), 114–15.

44. Mosquera, *Visiones de la espiritualidad afrocolombiana*.

45. See Natalia Quiceno Toro, María Ochoa Sierra, and Adriana Marcela Villamizar, "La Política del canto y el poder de las Alabaoras de Pogue (Bojayá, Chocó)," *Estudios Políticos*, no. 51 (July 2017): 175–95, https://doi.org/10.17533/udea.espo.n51a09; John Alexis Rengifo-Carpintero and Carmen Helena Díaz-Caicedo, "El canto como práctica pedagógica al interior de las comunidades afrodescendientes en la zona pacífico de Colombia," *Pensamiento palabra y obra*, no. 19 (June 2018): 62–75.

46. Hartman, *Scenes of Subjection*, 64.

47. Sergio Antonio Mosquera Mosquera, "Los procesos de manumisión en las provincias de Chocó," in *Afrodescendientes en las Américas: Trayectorias sociales e identitarias. 150 años de la abolición de la esclavitud en Colombia*, ed. Claudia Mosquera, Mauricio Pardo, and Odile Hoffman (Bogotá: Universidad Nacional de Colombia, 2002), 118, https://repositorio.unal.edu.co/handle/unal/2863.

48. For more on the significance of the "Black Christ of Bojayá" as a symbol of the 2002 Bojayá massacre, and the statue inspired by this symbol given by FARC members as a gift to the community during the peace process as a symbol of repentance, see Aurora Vergara-Figueroa and Jerónimo Botero Marino, "Singing Historical Reparations: Alabaoras Challenging the Spectacle of Forgiveness in Communities Affected by Deracination in Colombia," in *Postcoloniality and Forced Migration: Mobility, Control, Agency*, ed. Martin Lemberg-Pedersen et al. (Bristol: Bristol University Press, 2022), 198–208, https://doi.org/10.1332/policypress/9781529218190.003.0012.

49. Smith, *Decolonizing Methodologies*, 146.

50. Smith, 34.

51. Mosquera, "Los procesos de manumisión en las provincias de Chocó," 112.

52. Sergio Antonio Mosquera Mosquera and Ramón Mosquera Bermúdez, eds., *Afro Cineastas*, vol. 2, Cuadernos de Muntú Bantú (Quibdó: Muntú Bantú, 2014).

53. Zulia Mena García and Sergio Antonio Mosquera Mosquera, *Afrochocoanas Visibles: Un Enfoque de Género y Etnia* (Bogotá: Editorial Bolívar, 2015).

54. Sergio Antonio Mosquera Mosquera, *Antropofauna afro-chocoana: Un estudio cultural sobre la animalidad* (Quibdó: Universidad Tecnológica del Chocó Diego Luis Córdoba, 2009).

55. "Muntú Bantú. Museo Afrocolombiano," Muntú Bantú: El centro de memoria histórica afro más grande de Colombia, accessed January 28, 2023, https://www.muntubantu.com/.

56. Her poem "Muñeca negra" became a children's book that inspired her workshops: Mary Grueso Romero, *La muñeca negra*, illustrated by Vanessa Castillo (Bogotá:

Apidama Ediciones, 2011). More of her poetry is available in Vergara-Figueroa et al., *Descolonizando mundos*, 269–317, and Guiomar Cuesta and Alfredo Ocampo, eds., *Antología de Mujeres Poetas Afrocolombianas* (Bogotá: Ministerio de Cultura, 2010), 155–67, https://babel.banrepcultural.org/digital/collection/p17054coll7/id/15.

57. Muntú Bantú (@FunMuntuBantu), "Estimados, Hacemos Público Este Comunicado, y Agradecemos a Cada Persona Que Nos Ha Manifestado Su Apoyo En Este Momento Tan Frustrante Para El Libre Desarrollo de Nuestros Objetivos Misionales. ¡Somos Muntú Bantú! ¡Somos Unidad En La Diversidad!," X (formerly Twitter), January 13, 2023, https://twitter.com/FunMuntuBantu/status/1613953209608933379.

58. Laura Camila Arévalo Domínguez, "Muntú Bantú, el museo que cerró por amenazas de grupos armados en Quibdó," *El Espectador*, January 19, 2023, https://www.elespectador.com/el-magazin-cultural/muntu-bantu-el-museo-que-cerro-por-amenazas-de-grupos-armados-en-quibdo/.

59. "Statement on Afro-Colombian Historian Sergio Antonio Mosquera," Latin American Studies Association, February 6, 2023, https://lasaweb.org/en/news/statement-sergio-antonio-mosquera/.

60. "Muntú Bantú Foundation," Scholars at Risk, January 13, 2023, https://www.scholarsatrisk.org/report/2023-01-13-muntu-bantu-foundation/.

61. Gonzalo de la Torre Guerrero, "Los misioneros claretianos y sus cien años de presencia en el Chocó," *Anuario FUCLA* 1, no. 2, 2009, 63–69.

62. Gonzalo de la Torre Guerrero, "La fiesta franciscana que todos nos merecemos: Cómo actualizar y dinamizar nuestra fiesta," *Revista Mama Ú*, October 1, 2009.

63. Julio César Uribe Hermocillo has written more detailed texts about Gonzalo de la Torre's life and work, as well as the Muestra Bíblica in his blog "Gonzalo de la Torre: Una vida al servicio del pueblo (primera parte)," *El Guarengue* (blog), June 6, 2022, https://miguarengue.blogspot.com/2022/06/gonzalode-la-torre-una-vida-al-servicio.html; "Gonzalo de la Torre: Una vida al servicio del pueblo (segunda parte)," *El Guarengue* (blog), July 4, 2022, https://miguarengue.blogspot.com/2022/07/gonzalo-de-latorre-una-vida-deservicio.html.

64. Gonzalo de la Torre Guerrero, "La etnoeducación, sus bases antropológicas y su papel histórico" *Anuario FUCLA* 1, no. 1 (2008), 86..

65. Gonzalo de la Torre Guerrero, "COCOMACIA: Veinticinco años abriendo caminos . . . (Recuerdos históricos y visión de futuro)," *Anuario FUCLA* 1, no. 1 (2008): 144.

66. de la Torre Guerrero, "COCOMACIA."

67. Misioneros Claretianos Colombia Venezuela, "Muestra Bíblica Claretiana - P. Gonzalo de La Torre, CMF," October 19, 2018, 08:31, YouTube video, https://www.youtube.com/watch?v=vyEljm8eVPY.

68. "MUBIC—Museo bíblico claretiano," accessed July 21, 2023, https://museobiblico.uniclaretiana.edu.co/.

69. Gonzalo María de la Torre Guerrero, "En busca de una definición de espiritualidad que incluya el amplio horizonte de la espiritualidad afrodescendiente," *Revista Mamá Ú* 1, no. 10 (2012): 21.

70. bell hooks, *All About Love: New Visions* (New York: HarperCollins, 2000).
71. Ahmed, *The Cultural Politics of Emotion*, 33.
72. Nelson Fory Ferreira, "Obras," *Historia Contada Por Negros . . . Para Todos* (blog), March 24, 2012, http://historianuestracaballero.blogspot.com/.
73. Silvia Rivera Cusicanqui, "Experiencias de montaje creativo: De la historia oral a la imagen en movimiento ¿Quién escribe la historia oral?," *Chasqui*, December 2012, 14–18.

Chapter 4. Utopian Memories

1. Vergara-Figueroa, *Afrodescendant Resistance to Deracination in Colombia*, 70.
2. María Victoria Uribe, "Memory in Times of War," *Public Culture* 21, no. 1 (January 1, 2009): 4–5, https://doi.org/10.1215/08992363-2008-017.
3. Pilar Riaño and María Victoria Uribe, "Construyendo memoria en medio del conflicto: El grupo de memoria histórica de Colombia," *Revista de Estudios Colombianos* no. 50 (2017): 19.
4. Christina Sharpe, *In the Wake: On Blackness and Being* (Durham, NC: Duke University Press, 2016), 50.
5. Eduard Arriaga and Andrés Villar, *Afro-Latinx Digital Connections* (Gainesville: University of Florida Press, 2021), 121.
6. Sonya Donaldson, "The Ephemeral Archive: Unstable Terrain in Times and Sites of Discord," in *The Digital Black Atlantic*, ed. Roopika Risam and Kelly Baker Josephs (Minneapolis: University of Minnesota Press, 2021), 20.
7. Arriaga and Villar, *Afro-Latinx Digital Connections*, 166.
8. Carbajal and Caswell, "Critical Digital Archives," 1105.
9. Carbajal and Caswell, 1106.
10. Charo Mina Rojas et al., "Luchas del buen vivir por las mujeres negras del Alto Cauca," *Nómadas*, no. 43 (October 2015): 168, https://doi.org/10.30578/nomadas.n43a10.
11. Arriaga and Villar, *Afro-Latinx Digital Connections*, 120.
12. Escobar, *Territories of Difference*, 273.
13. Arriaga and Villar, *Afro-Latinx Digital Connections*, 147.
14. Carbajal and Caswell, "Critical Digital Archives," 1106.
15. Donaldson, "The Ephemeral Archive," 23.
16. Donaldson, 26.
17. "Quienes somos—memoriasdelatrato.org," Memorias del Río Atrato, accessed March 1, 2022, http://www.memoriasdelatrato.org/quienes-somos/.
18. "Quienes somos—memoriasdelatrato.org."
19. Andrés Lombana-Bermudez, "How Memory and Digital Media Can Pave the Way to Peace in Colombia," Global Voices, March 27, 2017, https://globalvoices.org/2017/03/27/how-memory-and-digital-media-can-pave-the-way-to-peace-in-colombia/.

20. Lucely RivasEspinoza, "La página web que cuenta 'Las Memorias del Atrato,'" *Semana*, December 15, 2017, https://www.semana.com/pagina-web-cuenta-la-historia-del-atrato/551282/.

21. Catherine Knight Steele, *Digital Black Feminism* (New York University Press, 2021).

22. Johnier Palacios Paneso, "Bojayá 12 Años—De Mi Tierra No Me Quiero Ir," Museo de Memoria de Colombia, accessed July 25, 2023, https://web.archive.org/web/20220804081123/https://museodememoria.gov.co/arte-y-cultura/bojaya-12-anos-de-mi-tierra-no-me-quiero-ir/.

23. "¿Apoya El Acuerdo Final Para La Terminación Del Conflicto y La Construcción de Una Paz Estable y Duradera?," Presidencia de la República, August 30, 2016, http://es.presidencia.gov.co/noticia.

24. Arriaga and Villar, *Afro-Latinx Digital Connections*, 34.

25. Arriaga and Villar, 34.

26. The list of participants, according to the video's credits, includes: Ana Virgelia Córdoba Palomeque, Damaris Palacios Becerra, Estuar María Blandón, Francisca Hurtado Mena, Juana Francisca Mosquera Mosquera, Julia Susana Mena Moreno, Lucely Rivas Espinoza, Luz Adonis Mena Becerra, Maira Alejandra Jayariyu, Marlenis Valencia Mena, Orfelina Cabrera Isarama, Rubiela Cuesta Córdoba, Yaila Yea Mena Pino, Yessica Monroy Cuesta, and Yotniced Zea Cuesta.

27. For more on T-622 of 2016 and the guardianes del atrato, see Diego Cagüeñas, María Isabel Galindo Orrego, and Sabina Rasmussen, "El Atrato y sus guardianes: Imaginación ecopolítica para hilar nuevos derechos," *Revista Colombiana de Antropología* 56, no. 2 (July 1, 2020): 169–96, https://doi.org/10.22380/2539472X.638.

28. Arriaga and Villar, *Afro-Latinx Digital Connections*, 34.

29. Natalia Quiceno Toro et al., *Comisión de género en la COCOMACIA: Las mujeres en la gestión del territorio en el medio Atrato* (Bogotá: Pontificia Universidad Javeriana, 2019), http://bibliotecadigital.udea.edu.co/handle/10495/13480.

30. Quiceno Toro et al., 23.

31. Cepeda, "Putting a 'Good Face on the Nation.'"

32. Eduard Arriaga, "Afrolatin@ Digital Humanities or Rethinking Inclusion in the Digital Humanities," in *Digital Humanities in Latin America: Reframing Media, Technology, and Culture in Latin/o America*, ed. Héctor Fernández L'Hoeste and Juan Carlos Rodríguez (Gainesville: University of Florida Press, 2020), 127, https://doi.org/10.5744/florida/9781683401476.003.0008.

33. Andrés Mauricio Mosquera Mosquera, "Nosotros," Enamórate del Chocó, accessed March 11, 2022, https://enamoratedelchoco.co/nuestra-labor/.

34. Paul Joseph López Oro, "Digitizing Ancestral Memory: Garifuna Settlement Day in the Americas and in Cyberspace," in *Indigenous Interfaces: Spaces, Technology, and Social Networks in Mexico and Central America*, ed. Jennifer Gómez Menjívar, Gloria Elizabeth Chacón, and Arturo Arias, Critical Issues in Indigenous Studies (Tucson: University of Arizona Press, 2019), 169–70.

35. Smith, *Afro-Paradise*, 79.

36. Arriaga, "Afrolatin@ Digital Humanities or Rethinking Inclusion in the Digital Humanities," 126.

37. Steele, *Digital Black Feminism*, 106.

38. Roopika Risam, *New Digital Worlds: Postcolonial Digital Humanities in Theory, Praxis, and Pedagogy* (Evanston, IL: Northwestern University Press, 2018).

39. Yarimar Bonilla and Jonathan Rosa, "#Ferguson: Digital Protest, Hashtag Ethnography, and the Racial Politics of Social Media in the United States," *American Ethnologist* 42, no. 1 (2015): 12, https://doi.org/10.1111/amet.12112.

40. Jessica Marie Johnson, "Social Stories: Digital Storytelling and Social Media," *Forum Journal* 32, no. 1 (August 23, 2018): 39.

41. Eduard Arriaga, "Temporalidades en red: representaciones artísticas de lo africano y lo afrodescendiente en la era digital," *Foro Hispánico* 58 (January 2018): 286, https://doi.org/10.1163/9789004364080_017.

42. For more details about religious festivals as resistance in Chocó, see José Óscar Córdoba Lizcano, *Resistencia festiva: Fiesta de San Antonio de Padua en Tanquí, Chocó en el contexto del conflicto armado (1996–2008)* (Quibdó: Editorial Uniclaretiana, 2019).

43. Steele, *Digital Black Feminism*, 109.

44. Velia Vidal, "Tributaries: The Chocó Collection and Afro-Colombia," *SDCELAR | Latin America at the British Museum* (blog), July 4, 2023, https://www.sdcelarbritishmuseum.org/projects/isthmo-colombia-and-nw-south-america/tributaries-the-choco-collection-and-afro-colombia/.

45. "BBC 100 Women 2022: Who Is on the List This Year?," *BBC News*, accessed July 25, 2023, https://www.bbc.co.uk/news/resources/idt-75af095e-21f7-41b0-9c5f-a96a5e0615c1.

46. Velia Vidal Romero, *Aguas de estuario* (eLibros Editorial, Laguna Libros, 2020), 16.

47. Vidal Romero, 13.

48. Vidal Romero, 13.

49. "En sesenta días arrancamos nuestro primer convenio, tenemos siete clubes infantiles de lectura operando, nos visitaron Maité Hontele y Teresita Gómez, hicimos un taller con maestros (Motete itinerante), tenemos un club de maestros con veintitrés integrantes, y hemos trabajado talleres con niños de ocho sedes educativas distintas en Quibdó," Vidal Romero, 13 [In sixty days we will start our first agreement, we have seven children's reading clubs operating, Maité Hontele and Teresita Gómez visited us, we did a workshop with teachers (itinerant Motete), we have a teachers club with twenty-three members, and we have held workshops with children from eight different schools in Quibdó].

50. Wade, "Anti-Racism in Mestizo Societies," 169.

51. Peter Wade, *Degrees of Mixture, Degrees of Freedom: Genomics, Multiculturalism, and Race in Latin America* (Durham, NC: Duke University Press, 2017).

52. Arriaga, "Afrolatin@ Digital Humanities or Rethinking Inclusion in the Digital Humanities," 2020, 127.

53. Vidal Romero, *Aguas de estuario*, 76–77.

54. Vidal Romero, 11.

55. Vidal Romero, 31.
56. Vidal Romero, 59.
57. Vidal Romero, 13.
58. Vidal Romero, 66.
59. Omaris Z. Zamora, "Black Latina Girlhood Poetics of the Body: Church, Sexuality and Dispossession," *Post45* (blog), January 21, 2020, https://post45.org/2020/01/black-latina-girlhood-poetics-of-the-body-church-sexuality-and-dispossession/.
60. Vidal Romero, *Aguas de estuario*, 76–77.
61. Vidal Romero, 76–77.
62. Vidal Romero, 66.
63. Vidal Romero, 66.
64. Vidal Romero, 81.
65. Vidal Romero, 40.
66. Vidal Romero, 82.
67. Vidal Romero, 33.
68. Grueso, "Escenarios de colonialismo y (de) colonialidad en la construcción del Ser Negro," 155.
69. Vidal Romero, *Aguas de estuario*, 76.
70. Smith, *Afro-Paradise*, 108.
71. Vidal, "Tributaries."

Chapter 5. Utopian Networks

1. Justa Germania Mena Córdoba, "Mujer que no cumpla su sueño, mujer que no ha nacido," *Mujeres Pacíficas*, 2013, http://www.mujerespacificas.org/stories#/justamena.
2. Lorde, "A Burst of Light: Living with Cancer," 82.
3. Ruth Wilson Gilmore, *Golden Gulag: Prisons, Surplus, Crisis, and Opposition in Globalizing California* (Berkeley: University of California Press, 2007), 28.
4. Lorde, "A Burst of Light: Living with Cancer," 144.
5. Sharpe, *In the Wake*.
6. Taylor, *The Archive and the Repertoire*.
7. Gimena Sánchez Garzoli, "Massacres and Killings of Social Leaders Impede Peace in Colombia: Second Alert," Advocacy for Human Rights in Latin America, Washington Office on Latin America (WOLA), December 23, 2020, https://www.wola.org/2020/12/massacres-and-killings-of-social-leaders-impede-peace-second-alert/.
8. Gimena Sánchez Garzoli and Kelsey Kotts, "Civilians and Social Leaders Require Protection in Colombia Part II," Washington Office on Latin America (WOLA), June 16, 2023, https://www.wola.org/2023/06/civilians-social-leaders-require-protection-colombia-part-ii/.
9. Cherríe Moraga and Gloria Anzaldúa, *This Bridge Called My Back: Writings by Radical Women of Color*, 4th ed. (Albany, NY: SUNY Press, 2015), 19.
10. Ahmed, *Living a Feminist Life*, 14.
11. Leah Lakshmi Piepzna-Samarasinha, *Care Work: Dreaming Disability Justice* (Vancouver: Arsenal Pulp Press, 2018).

12. Piepzna-Samarasinha, 141.
13. Jill Dolan, *Utopia in Performance: Finding Hope at the Theater* (Ann Arbor: University of Michigan Press, 2010), 65–66.
14. See Ana María Arango, "Espacios de educación musical en Quibdó (Chocó-Colombia)," *Revista Colombiana de Antropología* 44, no. 1 (June 2008): 157–89; de la Torre Guerrero, "La fiesta franciscana que todos nos merecemos."
15. Arango, "Espacios de educación musical en Quibdó (Chocó-Colombia)."
16. de la Torre Guerrero, "La fiesta franciscana que todos nos merecemos."
17. Taylor, *The Archive and the Repertoire*, 168.
18. Justa Victoria Sánchez Caballero, "Centro Cultural Mama Ú: Un lugar para la vida, la cultura, la resistencia y la esperanza," *Centro Cultural Mama Ú* (blog), 2012, https://centroculturalmamau.wordpress.com/mama-u/.
19. Adriana Marcela Villamizar Gelves et al., *Red departamental de mujeres Chocoanas* (Medellín: Universidad de Antioquia, 2019), https://bibliotecadigital.udea.edu.co/dspace/bitstream/10495/13469/1/VillamizarAdria_2019_%20RedDepartamentalMujeresChocoanas.pdf.
20. Natalia Quiceno Toro et al., *Ruta pacífica de las mujeres en el Chocó: Un camino de agua, tierra, selva y mar* (Medellín: Universidad de Antioquia, 2019), https://bibliotecadigital.udea.edu.co/bitstream/10495/13478/1/QuicenoNatalia_2019_RutaPacificaMujeres.pdf.
21. Wendy Harcourt and Arturo Escobar, "Women and the Politics of Place," *Development* 45, no. 1 (March 2002): 12, https://doi.org/10.1057/palgrave.development.1110308.
22. Ulrich Oslender, "Violence in Development: The Logic of Forced Displacement on Colombia's Pacific Coast," *Development in Practice* 17, no. 6 (November 1, 2007): 752–64, https://doi.org/10.1080/09614520701628147.
23. Immanuel Wallerstein, *The Capitalist World-Economy* (Cambridge: Cambridge University Press, 1979).
24. Juris and Khasnabish, "Introduction."
25. Escobar, *Territories of Difference*, 276.
26. Ochy Curiel, "Convirtiendo el dolor de las mujeres en solidaridades y esperanzas," América Latina en movimiento, June 12, 2005, https://www.alainet.org/es/articulo/113773.
27. Ruta Pacífica de las Mujeres, Carla Alfonso, and Carlos Martín Beristain, *Memory for Life: A Truth Commission Proposal from Women for Colombia*, 2015, 34, http://rutapacifica.org.co/documentos/Memoryforlife.pdf.
28. Ruta Pacífica de las Mujeres, Alfonso, and Martín Beristain, 11.
29. Ruta Pacífica de las Mujeres, Alfonso, and Martín Beristain, 163.
30. Kimberly Theidon, "Peace in Colombia: A Time to Believe?" *Current History* 115, no. 778 (2016): 54.
31. "¿Qué es la Comisión?," Ruta Pacífica de las Mujeres, accessed March 28, 2020, https://rutapacifica.org.co/wp/que-es-la-comision/.
32. Ruta Pacífica de las Mujeres, Alfonso, and Martín Beristain, *Memory for Life*.

33. Comisión de la verdad y memoria de las mujeres, *La verdad de las mujeres. Víctimas del conflicto armado en Colombia*, vol. 1 (Bogotá: Ruta Pacífica de las Mujeres, 2013), 75, http://rutapacifica.org.co/documentos/tomo-I.pdf.

34. "1000 voces," June 12, 2021, https://web.archive.org/web/20210612231951/http://1000voces.com/proyecto/.

35. Elizabeth Currans, *Marching Dykes, Liberated Sluts, and Concerned Mothers: Women Transforming Public Space* (Urbana: University of Illinois Press, 2017).

36. Tova Benski, "Breaching Events and the Emotional Reactions of the Public: Women in Black in Israel," in *Emotions and Social Movements*, ed. Helena Flam and Debra King (New York: Routledge, 2007), 57–78.

37. For more on protest as action's design, see Tali Hatuka, "Action's Design," in *Protest Cultures: A Companion*, ed. Kathrin Fahlenbrach, Martin Klimke, and Joachim Scharloth, Protest, Culture and Society 17 (New York: Berghahn Books, 2016), 213–20.

38. Maylei Blackwell, *Scales of Resistance: Indigenous Women's Transborder Activism* (Durham, NC: Duke University Press, 2023), 117–18.

39. Athena Athanasiou, *Agonistic Mourning: Political Dissidence and the Women in Black* (Edinburgh: Edinburgh University Press, 2017).

40. Cynthia Cockburn, *From Where We Stand: War, Women's Activism and Feminist Analysis* (London: Zed Books, 2007), 52.

41. Juris and Khasnabish, "Introduction," 8.

Chapter 6. Everyday Utopias

1. Eloísa Berman-Arévalo and Diana Ojeda, "Ordinary Geographies: Care, Violence, and Agrarian Extractivism in 'Post-Conflict' Colombia," *Antipode* 52, no. 6 (November 2020): 1584, https://doi.org/10.1111/anti.12667.

2. Oslender, *The Geographies of Social Movements*, 212.

3. Oslender, 213.

4. Paul Virilio, "On Georges Perec," in *The Everyday*, ed. Stephen Johnstone (London: Whitechapel, 2008), 141.

5. Silvia Federici, *Revolution at Point Zero: Housework, Reproduction, and Feminist Struggle* (Brooklyn: PM Press, 2012); Keeanga-Yamahtta Taylor, ed., *How We Get Free: Black Feminism and the Combahee River Collective* (Chicago: Haymarket Books, 2017); Lorena Cabnal, "Acercamiento a la construcción de la propuesta de pensamiento epistémico de las mujeres indígenas feministas comunitarias de Abya Yala," in *Feminismos diversos: El feminismo comunitario*, ed. ACSUR Las Segovias (Asociación para la cooperación con el Sur, 2010).

6. María Lugones, "Revising Gender: A Decolonial Approach," in *Theories of the Flesh: Latinx and Latin American Feminisms, Transformation, and Resistance*, ed. Andrea J. Pitts, Mariana Ortega, and José Medina (New York: Oxford University Press, 2020), 37.

7. Clara Han, *Life in Debt: Times of Care and Violence in Neoliberal Chile* (Berkeley: University of California Press, 2012), 128.

8. Das and Fassin, "Ordinary Ethics."

9. Lozano Lerma, "The Killing of Women and Global Accumulation," 169.

10. Lynette Hunter, *Disunified Aesthetics: Situated Textuality, Performativity, Collaboration* (Montreal: McGill-Queen's University Press, 2014).
11. Sedgwick and Frank, *Touching Feeling*.
12. Lizarazo, "Alongside Violence."
13. Michael Sheringham, "Configuring the Everyday," in *The Everyday*, ed. Stephen Johnstone (London: Whitechapel Gallery, 2008), 109.
14. Lozano, "Feminismo Negro—Afrocolombiano," 45.
15. Muñoz, *Disidentifications*.
16. Muñoz, 5.
17. Muñoz, 14.
18. Lizarazo et al., "Ethics, Collaboration, and Knowledge Production."
19. Muñoz, *Disidentifications*, 179.
20. Asher, *Black and Green*, 152–53.
21. Paredes, "Hilando fino desde el feminismo indígena comunitario."
22. Grueso, "Escenarios de colonialismo y (de) colonialidad."
23. Rubiela Cuesta Córdoba, "La historia de Rubiela," *Mujeres Pacíficas*, 2013, http://www.mujerespacificas.org/stories#/rubielacuesta.
24. Harcourt and Escobar, "Women and the Politics of Place," 8.
25. Juris and Khasnabish, "Introduction," 4.
26. Cuesta Córdoba, "La historia de Rubiela."
27. Lozano, "Feminismo Negro—Afrocolombiano."
28. Grueso, "Escenarios de colonialismo y (de) colonialidad."
29. Vergara Figueroa and Arboleda Hurtado, "Feminismo Afrodiaspórico."
30. Das and Fassin, "Ordinary Ethics."
31. Asher, *Black and Green*, 153.
32. Arturo Escobar, *Sentipensar con la tierra. Nuevas lecturas sobre desarrollo, territorio y diferencia*, Pensamiento vivo (Medellín: Ediciones UNAULA, 2014), 81.
33. Ana Rosa Heredia Cuesta, "La historia de Ana Rosa," *Mujeres Pacíficas*, 2013, http://www.mujerespacificas.org/stories#/anarosaheredia.
34. Cuesta Córdoba, "La historia de Rubiela."
35. Lozano, "Feminismo Negro—Afrocolombiano."
36. Blackwell, *Scales of Resistance*, 15–16.
37. Mujeres Creando, *La Virgen de los deseos* (Buenos Aires: Tinta Limón, 2005), 178.
38. Lozano, "Feminismo Negro—Afrocolombiano."
39. Toni Morrison, *Jazz* (New York: Knopf Doubleday, 1992), xvi.
40. Lozano Lerma, "The Killing of Women and Global Accumulation," 158.
41. Lozano Lerma, 161.
42. Rivera Cusicanqui, "Experiencias de montaje creativo," 16.

Conclusion. Performing Why Nots

1. Sandra Soler Castillo, "Racismo discursivo de élite en los textos escolares de ciencias sociales en Colombia," *Revista de Investigación. Universidad de la Salle* 6, no. 002 (2006): 255–60.

2. Arboleda Hurtado and Perea Perea, *La cátedra de estudios Afrocolombianos: Una apuesta jurídica de justicia étnico-racial en la escuela*.

3. Arocha, "Ley 70 de 1993," 168–69.

4. "Grupo de mineros se toma aeropuerto de Quibdó," *Semana*, July 19, 2013, https://www.semana.com/nacion/articulo/grupo-mineros-toma-aeropuerto-quibdo/351336-3/.

5. The comisionadas have shared some of the knowledge about the effects of mining for women and about ancestral food practices in Enyel Esteban Rodríguez García and Elisabet Pèriz Fernàndez, eds., *Risas, Sueños y Lamentos Del Río. Vivencias de Los Ríos Atrato y Baudó Desde La Mirada de Sus Guardianas* (Bogotá: Centro de Estudios para la Justicia Social Tierra Digna, 2019).

6. Christen A. Smith, *Afro-Paradise: Blackness, Violence, and Performance in Brazil* (Urbana: University of Illinois Press, 2016).

7. Constitutional Court of Colombia, *Judgment T-622/16 (The Atrato River Case)*, translated by the Dignity Rights Project, 2016, https://delawarelaw.widener.edu/files/resources/riveratratodecisionenglishdrpdellaw.pdf.

8. Lozano, "Feminismo Negro—Afrocolombiano," 45.

9. Marielle Franco, "Lo nuevo siempre viene," in *Afrodescendencias: Voces en resistencia*, ed. Rosa Campoalegre Septien (Buenos Aires: Consejo Latinoamericano de Ciencias Sociales, 2018), 177–80, https://doi.org/10.2307/j.ctvn96gn4.

10. Cacopardo, "'Nada sería posible si la gente no deseara lo imposible'. Entrevista a Silvia Rivera Cusicanqui," 191.

Index

Note: Page numbers in *italics* denote figures.

ACIA (Asociación Campesina Integral del Atrato). *See* COCOMACIA
activism, 7–12, 23–24, 35, 41, 46, 60–61, 143, 197–99; daily life as, 6, 13, 15, 65, 120, 158–59, 205, 207–8, 217–18; durational performance and, 25, 170; embodied knowledge and, 13–14, 63, 75, 90, 138, 165, 205, 216, 218; land ownership and, 83, 89, 119, 164, 188; networks of solidarity and, 25, 158, 160–61, 164, 182, 202, 219; NGOs and, 27, 44, 62, 152, 196. *See also* Asociación Vamos Mujeres; feminism; la Ruta Pacífica de las Mujeres; Women in Black / Mujeres de negro (WiB); *individual activists*
Adichie, Chimamanda Ngozi, 145
Afrocentric knowledge production, 24, 59; in museums and archives, 8, 17, 94–97, 112, 116, 124, 127–32, 139–40, 153–55, 217–19
Afrocolombianidad, 97–98, *107*, 111–12, 127, 129, 194, 197, 234n33. *See also* Blackness; colombianidad
Afro-Colombian studies, 12, 53, 95, *107*, 109, 111–12, 199; Cátedra de Estudios Afrocolombianos, 100, 212

Afrodescendants, 2, 41, 126–29, 167, 199; inclusion in national narratives, 97–100, 105, 110, 122, 144, 155, 212–13
Agamben, Giorgio, 38
agency, 18, 21, 43, 66–67, 86–87, 118, 144, 157, 178, 187; spaces of, 32, 40, 128; survival and, 8, 28, 49, 55–56, 90, 133, 191
Ahmed, Sara, 63–64, 120, 159
alabaos [mourning songs] and alabaoras [mourning singers], 62, 65–66, 106–9, 173, 230n12
Antioquia, 57, 177, 211; Murindó, 2, 32, 134, 230n20; Vigía del Fuerte, 2, 67, 139
archives, 25, 85, 105, 133, 136, 143, 148, 150, 172, 216; Afrocentric knowledge production and, 8, 17, 24, 94–96, 112, 124, 127–28, 140, 153–55, 217–19; Afro-Latinx digital connections through, 128–29; alternative archives, 12, 16, 77, 92–99, 120–24, 126, 128, 180, 213, 217; at Comisión de Género, 60–61, 70, 72, 91–93, 212; ephemerality of, 90, 92–93, 112, 130–32, 142, 144–46, 176; the everyday as, 23, 208; personal, 5, 60–61, 66, 70, 72, 77; slow, 19; the unarchivable, 14, 33, 82, 88, 158. *See also* Fotógrafas del Pacífico; Memorias del Río Atrato;

archives (*continued*): La Muestra Bíblica; Mujeres Pacíficas; Muntú Bantú
Arocha Rodríguez, Jaime, 36, 97–98, 107, 127
Arriaga, Eduard, 128–30, 134–35, 140, 142–44, 149
Asher, Kiran, 36; *Black and Green,* 53, 227n17
Asociación Dos de Mayo (ADOM), 135, 162
Asociación Vamos Mujeres [Let's Go Women Association], 24–31, 33, 42–49, 54–55, 164, 217
assassinations, 8–10, 31, 158–59, 169, 172, 194, 202, 216
Atrato River, 3, 26, 28, 32, 101, 113; Fotógrafas del Pacífico Instagram and, 141–44, 153–55; Memorias del Río Atrato website and, 130–36, 141; T-622 judgment (2016), 136, 215
Auto 092 of 2008, 162
Autodefensas Unidas de Colombia [United Self-Defense Groups of Colombia] (AUC), 46

Bahía Solano, 149, 153
Bailey, Moya, 18
Black feminism, 133–35, 146, 194–200, 203–4, 224n43; feminismo(s) en-lugar, 8, 194–95, 216. *See also* feminism
Blackness, 3, 19, 36, 39–41, 46, 97, 122, 127, 142; visibility and, 55, 74, 93–95, 99–100, 104–5, 124, 128. *See also* Afrocolombianidad
Black studies, 11, 39, 51–52, 54–55, 61, 98, 127, 141
Blackwell, Maylei, 178, 203
blanqueamiento [whitening], 3–4, 98, 100, 106, 108, 213. *See also* mestizaje; whitening
Bloustien, Geraldine, 21
Bogotá, 12, 43, 93, 112, 133, 154, 192, 219; mestizaje in, 3, 16, 30, 58, 97, 121, 124; Museo del Oro, 96, 101; Women in Black in, 156, 160, 170–80, 183
Bojayá massacre (2002), 45–46, 82, 107–10, 126, 132–35, 162, 192, 206
Bonilla, Yarimar, 143
British Museum, 96, 121, 154; Santo Domingo Centre for Excellence in Latin American Research (SDCELAR), 146

capitalism, 16, 157, 215–16; extractive, 13, 28–29, 48, 93, 146, 155, 164, 185, 204, 213–16; resistance to, 44–45, 64–65, 123, 164, 197, 205. *See also* slavery
care, 28, 32, 90, 130, 187–88, 192, 197; care politics, 43, 157–60, 163, 165, 172–73, 180–81, 194, 209, 218; care webs, 160; networks of, 5, 8, 19, 74, 124, 160, 163, 165, 178, 202, 215, 218; women's labor and, 53, 63, 67, 159–60, 181–82, 193, 195, 203, 206, 208
Carnavalenguas (National Carnival of Women's Languages, Voices and Letters), 50, 229n44
Carranza, María Mercedes: *El canto de las moscas,* 10, 81–82
Castillo, Yancy, 129
Catholicism, 4, 98, 107–8, 134, 213; Claretian mission, 113–15, 119, 163, 188
Cauca, 129, 138, 159, 174, 216; Consejo Regional Indígena del Cauca [Regional Indigenous Council of Cauca], 177
Centro Cultural Gabriel García Márquez, 170–71
Centro Nacional de Memoria Histórica, 130
Cepeda, María Elena, 11
Cimarrón Movimiento Nacional por los Derechos Humanos de las Comunidades Negras de Colombia [National Movement for Black Communities' Rights in Colombia], 93–94, 104
Claretian mission, 113–15, 119, 163, 188
COCOMACIA (Consejo Comunitario Mayor de la Asociación Campesina Integral del Atrato [Main Community Council of the Integral Peasant Association of the Atrato River]), 5–6, 48, 51, 77, 184–87, 230n20; archives of, 19, 60–61, 72, 91–93, 129–30, 219; Comisión Juvenil de COCOMACIA (COJUCOMA), 32, 80; as el proceso, 33–34, 36, 52, 62, 76, 78–81, 84–87, 189, 193–95, 202–4; funding and, 33, 58, 70, 188–91, 193, 201, 214–17; General Assembly (2013), 17, 73, 84; Geographic Information System (GIS) division, 70–71; offices of, 1, 3, 8, 32–37, 37, 50, 50–51, 58, 72, 91–93, 113, 162, 189, 205, 211–12; origins of, 2, 113; ownership of Memorias del Río Atrato,

130, 132–37; radio station (Stereo), 74, 84, 89, 135; restaurant, 61, 73, 88, 151–52, 205–6, 214; significance of everyday practices in, 16, 19, 27–29, 32–33, 70–71, 151, 157, 197, 209, 214; significance of storytelling in, 14–17, 24, 59–64, 66–69, 75–76, 83–84, 130, 132, 210, 215. *See also* Comisión de Género; *individual members, locations, and projects*

cocreation, 28–29, 55, 59–61, 74, 81, 213

collaboration, 72, 117, 124, 127, 142, 150–51, 172; audience and, 5, 18–19, 22, 68–69, 71, 76, 196; embodied knowledge and, 14, 20, 22–25, 62, 157, 218; ethics and, 15, 17–18, 25, 89–90, 119, 207, 218; failure and, 18, 20, 25, 49, 55–56, 66–67, 80, 206–7, 214, 217–18; for funding, 6, 12, 17, 58, 75–76, 91–92, 135–36, 138, 165, 196–97; methodological significance of, 16–25, 41, 59, 62, 64–69, 95, 98, 111, 127; power relations in, 67, 71, 117, 165–66, 181–83, 196; solidarity and, 8, 123, 161, 183, 197, 202; survival and, 6, 13, 19–20, 25, 51, 55–56, 60, 82, 197, 219–20; untranslatability and, 43, 207, 212, 217. *See also individual organizations and projects*

collective territories, 4–5, 8, 79, 81, 128, 134–36, 155–56, 160, 214; governance structure in, 2, 28, 130, 133, 151, 230n20. *See also* Antioquia; Atrato River; Bojayá massacre; Medio Atrato

Colombian Constitution (1991), 4, 123; Transitory Article 55, 2, 29

colombianidad [Colombianness], 11, 60, 105, 155, 213. *See also* Afrocolombianidad

colonialism, 23, 93, 96, 120–21, 143–44; author positionality and, 16, 58; enduring resonance of, 12, 15–16, 27, 40, 44, 55, 115–17, 123, 154–55, 203–4, 207–8, 215

Comisión de Estudios sobre la Violencia [Commission for the Study of Violence], 10

Comisión de Género [Gender Commission] of COCOMACIA, 5–6, 81, 112, 196–98, 200, 206–10, 213–17, 219, 227n17; 2013 events in Tanguí, 27, 33, 49, 53–55, 70, 75–76, 190–91, 193–94, 201–2, 204; *Comisión de Género en la COCOMACIA*, 138; inclusion of men, 33, 161, 191, 204; lists of comisionadas, 36, 61, 68, 135–36, 138, 238n25; methodology of book and, 13–16, 18–22, 24, 59, 67, 69, 72–73, 80, 90; offices of, 33, 36–37, 49–51, 59, 72, 78, 82, 91–93, 162, 212; online presence, 129, 145; origins of, 2, 227n17; paper archive of, 60–61, 70, 72, 91–93, 212; San Pacho festival and, 161–62; significance of the everyday in, 16–19, 27–29, 32–35, 186; women in leadership and, 188–90, 195, 199; women of Ichó and, 44, 47–48; work in radio, 84. *See also* COCOMACIA; *individual comisionadas, projects, and actions*

Comisión Nacional de Memoria Histórica [Historical Memory National Commission], 82

Community Council of Buchadó, 67, 188

complex personhood, 35

Conferencia Nacional de Organizaciones Afrocolombianas [National Assembly of Afro-Colombian organizations] (CNOA), 129

Consejo Nacional de Paz Afrocolombiana (CONPA), 112

Córdoba, Piedad, 111, 173

COVID-19 pandemic, 9, 215, 219–20

crip-of-color critique, 18, 225n60

Cuesta Córdoba, Rubiela, 36, 52, 61, 63, 68, 70, 136, 138, 185–86, 193, 214–16; "La historia de Rubiela," 80, 125, 159, 197–99, 202–3, 205, 219

Curiel, Ochy, 30, 166

damage-centered vs. desire-based research, 22

Das, Veena, 53, 188, 199

death, 3, 30, 36, 92, 98, 104, 117, 157; alabaos and alabaoras, 62, 65–66, 106–9, 173, 230n12; everyday presence of, 73, 107–8, 125–26, 158, 162, 188, 209, 220; state distribution of, 12, 41, 43–44. *See also* Bojayá massacre (2002)

decolonial feminism, 14–15, 30, 166, 194, 204

digital storytelling, 16–18, 23–24, 50–51, 61–62, 65, 68, 80–82, 130, 143, 217; as genre, 19–20, 59, 69, 140–41. *See also* Fotógrafas del Pacífico; *Mujeres Pacíficas*

disability studies, 18, 160. *See also* crip-of-color critique
disidentification, 52, 195–97, 210
displacement, 4, 12, 27, 49, 63, 66, 133, 172, 180, 191; Bojayá massacre and, 82–83, 116, 133, 162, 192, 206; in comisionadas' stories, 3, 8, 46–47, 72, 76–77, 81–83, 185, 193–94, 202, 206; disidentification and, 196; due to guerrilla and paramilitary conflict, 10, 29–30, 116, 185, 193–94; solidarity at Feria Alternativa and, 163–64; Vamos Mujeres' reactions to, 29–30, 35–36, 45–47
dispossession, 3, 55, 83, 100, 157, 180
Dolan, Jill, 160
Donaldson, Sonya, 131, 139
drugs, 5, 9–11, 31
Duque, Iván, 9
durational performance, 14, 25, 156–57, 169–71, 175, 203, 216. *See also* encuentros [encounters]

Ejército de Liberación Nacional [National Liberation Army] (ELN), 9, 15, 29, 152
El Alemán, 31
embodied knowledge, 32–33, 78, 80, 88–89, 95, 164, 193, 215; activism and, 13–14, 63, 75, 90, 138, 165, 205, 216, 218; collaboration and, 14, 20, 22–25, 62, 157, 218; racialization and, 58, 99, 140; value of the everyday and, 16, 22–25, 29, 157–58, 187, 189, 203, 212
embodiment, 7, 31, 34, 81, 84, 136, 140, 166, 179, 217; author positionality and, 27, 43, 58; as challenge to academic writing, 63; embodied knowledge (*see* embodied knowledge); embodied memory, 14, 62, 93, 95–96, 130, 150, 160, 169; embodied research, 65; embodied theory, 159; humanitarian rhetoric and, 38; national myths and, 4, 167; peacemaking and, 166, 170; racism and, 100, 105; rehearsal and, 69, 198; spirituality and, 102, 118; survival as embodied practice, 6, 9, 15, 29, 40, 49, 55, 190, 192, 214, 219
encuentros [encounters], 26, 212; with military, 184–86, 192; Muntú Bantú as space of, 111–12; of Women in Black in Bogotá, 156, 160, 170–80, 183; of Women in Black in Montevideo, 160, 177–80, 182–83
endurance, 28–29, 33, 49, 69, 82, 88, 157, 169–70, 173, 197; enduring performances, 203, 207, 210, 215, 218. *See also* durational performance; encuentros
Escobar, Arturo, 129, 163, 200
estar en todo [to be everything], 202–3, 215
ethics, 7, 11, 51, 104, 186–87, 197–98, 208, 214, 216–17; care and, 50, 53, 67, 90, 119, 159, 178, 181, 209; feminist, 13, 15, 30, 32, 159; normative, 25, 32, 53, 199, 218; ordinary ethics, 25, 53, 189, 199–201; rehearsals and, 20, 25, 28–30, 53, 189, 200, 202–3, 207, 218; in research and writing practices, 15, 17–18, 30, 32, 39–41, 89–90; spaces of memory and, 118–21, 124, 129–30; storytelling and, 12, 19, 81, 127–30, 207, 219
ethno-education, 115–16
ethnography, 16, 18, 22, 35, 41, 95, 97, 127; extractive, 17
Etnia Company: "De mi tierra no me quiero ir," 133
extractive ethnography, 17
extractive practices, 2, 4, 28, 93, 137–38, 155, 157, 164, 185, 214. *See also* mining

Facebook, 112, 129, 145, 192
femicide, 163, 172, 179
feminism, 13, 24, 167–69, 207; Black feminism, 133–35, 146, 194–200, 203–4, 224n43; decolonial feminism, 14–15, 30, 166, 194, 204; feminismo(s) en-lugar [feminism(s) in place], 8, 194–95, 216; genealogies in, 30, 32, 39, 55; knowledge production and, 5, 7–8, 14–15, 23, 133, 146, 159–60, 183, 197–99, 219, 224n43; networks of solidarity and, 8, 19, 25, 111, 135, 158–61, 164–65, 178, 183, 202–4, 218–19; social movements and, 19, 23, 25, 32–33, 39, 160, 170–71, 176–83, 195–200, 229n44; teoría de las mujeres [women's theory], 14. *See also* activism; *individual feminists and organizations*
Ferry, Stephen: *Violentology: A Manual of the Colombian Conflict*, 37–38

Fiesta de la Lectura y la Escritura del Chocó (FLECHO), 147–48
Foro Interétnico Solidaridad Chocó (FISCH), 32, 79, 112
Fory Ferreira, Nelson, 121
Fotógrafas del Pacífico, 24, 129, 142, 153–55, 217; Enamórate de Buenaventura (@enamoratebuenaventura), 139; Enamórate del Chocó (@enamoratechoco), 139–40; Enamórate del Pacífico (@enamoratedelpacifico), 139; @fotografasdelpacifico, 139–41, 144; #fotógrafasdelpacífico, 128, 143
Fouché, Rayvon, 133
Franco, Marielle, 216
de Friedemann, Nina, 36, 95, 97–98, 107, 127
Fundación Mujer y Vida, 135, 162
Fundación Muntú Bantú, 24, 96, 113, 121, 123, 154, 217, 219; addressing slavery, 101–3, 105, 107–11, 122; centering transnational Black icons, 104–6, 111–12, 122; religious iconography and, 106–10, 115, 122

Gaitán, Jorge Eliécer, 10
Gamboa de Córdoba, Benilda, 45, 48
gender, 27, 31, 78, 97, 105–6, 134, 185; equality, 48, 54, 63, 89, 115, 118, 200, 205, 209; feminized labor, 159–60, 164, 182, 206, 208; language and, 167, 197, 222n8, 230n20; Law 1257 and, 62–63, 65, 84, 162; leadership and, 42, 47, 87, 138, 166, 188–89, 193–99, 202, 204–6, 216; new masculinities, 161, 193; participative research on, 135–36; patriarchy and, 48, 51, 54, 157, 167, 178–79, 195, 197–200, 208; in religious iconography, 117–18; traditional roles, 11, 42, 47–48, 75, 87–89, 135, 179, 194–99, 208, 210, 213; victimhood and, 14, 32, 52, 167–69, 214; violence and, 3, 11, 33, 49–50, 62–64, 138, 161–63, 191, 194–95, 229nn43–44 (*see also* femicide). *See also* Comisión de Género [Gender Commission]
Gilmore, Ruth Wilson, 157
Global North, 12, 16, 30, 58, 165, 176–77
Global South, 12, 30, 137, 165, 181
Gómez Murillo, Teresita, 177, 239n49

Gordon, Avery, 35, 65
Grueso, Libia, 199, 224n43
Grueso Romero, Mary, 112, 235n56
Grupo de Memoria Histórica, 11, 126
Guardianes del Atrato, 32, 136, 215–16
guerrilla groups, 4, 11, 16, 30–31, 45, 91, 171, 185–86, 193–94; Ejército de Liberación Nacional [National Liberation Army], 9, 15, 29, 152; FARC (*see* Revolutionary Armed Forces of Colombia); M-19, 9–10

Han, Clara, 187–88
Harcourt, Wendy, 163
Hartman, Saidiya, 22, 39, 52, 57, 109
Havana, 166, 170, 182
Heredia Cuesta, Ana Rosa, 36, 61, *68*, 138, 170, *186*, 200, 211, 230n20; "La historia de Ana Rosa," 82–83, 208–9, 211
heteropatriarchy, 11, 23, 99, 105
Hontele, Maité, 239n48
hope, 7–9, 52–53, 160, 171, 177, 183, 184, 186, 191; as practice of giving, 28, 32, 203; stories of, 32, 48, 50, 61, 88–89, 157, 205, 207; in uncertainty, 18, 46
humanitarian economy, 6, 12, 27, 44–45, 135–38, 152, 190–91, 196, 207–8, 214, 216
human rights, 4, 10, 36, 46, 159, 187, 216
Hunter, Lynette, 189

Ichó (San Francisco de Ichó), 24, 28–30, 41–45, 47, 55, 156, 164, 217
imagining otherwise, 25, 121, 124, 129, 151, 164, 216; imagined futures, 7, 77, 103, 128, 144–45, 153, 158, 219–20; as imagining peace, 2, 6, 9, 15–16, 19, 31, 60, 135, 154, 181, 205, 210, 218; impossibility and, 2, 5–7, 19, 103, 200, 210, 217, 219–20; as reimagining the past, 65, 78, 130; storytelling for, 20, 23–24, 32, 65, 78, 90, 210, 219
impossibility, 31, 42, 77, 126, 130, 138, 164, 169, 179–80, 194; failure and, 5, 18; imagining otherwise and, 2, 5–7, 19, 103, 200, 210, 217, 219–20; pushing against, 22, 65, 87, 103
improvisation, 17, 19, 33, 63, 66, 69, 170, 196; in storytelling, 75, 79–80, 84, 89–90, 217

Indigenous communities, 28, 31, 57, 70, 93, 95, 130, 132; Dóbida, 113, 148; Embera, 114, 135, 148; Kogui, 167; missionary work and, 113, 188; motete in, 147–48; othering of, 99, 148; racial binaries and, 124, 128; Wayuú, 135; women in, 4, 137–39, 168, 177, 180, 203

Instagram, 24, 74, 112; Fotógrafas del Pacífico and, 128–29, 139–42; Motete on (@nuestromotete), 128, 145–46, 218

International Day for the Elimination of Violence Against Women, 111

invisibility: Afro-Colombian communities and, 12, 17, 99, 110, 128, 144, 148–49; Blackness and, 3, 55, 74, 95; of labor, 130, 192, 194, 207, 209; power in, 67

Johnson, Jessica Marie, 143

justice, 6, 11, 14–15, 29, 62–63, 180–82, 198; in activist messaging, 36, 82, 86, 161, 166, 168–69, 171–72, 214; care webs and, 160; environmental, 138; "Justice and Peace" law (Law 975), 31; museum exhibits and, 110, 118–19

knowledge production, 17–18, 40, 80, 93, 127, 195, 213; Afrocentrism and (see Afrocentric knowledge production); Afro-Latinx digital connections, 128–29; embodiment and (see embodied knowledge); feminist, 5, 7–8, 14–15, 23, 133, 146, 159–60, 183, 197–99, 219, 224n43; Fotógrafas del Pacífico and, 140, 142–44; Motete and, 146–47; *Mujeres Pacíficas* and, 19–20, 59–60, 63, 66, 69 74–75; museums and, 96, 103, 108, 113, 120, 123

Kumar, Corinne, 181

Lambert, Joe, 20–21, 68

Law 70: "La Ley de Comunidades Negras" (1993), 2, 95, 97–98, 100, 123–24, 186, 200, 212–13, 221n4, 227n17

Law 1257, 62–63, 66, 84, 162

LGBTQIA identities / sexual diversity, 97, 167, 196

Llórens, Hilda, 103

López Oro, Paul Joseph, 141

Lorde, Audre, 13, 33, 51; "A Litany for Survival," 14

Lozano Lerma, Betty Ruth, 189, 194–95, 199, 203–4, 224n43

M-19 guerilla group, 9–10

Madres de Plaza de Mayo, 179, 182

Majul, Alí, 130

malecón [waterfront], 191, 193. See also Atrato River

Mama Ú, 163–64

Márquez Mina, Francia, 9, 111, 138, 159, 216

Mbembe, Achille, 12, 41

Medellín, 3, 28, 43, 49, 93, 119, 146, 156, 192

Medio Atrato, 2, 138, 162

Memorias del Río Atrato, 24, 128–29, 138–42, 153–55, 217; relation to COCOMACIA, 130, 132–37; YouTube presence, 131, 135, 137

memory, 5–6, 25, 30, 39, 51, 118, 208–9, 215; archives and, 16–17, 19, 61, 66, 72–73, 81–82, 91–96, 148, 150, 158, 213; collective, 17, 24, 96, 103–4, 110, 125–26, 128–29, 138, 145, 177, 183; embodied, 14, 62, 93, 130, 150, 169; museums and, 24, 95–100, 102–5, 108, 110–13, 115, 120–24, 126–29, 133–34, 158; national, 19, 65, 75, 93–96, 99–100, 105, 126, 128, 133–34, 210; performativity and, 64–65, 75, 77–78, 90, 142, 160, 163, 165, 175, 218, 229n44; La Ruta's Truth and Memory Commission, 166–68; trauma and, 82, 90, 96–97, 106–10, 115, 120–23, 126, 172, 175, 218; untranslatability of, 207. See also Fotógrafas del Pacífico; Memorias del Río Atrato; La Muestra Bíblica; *Mujeres Pacíficas*; Muntú Bantú

Mena Becerra, Luz Adonis, 5, 36, 61, 134–35, 138, 192, 213–14, 219, 230n20; "La historia de Adonis," 77–78, 85

Mena Córdoba, Justa Germania, 1, 3, 63, 66, 79–80, 190, 211; "Mujer que no compla su sueño, mujer que no ha nacido," 50, 171, 215; presence at COCOMACIA offices, 33–37, 50, 72, 92; storytelling and, 50–51, 61, 64, 68,

71, 73–75, 157, 210, 215; at Tanguí workshop, 33, 53, 158
Mena García, Zulia: *Afrocolombianas visibles: Un enfoque de género y etnia*, 111
Mena Moreno, Julia Susana, 36, 52, 111–12, 147; "La historia de Julia," 85, 89, 91, 107; *Mujeres Pacíficas* and, 61, *68*, 70, 85, 89, 135–37, 217; in Tanguí workshop, 49–50, 54, 76
Menchú, Rigoberta, 89
mestizaje [ethnoracial mixture], 2, 19, 25, 28, 31, 95, 155, 168, 171, 205; author positionality and, 16, 27, 30, 40, 57, 145, 211–12; homogenization of, 3, 60, 97, 99, 110, 126, 128, 148–49, 154; in popular media, 94, 104, 111, 139–40; racial supremacy and, 3–5, 23, 58, 65, 97–101, 121, 124, 154, 208, 217–18. *See also* blanqueamiento [whitening]
methodology of book, 13–14, 24; audiovisual methodologies and, 16, 19–23, 25, 59, 69, 72–73, 80, 90, 95, 127, 136; author positionality, 16, 18, 27, 30, 40–41, 43–44, 57–59, 69–71, 75–76, 178; collaboration and, 16–25, 41, 59, 62, 64–69, 95, 98, 111, 127; ethnography and, 16–18, 22, 35, 41, 97, 127; lists of participants, 36, 61, *68*, 238n25; participatory research, 19–21, 69, 136, 168; research questions, 15; slow scholarship and, 18–19
militarization, 2, 6, 11–12, 30–31, 63, 192, 207, 214; activism amid, 7, 29, 48, 55, 166, 173, 176, 179–83; museum exhibits about, 111, 118, 124; survival amid, 14, 23, 27, 29, 40, 48–49, 55–56, 158, 185, 189
mining, 13, 29, 48, 104, 137, 204, 208, 215; strike (2013), 121, 213–14; for gold, 2, 11, 44, 85, 96; traditional practices of, 85, 88, 155, 214
Misioneros Claretianos Colombia Venezuela, 119
misogyny, 117–18, 185
missionaries, 86, 91, 96, 113–14, 117, 119, 163, 217. *See also* de la Torre Guerrero, Gonzalo

monocultures, 2, 185–86
Montevideo, 160, 176–80, 182
Morrison, Toni: *Jazz*, 205
Mosquera Mosquera, Sergio Antonio, 24, 36, 40, 96, 101–2, 104, 109–10, 113, 120–22; *Afro Cineastas*, 111; *Afrocolombianas visibles*, 111; *Antropofauna afrochocoana*, 112; *Visiones de la espiritualidad afrocolombiana*, 107
Mosquera Navia, Pedro Luis, 45
Mosquera Pérez, María del Socorro, 1, 36, 60–62, 74; "La historia de María del Socorro," 13, 219
Mosquera Rosero-Labbé, Claudia, 11–12, 105
Moten, Fred, 54–55
Motete, 24, 129, 147–55, 239n49; on Instagram (@nuestromotete), 128, 145–46, 218
Moya Cuesta, Mariluz (Pancha), 61, *68*, 86, 206; "La historia de Mariluz," 87–88
Moya Cuesta, Miriam, 61, *68*, 87–89, 211; "La historia de Miriam," 205–8, 210
La Muestra Bíblica, 24, 96, 114–20, 123, 127, 154
Mujeres creando, 203–4
Mujeres Pacíficas, 6, 17–18, 22–23, 90, 215; creative process, 21, 69–74, 76, 203, 213; hope and, 5, 50, 61, 205; individual stories from, 13, *50*, 63–65, 67–68, *68*, 73, 77–89, 159–60, 197–200, 202, 206–10, 219; knowledge production and, 19–20, 59–60, 63, 66, 69, 74–75; Memorias del Río Atrato and, 127, 132, 136–37; self-representation and, 24, 50, 62, 72, 75, 77–78, 80, 85, 88–89, 211–12, 217. *See also individual participants*
Muñoz, José Esteban, 52, 196–97
Museo Bíblico Claretiano (MUBÍC), 119
Museo Nacional de Colombia [National Museum of Colombia], 96–99, 101, 105, 112, 121, 154–55

Navia, Fernelis, 104
Navia Mena, Carmen Aides, 61, *68*, 83–84
necropolitics, 12, 41
Neguá river, 28

nongovernmental organizations (NGOs), 38, 62, 76, 91, 93, 101, 164, 196, 200, 210; bureaucracy of, 27, 29, 44, 190, 193, 212; friction with local organizations, 137, 152, 196, 206; humanitarian economy and, 12, 27, 44, 190, 196; reproducing hierarchies, 12, 44, 58, 152, 208; supporting Vamos Mujeres, 29, 33, 42, 44, 47; Vamos Mujer, Medellín, 43, 156

Ochoa Palacios, Teresa, 163–64
orality, 17, 20, 22, 38, 69, 71, 79, 147, 230n12, 232n43; centering traditions of, 59–61, 63, 75, 120, 130, 133, 135, 141, 147, 210
ordinariness, 28, 34–35, 80, 105–6, 187, 218; ordinary ethics, 25, 53, 189, 199–201
orishas (deities in African diasporic spirituality), 213
Orozco, Paula (@pau_orozco8), 141, 144
Oslender, Ulrich, 36, 61

Pachakuti, 7, 144
paisa, 57–58, 75–76, 211–12
Palacios Paneso, Johnier, 133
Palacios Romaña, Yenny, 26, 33–34, 36, 61, 68, 84, 88–89, 137, 192, 212; "La historia de Yenny," 67
paramilitaries, 36, 116, 118, 126, 185, 190, 194, 214; agribusiness and, 4; Autodefensas Unidas de Colombia [United Self-Defense Groups of Colombia] (AUC), 45–46; as BACRIM (bandas criminals [criminal gangs]), 209; drug lords and, 9, 11, 31
Paredes, Julieta, 14, 197–98
Paredes, Luisa, 144
Parroquia Claretiana de Jesús Nazareno (Medellín), 119
participatory action research, 168
patriarchy, 8, 83, 86, 117, 169, 188; heteropatriarchy, 11, 23, 99, 105; militarization and, 192–93; traditional gender roles and, 48, 51, 54, 157, 167, 178–79, 195, 197–200, 208
peacemaking, 2, 8, 13, 25, 49, 123, 129, 150, 202, 210; peace accords (2016), 9, 12, 31, 127, 134–35, 141, 159, 167, 190, 219; gender in, 167–70, 179; imagining peace, 6, 9, 15–16, 19, 23, 60, 62, 135, 154, 170, 181, 205, 217–18; negotiations in, 15, 23, 31, 110, 112, 166–67, 170, 183, 215, 235n48

pedagogy, 38, 84, 86, 105, 109, 111, 119–20, 124, 127, 155, 164
Peláez López, Alán, 55
performance studies, 14, 20, 22, 65, 189
performativity, 8, 24, 49, 99, 126, 140, 193, 195; ethics and, 120, 187, 201, 207; of racism, 142; showing up and, 25, 33, 86, 90, 156–58, 160, 183, 194, 210, 218; silence and, 21, 25, 63–66, 89, 158, 169–71, 175–76, 180, 189, 207–13; solidarity and, 6, 25, 158, 183, 197, 218, 229n44; of storytelling, 75–78, 80–81, 86, 89–90, 218; trauma and, 55, 82–83, 108, 162–63, 165–66, 168, 172, 180, 191, 202–3, 218
Phelan, Peggy, 65
Piepzna-Samarasinha, Leah Lakshmi, 160
postconflict utopias, definition, 6–9
Premio Amparo Díaz Uribe [Amparo Díaz Award], 132
Premio Nacional de Paz [National Peace Prize], 165–66

Quejada Palacios, Teresa, 162
Quibdó, Chocó, 2, 4, 12, 48, 55, 77, 156, 170, 176, 201; mining strike (2013) in, 213–14; author positionality in, 16, 30, 57–58, 101, 145, 163, 211–12; COCOMACIA offices in, 1, 3, 8, 32, 35, 35–36, 50, 50–51, 58, 92–93, 113, 162, 211–12; Diócesis of, 44, 113; Dos de mayo neighborhood, 135, 206; Fotógrafas del Pacífico in, 141, 143–44; location of La Muestra Bíblica, 24, 96, 113–14, 116, 124, 127, 217; location of Muntú Bantú, 24, 96, 101–3, 106–7, 107, 109, 111, 124, 127, 217; Memorias del Río Atrato and, 134, 136; Motete in, 128, 146–47, 151–53, 239n48; purchasing goods in, 26–27, 85, 113, 184; rain and humidity in, 92, 125, 153; traditions in, 85, 92, 144, 161, 165

race and racialization. *See* Blackness; mestizaje [ethnoracial mixture]; racism; whitening
racism, 15–16, 38, 46, 49, 138, 157–58, 216; genocide of Afrodescendants, 115; performativity of, 142; race-denial in national narratives, 12, 74, 94–95, 99–100, 105, 110, 126–28, 148–49; region and,

3–4, 11–12, 23, 31–32, 54, 57–58, 97, 231n20. *See also* whitening
Ramírez, Hanna, 18
Red Departamental de Mujeres Chocoanas, La, 25, 160–62, 170, 173, 177, 183, 218; Feria Alternativa Justa y Solidaria, 163–65
re-existencia, 13, 24, 153, 199
rehearsals, 5, 18–19, 39, 61, 69, 74–75, 78, 80, 182, 210; of care politics, 157, 181; as durational performance, 169, 175; ethics and, 20, 25, 28–30, 53, 189, 200, 202–3, 207, 218; gender and, 89, 161, 198; peace and, 9, 25, 32, 135, 142, 150, 181, 187, 205; of racialized narratives, 99–100; of solidarity, 15, 104; of survival, 13, 28, 42, 63, 66, 83, 90, 175, 217; utopian, 6–7, 13, 55, 96, 129, 150, 157, 217; victimhood and, 36, 38; writing and, 22–24, 30, 40, 42, 44, 48–49
repertoire, 16, 55, 61, 96, 148, 158, 175, 180, 226n5
Restrepo, Luis Carlos, 31
Revolutionary Armed Forces of Colombia (FARC), 36, 45–46, 126, 185, 214; peace accords (2016), 9, 12, 31, 127, 134–35, 141, 159, 167, 190, 219; negotiations with, 12, 15, 23, 31, 110, 112, 170, 190, 219, 235n48; popularization of, 10–11
Riaño, Pilar, 126
Risam, Roopika, 143
Rivas Espinoza, Lucely, 132–33, 135–39, 238n25
Rivas López, Banessa, 28, 32, 36, 61, *68*, 79–80, 84, 88, 160, 184, 213–15, 219
Rivas, William, 122–23
Rivera Cusicanqui, Silvia, 7, 23, 100, 123, 144, 203, 210, 219, 222n8; Pachakuti, 7, 144
Rivera, Rosa, 43, 156
Rosa, Johnathan, 143
Ruta Pacífica de las Mujeres, La, 25, 135, 156, 158, 160, 162, 229n44; alliances with other organizations, 163, 165, 170–71, *173*, 173–74, 176–77, 183, 218–19; *Memory for Life*, 166–67; *La verdad de las mujeres*, 168–69; winning Premio Nacional de Paz [National Peace Prize], 165–66; Women's Truth and Memory Commission, 166–69

Salas Lenis, Fanny Rosmira, 61, 85, 188; "La historia de Rosmira," 86, 88
Sánchez, Freddy, 117
Sánchez, Justa (Justi), 163
San Pacho (Saint Francis of Assisi), 108, 144, 161–62, 164–65, 214
Scarry, Elaine, 38
Segato, Rita Laura: *La guerra contra las mujeres*, 7, 187
self-representation, 21, 146, 149, 155, 188; *Mujeres Pacíficas* and, 24, 50, 62, 72, 75, 77–78, 80, 85, 88–89, 211–12
Sexualidades Campesinas, 20, 231n22
Sharpe, Christina, 127
showing up, 14, 22–23, 63, 69, 98, 114, 153, 172, 187, 214; barriers to, 191–95; hope as consequence of, 53; performativity and, 25, 33, 86, 90, 156–58, 160, 183, 194, 210, 218; as political, 2, 56, 80, 90, 93, 160, 163, 168, 178–83, 218; power of presence and, 33, 158–60, 165, 168, 176, 202, 204–5
sicaresca literary genre, 10–11
silence, 41, 59, 73, 80, 114, 199, 232n43; in official narratives, 12, 14, 95–96, 99–100, 105, 110, 115, 121, 123, 126, 143; as resistant performance, 21, 25, 63–66, 89, 158, 169–71, 175–76, 180, 189, 207–13
slavery, 11–12, 23, 41, 49, 51, 64, 74, 127, 154, 234n37; absent from Museo del Oro, 96; addressed by Fundación Muntú Bantú, 101–3, 105, 107–11, 115, 122; slaver-capitalist knowledge, 40
slow scholarship, 18–19
Smith, Christen, 12, 99, 154, 214
Smith, Linda Tuhiwai, 106
social media, 21, 39, 112, 142–46, 149, 154–55. *See also* Facebook; Instagram; Twitter; YouTube
solidarity, 34, 47, 76, 82, 92, 113, 142, 169, 174; feminist networks of, 8, 19, 25, 111, 135, 158–61, 164–65, 178, 183, 202–4, 218–19; Feria Alternativa Justa y Solidaria, 163–65; Foro Interétnico Solidaridad Chocó (FISCH), 32, 79, 112; performance and, 6, 25, 158, 183, 197, 218, 229n44; transnational, 8, 14–15, 19, 25, 104–5, 130, 170, 178–83, 198, 217–19; visibility and, 104, 135–37, 158–59, 165, 175, 177–79, 182–83. *See also* activism; encuentros [encounters]; feminism

Soweto. *See* Cimarrón
state of exception, 38, 41
Steele, Catherine Knight, 133, 143, 146
survival technologies, 8–9, 127, 133, 137, 153–54, 165

T-622/16 judgment (Atrato River Case, 2016), 136, 215
Tanguí, 27, 33, 49, 53–55, 70, 75–76, 190–91, 193–94, 201–2, 204; military encounter in, 184–86, 192
Taylor, Diana, 14, 43, 158, 162, 226n5
teoría de las mujeres [women's theory], 14
teoría socioterritorial en movimiento (TStM), 129
Theidon, Kimberly, 168
de la Torre Guerrero, Gonzalo, 24, 36, 85–86, 91, 96, 113–22, 148, 163, 188, 217
Torres, Ana Victoria, 35, 35–36, 227n17
transnational solidarity, 25, 104–5, 130, 170, 178–83, 198, 218–19
trauma, 11–12, 15–16, 38, 45, 71, 152; hope and, 61, 88; labor of survival after, 17, 27, 30, 32, 39, 49–50, 55, 67, 166, 191, 208–9; memorialization and, 82, 90, 96–97, 106–10, 115, 120–23, 126, 165, 172, 175, 218; performance and, 55, 82–83, 108, 162–63, 165–66, 168, 172, 180, 191, 202–3, 218; revictimization and, 5, 43, 55, 81, 108, 126, 215, 218; untranslatability of, 207
Trujillo, César Gaviria, 4
Tutunendo, 26, 144
Twitter, 112–13, 143, 146

UNESCO: Representative List of the Intangible Cultural Heritage of Humanity, 161
Uniclaretiana (formerly FUCLA), 113, 163–64
United Nations High Commissioner for Refugees (UNHCR), 4, 27, 46, 190–91, 204
United Nations Security Council Resolution 1325, 181–82
United Nations (UN) Women, 135–36
United States, 95, 101, 112, 140, 170, 182, 212, 222n7; in author positionality, 58, 178; militarization by, 9, 30–32; Plan Colombia (now Peace Colombia), 5, 10, 31; popular culture of, 10, 94, 111; presidential election (2016), 134
United States Agency for International Development (USAID), 6, 130
untranslatability, 24, 43, 207, 212, 217
Uribe, Álvaro, 5, 62, 134, 185–86
Uribe, Gloria, 163
Uribe, Julio César, 164
Uribe, María Victoria, 126

Vergara-Figueroa, Aurora, 36, 126, 235n48
victimhood, 3, 19, 42, 55, 132, 154, 173–74, 178, 181; feminization and, 14, 32, 52, 167–69, 214; moving beyond, 16, 23, 35–36, 38–40, 45, 52, 68; revictimization, 5, 28, 43, 55, 81, 108, 126, 215, 218; self-identification and, 97, 108, 193, 196, 216
Vidal Romero, Velia, 36, 57; *Aguas de estuario*, 24, 129, 145–47, 149, 152–55, 218; Motete, 24, 128–29, 145–55, 218, 239n48
Villar, Andrés, 128, 130, 134–35
La Violencia, 10, 12
La Violencia en Colombia (Campos, Fals-Borda, and Luna), 10, 38
violentología [study of violence in Colombia] and violentólogos, 10, 39–40; *Violentology: A Manual of the Colombian Conflict* (Ferry), 37–38
visibility, 7–8, 30, 34, 55, 151, 209, 212; digital tools and, 62, 65, 87, 124, 127, 132, 137, 139, 141–43, 146; museums and, 96, 99–100, 103–4, 108, 120, 123–24; National Peace Prize recognition, 165–66; politics of, 17, 52, 61–62, 64–65, 67, 85, 87, 207, 213; solidarity and, 104, 135–37, 158–59, 165, 175, 177–79, 182–83; visual narratives, 1, 19, 22, 59, 90, 95, 99, 120, 144
Vivanco, Dora Inés, 129
Viveros Vigoya, Mara, 36, 57–58
Vivienne, Son, 69
vivir bien [to live well], 197–98
vulnerability, 17, 41, 52, 152, 161, 166, 175, 182, 214; alongside agency, 28, 49, 55, 67; digital memories and, 24, 92–93, 121–22, 124, 146, 169, 217; museum spaces and, 24, 39, 113, 121–22, 124, 134,

158; showing up and, 54, 157–58, 165, 202, 216; storytelling and, 21, 39, 55, 61, 69, 84–85, 87, 183, 202, 217

Wade, Peter, 16, 36, 97, 140, 148
Waosolo (Andrés Mauricio Mosquera Mosquera), 139–40. *See also* Fotógrafas del Pacífico
War on Drugs, 19
whitening, 60, 110–11, 121, 139–40, 154, 230n20; as blanqueamiento, 3–4, 98, 100, 106, 108, 213
why nots, 7, 14–15, 18, 76, 201, 210; expressed by María del Socorro Mosquera Pérez, 1–2, 5, 8, 25, 74, 132, 141, 198, 203, 205, 219–20

Wilderson, Frank, II, 52
Women in Black / Mujeres de negro (WiB), 6, 25, 160, 214, 218–19; encuentro in Montevido, 160, 177–80, 182–83; XV Encuentro Internacional, 156, 160, 170–79, 183
worldmaking, 7–8, 64, 142, 157, 160, 189, 207, 220

YouTube, 112, 119, 131, 135, 137

Zajović, Staša, 178
Zamora, Omaris, 150
Zapata Olivella, Manuel, 102

TANIA LIZARAZO is an associate professor in the Department of Modern Languages, Linguistics, and Intercultural Communication at the University of Maryland, Baltimore County.

The University of Illinois Press
is a founding member of the
Association of University Presses.
———————————————

University of Illinois Press
1325 South Oak Street
Champaign, IL 61820-6903
www.press.uillinois.edu